# Fruits Basket™

## Volume 10

Natsuki Takaya

# Fruits Basket Vol. 10
## Created by Natsuki Takaya

Translation - Alethea Nibley and Athena Nibley
English Adaptation - Jake Forbes
Contributing Writer - Adam Arnold
Associate Editor - Peter Ahlstrom
Retouch and Lettering - Deron Bennett
Production Artist - Jose Macasocol, Jr.
Cover Design - Christian Lownds

Editor - Paul Morrissey
Digital Imaging Manager - Chris Buford
Production Managers - Jennifer Miller and Mutsumi Miyazaki
Managing Editor - Jill Freshney
VP of Production - Ron Klamert
Publisher and E.I.C. - Mike Kiley
President and C.O.O. - John Parker
C.E.O. - Stuart Levy

A  Manga

TOKYOPOP Inc.
5900 Wilshire Blvd. Suite 2000
Los Angeles, CA 90036

E-mail: info@TOKYOPOP.com
Come visit us online at www.TOKYOPOP.com

ISBN: 1-59532-405-4

First TOKYOPOP printing: July 2005
10 9 8 7 6 5 4
Printed in the USA

# Fruits Basket™

## Volume 10

## By
## Natsuki Takaya

HAMBURG // LONDON // LOS ANGELES // TOKYO

# Fruits Basket™

## Table of Contents

# STORY SO FAR...

Hello, I'm Tohru Honda and I have come to know a terrible secret. After the death of my mother, I was living by myself in a tent, when the Sohma family took me in. I soon learned that the Sohma family lives with a curse! Each family member is possessed by the vengeful spirit of an animal from the Chinese Zodiac. Whenever one of them becomes weak or is hugged by a member of the opposite sex, they change into their Zodiac animal!

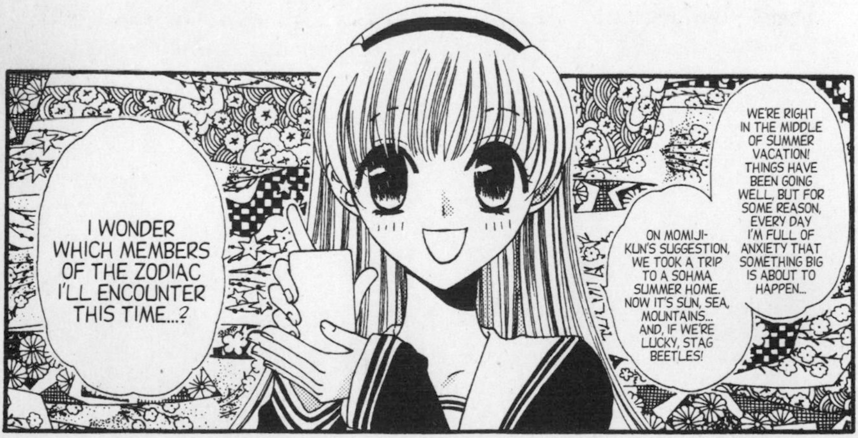

WE'RE RIGHT IN THE MIDDLE OF SUMMER VACATION! THINGS HAVE BEEN GOING WELL, BUT FOR SOME REASON, EVERY DAY I'M FULL OF ANXIETY THAT SOMETHING BIG IS ABOUT TO HAPPEN...
ON MOMIJI-KUN'S SUGGESTION, WE TOOK A TRIP TO A SOHMA SUMMER HOME. NOW IT'S SUN, SEA, MOUNTAINS... AND, IF WE'RE LUCKY, STAG BEETLES!
I WONDER WHICH MEMBERS OF THE ZODIAC I'LL ENCOUNTER THIS TIME...?

# Tohru Honda

The ever-optimistic hero of our story.
An orphan, she now lives in Shigure's
house, along with Yuki and Kyo, and
is the only person outside of the family
who knows the Sohma family's curse.

# Yuki Sohma, the Rat

Soft-spoken. Self-esteem issues.
At school he's called "Prince Yuki."

# Kyo Sohma, the Cat

The Cat who was left out of the Zodiac.
Hates Yuki, leeks and miso. But mostly
Yuki.

# Kagura Sohma, the Boar

Bashful, yet headstrong. Determined to
marry Kyo, even if it kills him.

# Fruits Basket Characters

## Mabudachi Trio

### Shigure Sohma, the Dog
Enigmatic, mischievous and a little perverted. A popular novelist.

### Hatori Sohma, the Dragon
Family doctor to the Sohmas. Only thing he can't cure is his broken heart.

### Ayame Sohma, the Snake
Yuki's older brother. A proud and playful drama queen...er, king. Runs a costume shop.

### Saki Hanajima
"Hana-chan." Can sense people's "waves." Goth demeanor scares her classmates.

### Arisa Uotani
"Uo-chan." A tough-talking "Yankee" who looks out for her friends.

**Tohru's Best Friends**

## Momiji Sohma, the Rabbit

Half-German. He's older than he looks.
Mother rejected him because of the Sohma curse.

## Hatsuharu Sohma, the Ox

The nicest of guys, except when he goes "Black."
Then you'd better watch out.

## Kisa Sohma, the Tiger

Kisa became shy and self-conscious due to constant
teasing by her classmates. Yuki, who has similar
insecurities, feels particularly close to Kisa.

# Fruits Basket Characters

## Hiro Sohma, the Ram (or sheep)

This caustic tyke is skilled at throwing verbal barbs, but he has a soft spot for Kisa.

## Ritsu Sohma, the Monkey

This shy kimono-wearing member of the Sohma family is gorgeous. But this "she" is really a he!! Crossdressing calms his nerves.

## Akito Sohma

The head of the Sohma clan. A dark figure of many secrets. Treated with fear and reverence.

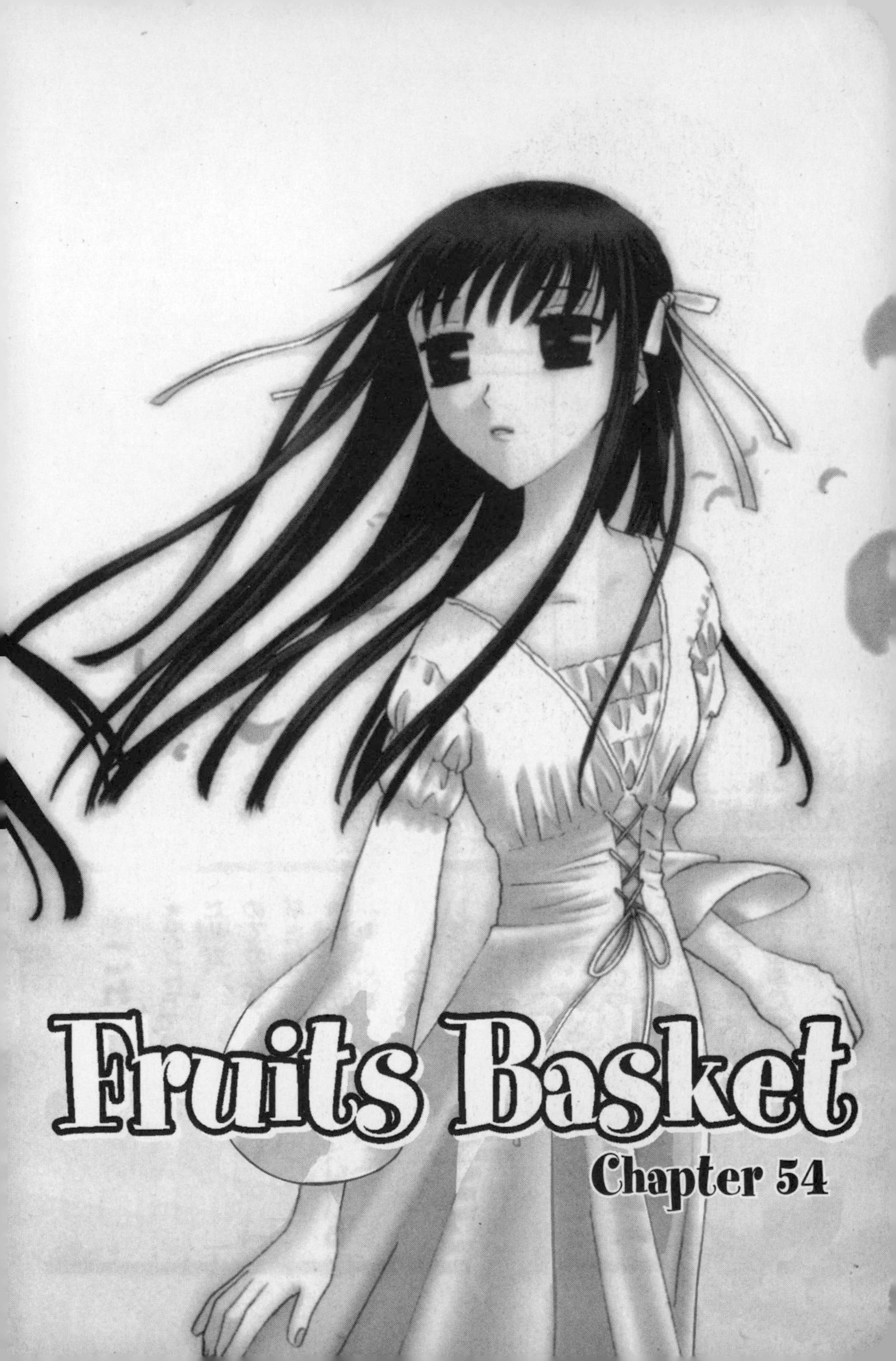
Fruits Basket
Chapter 54

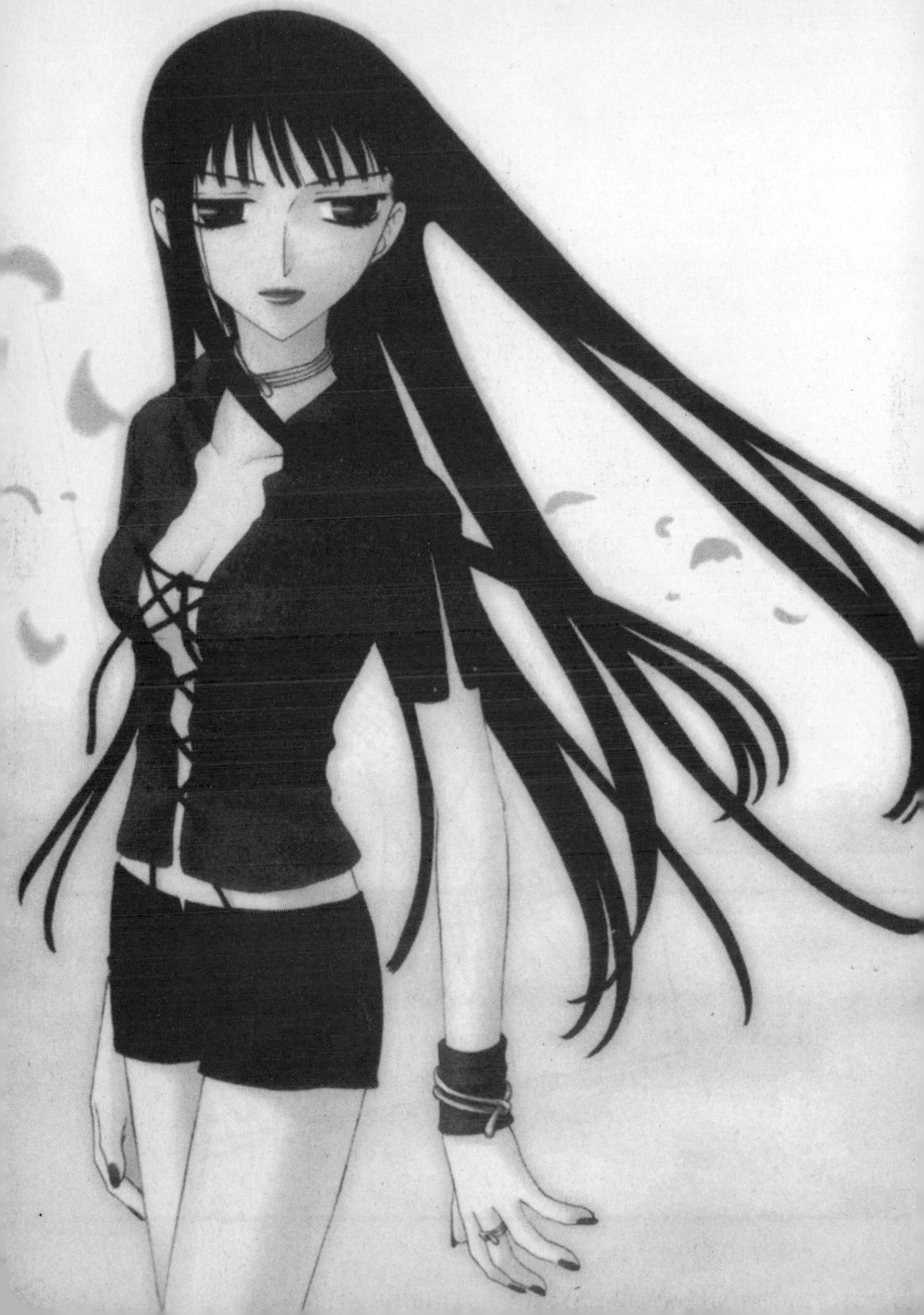

Filler
Sketch

I couldn't decide until the very last minute whether to give her a bikini or a one-piece... (Either would be fine...)

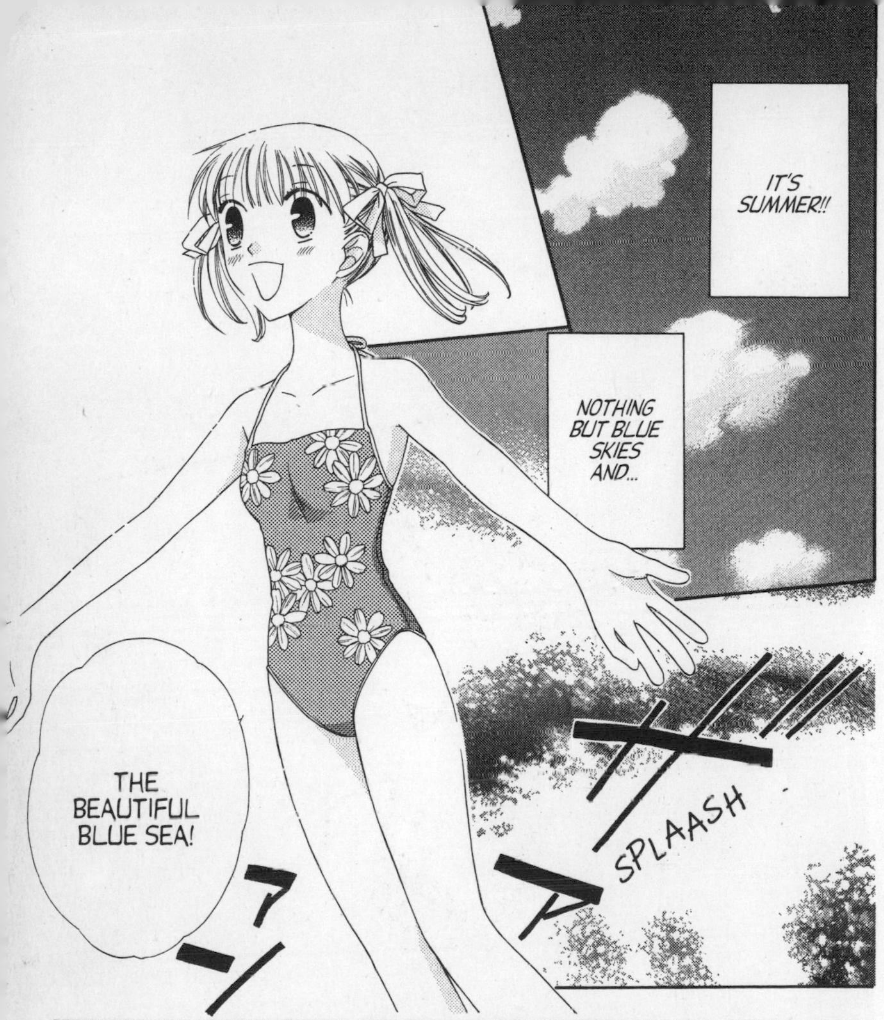
IT'S SUMMER!!
NOTHING BUT BLUE SKIES AND...
THE BEAUTIFUL BLUE SEA!
SPLAASH

## BLAH, BLAH, BLAH 1

Recently, I received some fan letters written on homemade rabbit stationery--it was so precious, I was embarrassed! (laugh) When I get hand-knit scarves and hats, I get embarrassed, too. It's like, "Ah, this feels like Toki-Memo*...!" (Really?) Thank you. I treasure them.

*Tokimeki Memorial: A popular series of dating sim games.

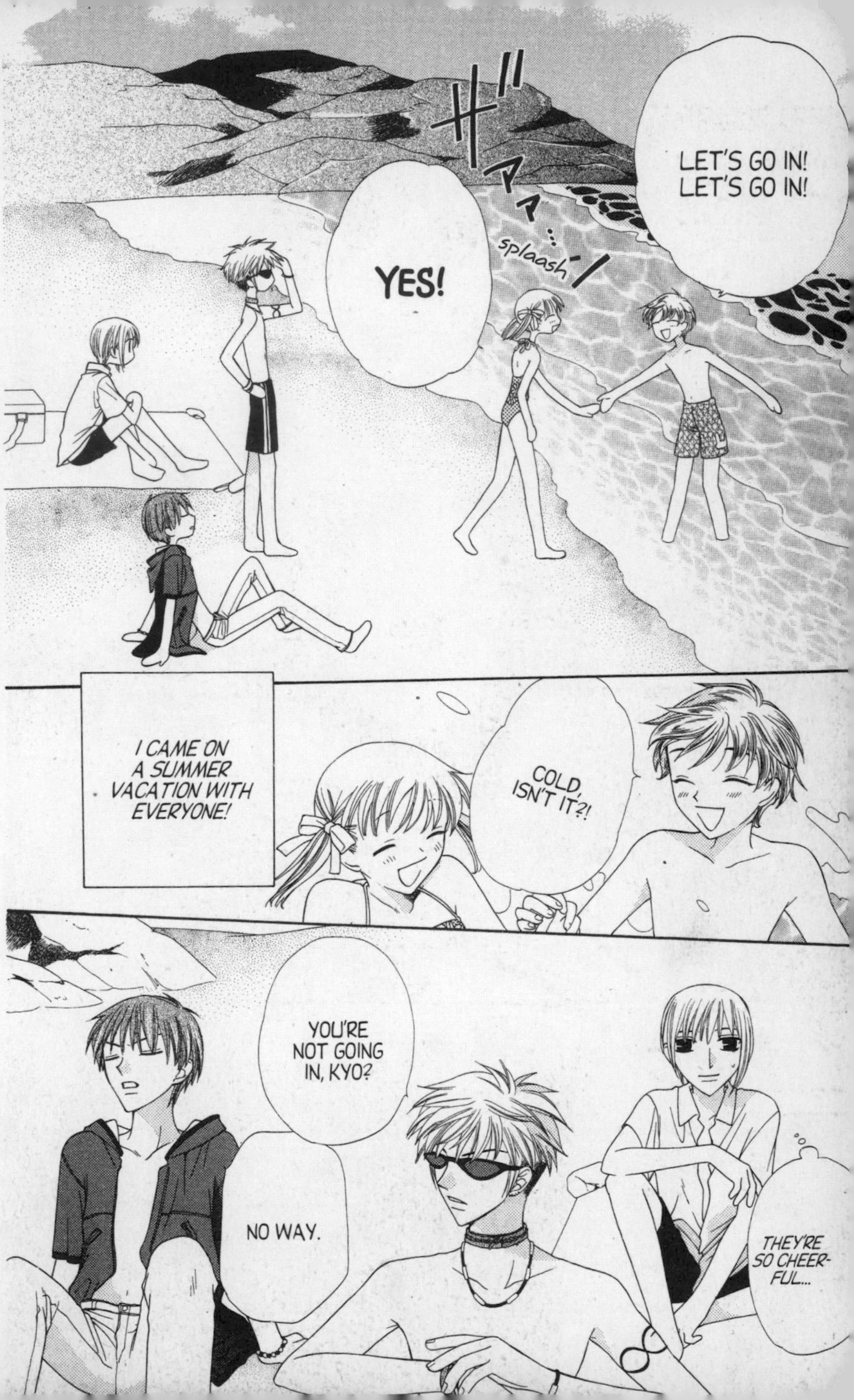
ザァ…
splaash
LET'S GO IN! LET'S GO IN!
YES!
I CAME ON A SUMMER VACATION WITH EVERYONE!
COLD, ISN'T IT?!
YOU'RE NOT GOING IN, KYO?
NO WAY.
THEY'RE SO CHEERFUL...

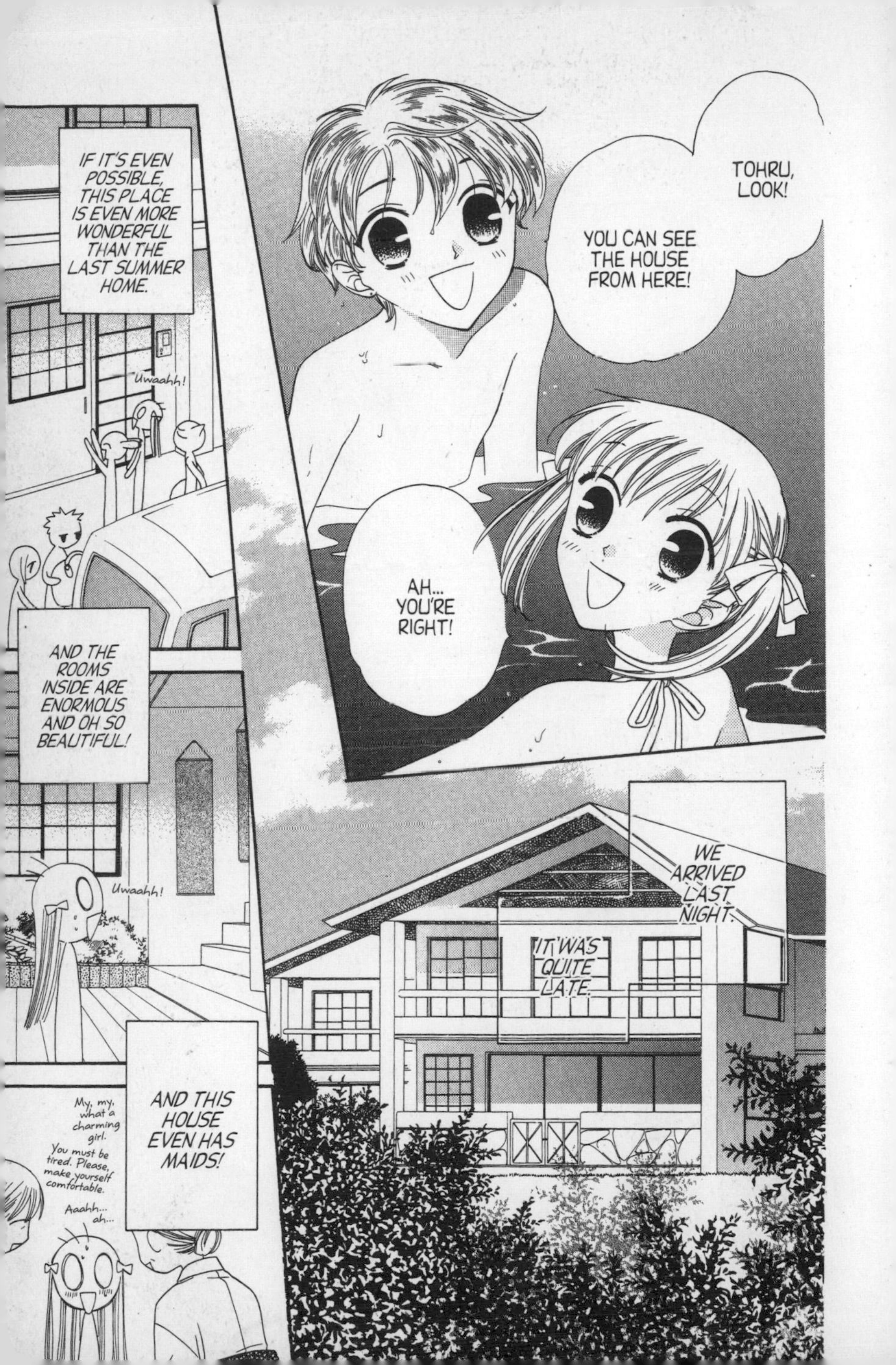

TOHRU, LOOK!
YOU CAN SEE THE HOUSE FROM HERE!
AH... YOU'RE RIGHT!
WE ARRIVED LAST NIGHT.
IT WAS QUITE LATE.
IF IT'S EVEN POSSIBLE, THIS PLACE IS EVEN MORE WONDERFUL THAN THE LAST SUMMER HOME.
Uwaahh!
AND THE ROOMS INSIDE ARE ENORMOUS AND OH SO BEAUTIFUL!
Uwaahh!
AND THIS HOUSE EVEN HAS MAIDS!
My, my, what a charming girl.
You must be tired. Please, make yourself comfortable.
Aaahh... ah...

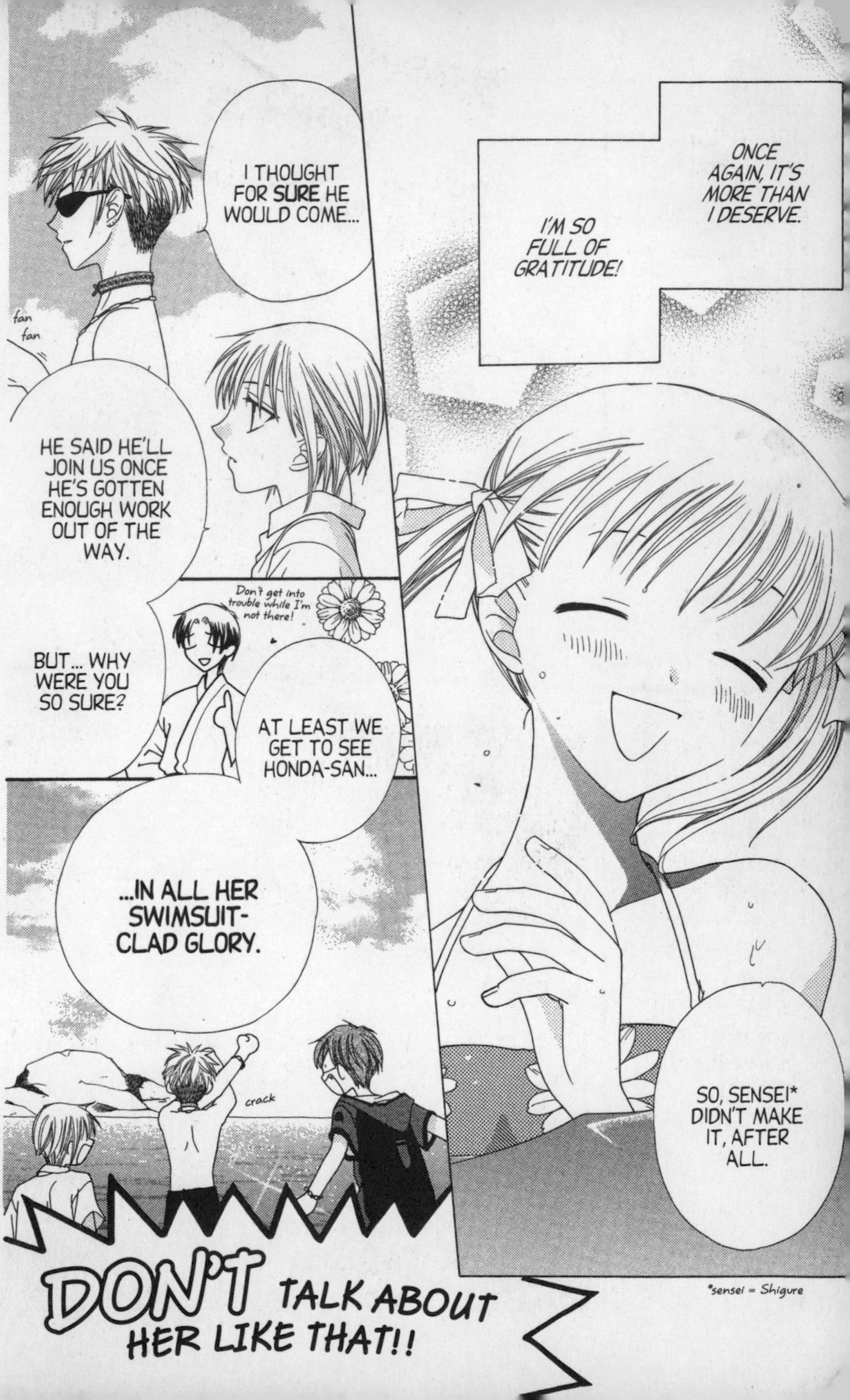
ONCE AGAIN, IT'S MORE THAN I DESERVE.
I'M SO FULL OF GRATITUDE!
SO, SENSEI* DIDN'T MAKE IT, AFTER ALL.
I THOUGHT FOR SURE HE WOULD COME...
fan fan
HE SAID HE'LL JOIN US ONCE HE'S GOTTEN ENOUGH WORK OUT OF THE WAY.
Don't get into trouble while I'm not there!
BUT... WHY WERE YOU SO SURE?
AT LEAST WE GET TO SEE HONDA-SAN...
...IN ALL HER SWIMSUIT-CLAD GLORY.
crack
DON'T TALK ABOUT HER LIKE THAT!!

*sensei = Shigure

**Fruits Basket 10**
**Part 1:**

Hajimemashite and konnichiwa! Takaya, here! Furuba has made it to Volume 10 at last! Uwaaaahh! Ten volumes... Clap clap! Volume 10 features Kisa. Recently, she has become remarkably cheerful. It's not that her situation has really changed... yet. But as long as there are people who understand her, she won't give up on walking forward.

Well now, volume ten is "Summer Vacation in a Summer Home." Please enjoy.

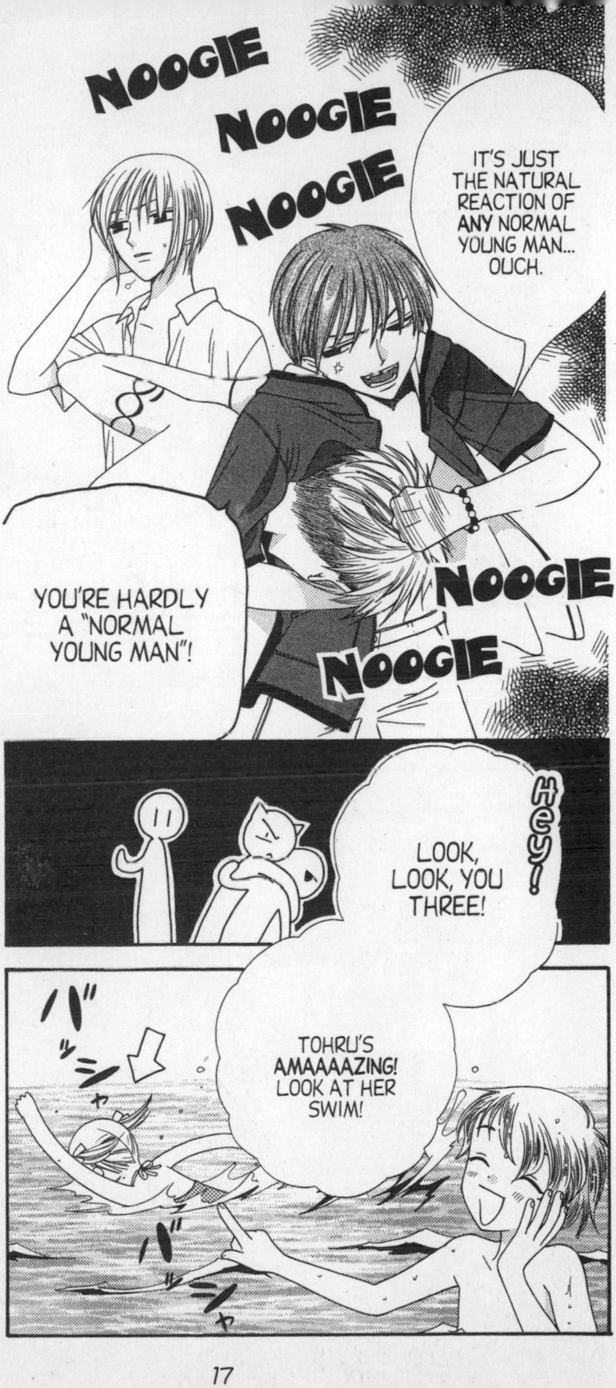
NOOGIE
NOOGIE
NOOGIE
IT'S JUST THE NATURAL REACTION OF ANY NORMAL YOUNG MAN... OUCH.
NOOGIE
NOOGIE
YOU'RE HARDLY A "NORMAL YOUNG MAN"!
Hey!
LOOK, LOOK, YOU THREE!
TOHRU'S AMAAAAZING! LOOK AT HER SWIM!

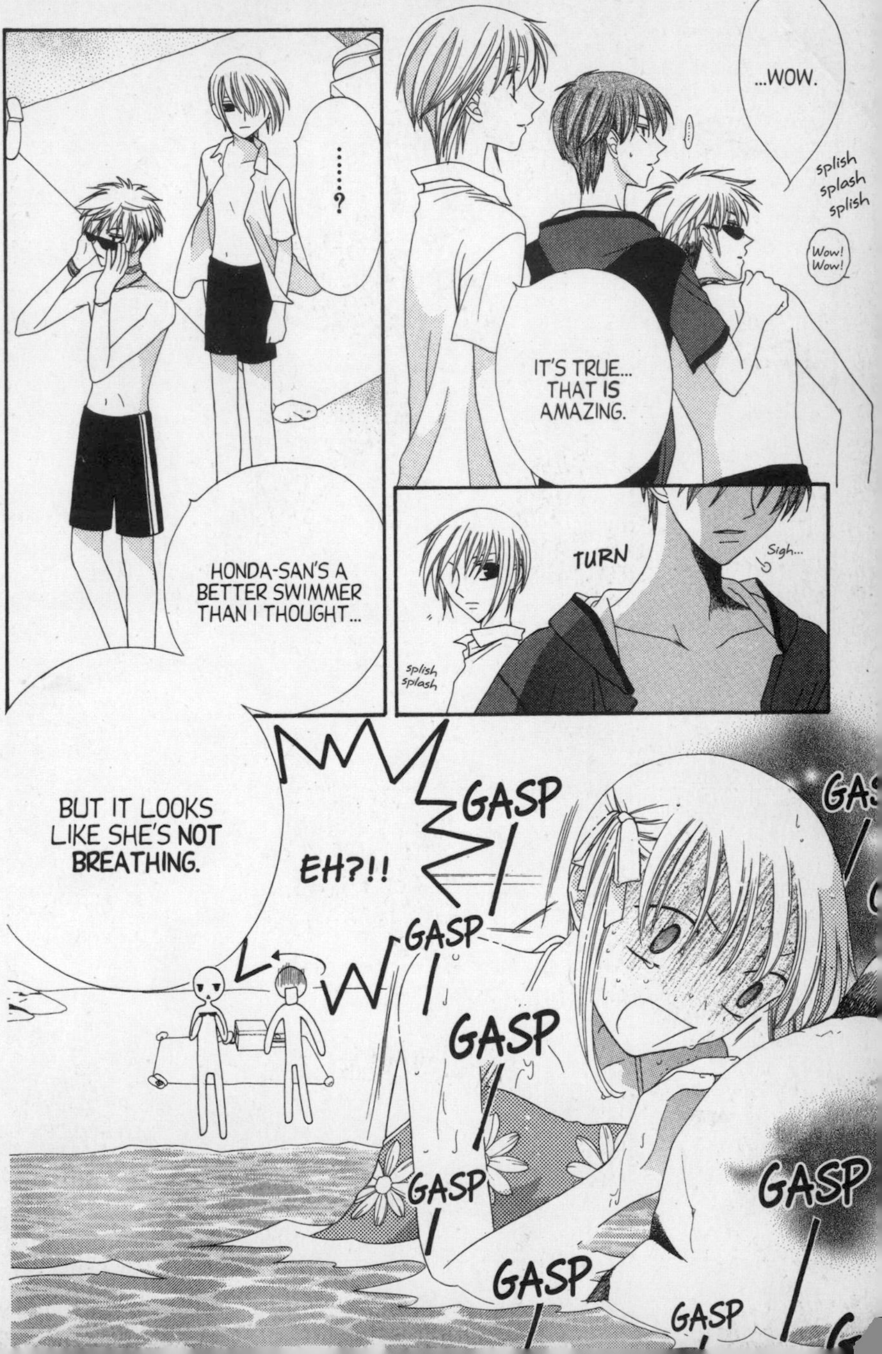

...WOW.
splish splash splish
Wow! Wow!
!
IT'S TRUE... THAT IS AMAZING.
TURN
Sigh...
splish splash
......?
HONDA-SAN'S A BETTER SWIMMER THAN I THOUGHT...
BUT IT LOOKS LIKE SHE'S NOT BREATHING.
EH?!!
GASP
GASP
GASP
GASP
GASP
GASP
GASP

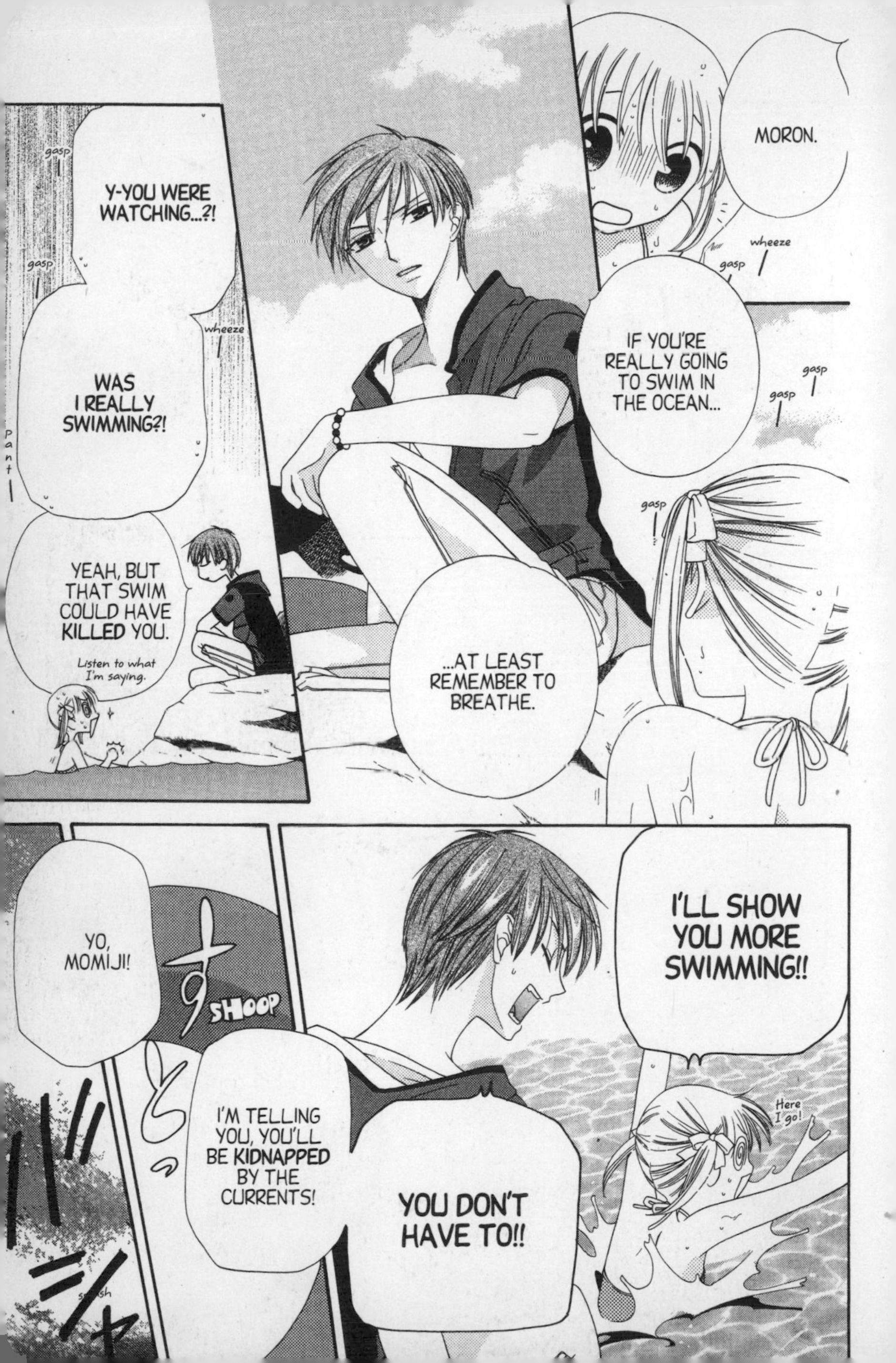
MORON.
wheeze
gasp
IF YOU'RE REALLY GOING TO SWIM IN THE OCEAN...
gasp
gasp
gasp
...AT LEAST REMEMBER TO BREATHE.
gasp
Y-YOU WERE WATCHING...?!
gasp
wheeze
WAS I REALLY SWIMMING?!
Pant
YEAH, BUT THAT SWIM COULD HAVE KILLED YOU.
Listen to what I'm saying.
I'LL SHOW YOU MORE SWIMMING!!
Here I go!
YOU DON'T HAVE TO!!
I'M TELLING YOU, YOU'LL BE KIDNAPPED BY THE CURRENTS!
SHOOP
YO, MOMIJI!
splash

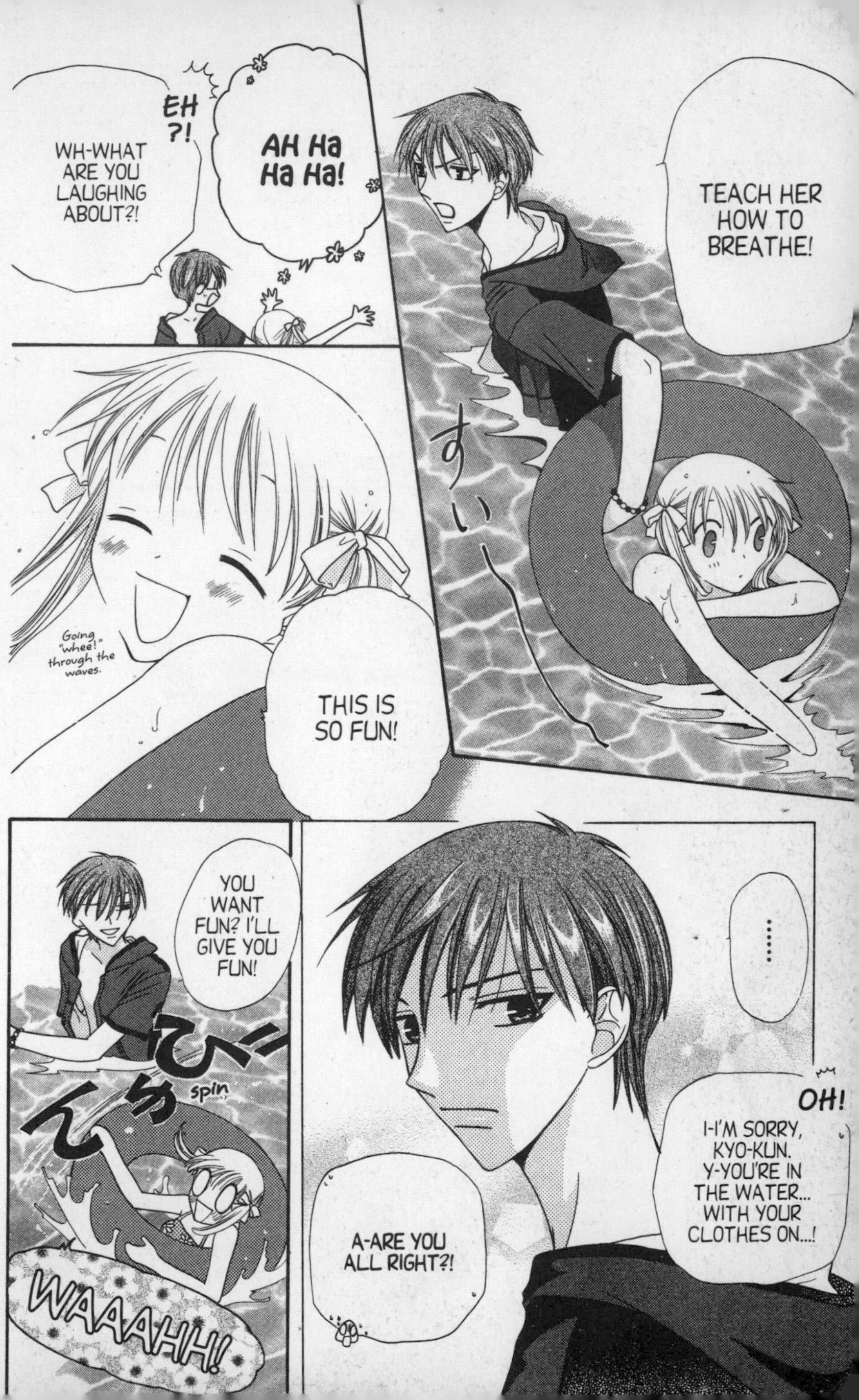
TEACH HER HOW TO BREATHE!
すいー
AH Ha Ha Ha!
EH ?!
WH-WHAT ARE YOU LAUGHING ABOUT?!
THIS IS SO FUN!
Going "whee!" through the waves.
......
OH!
I-I'M SORRY, KYO-KUN. Y-YOU'RE IN THE WATER... WITH YOUR CLOTHES ON...!
A-ARE YOU ALL RIGHT?!
YOU WANT FUN? I'LL GIVE YOU FUN!
ひゅーん
spin
WAAAHH!

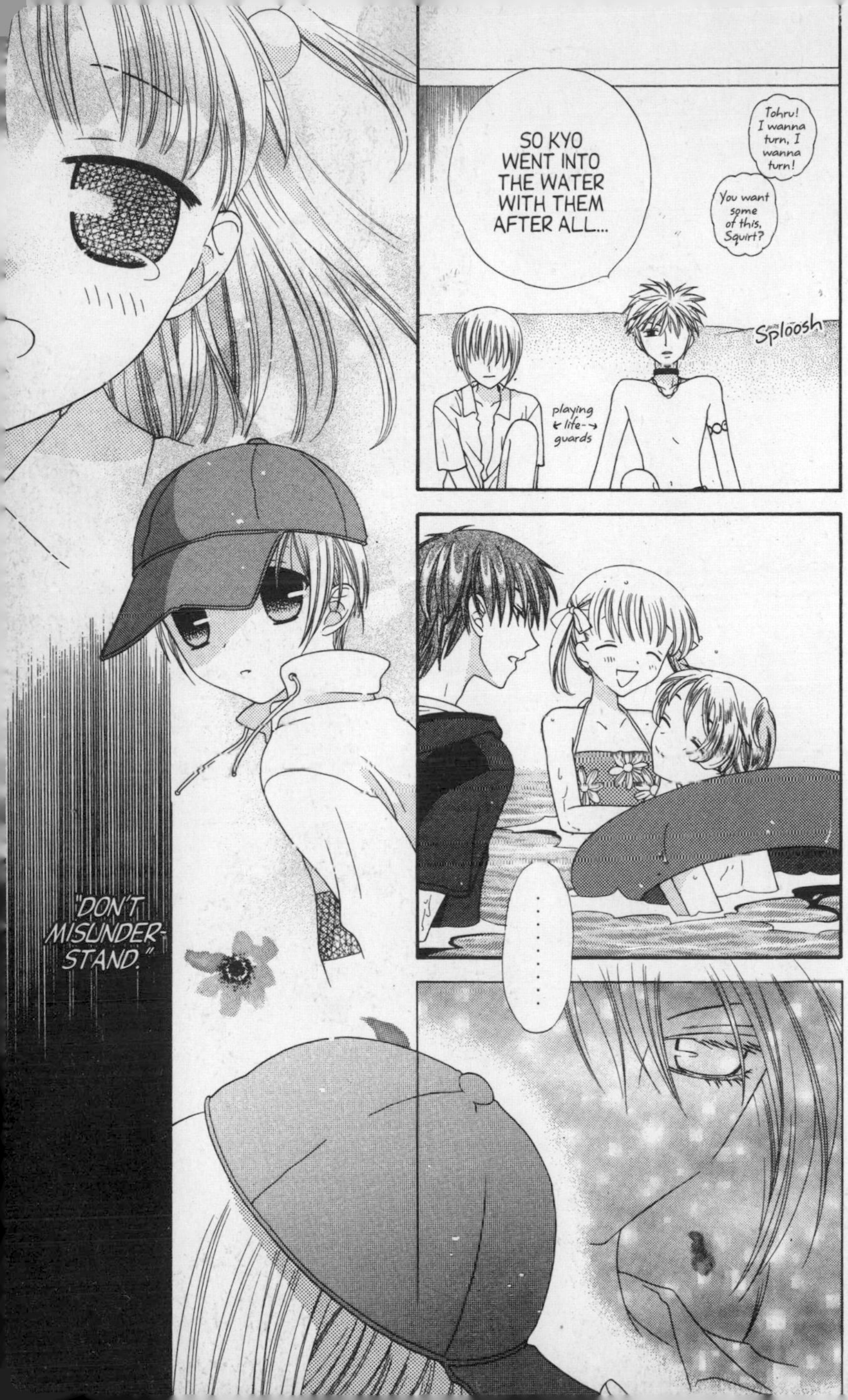
SO KYO WENT INTO THE WATER WITH THEM AFTER ALL...
Tohru! I wanna turn, I wanna turn!
You want some of this, Squirt?
Sploosh
playing life-guards
......
"DON'T MISUNDER-STAND."

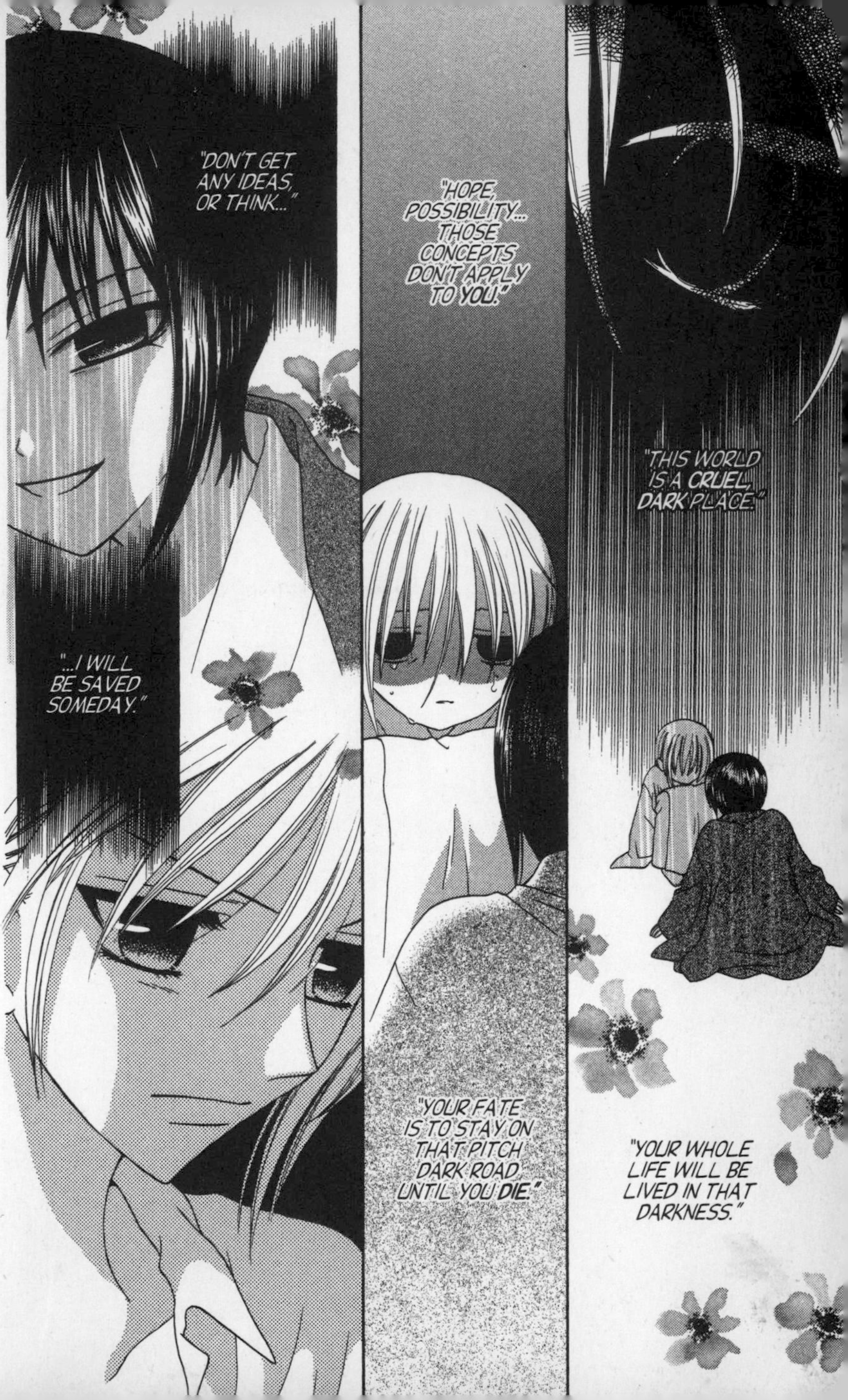
"THIS WORLD IS A CRUEL, DARK PLACE."
"YOUR WHOLE LIFE WILL BE LIVED IN THAT DARKNESS."
"HOPE, POSSIBILITY... THOSE CONCEPTS DON'T APPLY TO YOU."
"YOUR FATE IS TO STAY ON THAT PITCH DARK ROAD UNTIL YOU DIE."
"DON'T GET ANY IDEAS, OR THINK..."
"...I WILL BE SAVED SOMEDAY."

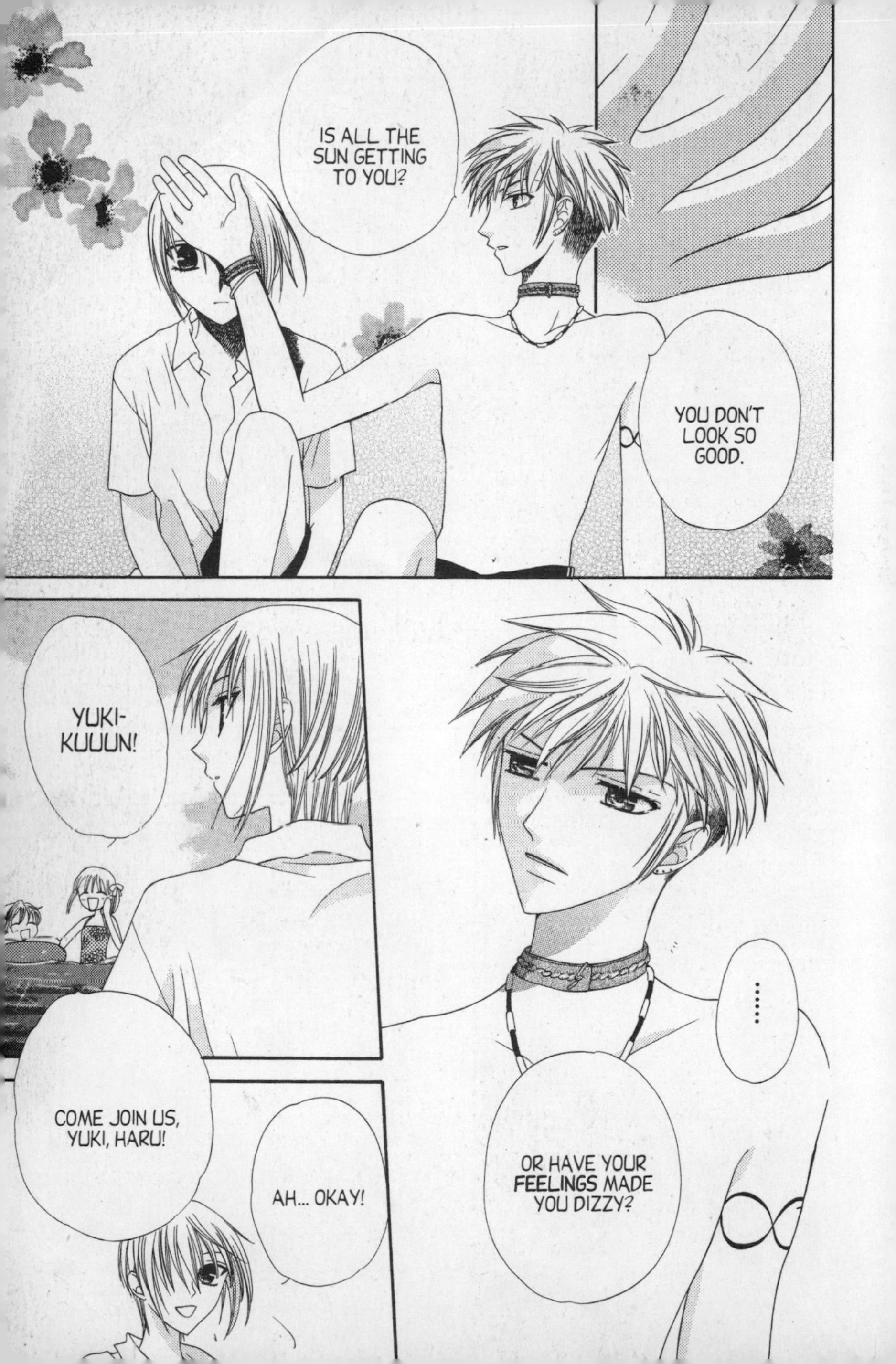
YOU DON'T LOOK SO GOOD.
IS ALL THE SUN GETTING TO YOU?
......
OR HAVE YOUR FEELINGS MADE YOU DIZZY?
YUKI-KUUUN!
COME JOIN US, YUKI, HARU!
AH... OKAY!

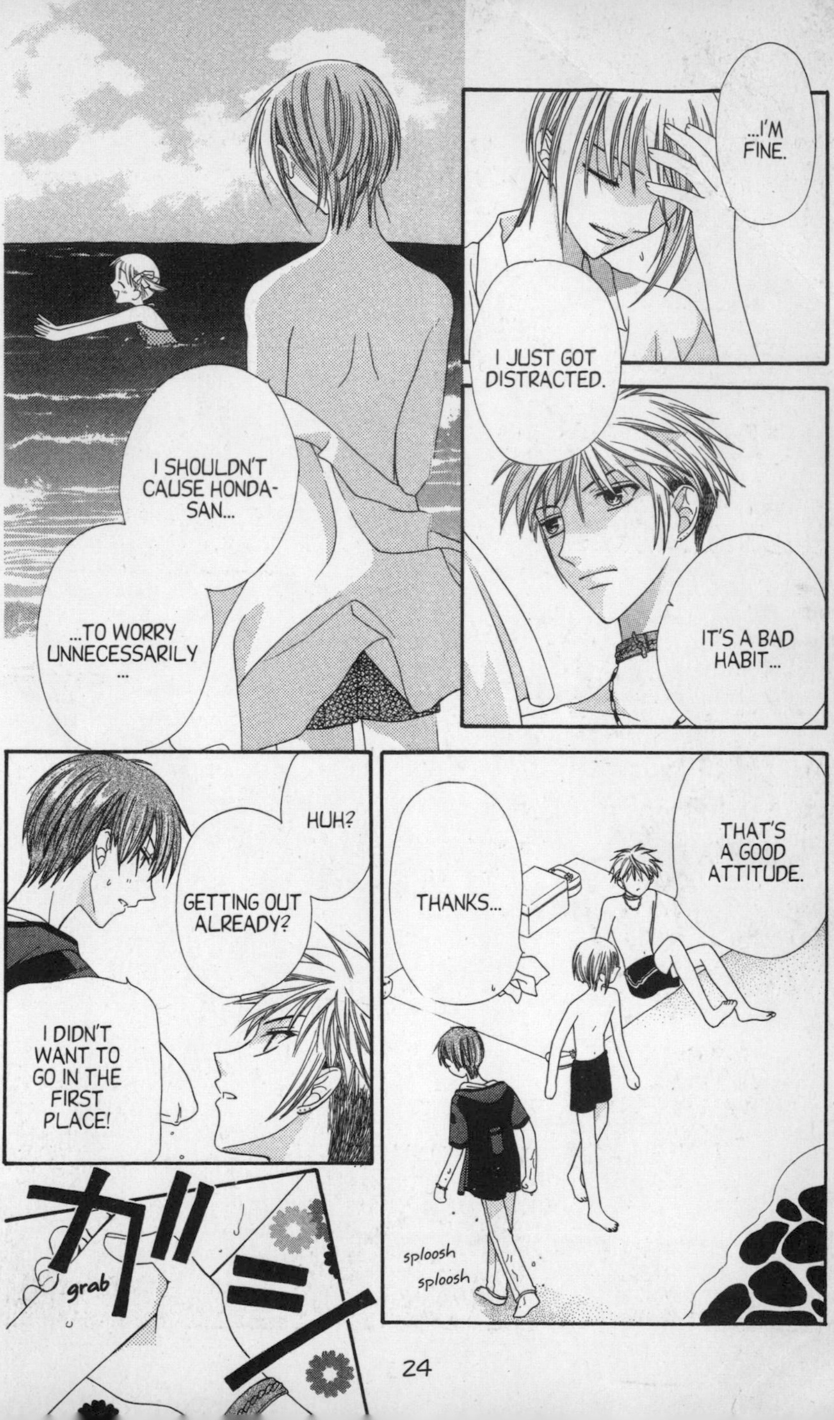
...I'M FINE.
I JUST GOT DISTRACTED.
IT'S A BAD HABIT...
I SHOULDN'T CAUSE HONDA-SAN...
...TO WORRY UNNECESSARILY ...
THAT'S A GOOD ATTITUDE.
THANKS...
sploosh
sploosh
HUH?
GETTING OUT ALREADY?
I DIDN'T WANT TO GO IN THE FIRST PLACE!
grab

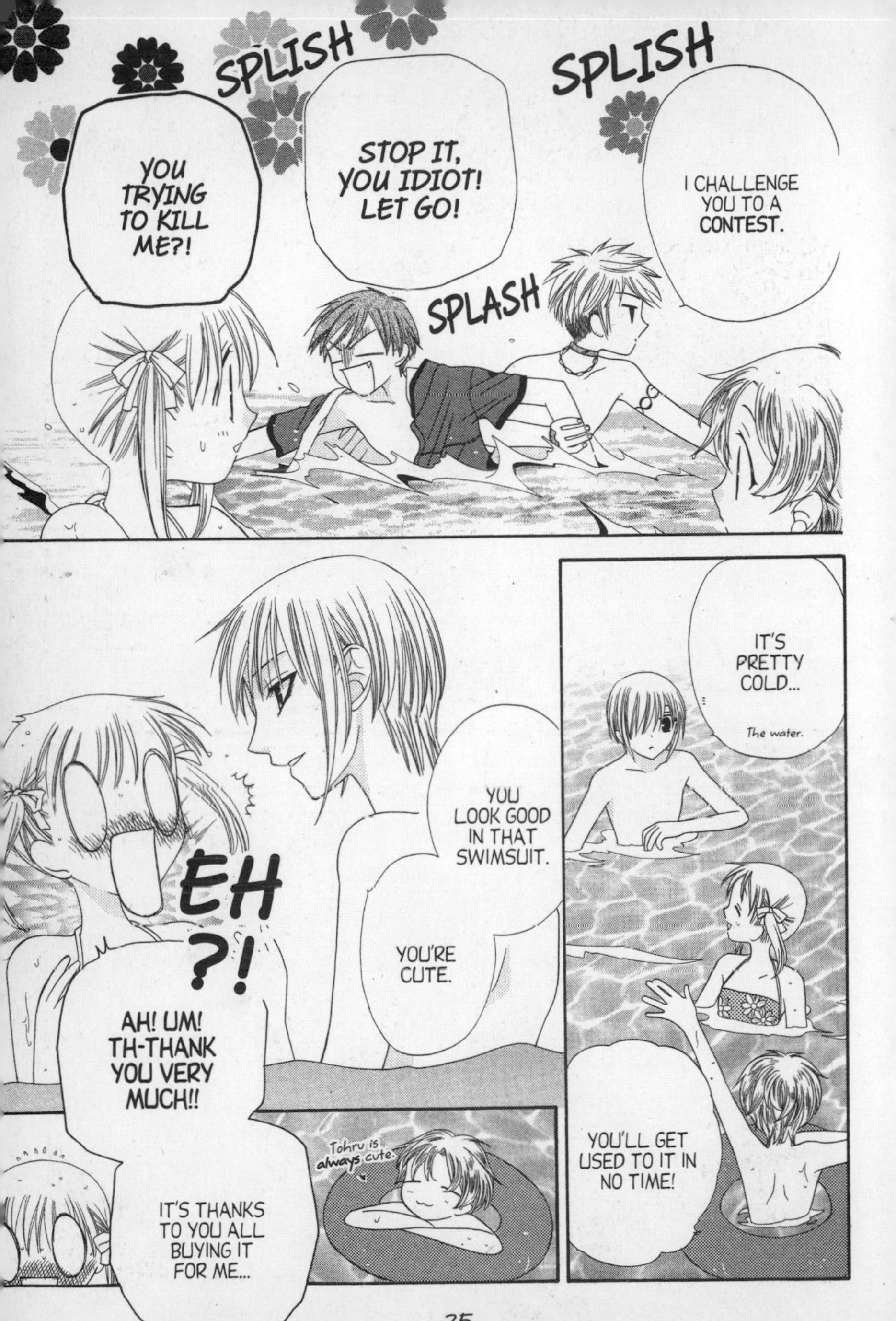
SPLISH
SPLISH
I CHALLENGE YOU TO A CONTEST.
STOP IT, YOU IDIOT! LET GO!
YOU TRYING TO KILL ME?!
SPLASH
IT'S PRETTY COLD...
The water.
YOU'LL GET USED TO IT IN NO TIME!
YOU LOOK GOOD IN THAT SWIMSUIT.
YOU'RE CUTE.
EH ?!
AH! UM! TH-THANK YOU VERY MUCH!!
Tohru is always cute.
IT'S THANKS TO YOU ALL BUYING IT FOR ME...

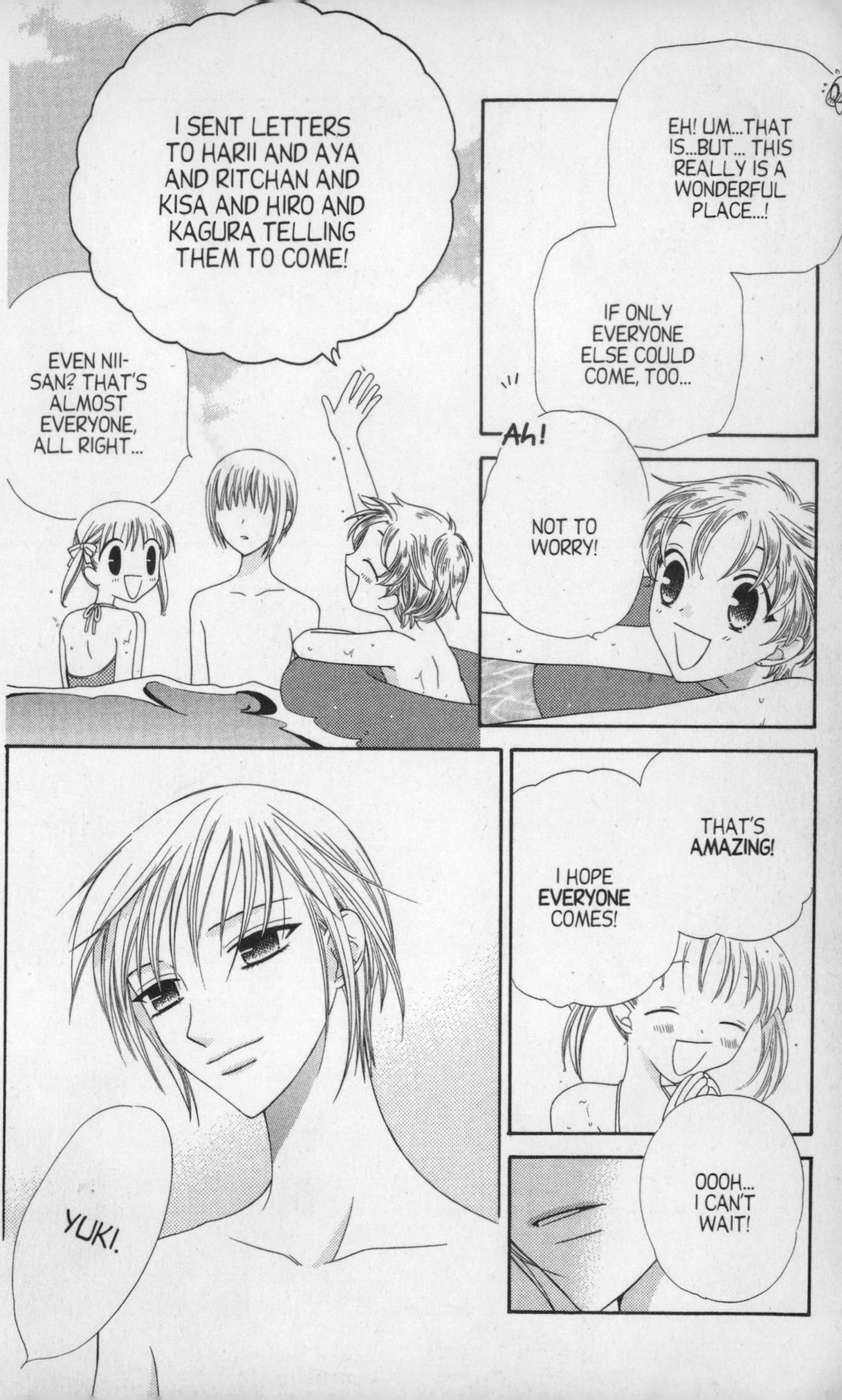
EH! UM...THAT IS...BUT... THIS REALLY IS A WONDERFUL PLACE...!
IF ONLY EVERYONE ELSE COULD COME, TOO...
Ah!
NOT TO WORRY!
I SENT LETTERS TO HARII AND AYA AND RITCHAN AND KISA AND HIRO AND KAGURA TELLING THEM TO COME!
EVEN NII-SAN? THAT'S ALMOST EVERYONE, ALL RIGHT...
THAT'S AMAZING!
I HOPE EVERYONE COMES!
OOOH... I CAN'T WAIT!
YUKI!

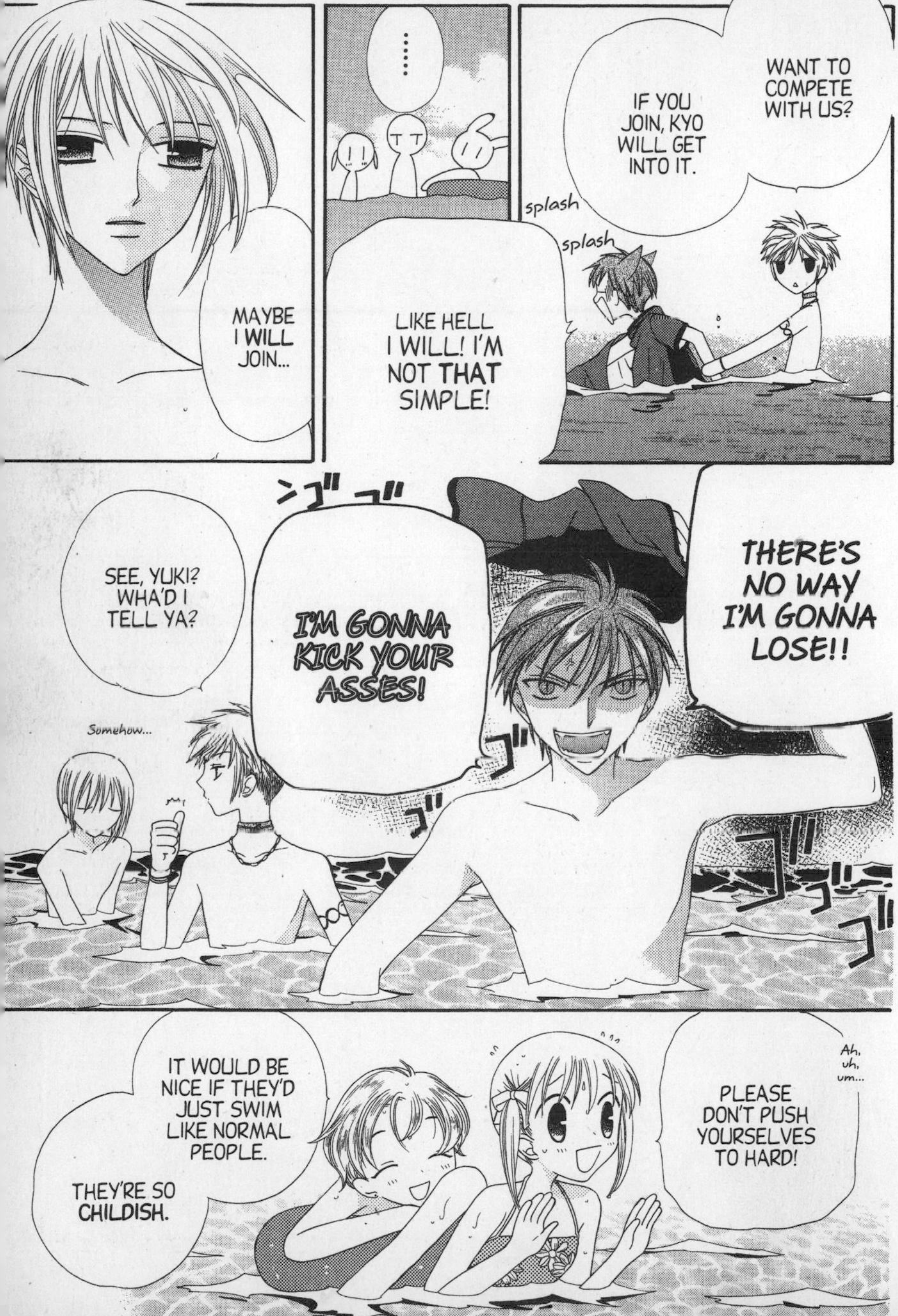
WANT TO COMPETE WITH US?
IF YOU JOIN, KYO WILL GET INTO IT.
splash
splash
......
LIKE HELL I WILL! I'M NOT THAT SIMPLE!
MAYBE I WILL JOIN...
THERE'S NO WAY I'M GONNA LOSE!!
I'M GONNA KICK YOUR ASSES!
SEE, YUKI? WHA'D I TELL YA?
Somehow...
Ah, uh, um...
PLEASE DON'T PUSH YOURSELVES TO HARD!
IT WOULD BE NICE IF THEY'D JUST SWIM LIKE NORMAL PEOPLE.
THEY'RE SO CHILDISH.

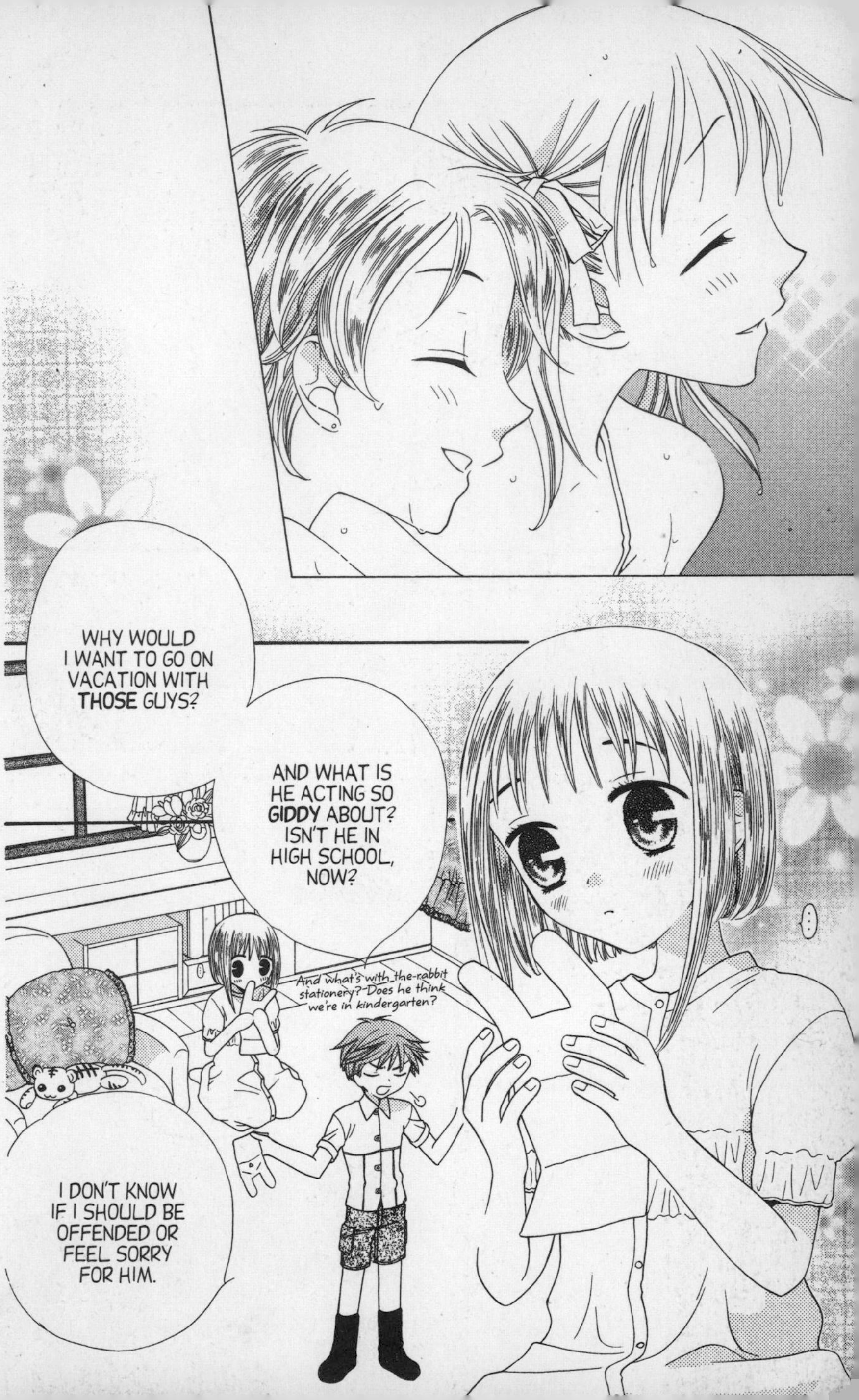
WHY WOULD I WANT TO GO ON VACATION WITH THOSE GUYS?
AND WHAT IS HE ACTING SO GIDDY ABOUT? ISN'T HE IN HIGH SCHOOL, NOW?
...
And what's with the rabbit stationery? Does he think we're in kindergarten?
I DON'T KNOW IF I SHOULD BE OFFENDED OR FEEL SORRY FOR HIM.

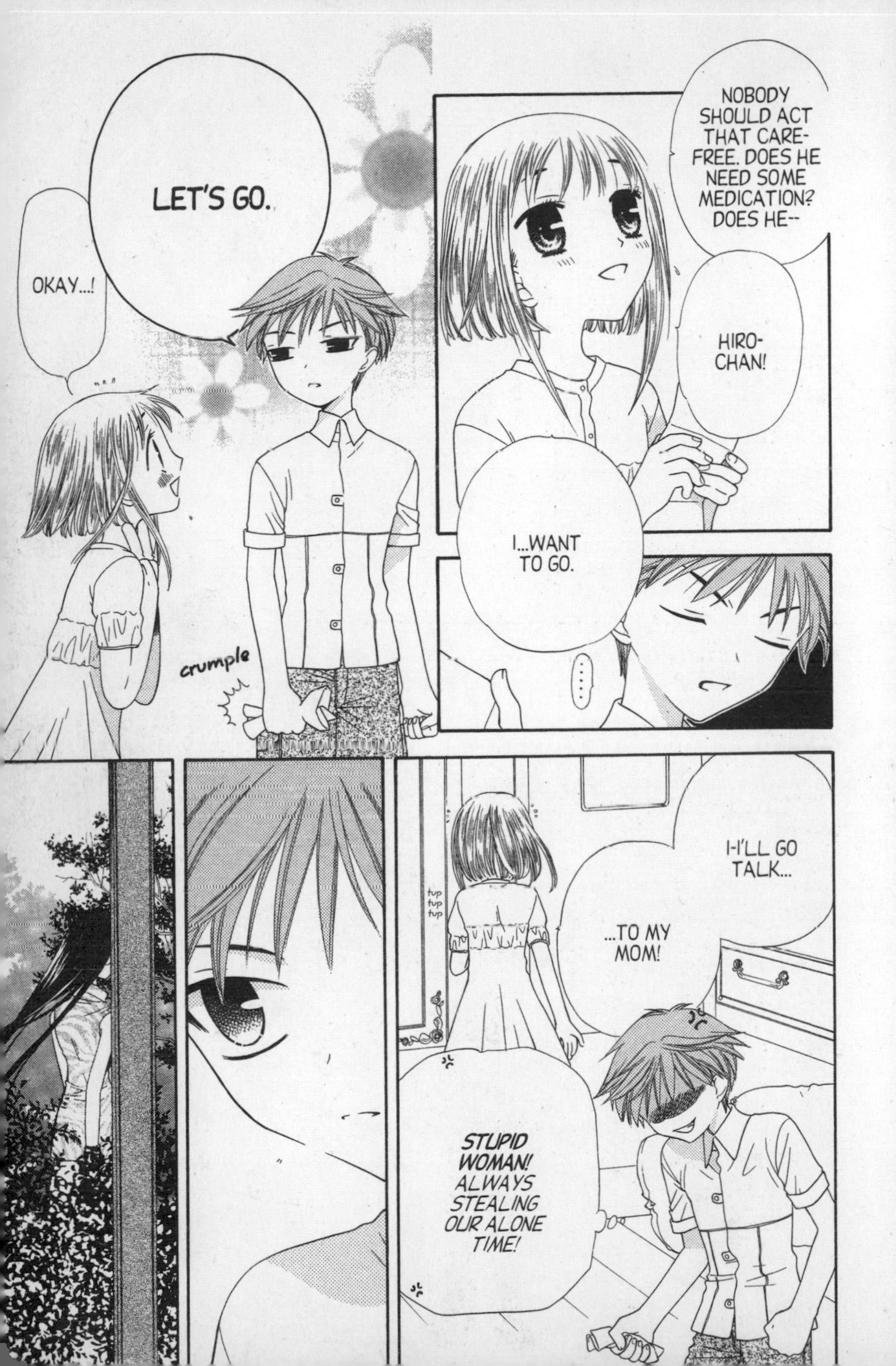
NOBODY SHOULD ACT THAT CARE-FREE. DOES HE NEED SOME MEDICATION? DOES HE--
HIRO-CHAN!
I...WANT TO GO.
.....
LET'S GO.
OKAY...!
crumple
I-I'LL GO TALK...
...TO MY MOM!
tup tup tup
STUPID WOMAN! ALWAYS STEALING OUR ALONE TIME!

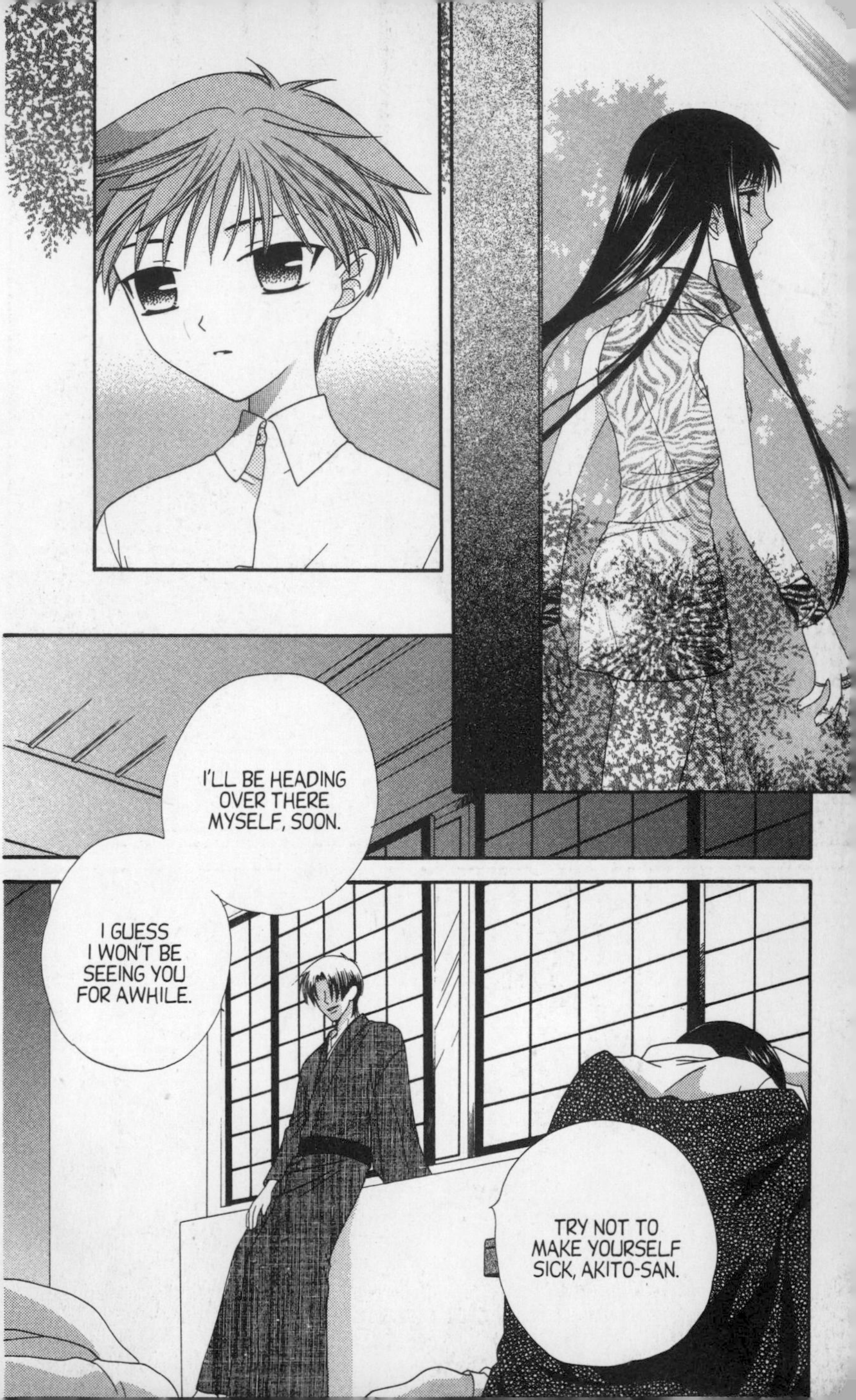
I'LL BE HEADING OVER THERE MYSELF, SOON.
I GUESS I WON'T BE SEEING YOU FOR AWHILE.
TRY NOT TO MAKE YOURSELF SICK, AKITO-SAN.

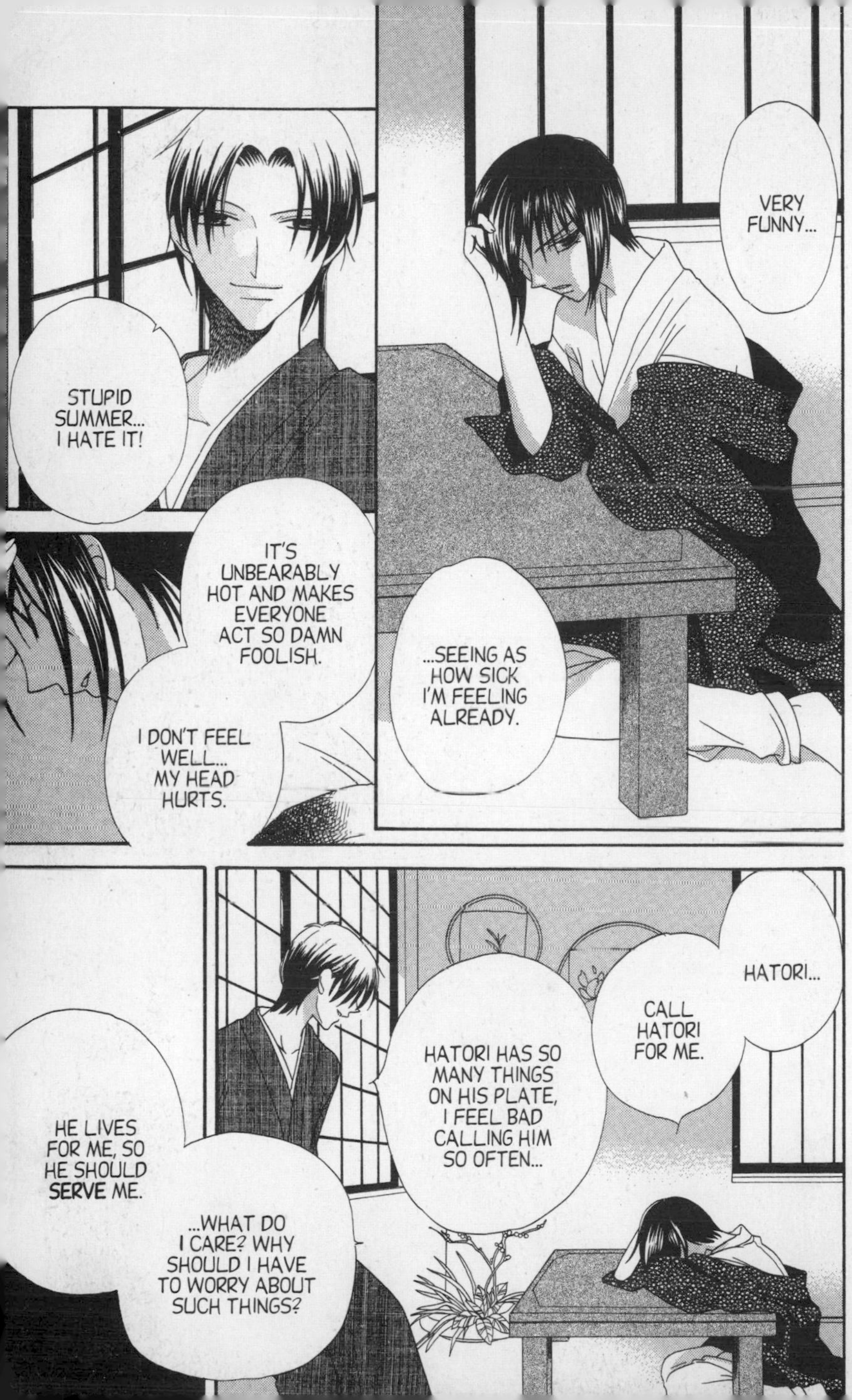
VERY FUNNY...
...SEEING AS HOW SICK I'M FEELING ALREADY.
STUPID SUMMER... I HATE IT!
IT'S UNBEARABLY HOT AND MAKES EVERYONE ACT SO DAMN FOOLISH.
I DON'T FEEL WELL... MY HEAD HURTS.
HATORI...
CALL HATORI FOR ME.
HATORI HAS SO MANY THINGS ON HIS PLATE, I FEEL BAD CALLING HIM SO OFTEN...
...WHAT DO I CARE? WHY SHOULD I HAVE TO WORRY ABOUT SUCH THINGS?
HE LIVES FOR ME, SO HE SHOULD **SERVE** ME.

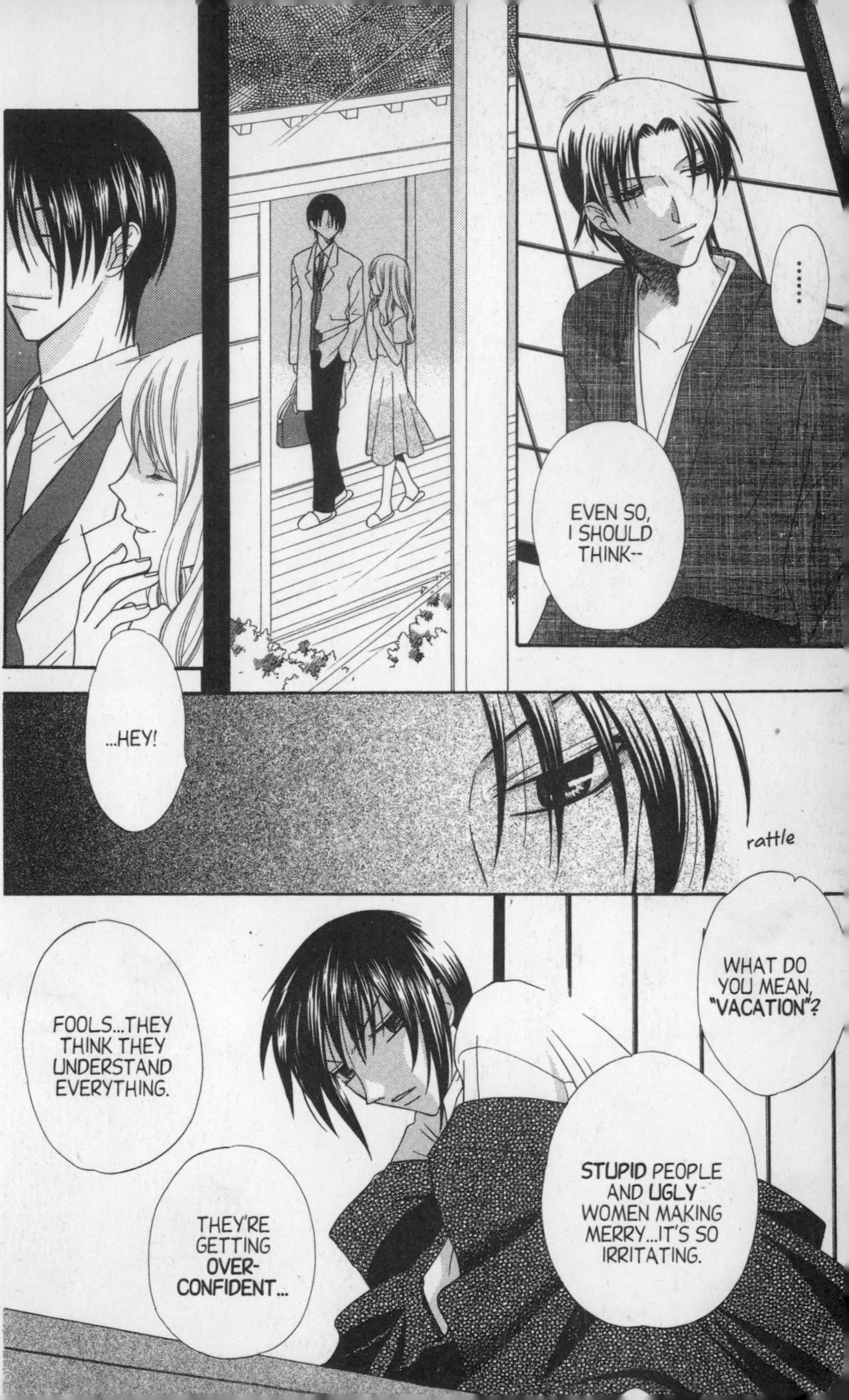
......
EVEN SO, I SHOULD THINK--
...HEY!
rattle
WHAT DO YOU MEAN, "VACATION"?
STUPID PEOPLE AND UGLY WOMEN MAKING MERRY...IT'S SO IRRITATING.
FOOLS...THEY THINK THEY UNDERSTAND EVERYTHING.
THEY'RE GETTING OVER-CONFIDENT...

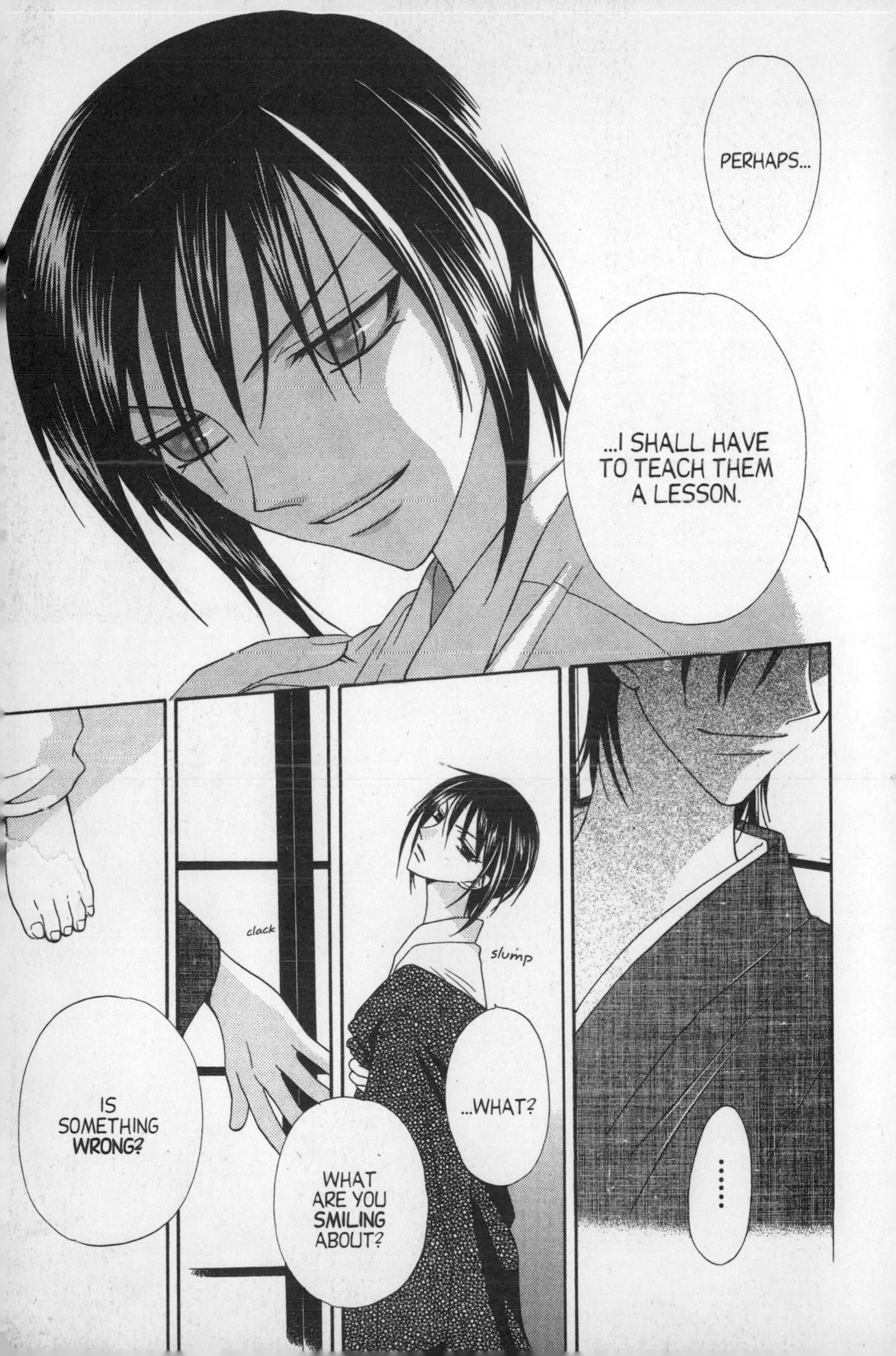
PERHAPS...
...I SHALL HAVE TO TEACH THEM A LESSON.
......
slump
...WHAT?
WHAT ARE YOU SMILING ABOUT?
clack
IS SOMETHING WRONG?

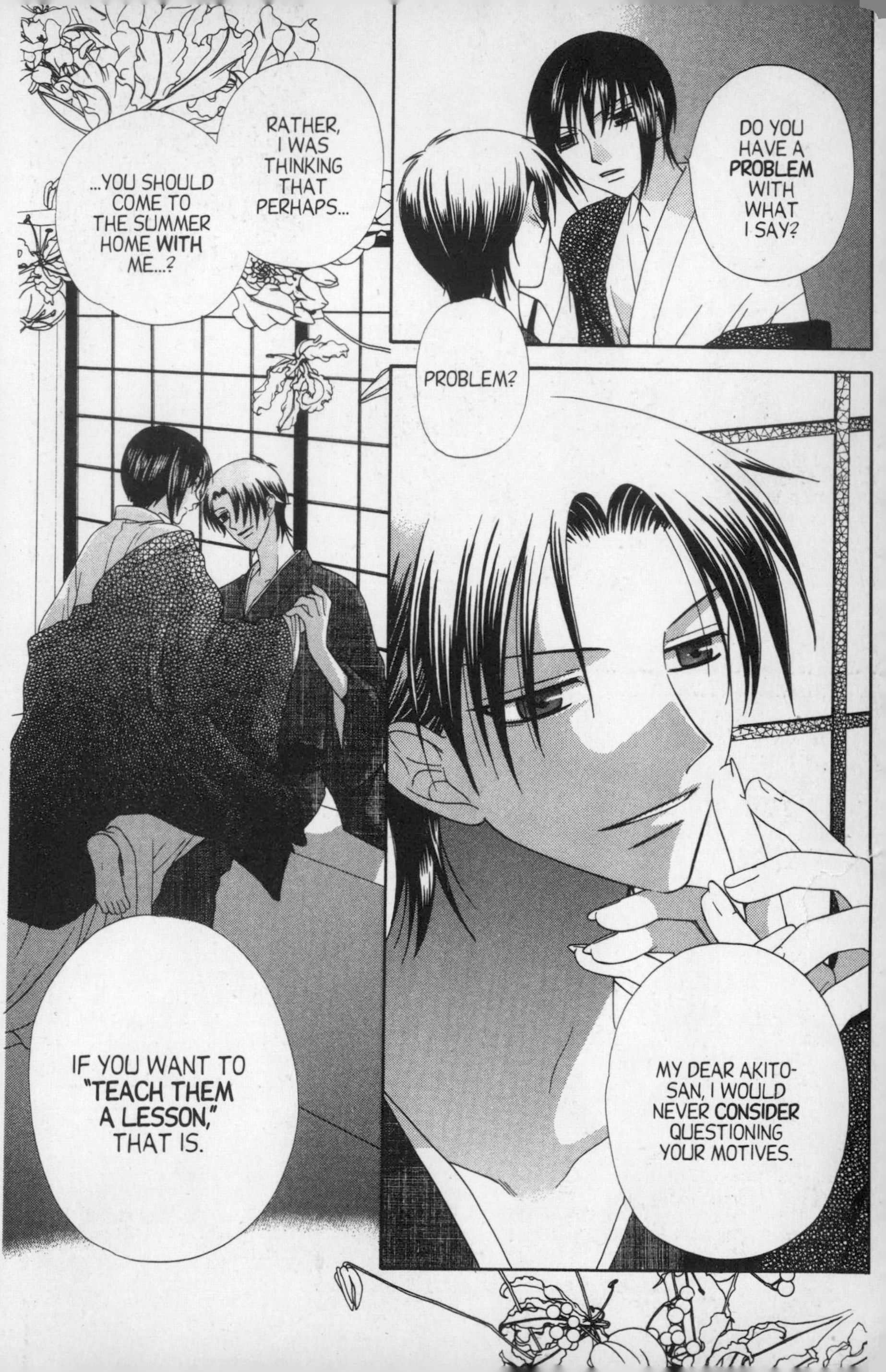
DO YOU HAVE A PROBLEM WITH WHAT I SAY?
PROBLEM?
MY DEAR AKITO-SAN, I WOULD NEVER CONSIDER QUESTIONING YOUR MOTIVES.
RATHER, I WAS THINKING THAT PERHAPS...
...YOU SHOULD COME TO THE SUMMER HOME WITH ME...?
IF YOU WANT TO "TEACH THEM A LESSON," THAT IS.

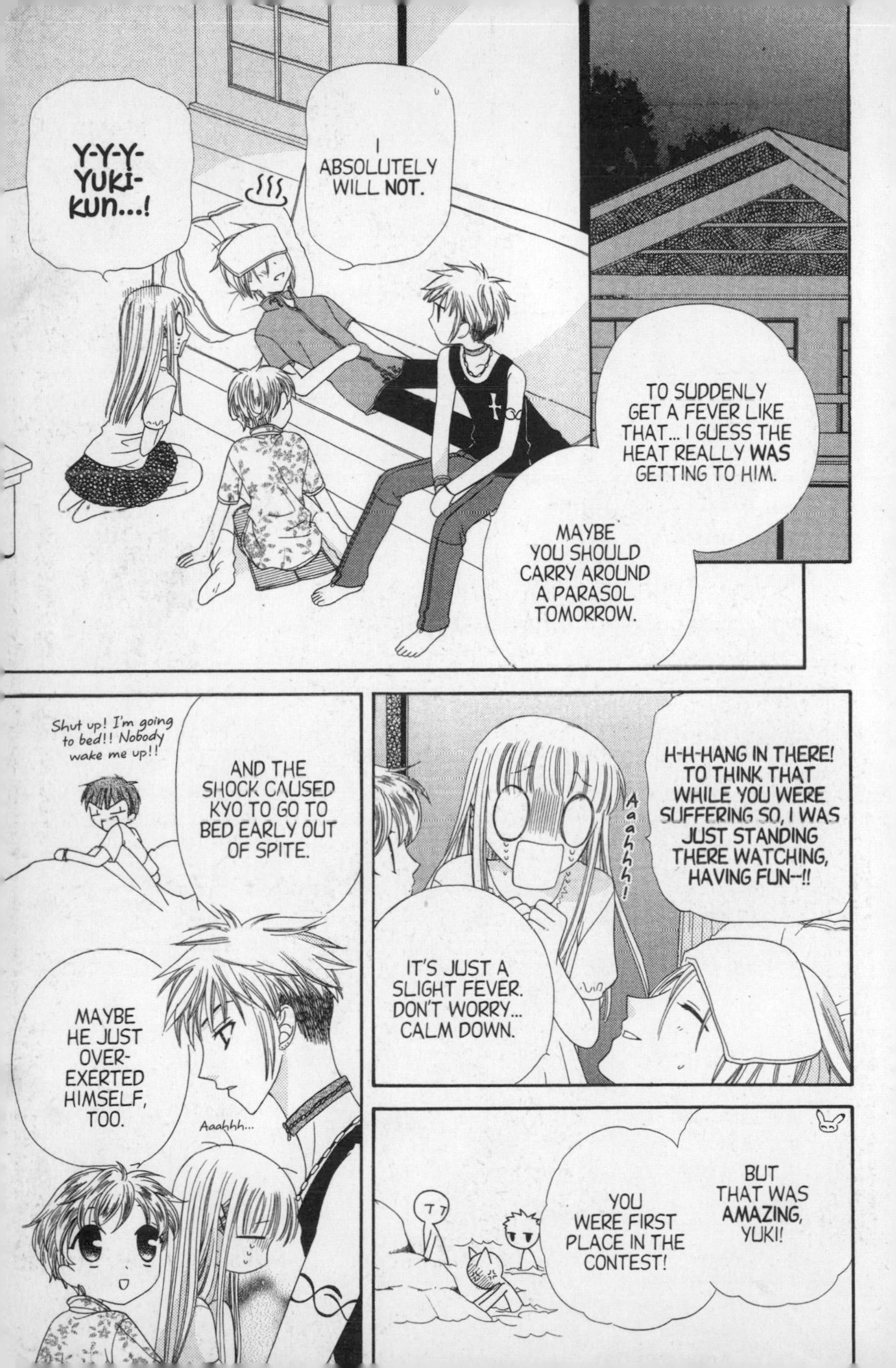
TO SUDDENLY GET A FEVER LIKE THAT... I GUESS THE HEAT REALLY WAS GETTING TO HIM.
MAYBE YOU SHOULD CARRY AROUND A PARASOL TOMORROW.
I ABSOLUTELY WILL NOT.
Y-Y-Y-YUKI-KUN...!
H-H-HANG IN THERE! TO THINK THAT WHILE YOU WERE SUFFERING SO, I WAS JUST STANDING THERE WATCHING, HAVING FUN--!!
Aaahhh!
IT'S JUST A SLIGHT FEVER. DON'T WORRY... CALM DOWN.
AND THE SHOCK CAUSED KYO TO GO TO BED EARLY OUT OF SPITE.
Shut up! I'm going to bed!! Nobody wake me up!!
MAYBE HE JUST OVER-EXERTED HIMSELF, TOO.
Aaahhh...
BUT THAT WAS AMAZING, YUKI!
YOU WERE FIRST PLACE IN THE CONTEST!

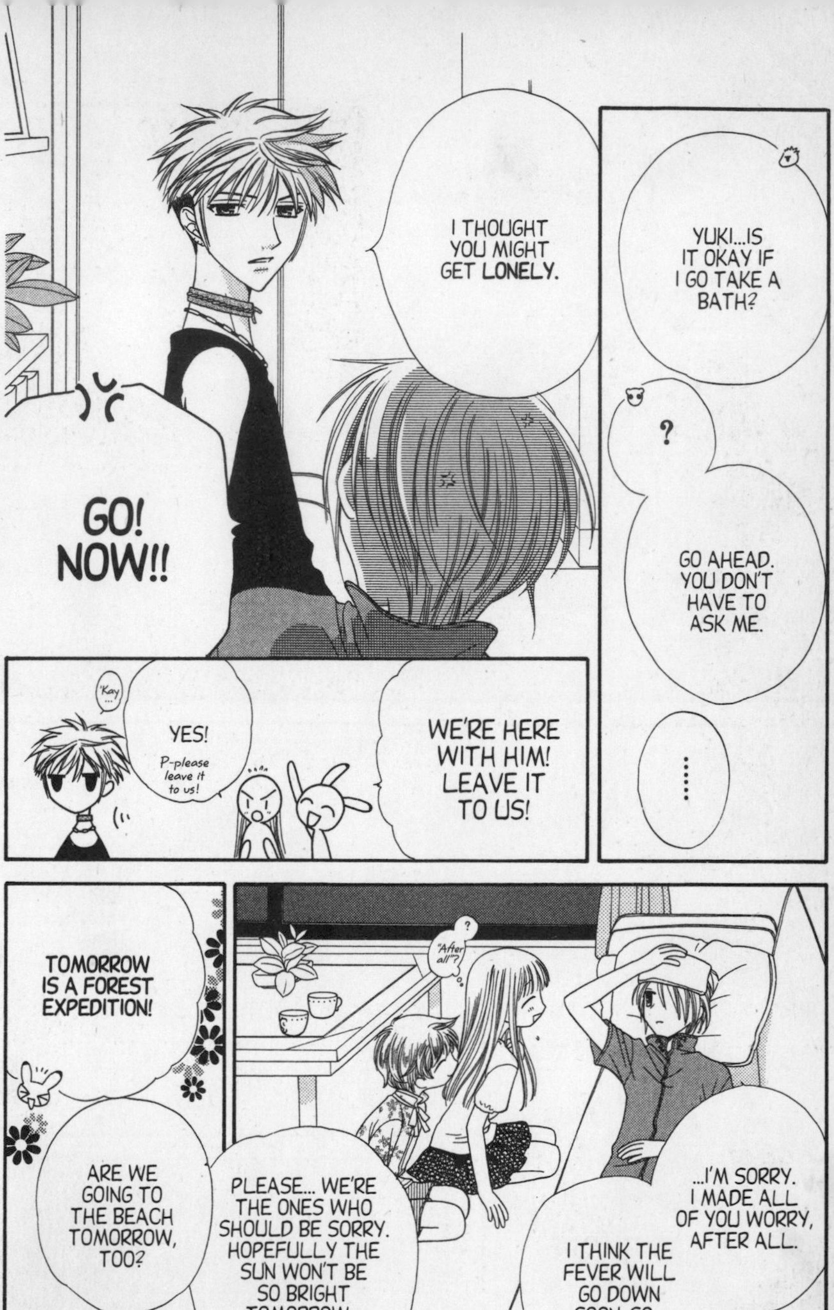
YUKI...IS IT OKAY IF I GO TAKE A BATH?
?
GO AHEAD. YOU DON'T HAVE TO ASK ME.
......
I THOUGHT YOU MIGHT GET LONELY.
GO! NOW!!
WE'RE HERE WITH HIM! LEAVE IT TO US!
YES!
P-please leave it to us!
'Kay...
...I'M SORRY. I MADE ALL OF YOU WORRY, AFTER ALL.
?
"After all"?
I THINK THE FEVER WILL GO DOWN SOON, SO...
PLEASE... WE'RE THE ONES WHO SHOULD BE SORRY. HOPEFULLY THE SUN WON'T BE SO BRIGHT TOMORROW...
ARE WE GOING TO THE BEACH TOMORROW, TOO?
TOMORROW IS A FOREST EXPEDITION!

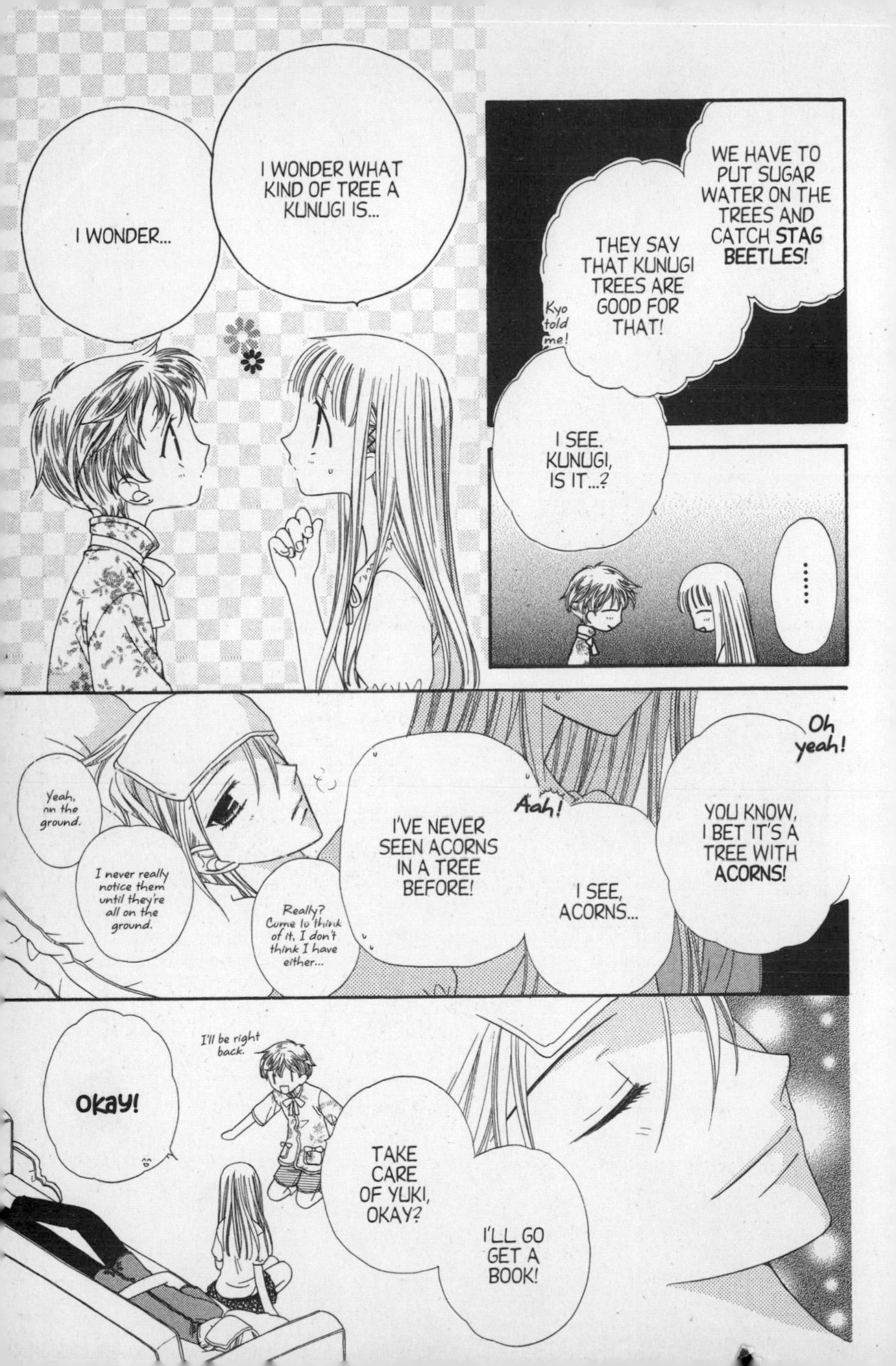
WE HAVE TO PUT SUGAR WATER ON THE TREES AND CATCH STAG BEETLES!
THEY SAY THAT KUNUGI TREES ARE GOOD FOR THAT!
Kyo told me!
I SEE. KUNUGI, IS IT...?
......
I WONDER WHAT KIND OF TREE A KUNUGI IS...
I WONDER...
Oh yeah!
YOU KNOW, I BET IT'S A TREE WITH ACORNS!
Aah!
I SEE, ACORNS...
I'VE NEVER SEEN ACORNS IN A TREE BEFORE!
Really? Come to think of it, I don't think I have either...
I never really notice them until they're all on the ground.
Yeah, on the ground.
I'LL GO GET A BOOK!
TAKE CARE OF YUKI, OKAY?
I'll be right back.
OKAY!

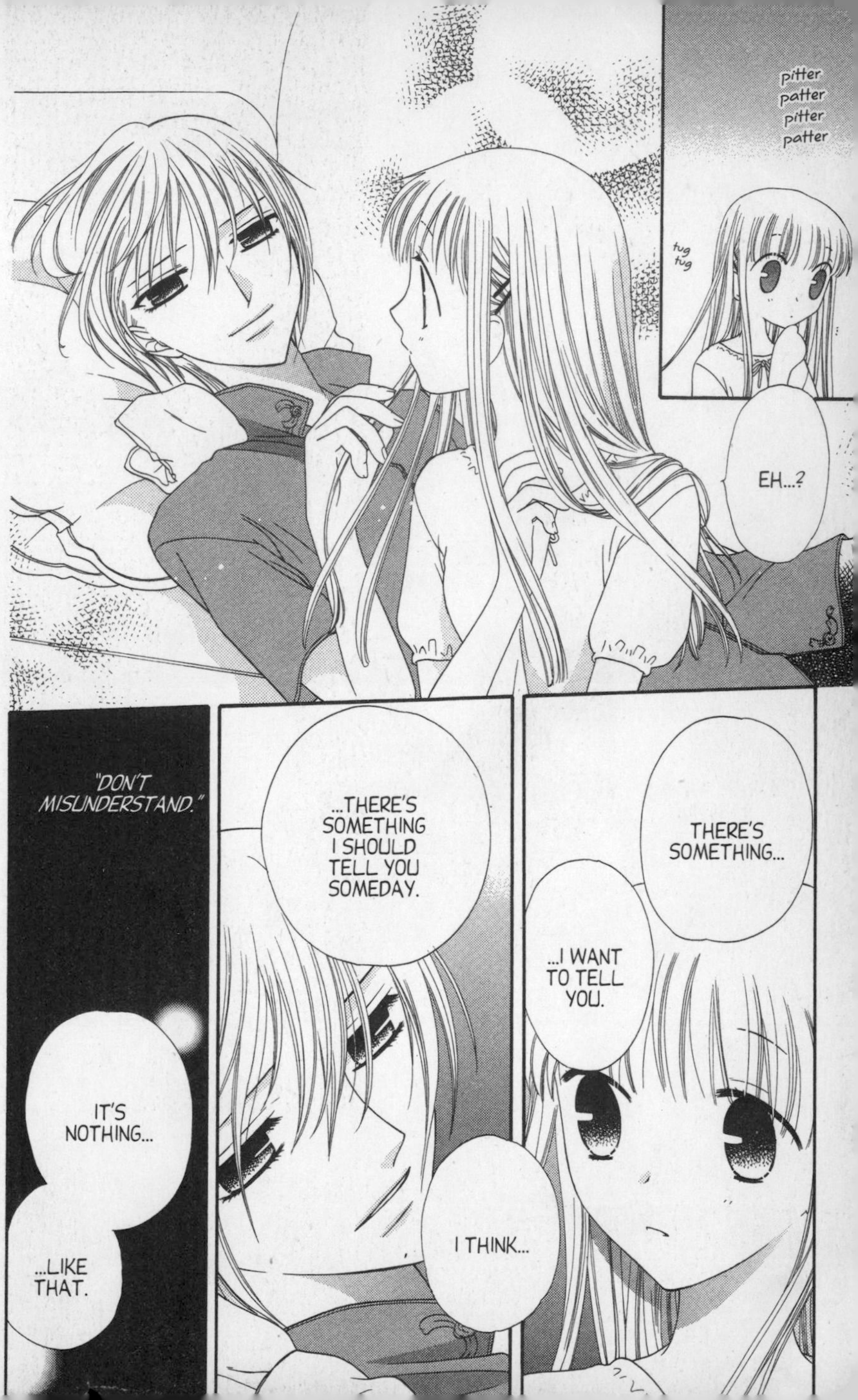
pitter patter pitter patter
tug tug
EH...?
THERE'S SOMETHING...
...I WANT TO TELL YOU.
...THERE'S SOMETHING I SHOULD TELL YOU SOMEDAY.
I THINK...
"DON'T MISUNDERSTAND."
IT'S NOTHING...
...LIKE THAT.

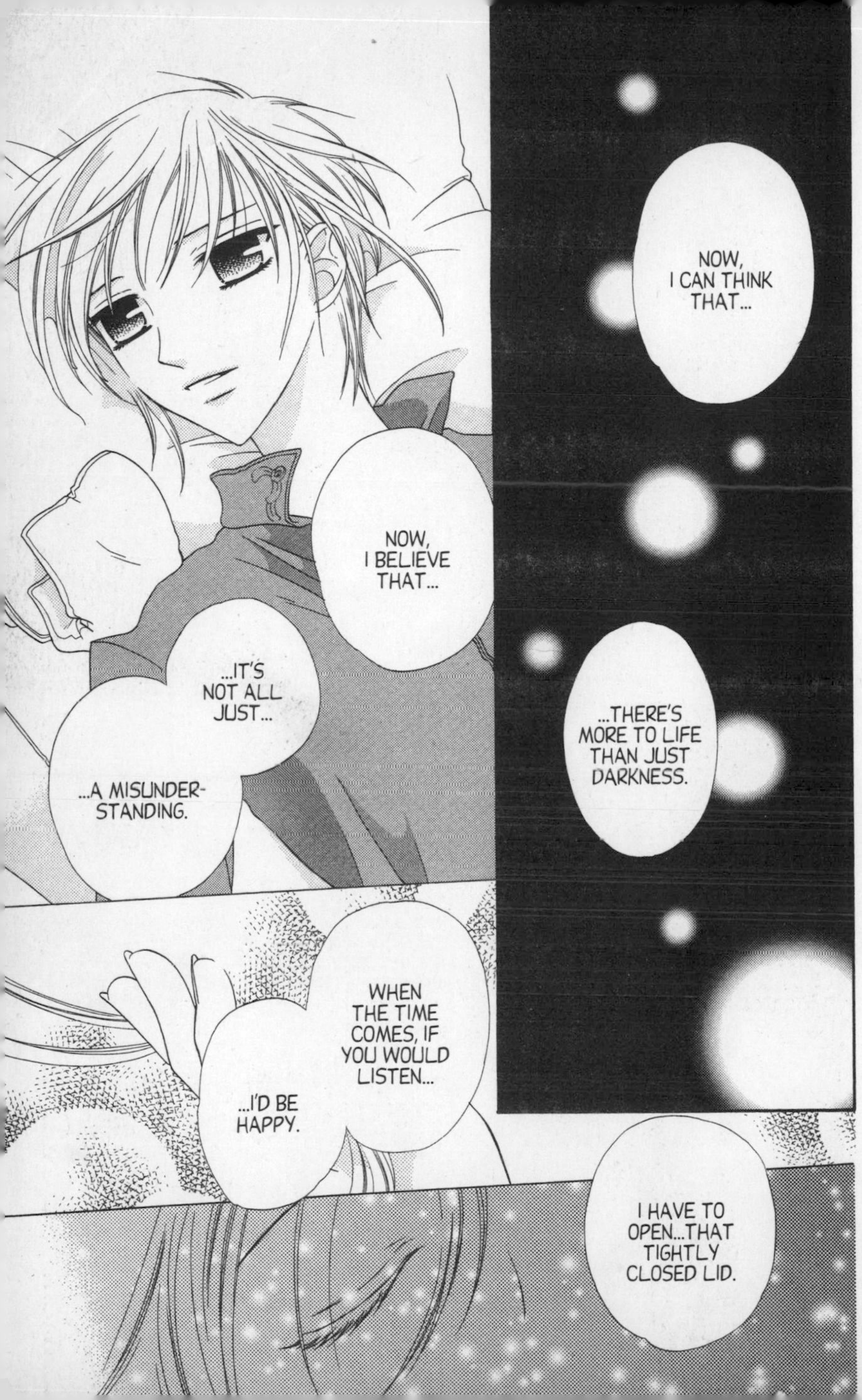
NOW, I CAN THINK THAT...
...THERE'S MORE TO LIFE THAN JUST DARKNESS.
NOW, I BELIEVE THAT...
...IT'S NOT ALL JUST...
...A MISUNDER-STANDING.
WHEN THE TIME COMES, IF YOU WOULD LISTEN...
...I'D BE HAPPY.
I HAVE TO OPEN...THAT TIGHTLY CLOSED LID.

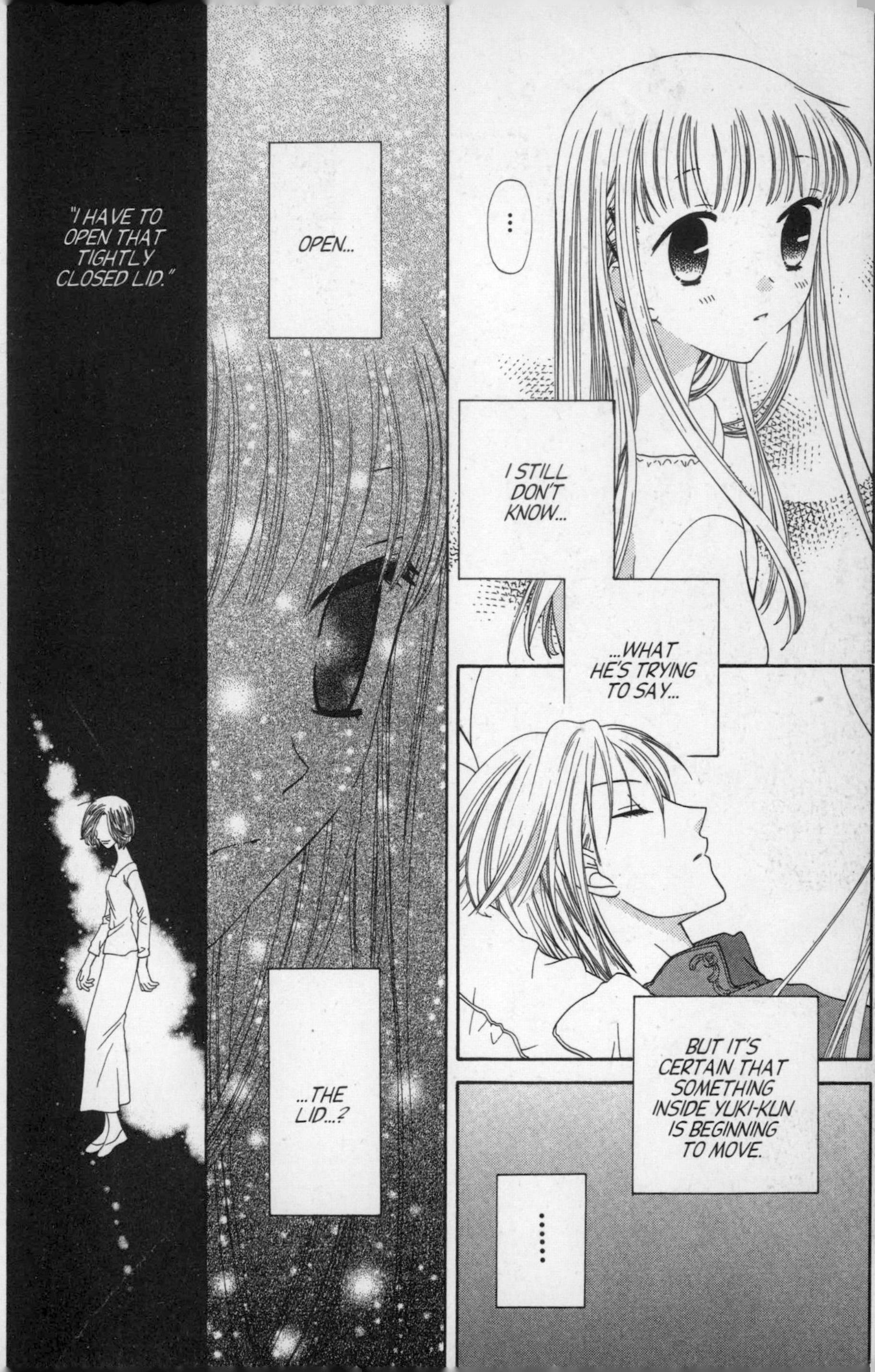
…
I STILL DON'T KNOW…
…WHAT HE'S TRYING TO SAY…
BUT IT'S CERTAIN THAT SOMETHING INSIDE YUKI-KUN IS BEGINNING TO MOVE.
……
OPEN…
…THE LID…?
"I HAVE TO OPEN THAT TIGHTLY CLOSED LID."

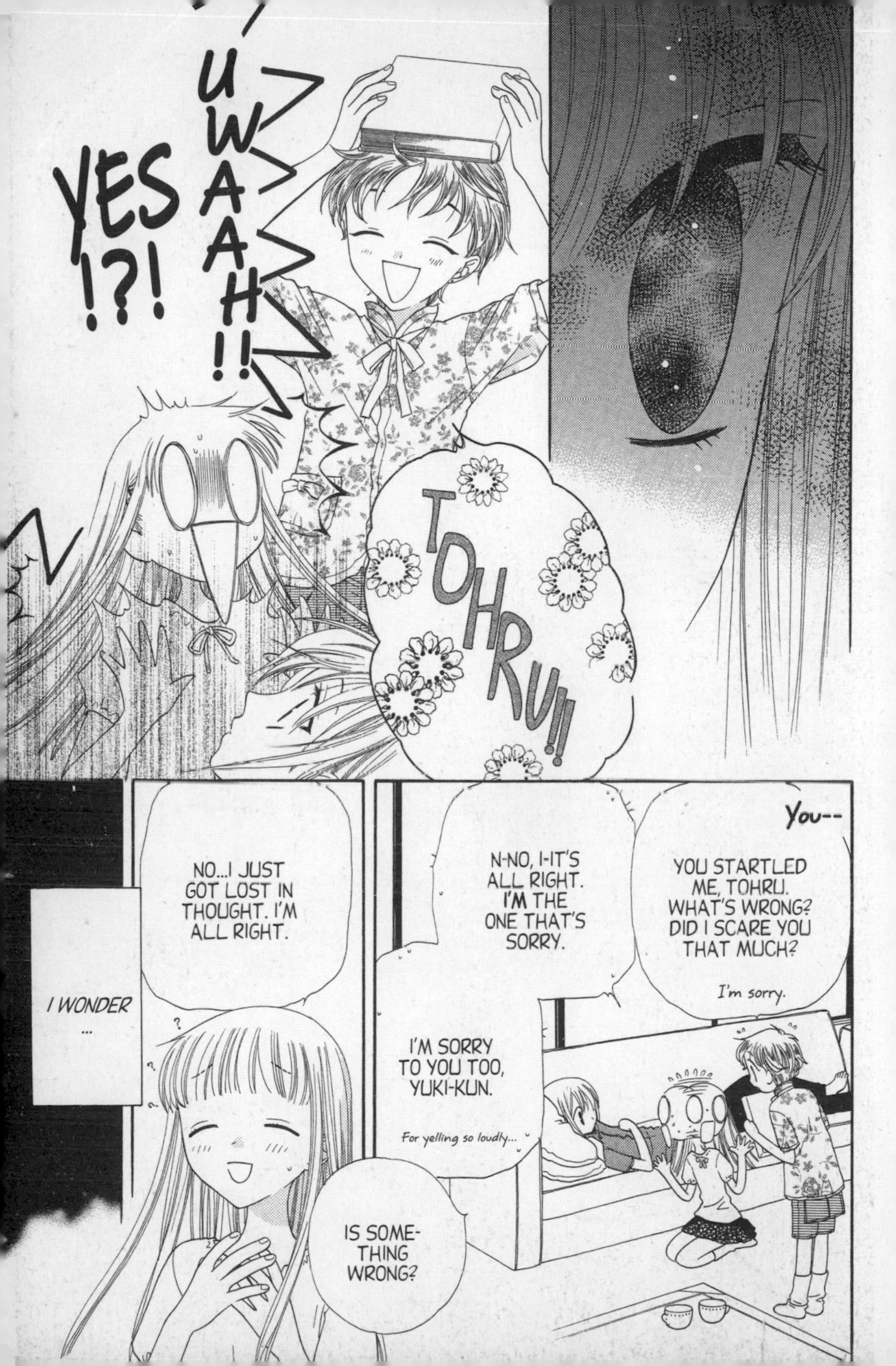
TOHRU!!
UWAAAH!!
YES!?!
You--
YOU STARTLED ME, TOHRU. WHAT'S WRONG? DID I SCARE YOU THAT MUCH?
I'm sorry.
N-NO, I-IT'S ALL RIGHT. I'M THE ONE THAT'S SORRY.
I'M SORRY TO YOU TOO, YUKI-KUN.
For yelling so loudly...
NO...I JUST GOT LOST IN THOUGHT. I'M ALL RIGHT.
IS SOME-THING WRONG?
I WONDER ...

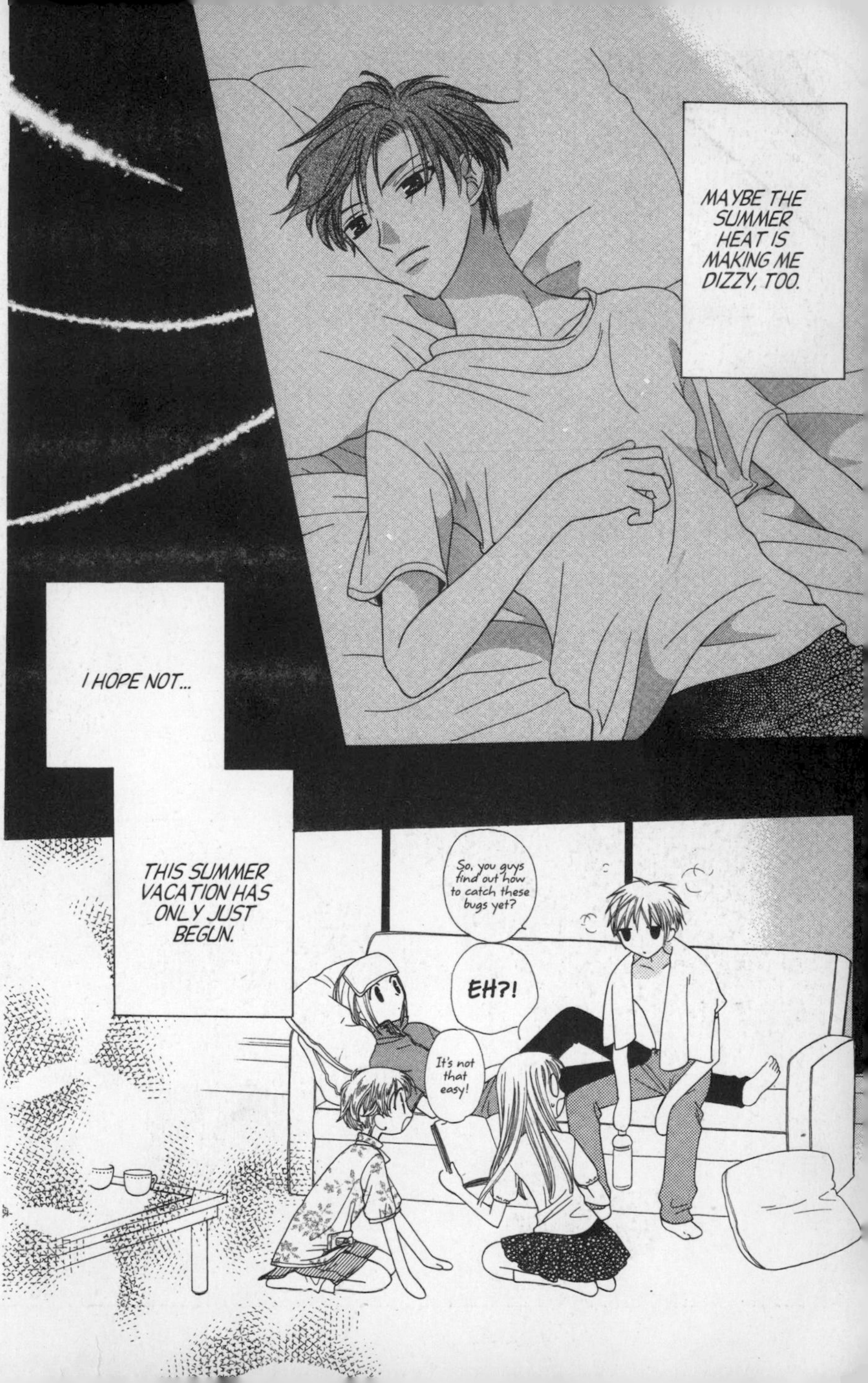
MAYBE THE SUMMER HEAT IS MAKING ME DIZZY, TOO.
I HOPE NOT...
THIS SUMMER VACATION HAS ONLY JUST BEGUN.
So, you guys find out how to catch these bugs yet?
EH?!
It's not that easy!

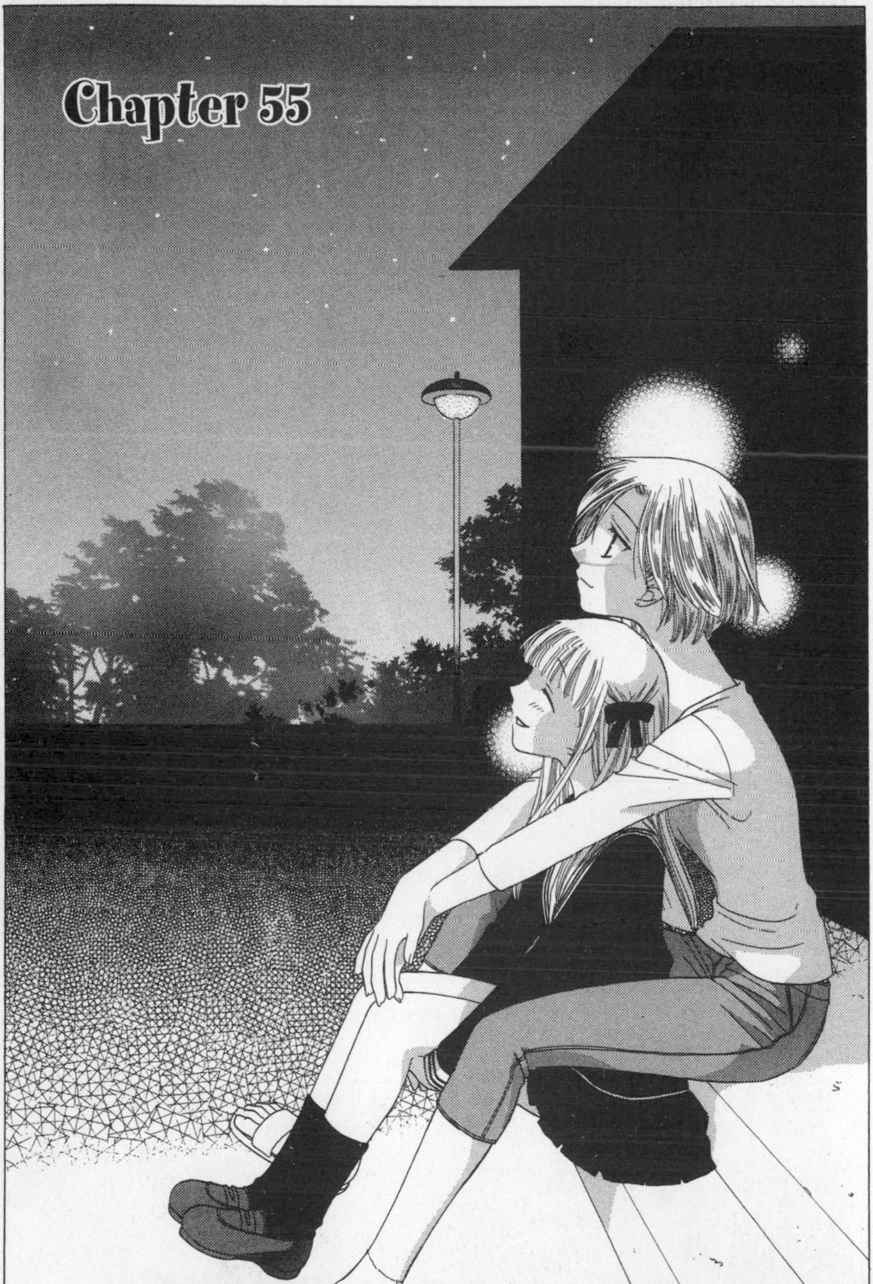
Chapter 55

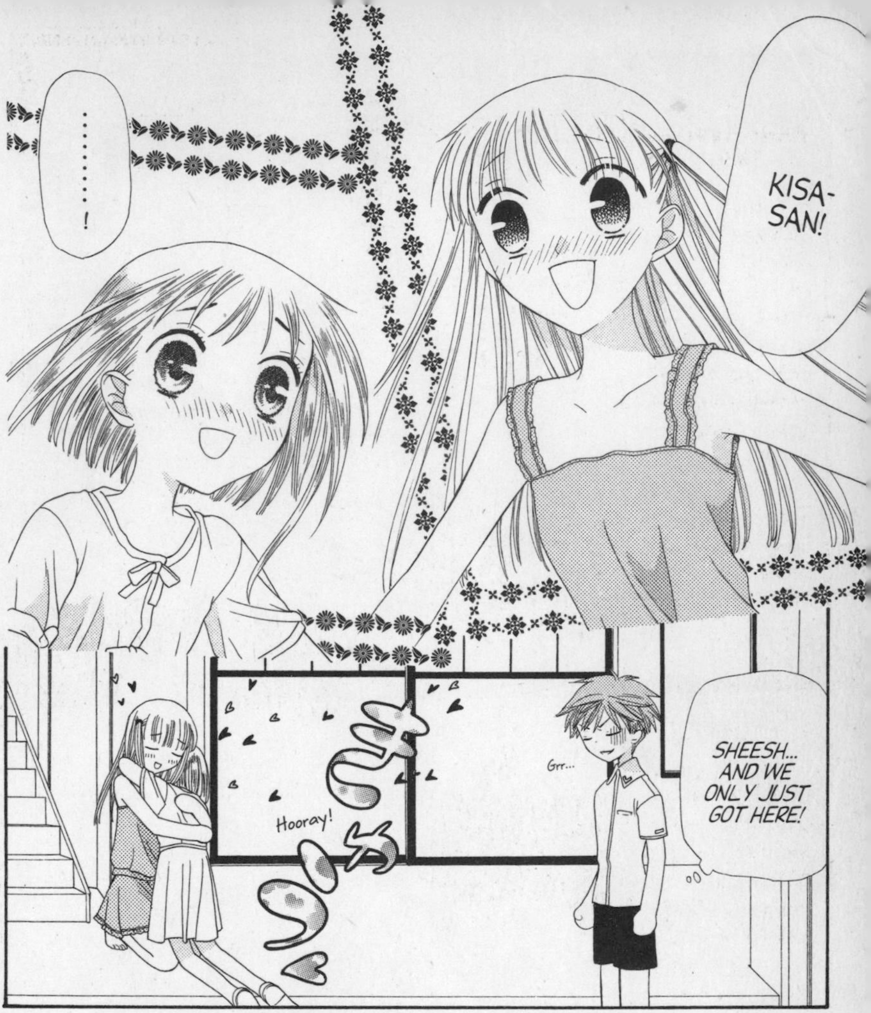
KISA-SAN!
......!
SHEESH... AND WE ONLY JUST GOT HERE!
Grr...
Hooray!

**BLAH, BLAH, BLAH 2**

I like drawing small children. But I guess Kisa and Hiro are at about that age where they'll be getting bigger soon. I look forward to drawing **that,** too!

**Fruits Basket 10 Part 2:**

*Now that Furuba has made it to volume 10, there aren't that many characters left to be introduced. I don't know if I think, "Finally!" or, "Already?" but, when I look back, I can't help but feel as if there are a lot of characters. And yet, I still find myself thinking that there aren't enough...*
*I think I'll start using this space to talk about the characters—give you all some of the worthless trivia that doesn't always come up in the stories themselves. Let's start with the famous Furuba "lost" side characters.*
*So, until the next chapter... Let's go!*

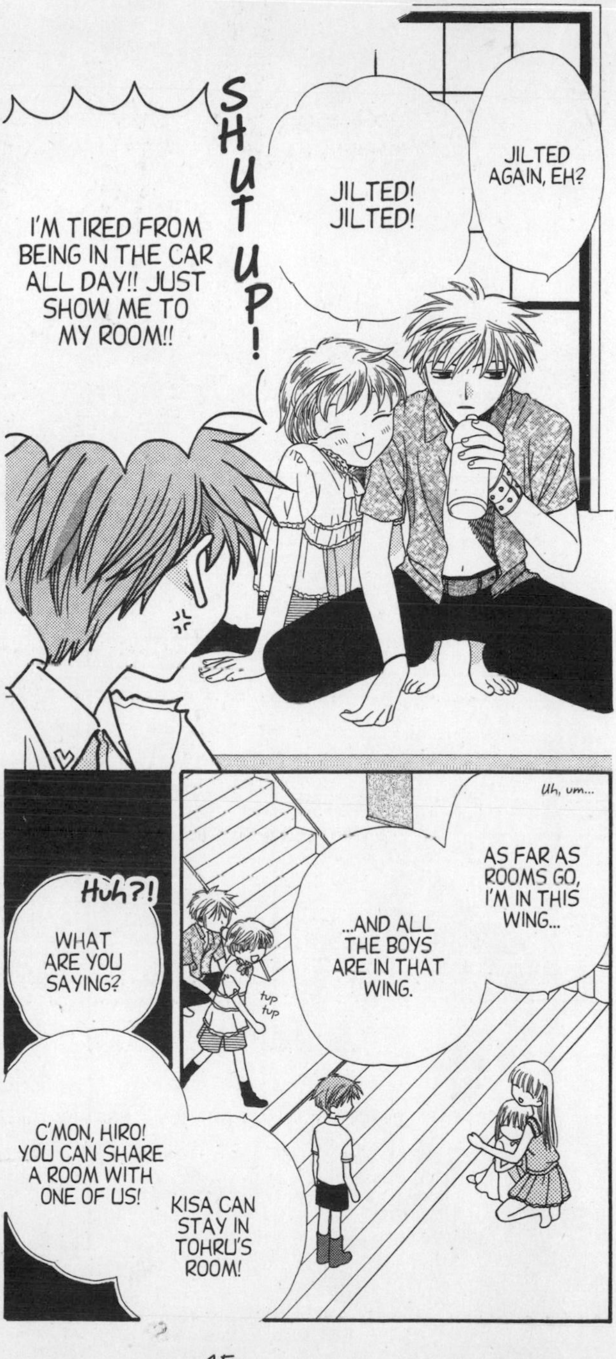
JILTED AGAIN, EH?
JILTED! JILTED!
SHUT UP!
I'M TIRED FROM BEING IN THE CAR ALL DAY!! JUST SHOW ME TO MY ROOM!!
Uh, um...
AS FAR AS ROOMS GO, I'M IN THIS WING...
...AND ALL THE BOYS ARE IN THAT WING.
Huh?!
WHAT ARE YOU SAYING?
tup tup
KISA CAN STAY IN TOHRU'S ROOM!
C'MON, HIRO! YOU CAN SHARE A ROOM WITH ONE OF US!

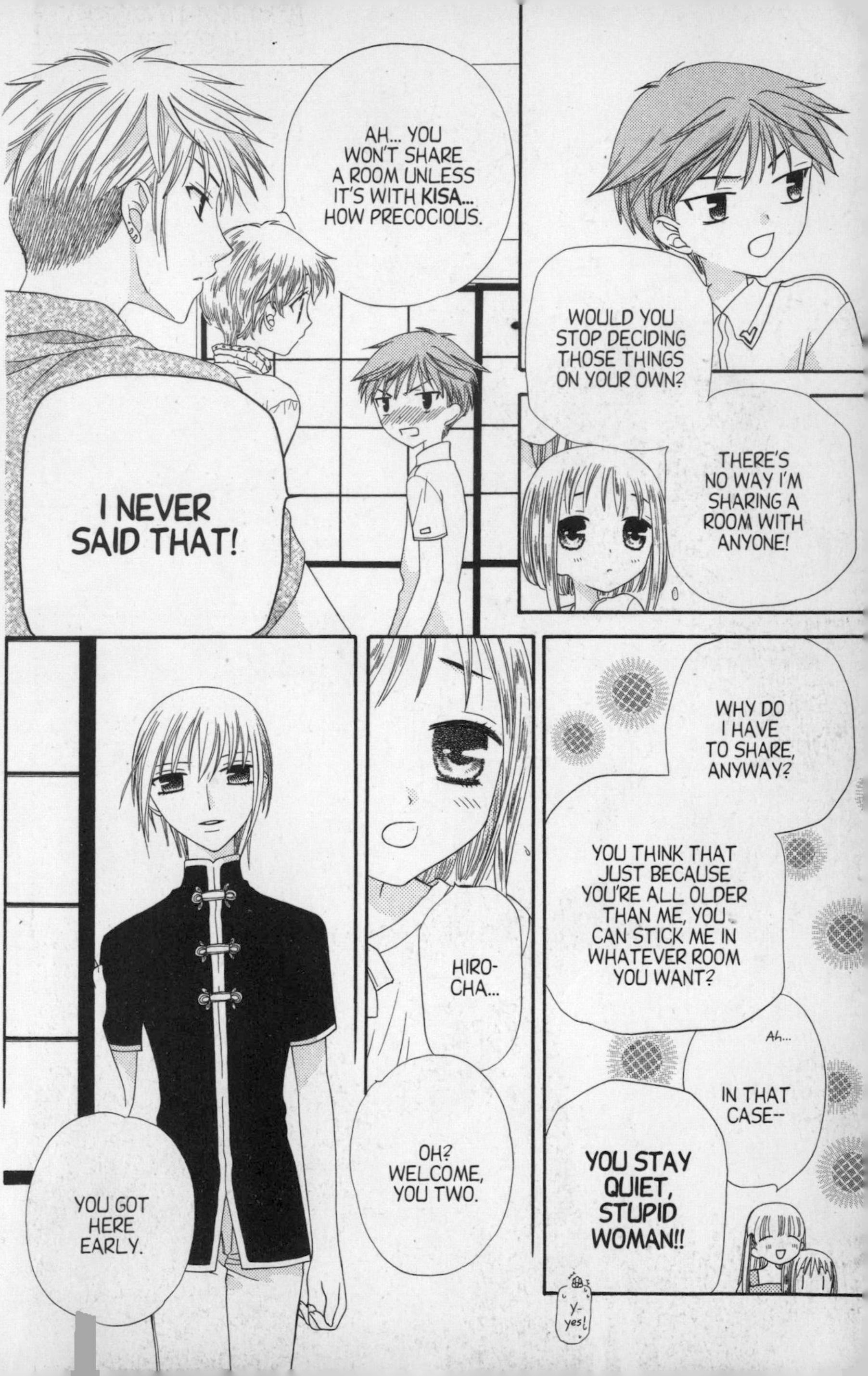
WOULD YOU STOP DECIDING THOSE THINGS ON YOUR OWN?
THERE'S NO WAY I'M SHARING A ROOM WITH ANYONE!
AH... YOU WON'T SHARE A ROOM UNLESS IT'S WITH KISA... HOW PRECOCIOUS.
I NEVER SAID THAT!
WHY DO I HAVE TO SHARE, ANYWAY?
YOU THINK THAT JUST BECAUSE YOU'RE ALL OLDER THAN ME, YOU CAN STICK ME IN WHATEVER ROOM YOU WANT?
Ah...
IN THAT CASE--
YOU STAY QUIET, STUPID WOMAN!!
Y-yes!
HIRO-CHA...
OH? WELCOME, YOU TWO.
YOU GOT HERE EARLY.

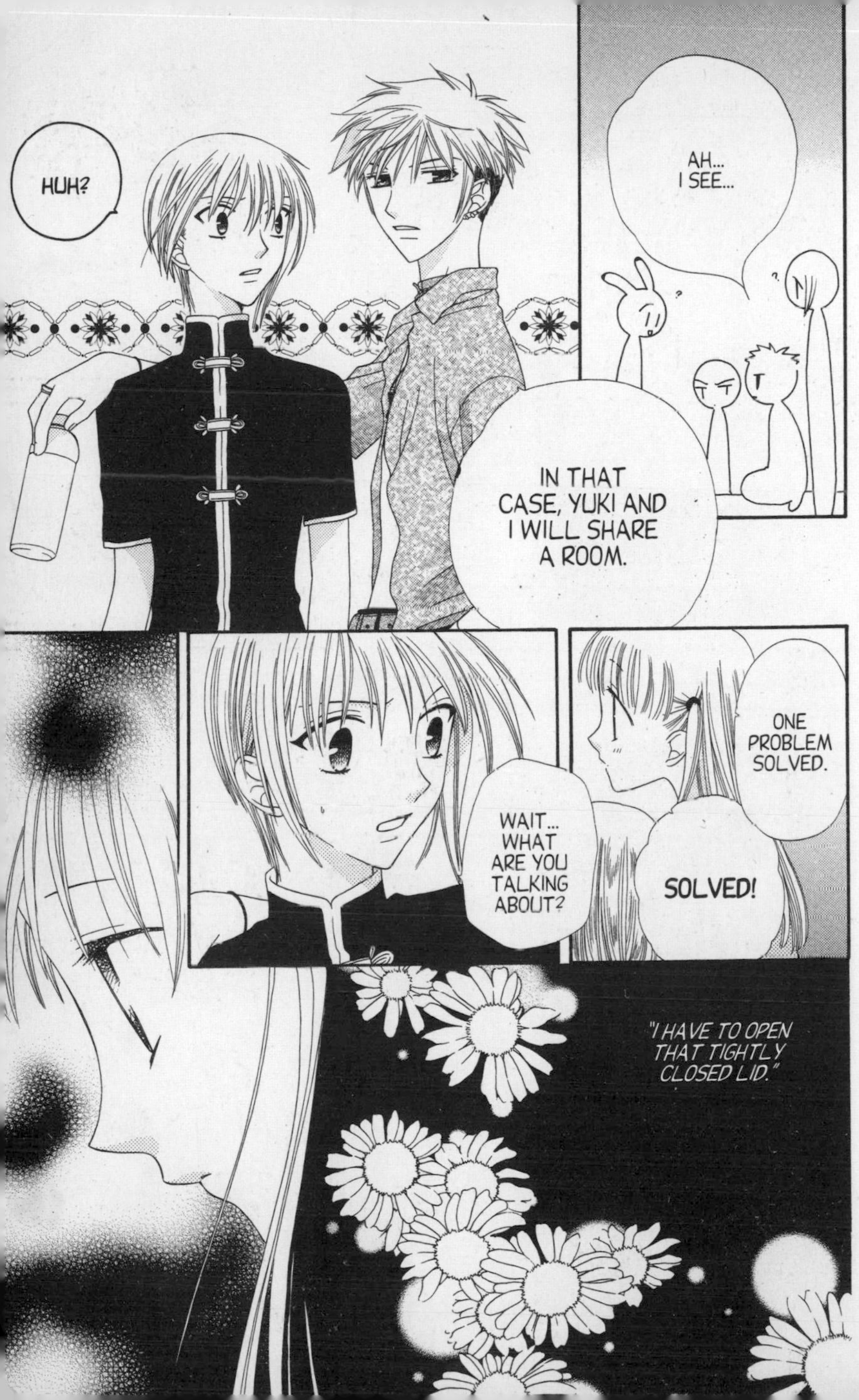
AH... I SEE...
IN THAT CASE, YUKI AND I WILL SHARE A ROOM.
HUH?
ONE PROBLEM SOLVED.
SOLVED!
WAIT... WHAT ARE YOU TALKING ABOUT?
"I HAVE TO OPEN THAT TIGHTLY CLOSED LID."

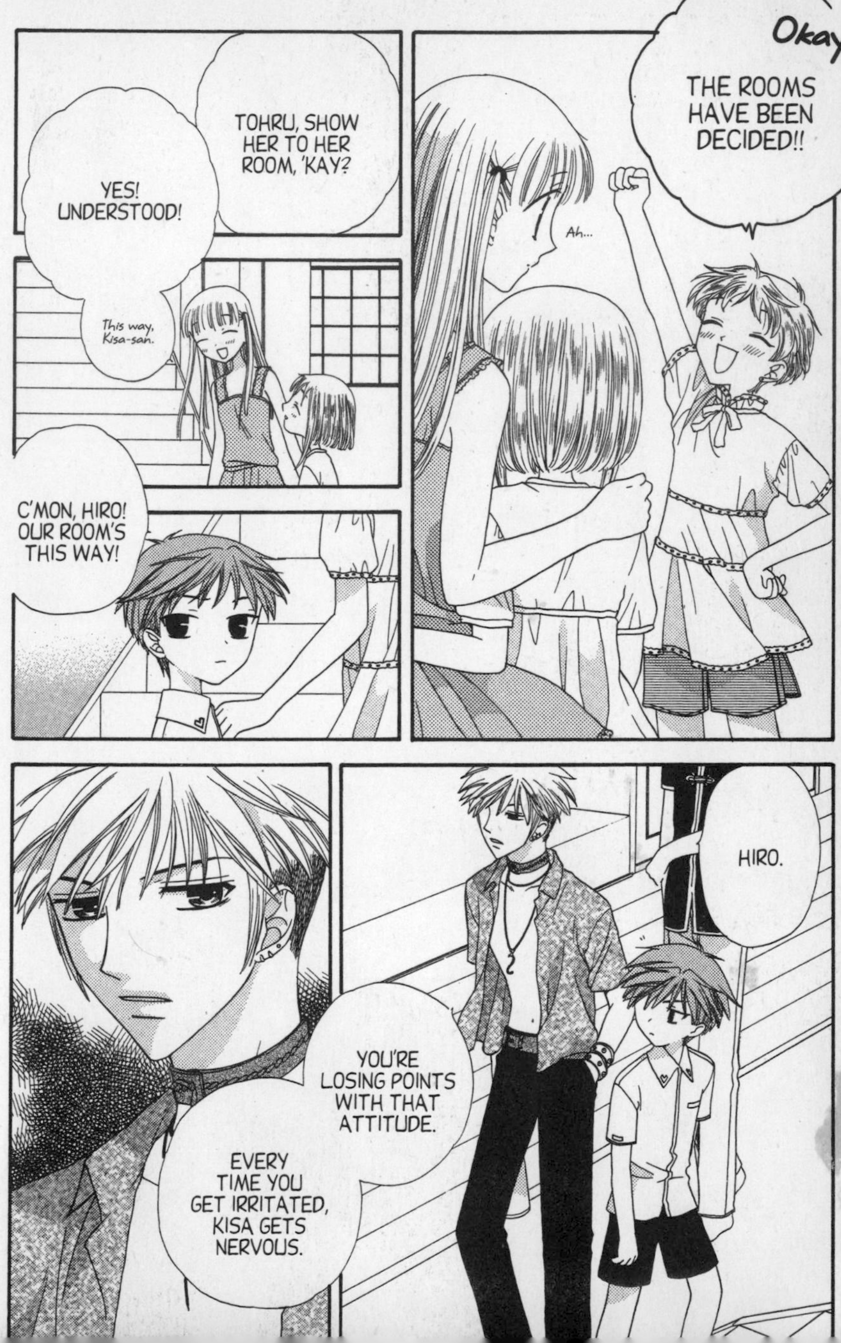
Okay!
THE ROOMS HAVE BEEN DECIDED!!
Ah...
TOHRU, SHOW HER TO HER ROOM, 'KAY?
YES! UNDERSTOOD!
This way, Kisa-san.
C'MON, HIRO! OUR ROOM'S THIS WAY!
HIRO.
YOU'RE LOSING POINTS WITH THAT ATTITUDE.
EVERY TIME YOU GET IRRITATED, KISA GETS NERVOUS.

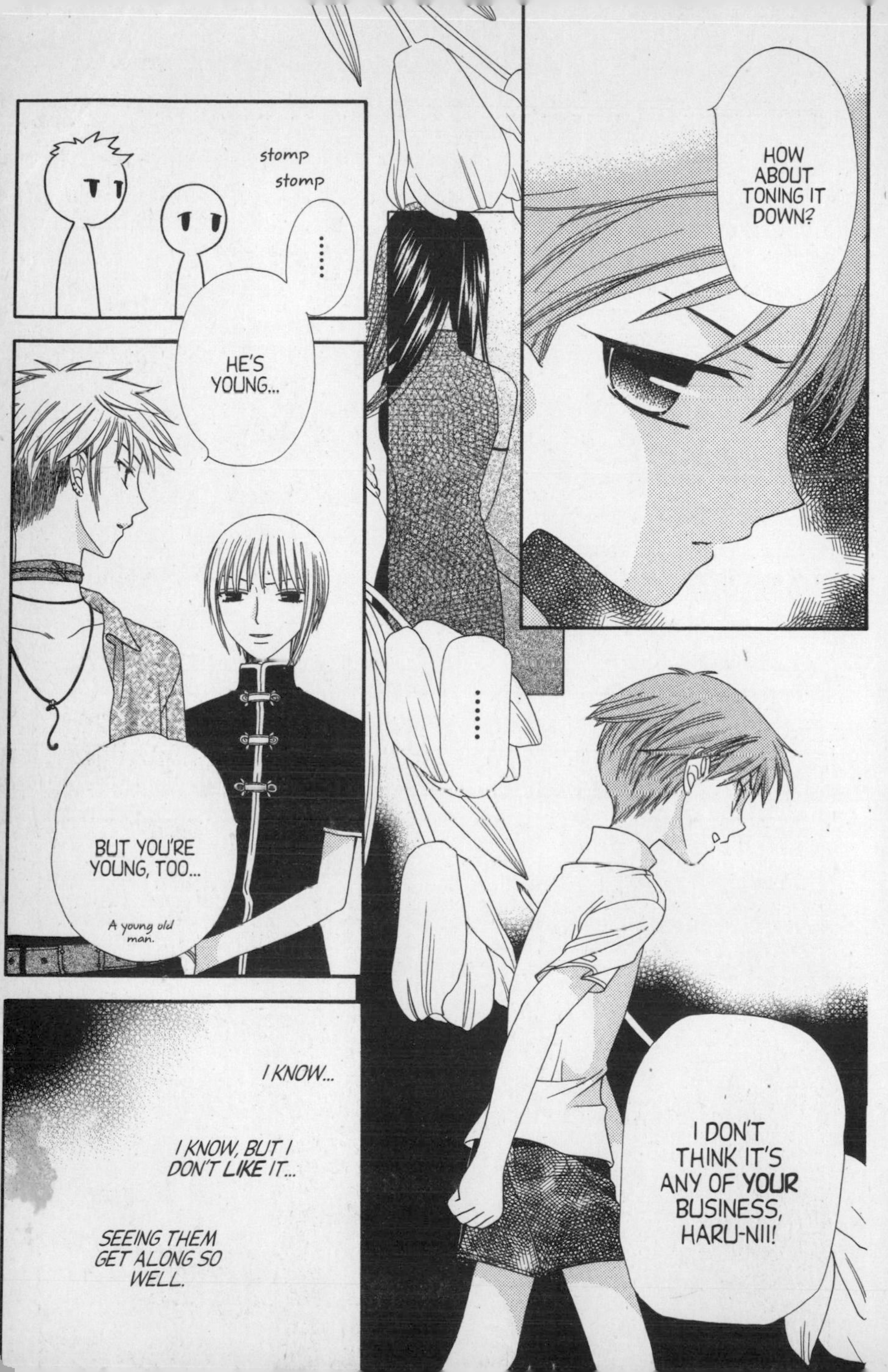
HOW ABOUT TONING IT DOWN?
......
I DON'T THINK IT'S ANY OF **YOUR** BUSINESS, HARU-NII!
stomp
stomp
......
HE'S YOUNG...
BUT YOU'RE YOUNG, TOO...
A young old man.
I KNOW...
I KNOW, BUT I DON'T **LIKE** IT...
SEEING THEM GET ALONG SO WELL.

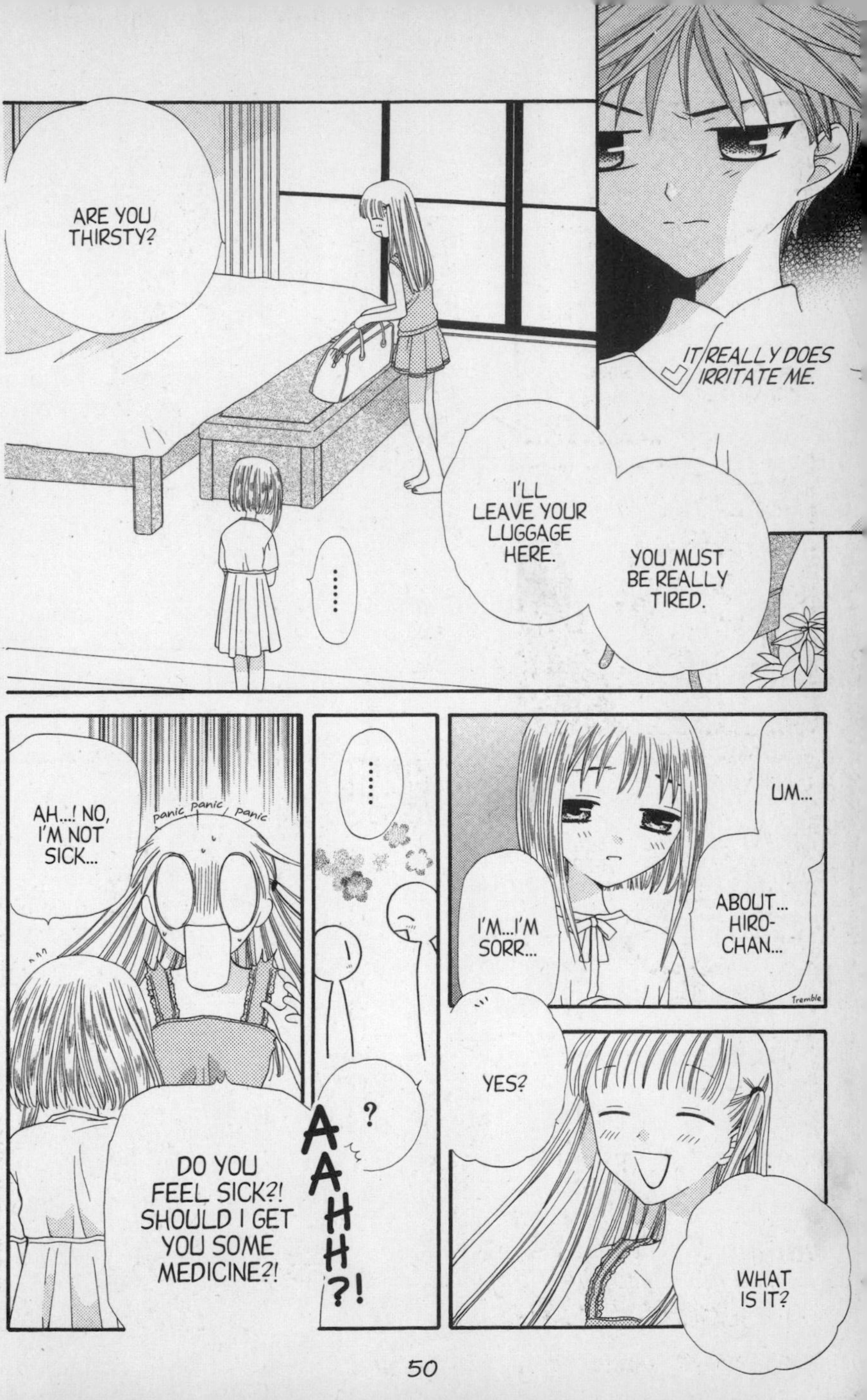
IT REALLY DOES IRRITATE ME.
I'LL LEAVE YOUR LUGGAGE HERE.
YOU MUST BE REALLY TIRED.
......
ARE YOU THIRSTY?
UM...
ABOUT... HIRO-CHAN...
I'M...I'M SORR...
Tremble
YES?
WHAT IS IT?
......
?
AAHH?!
DO YOU FEEL SICK?! SHOULD I GET YOU SOME MEDICINE?!
AH...! NO, I'M NOT SICK...
panic panic panic

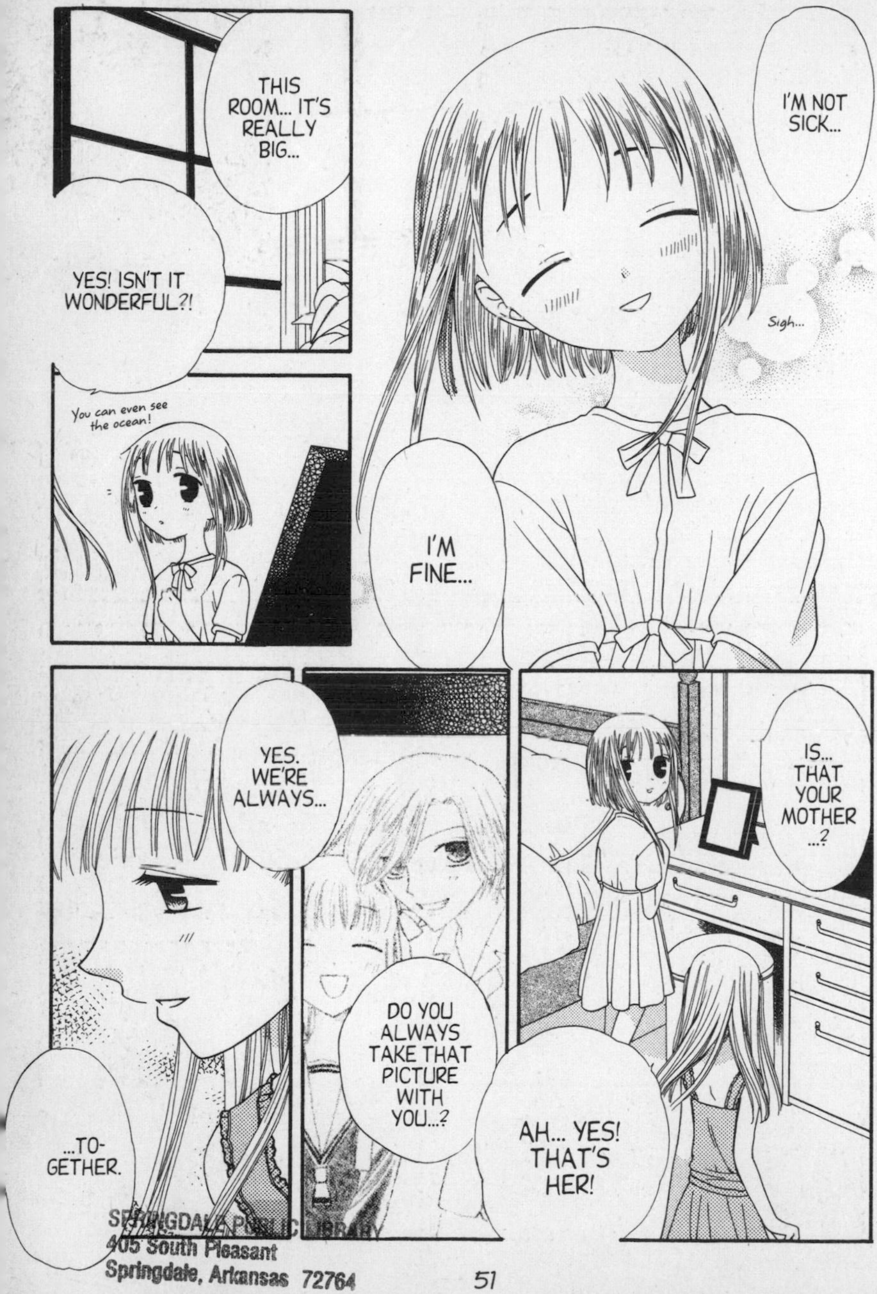
I'M NOT SICK...
Sigh...
I'M FINE...
THIS ROOM... IT'S REALLY BIG...
YES! ISN'T IT WONDERFUL?!
You can even see the ocean!
IS... THAT YOUR MOTHER ...?
AH... YES! THAT'S HER!
DO YOU ALWAYS TAKE THAT PICTURE WITH YOU...?
YES. WE'RE ALWAYS...
...TO-
GETHER.

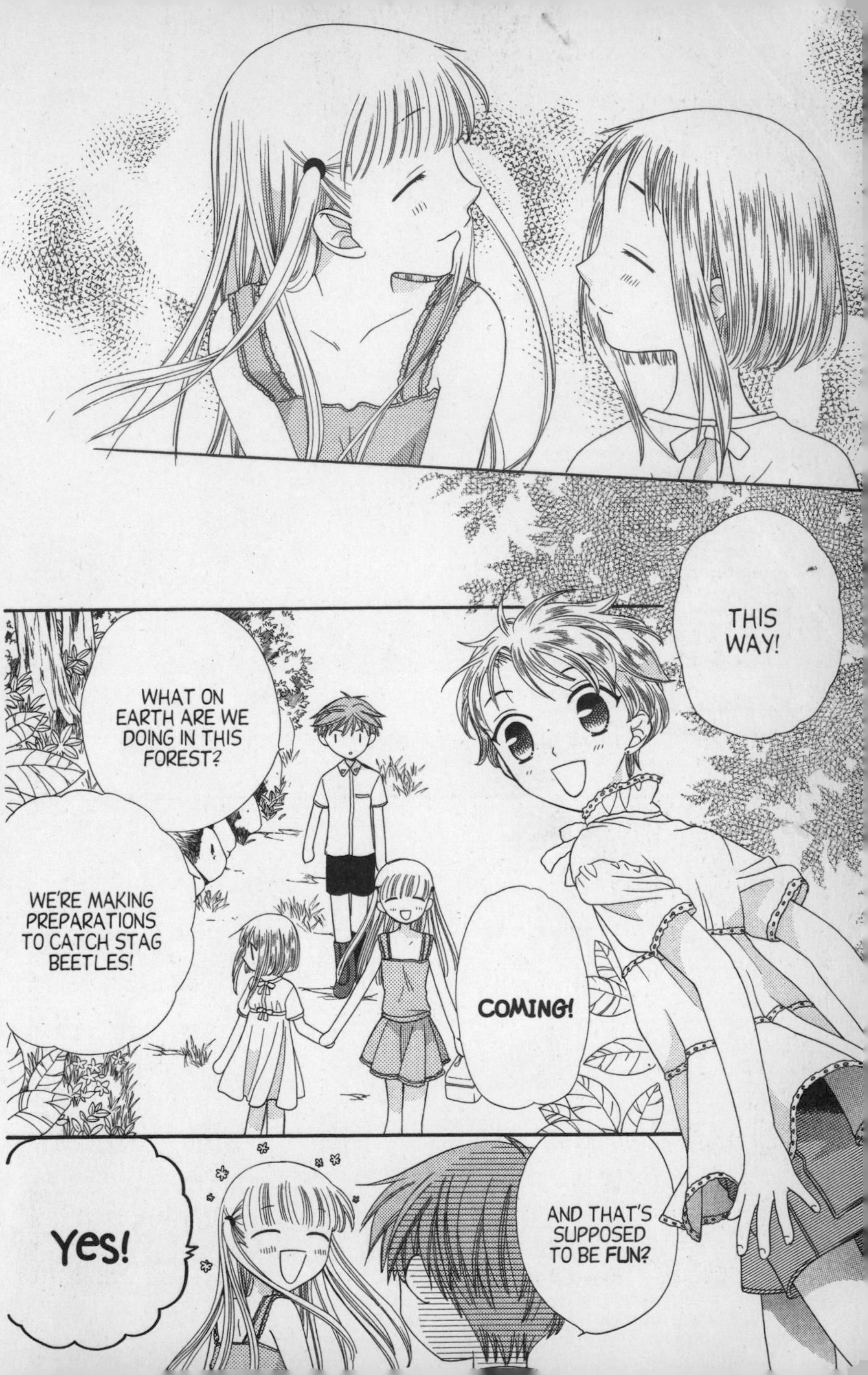
THIS WAY!
COMING!
WHAT ON EARTH ARE WE DOING IN THIS FOREST?
WE'RE MAKING PREPARATIONS TO CATCH STAG BEETLES!
AND THAT'S SUPPOSED TO BE FUN?
Yes!

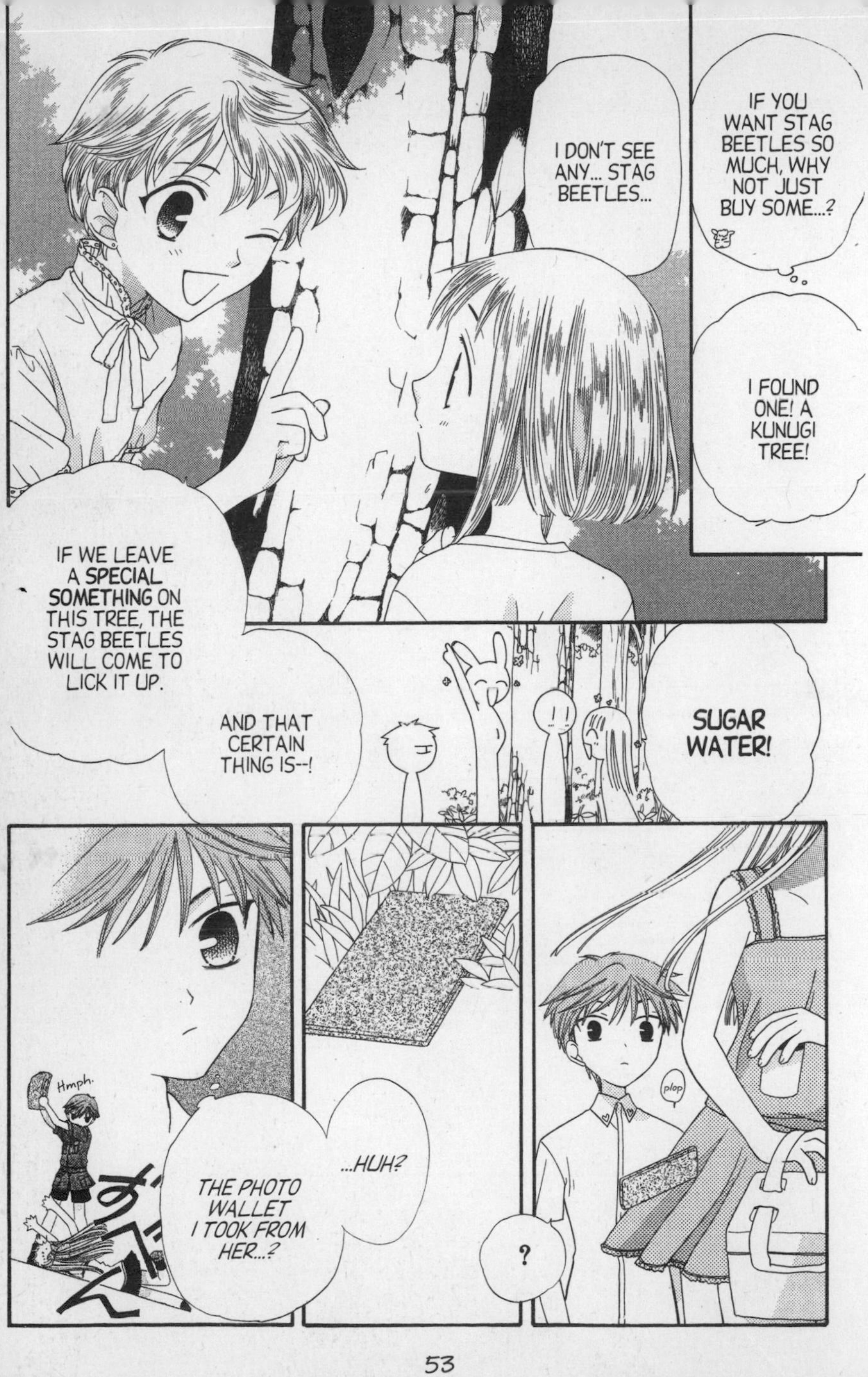
IF YOU WANT STAG BEETLES SO MUCH, WHY NOT JUST BUY SOME...?
I FOUND ONE! A KUNUGI TREE!
I DON'T SEE ANY... STAG BEETLES...
IF WE LEAVE A SPECIAL SOMETHING ON THIS TREE, THE STAG BEETLES WILL COME TO LICK IT UP.
AND THAT CERTAIN THING IS--!
SUGAR WATER!
plop
?
...HUH?
THE PHOTO WALLET I TOOK FROM HER...?
Hmph.

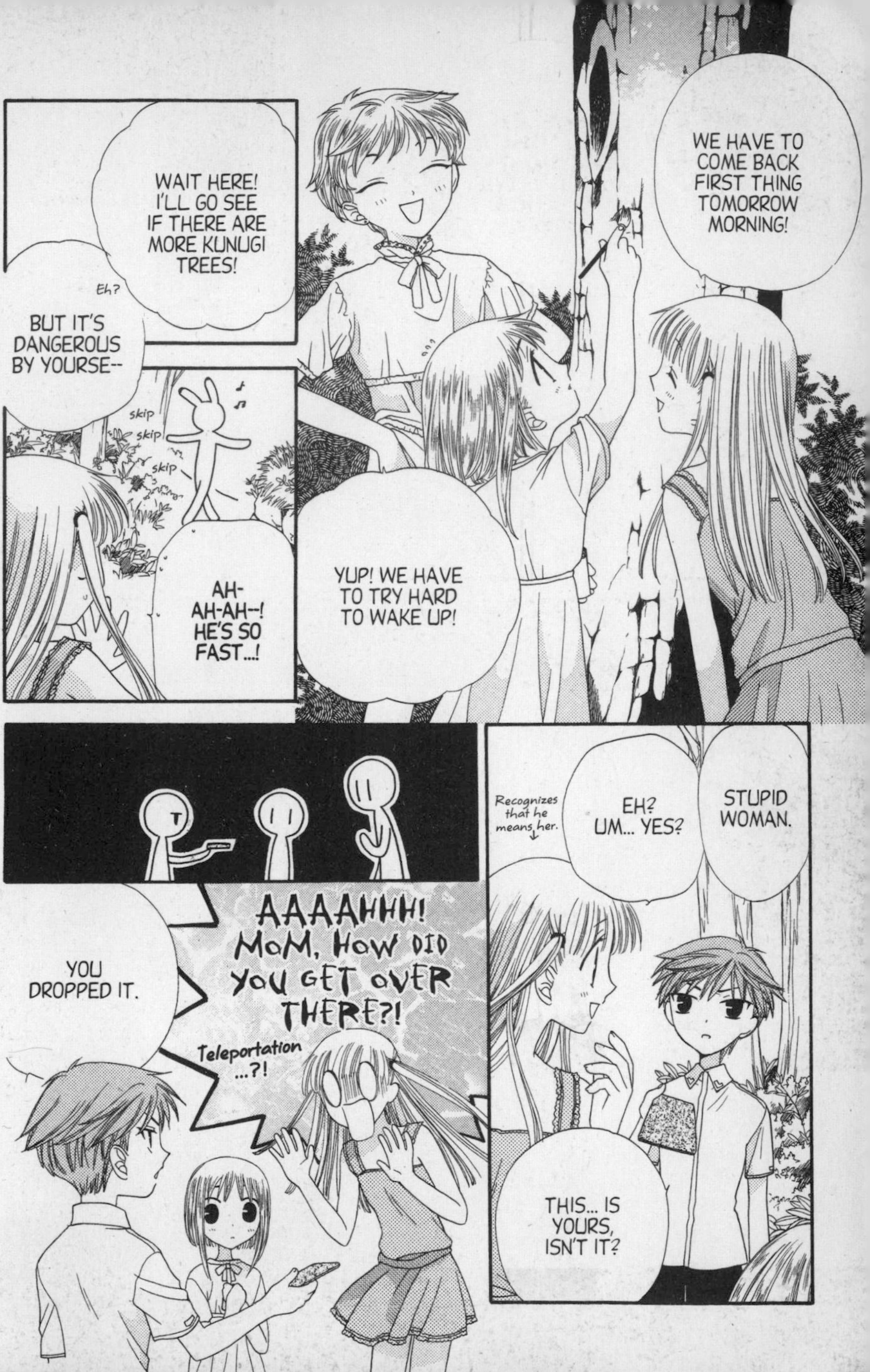
WE HAVE TO COME BACK FIRST THING TOMORROW MORNING!
YUP! WE HAVE TO TRY HARD TO WAKE UP!
WAIT HERE! I'LL GO SEE IF THERE ARE MORE KUNUGI TREES!
Eh?
BUT IT'S DANGEROUS BY YOURSE--
skip
skip
skip
AH-AH-AH--! HE'S SO FAST...!
STUPID WOMAN.
EH? UM... YES?
Recognizes that he means her.
THIS... IS YOURS, ISN'T IT?
YOU DROPPED IT.
AAAAHHH! MOM, HOW DID YOU GET OVER THERE?!
Teleportation ...?!

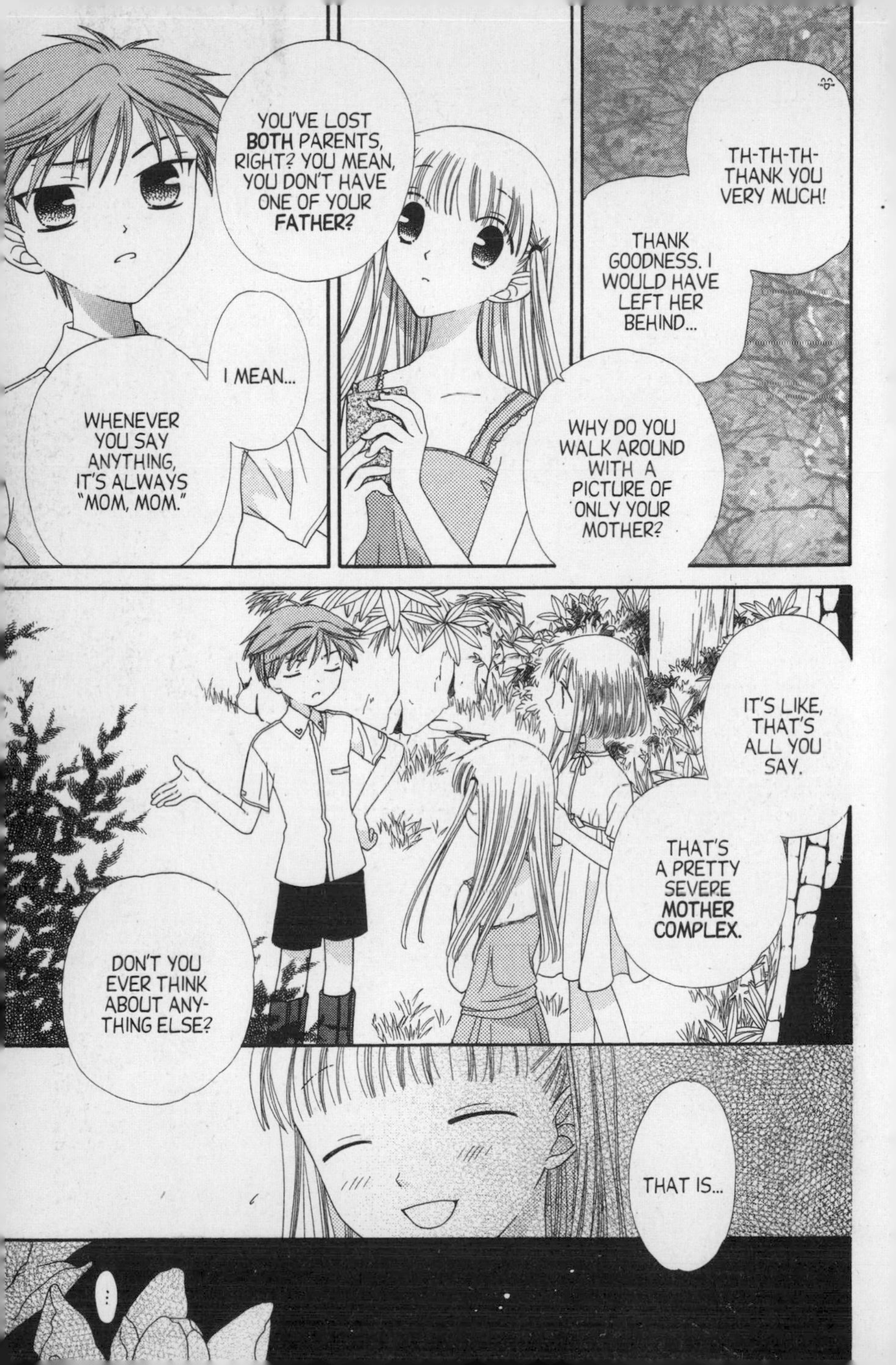
TH-TH-TH-THANK YOU VERY MUCH!
THANK GOODNESS. I WOULD HAVE LEFT HER BEHIND...
WHY DO YOU WALK AROUND WITH A PICTURE OF ONLY YOUR MOTHER?
YOU'VE LOST BOTH PARENTS, RIGHT? YOU MEAN, YOU DON'T HAVE ONE OF YOUR FATHER?
I MEAN...
WHENEVER YOU SAY ANYTHING, IT'S ALWAYS "MOM, MOM."
IT'S LIKE, THAT'S ALL YOU SAY.
THAT'S A PRETTY SEVERE MOTHER COMPLEX.
DON'T YOU EVER THINK ABOUT ANY-THING ELSE?
THAT IS...
...

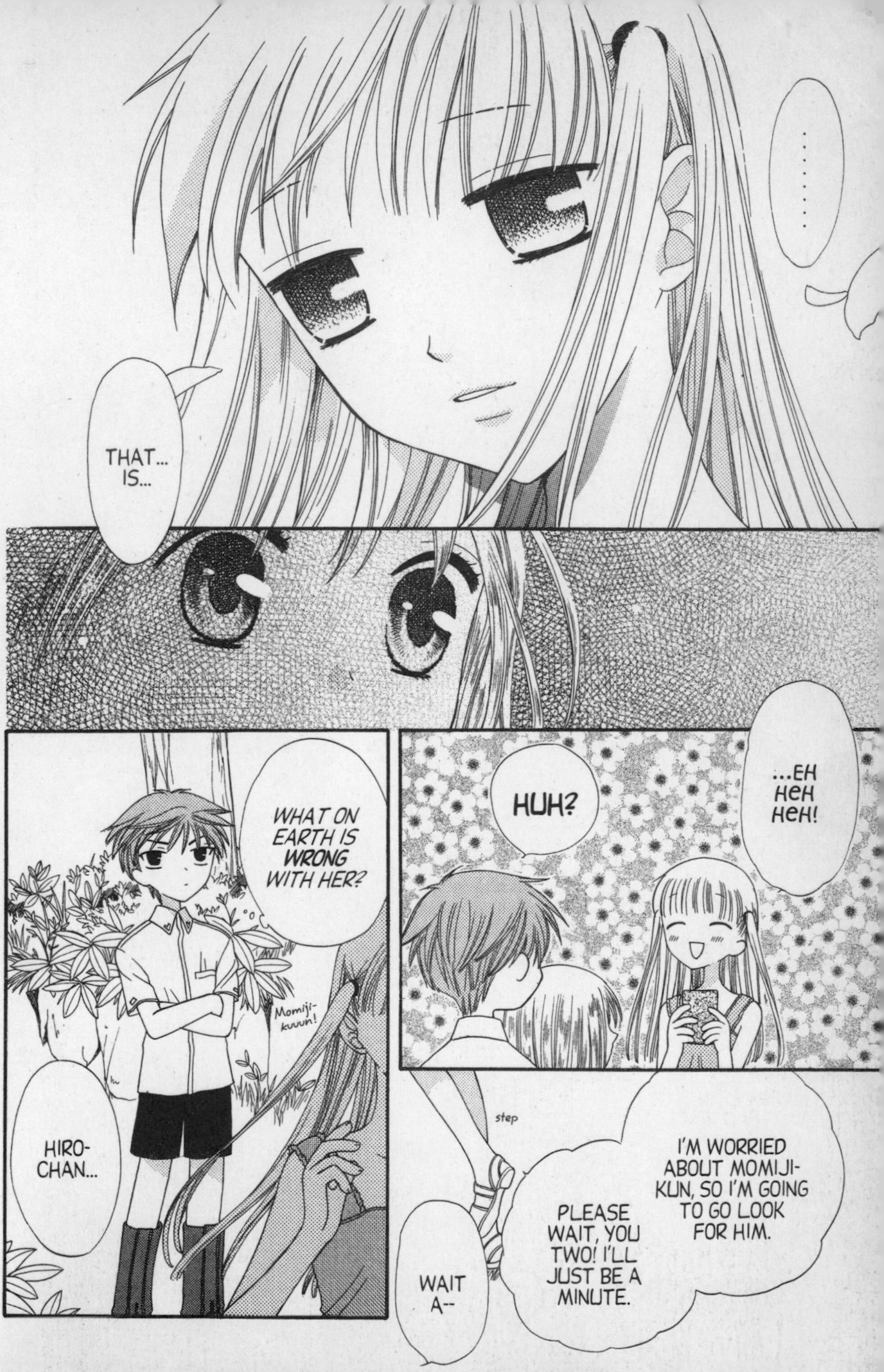
......
THAT... IS...
...EH HEH HEH!
HUH?
WHAT ON EARTH IS WRONG WITH HER?
Momiji-kuuun!
HIRO-CHAN...
step
I'M WORRIED ABOUT MOMIJI-KUN, SO I'M GOING TO GO LOOK FOR HIM.
PLEASE WAIT, YOU TWO! I'LL JUST BE A MINUTE.
WAIT A--

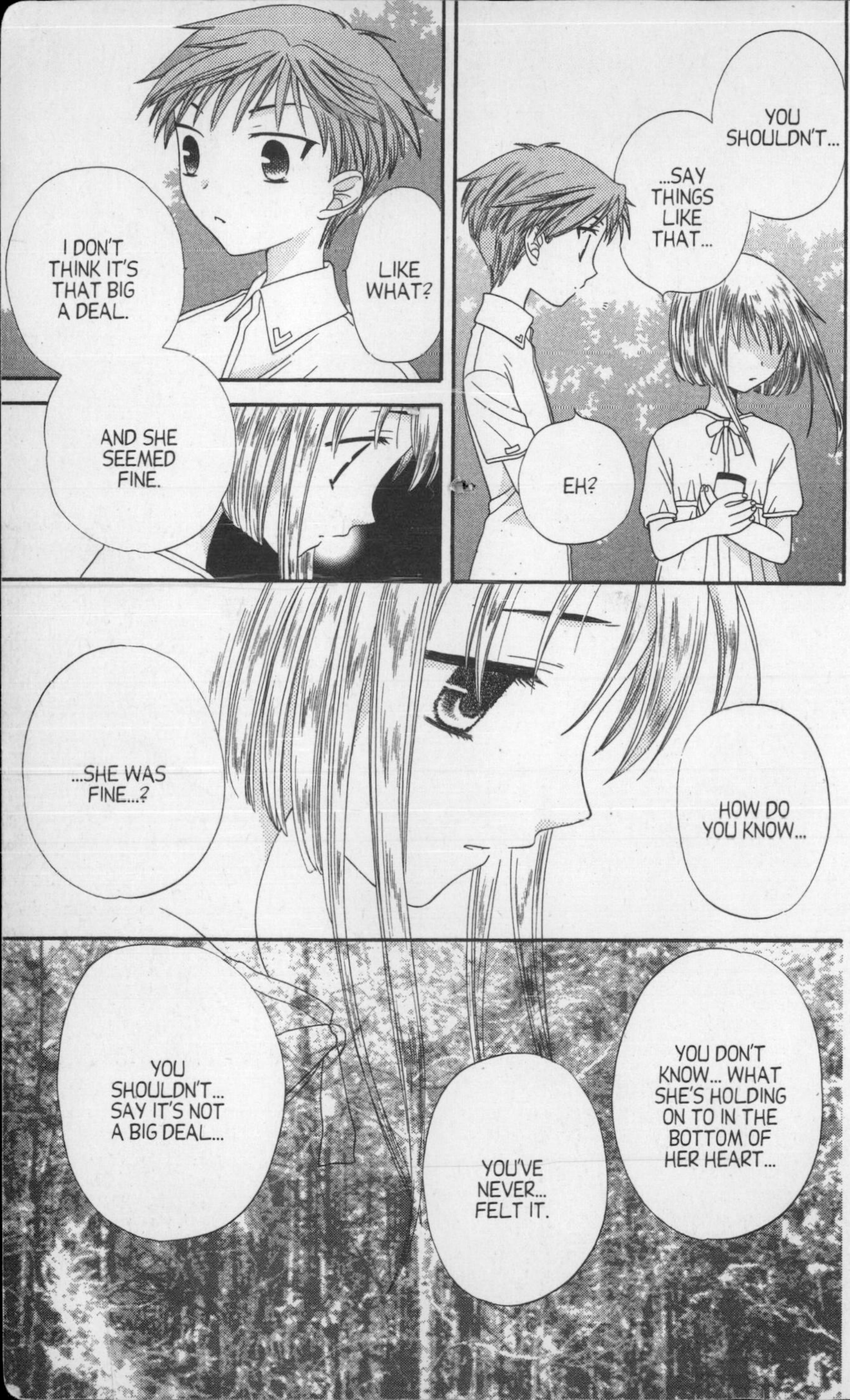
YOU SHOULDN'T...
...SAY THINGS LIKE THAT...
EH?
LIKE WHAT?
I DON'T THINK IT'S THAT BIG A DEAL.
AND SHE SEEMED FINE.
HOW DO YOU KNOW...
...SHE WAS FINE...?
YOU DON'T KNOW... WHAT SHE'S HOLDING ON TO IN THE BOTTOM OF HER HEART...
YOU'VE NEVER... FELT IT.
YOU SHOULDN'T... SAY IT'S NOT A BIG DEAL...

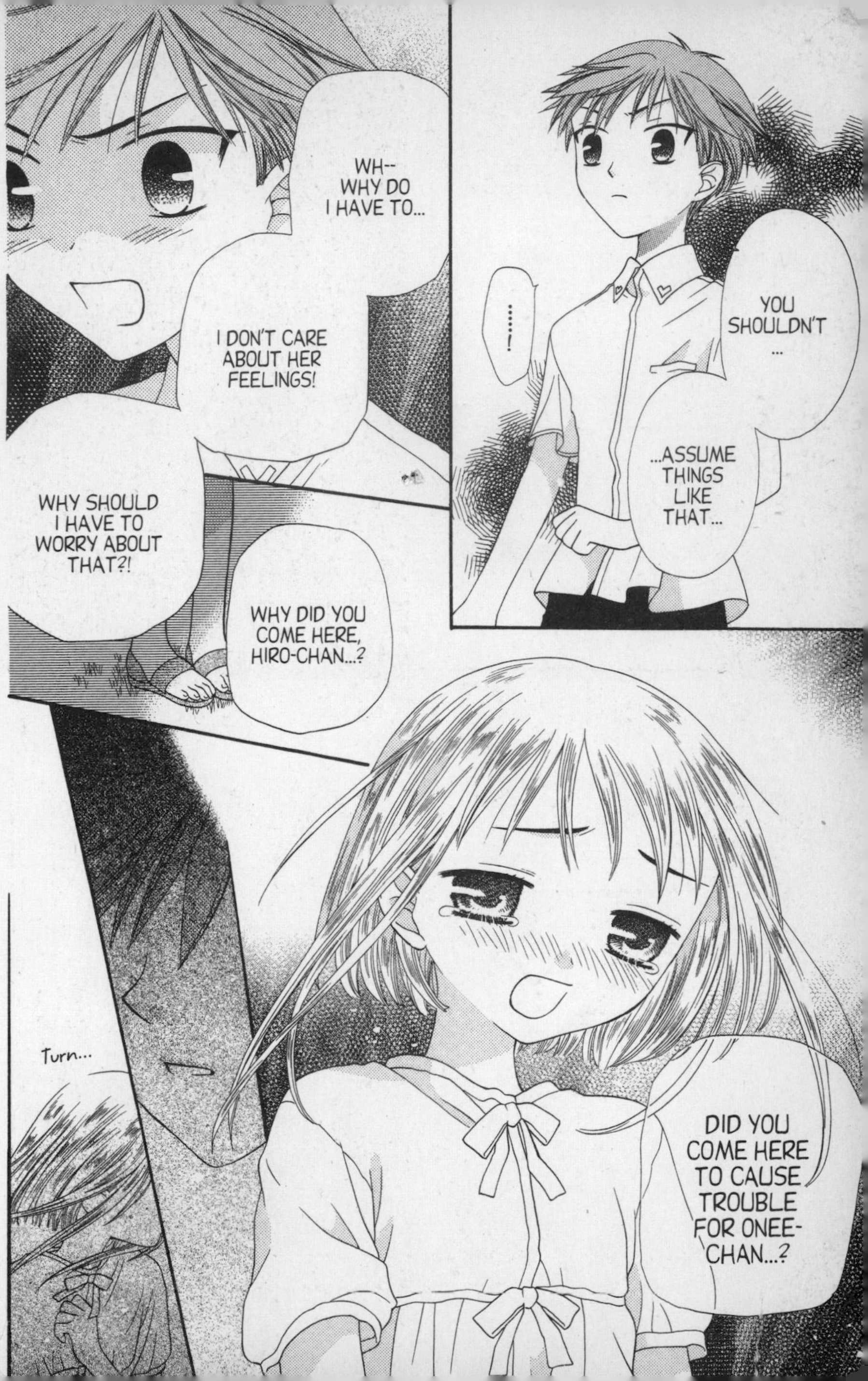
YOU SHOULDN'T ...
...ASSUME THINGS LIKE THAT...
......!
WH-- WHY DO I HAVE TO...
I DON'T CARE ABOUT HER FEELINGS!
WHY SHOULD I HAVE TO WORRY ABOUT THAT?!
WHY DID YOU COME HERE, HIRO-CHAN...?
DID YOU COME HERE TO CAUSE TROUBLE FOR ONEE-CHAN...?
Turn...

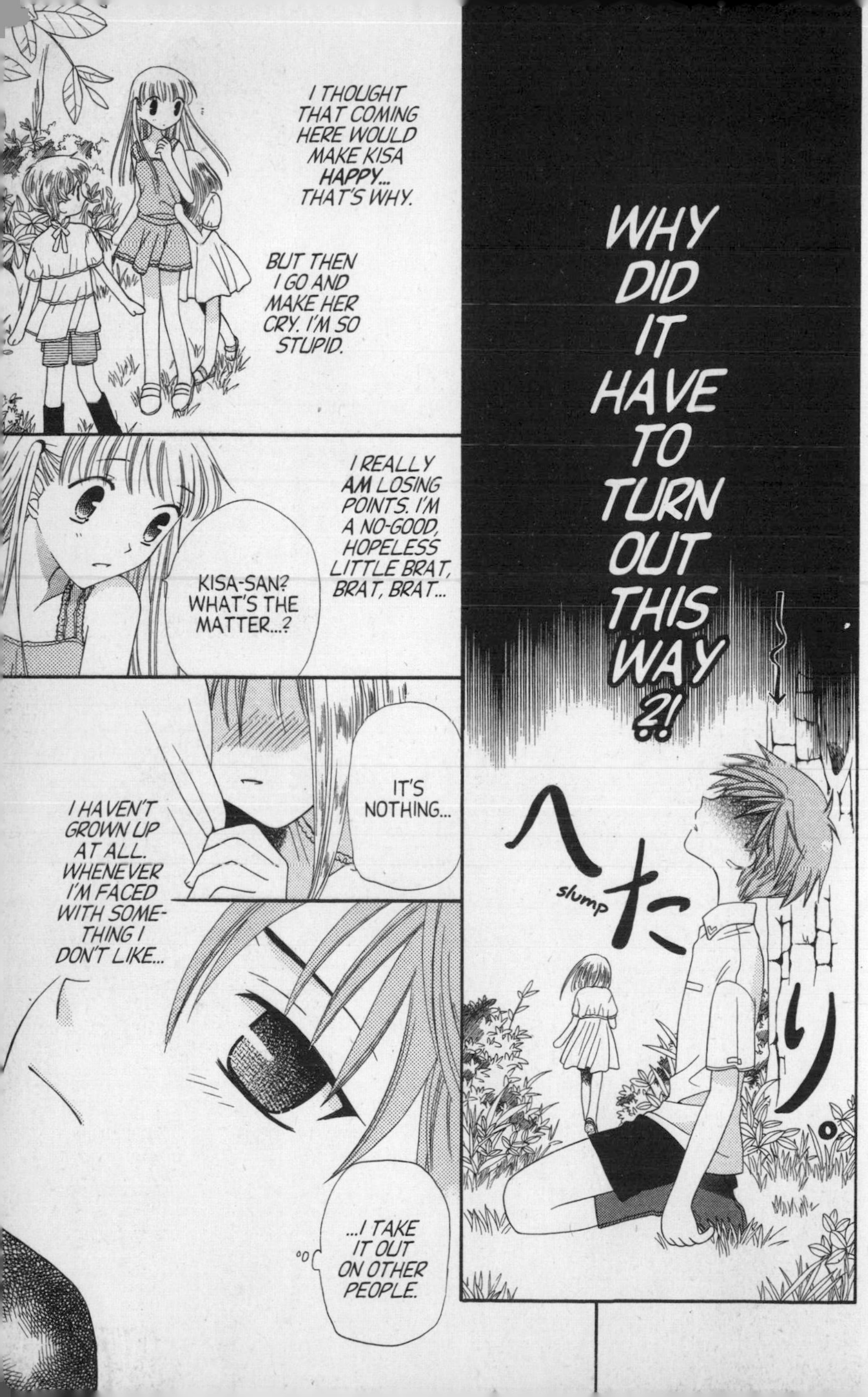
WHY DID IT HAVE TO TURN OUT THIS WAY?!
へたり。
slump
I THOUGHT THAT COMING HERE WOULD MAKE KISA HAPPY... THAT'S WHY.
BUT THEN I GO AND MAKE HER CRY. I'M SO STUPID.
I REALLY AM LOSING POINTS. I'M A NO-GOOD, HOPELESS LITTLE BRAT, BRAT, BRAT...
KISA-SAN? WHAT'S THE MATTER...?
IT'S NOTHING...
I HAVEN'T GROWN UP AT ALL. WHENEVER I'M FACED WITH SOME-THING I DON'T LIKE...
...I TAKE IT OUT ON OTHER PEOPLE.

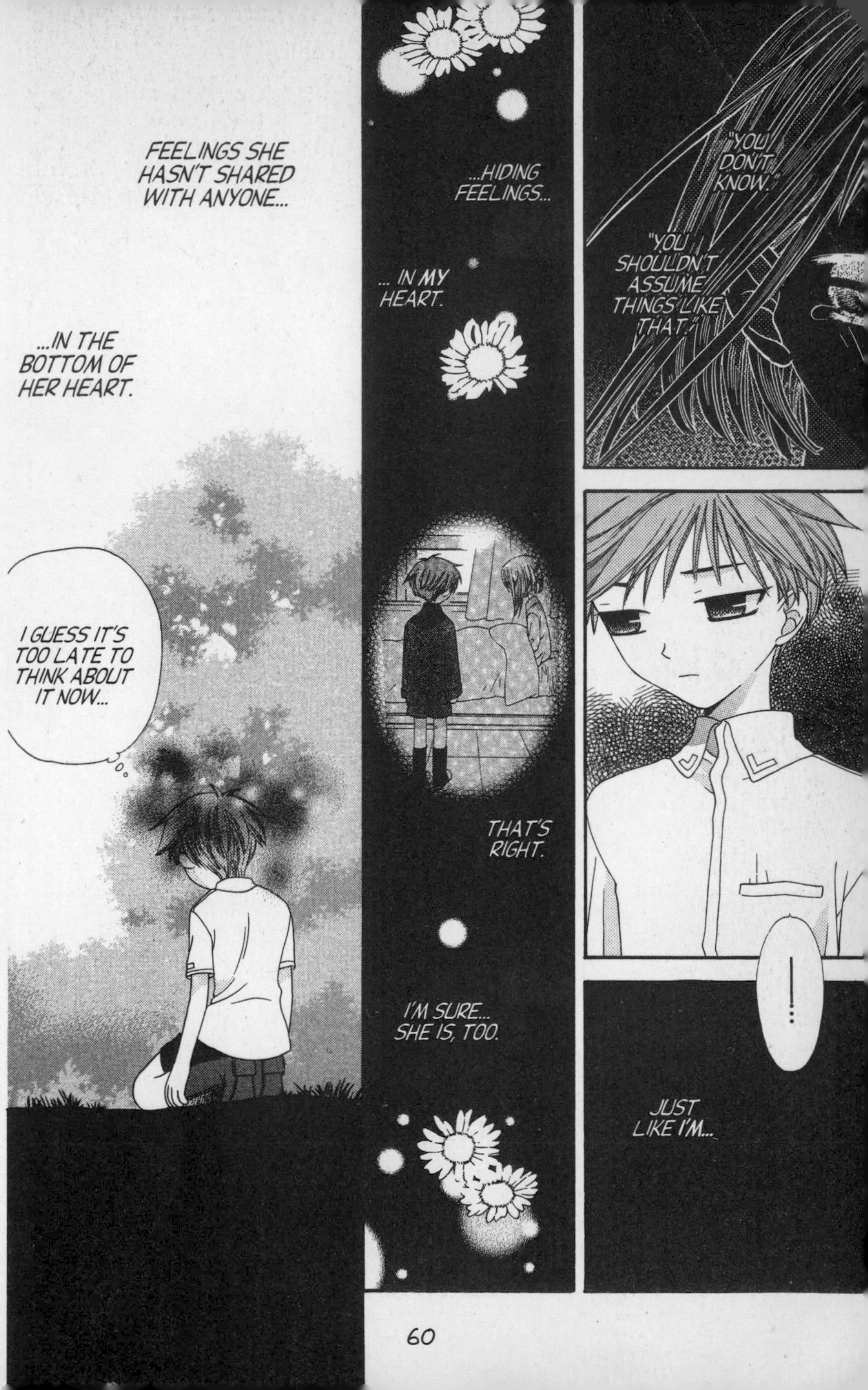
"YOU DON'T KNOW."
"YOU SHOULDN'T ASSUME THINGS LIKE THAT."
...!
JUST LIKE I'M...
...HIDING FEELINGS...
... IN MY HEART.
THAT'S RIGHT.
I'M SURE... SHE IS, TOO.
FEELINGS SHE HASN'T SHARED WITH ANYONE...
...IN THE BOTTOM OF HER HEART.
I GUESS IT'S TOO LATE TO THINK ABOUT IT NOW...

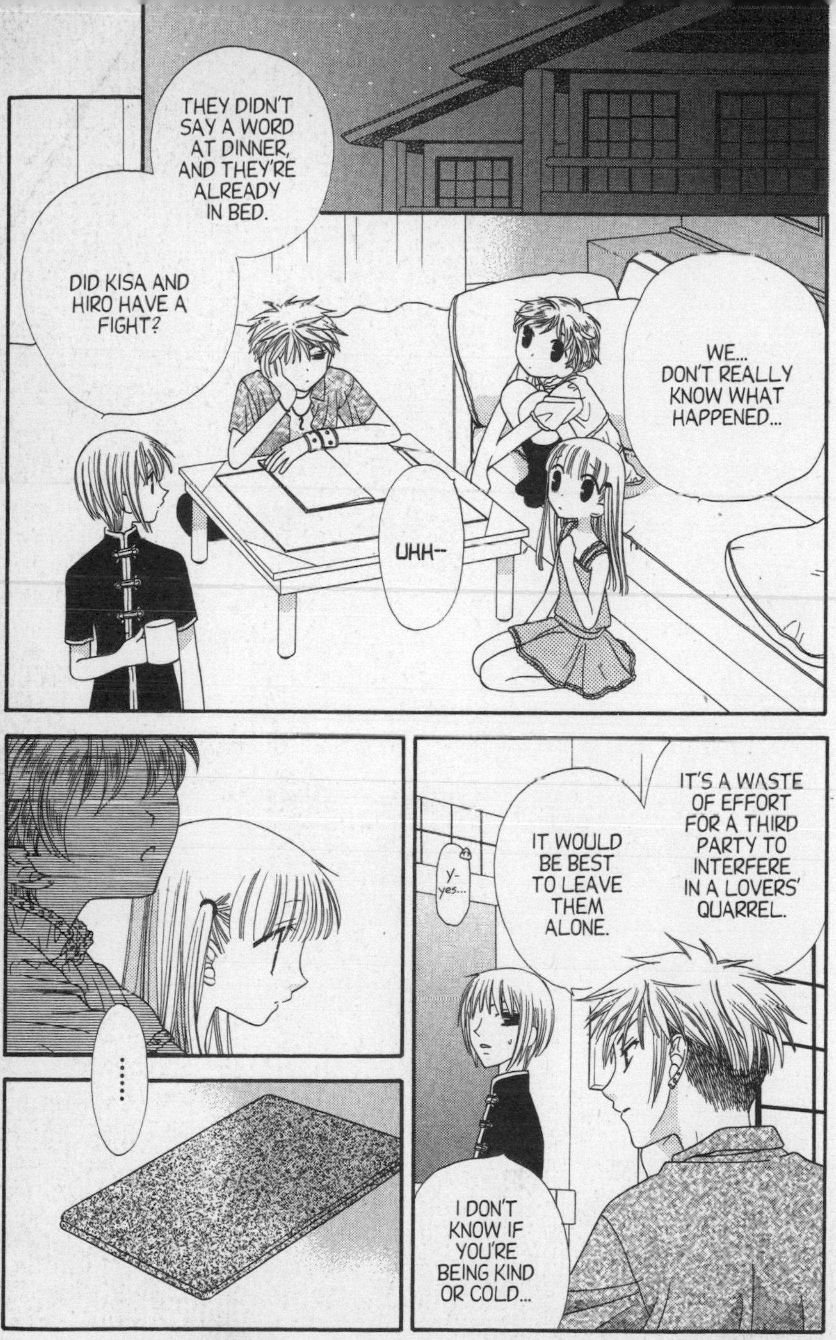
THEY DIDN'T SAY A WORD AT DINNER, AND THEY'RE ALREADY IN BED.
DID KISA AND HIRO HAVE A FIGHT?
WE... DON'T REALLY KNOW WHAT HAPPENED...
UHH--
IT'S A WASTE OF EFFORT FOR A THIRD PARTY TO INTERFERE IN A LOVERS' QUARREL.
IT WOULD BE BEST TO LEAVE THEM ALONE.
Y-yes...
I DON'T KNOW IF YOU'RE BEING KIND OR COLD...
......

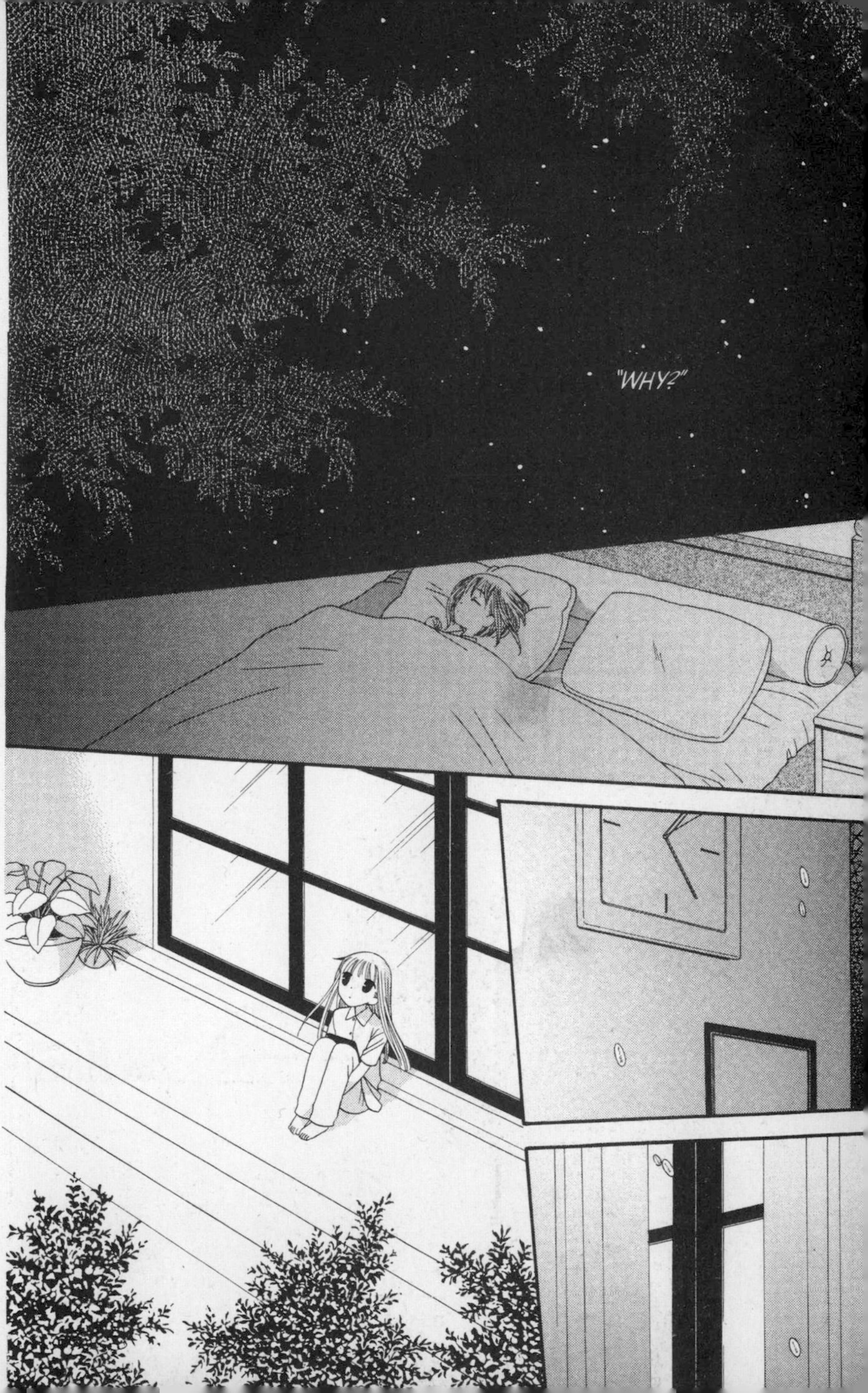
"WHY?"

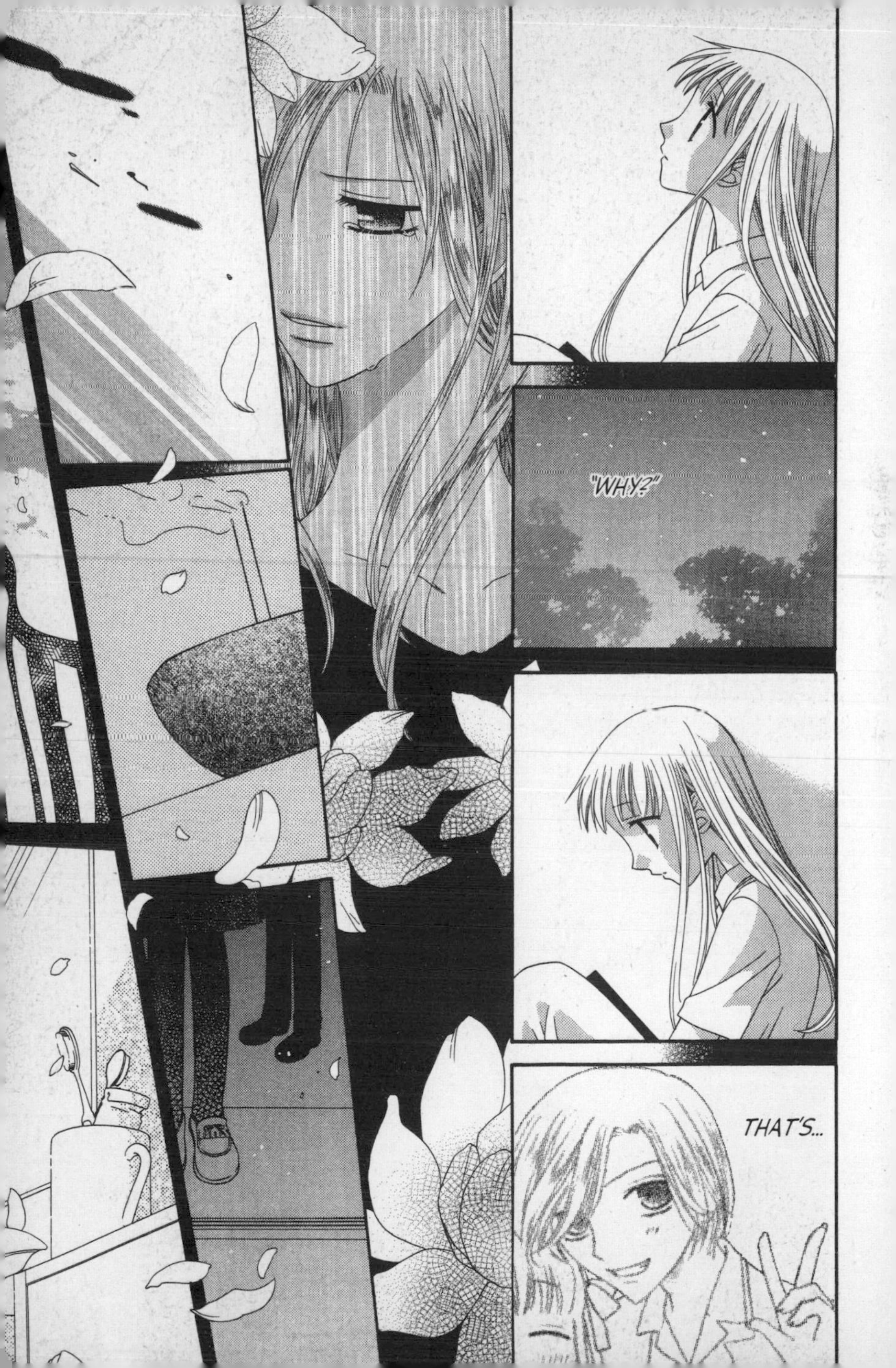

"WHY?"
THAT'S...

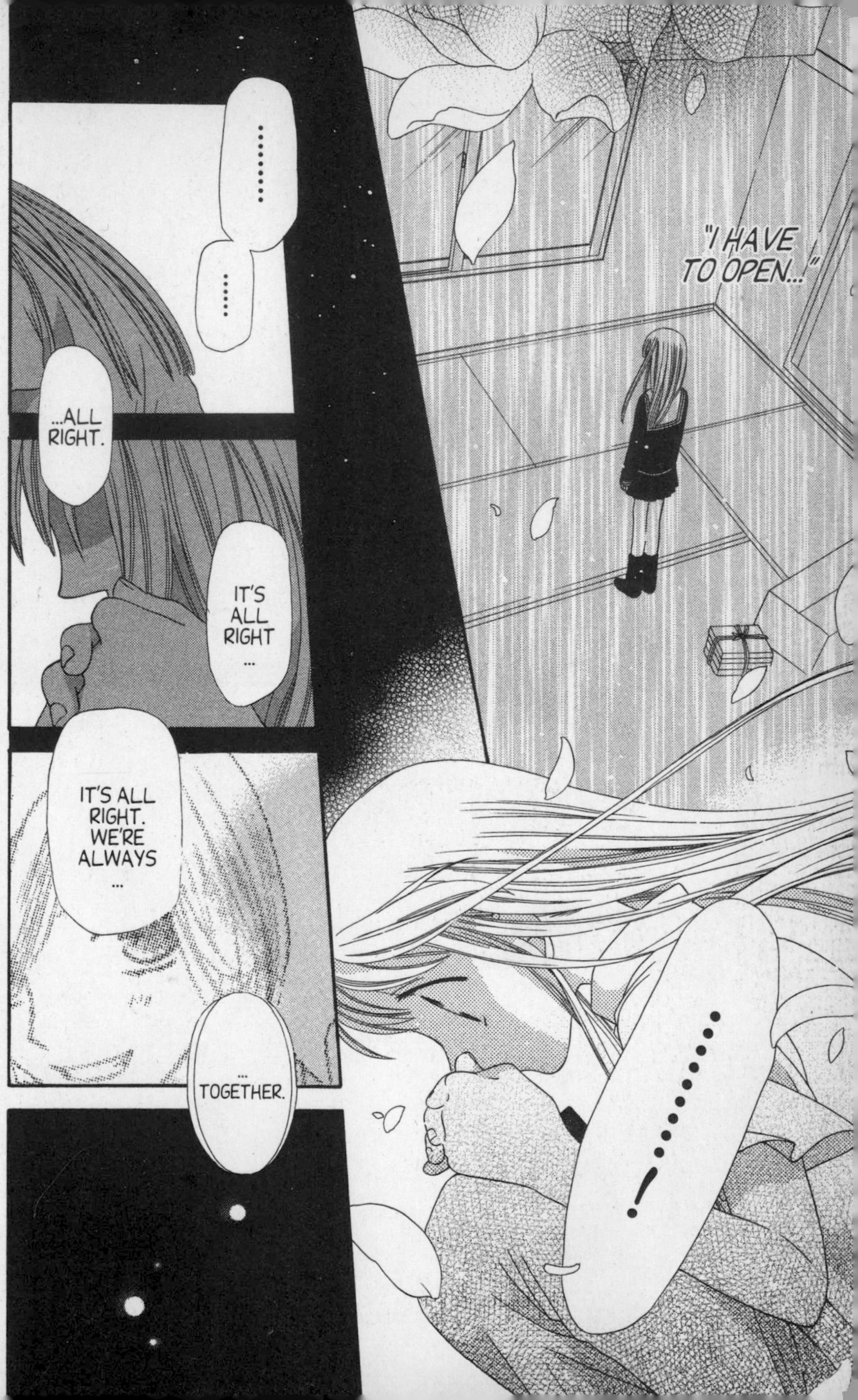
"I HAVE TO OPEN...!"
......!
......
......
...ALL RIGHT.
IT'S ALL RIGHT...
IT'S ALL RIGHT. WE'RE ALWAYS...
...TOGETHER.

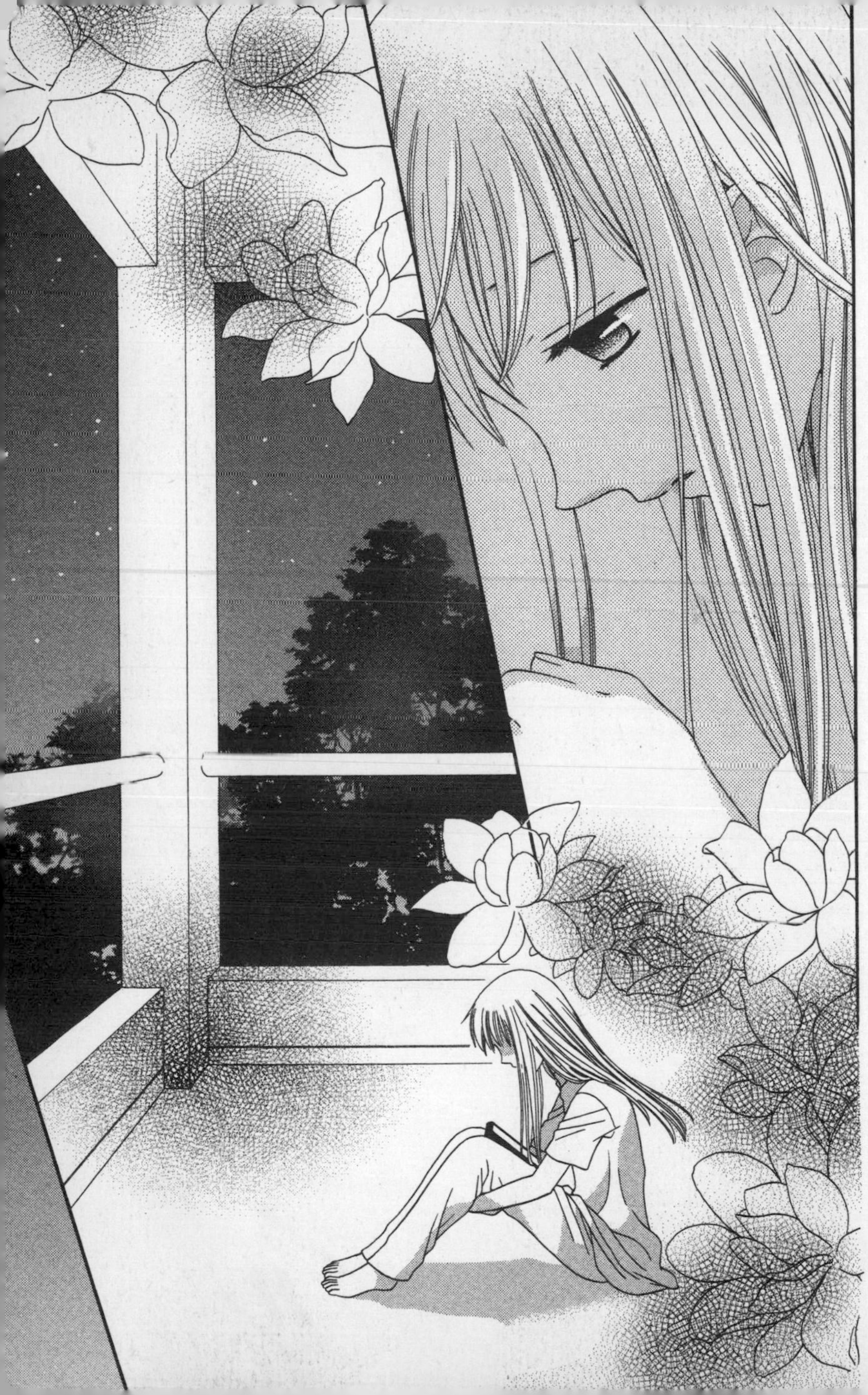

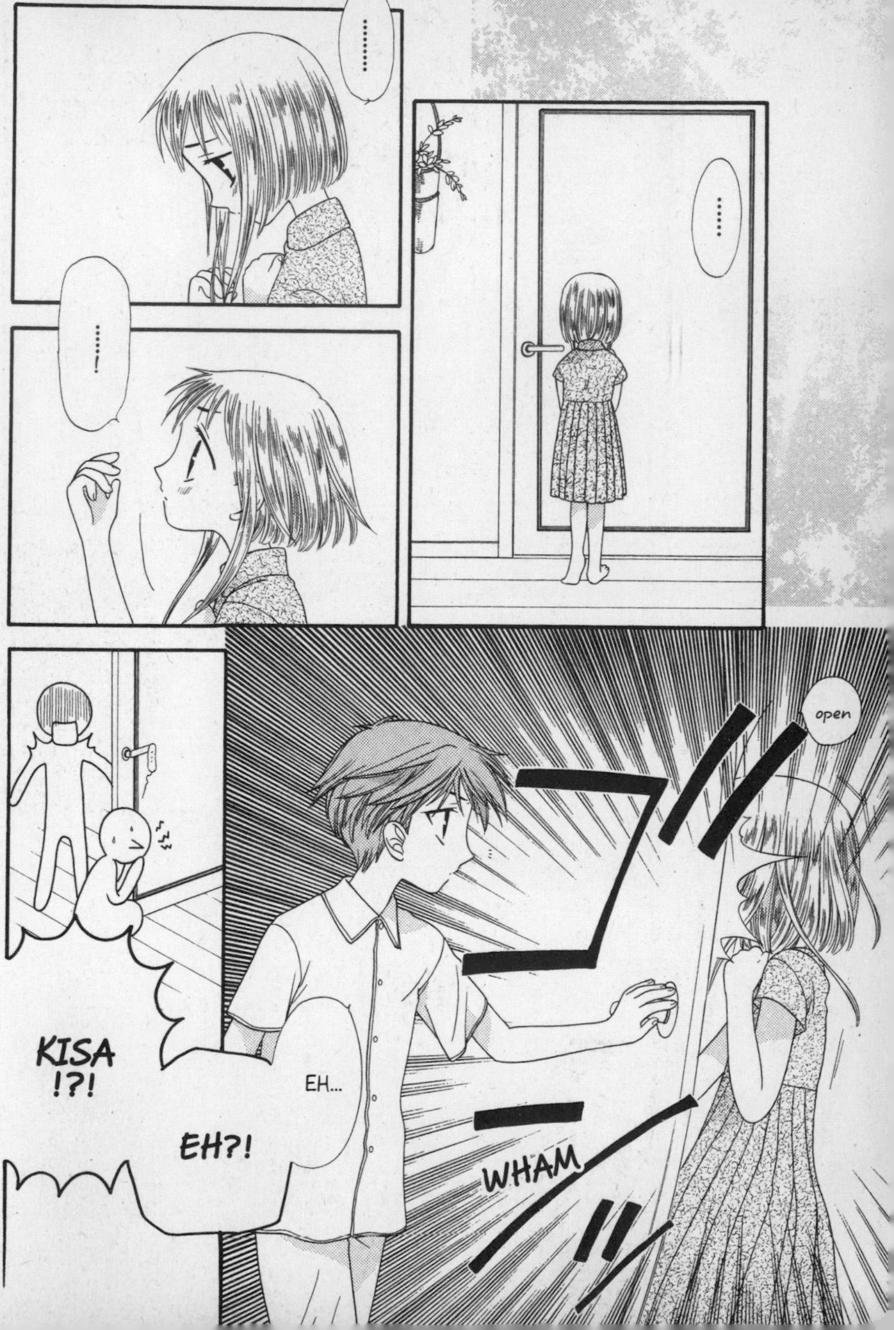

......
......
......!
open
WHAM
EH...
EH?!
KISA !?!

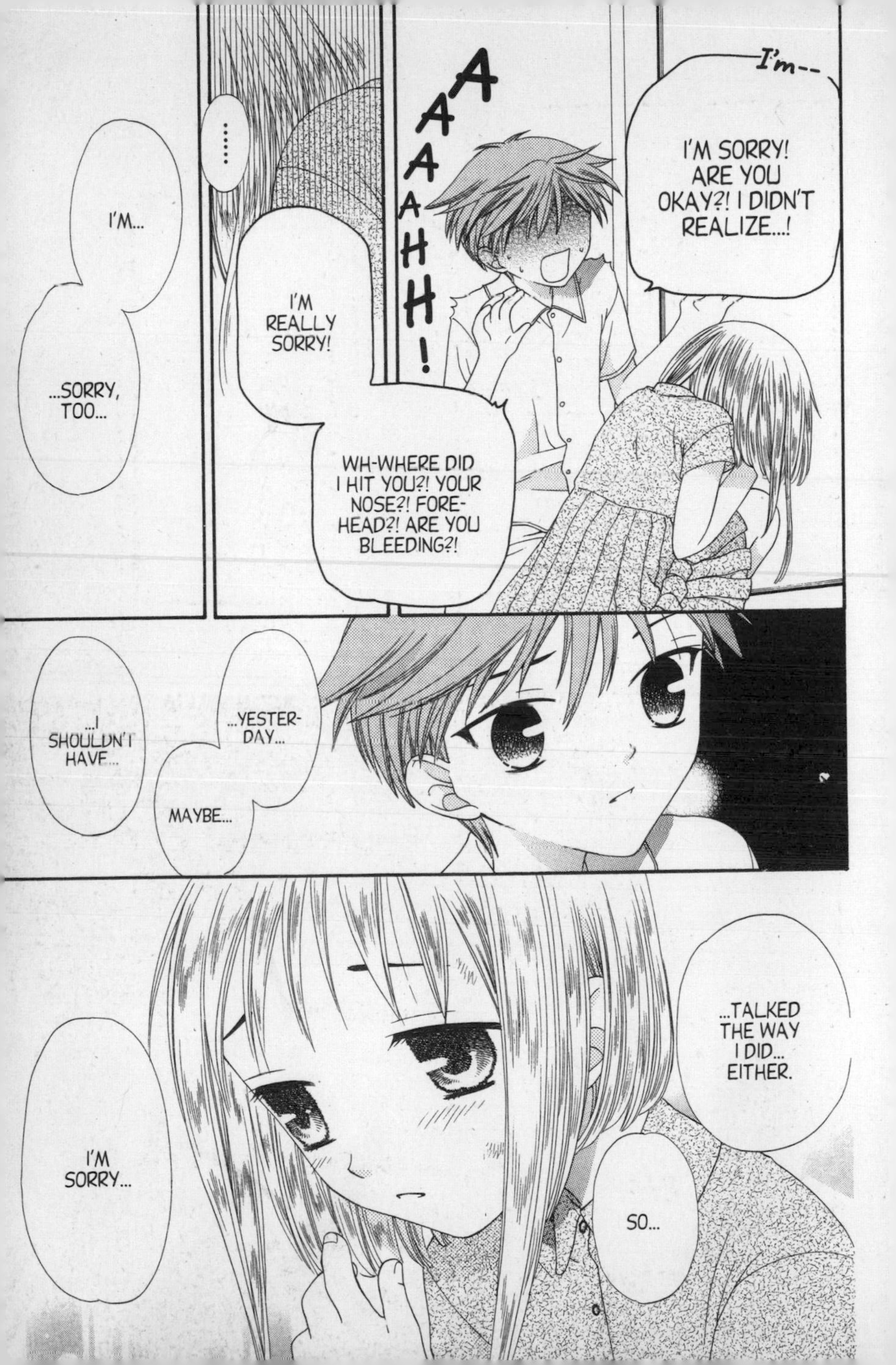
I'm--
I'M SORRY! ARE YOU OKAY?! I DIDN'T REALIZE...!
AAAAHH!
I'M REALLY SORRY!
WH-WHERE DID I HIT YOU?! YOUR NOSE?! FORE-HEAD?! ARE YOU BLEEDING?!
......
I'M...
...SORRY, TOO...
...YESTER-DAY...
MAYBE...
...I SHOULDN'T HAVE...
...TALKED THE WAY I DID... EITHER.
SO...
I'M SORRY...

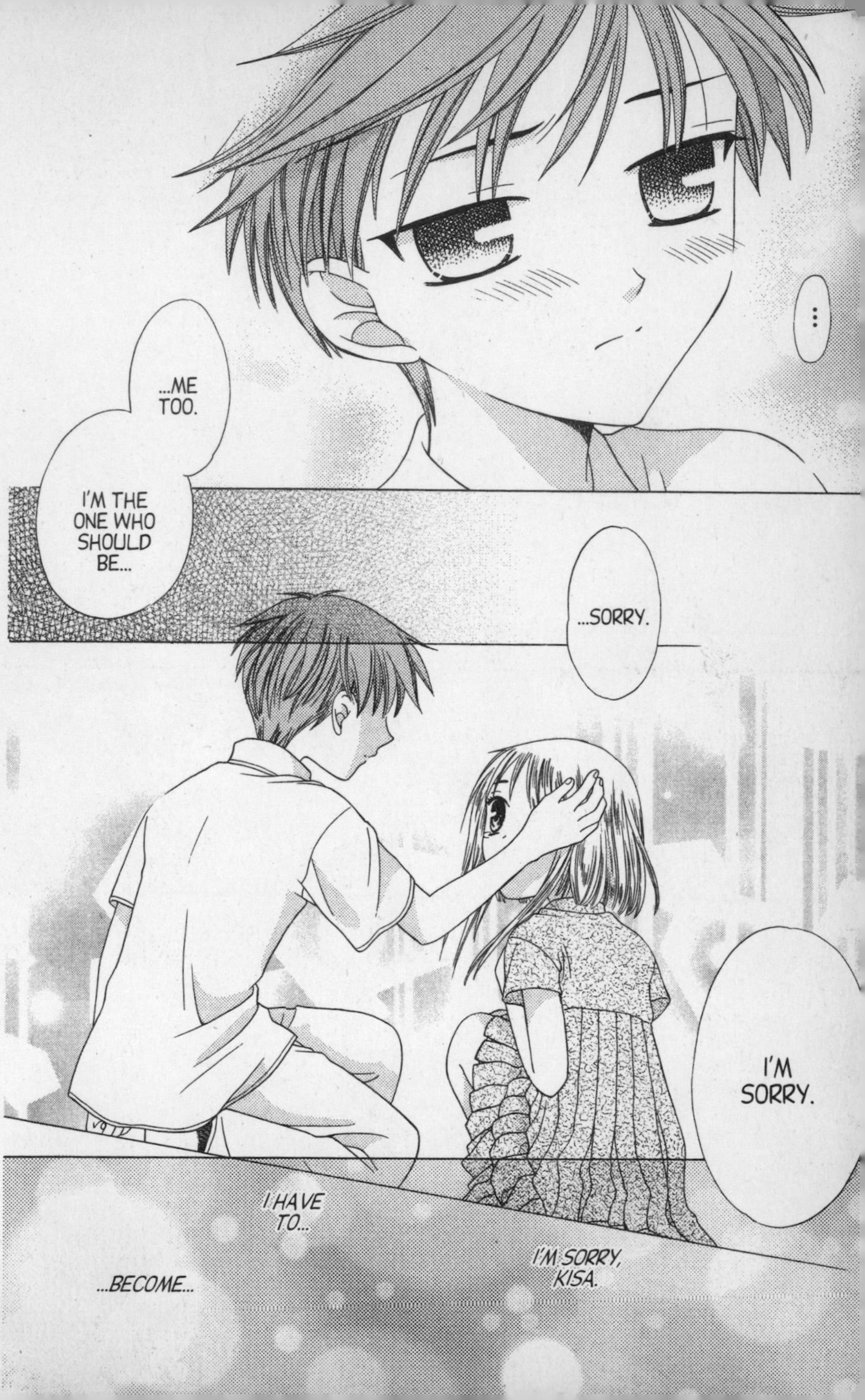
...
...ME TOO.
I'M THE ONE WHO SHOULD BE...
...SORRY.
I'M SORRY.
I'M SORRY, KISA.
I HAVE TO...
...BECOME...

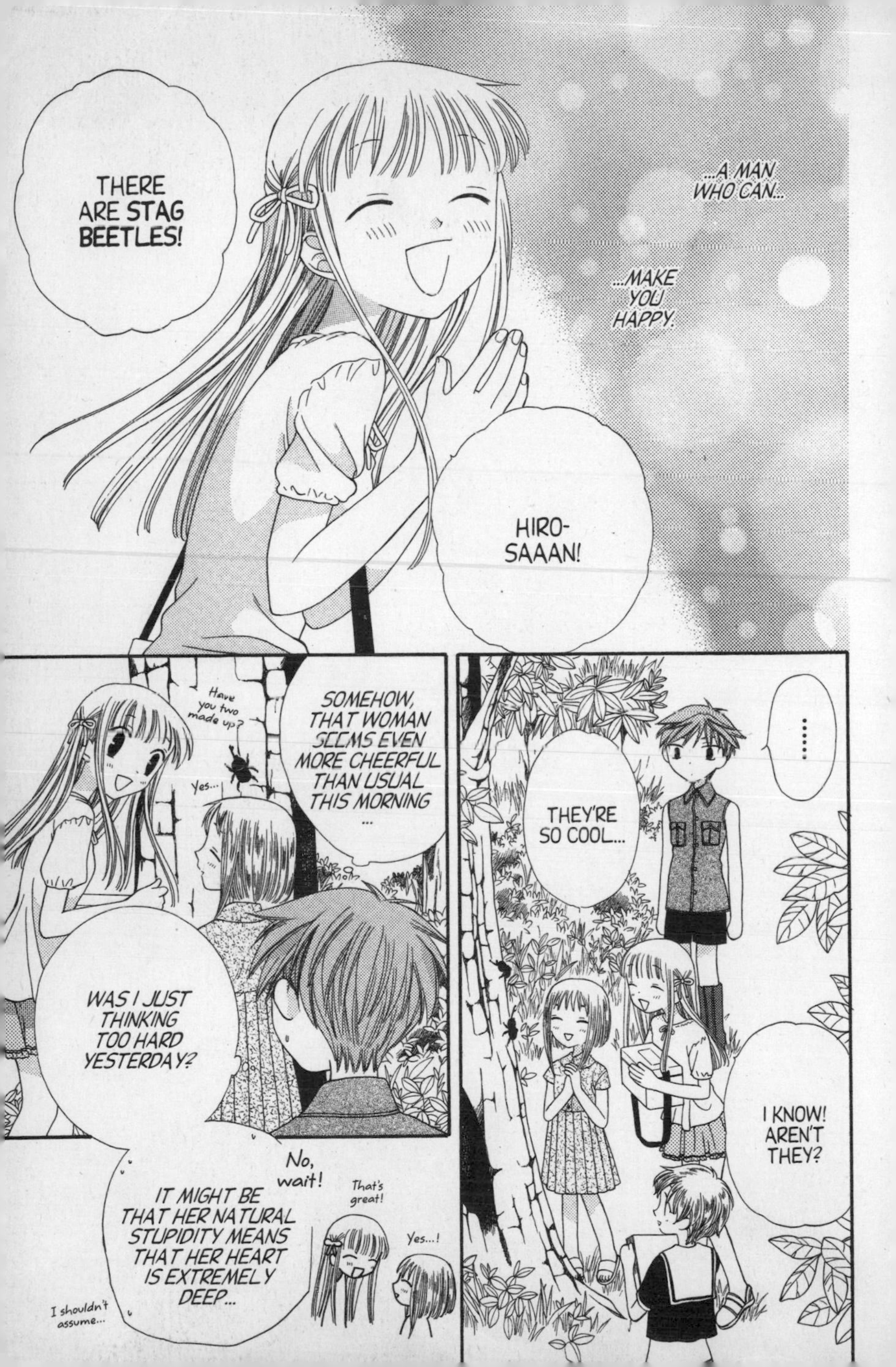
...A MAN WHO CAN...
...MAKE YOU HAPPY.
THERE ARE STAG BEETLES!
HIRO-SAAAN!
......
THEY'RE SO COOL...
I KNOW! AREN'T THEY?
SOMEHOW, THAT WOMAN SEEMS EVEN MORE CHEERFUL THAN USUAL THIS MORNING...
Have you two made up?
Yes...
WAS I JUST THINKING TOO HARD YESTERDAY?
No, wait!
IT MIGHT BE THAT HER NATURAL STUPIDITY MEANS THAT HER HEART IS EXTREMELY DEEP...
That's great!
Yes...!
I shouldn't assume...

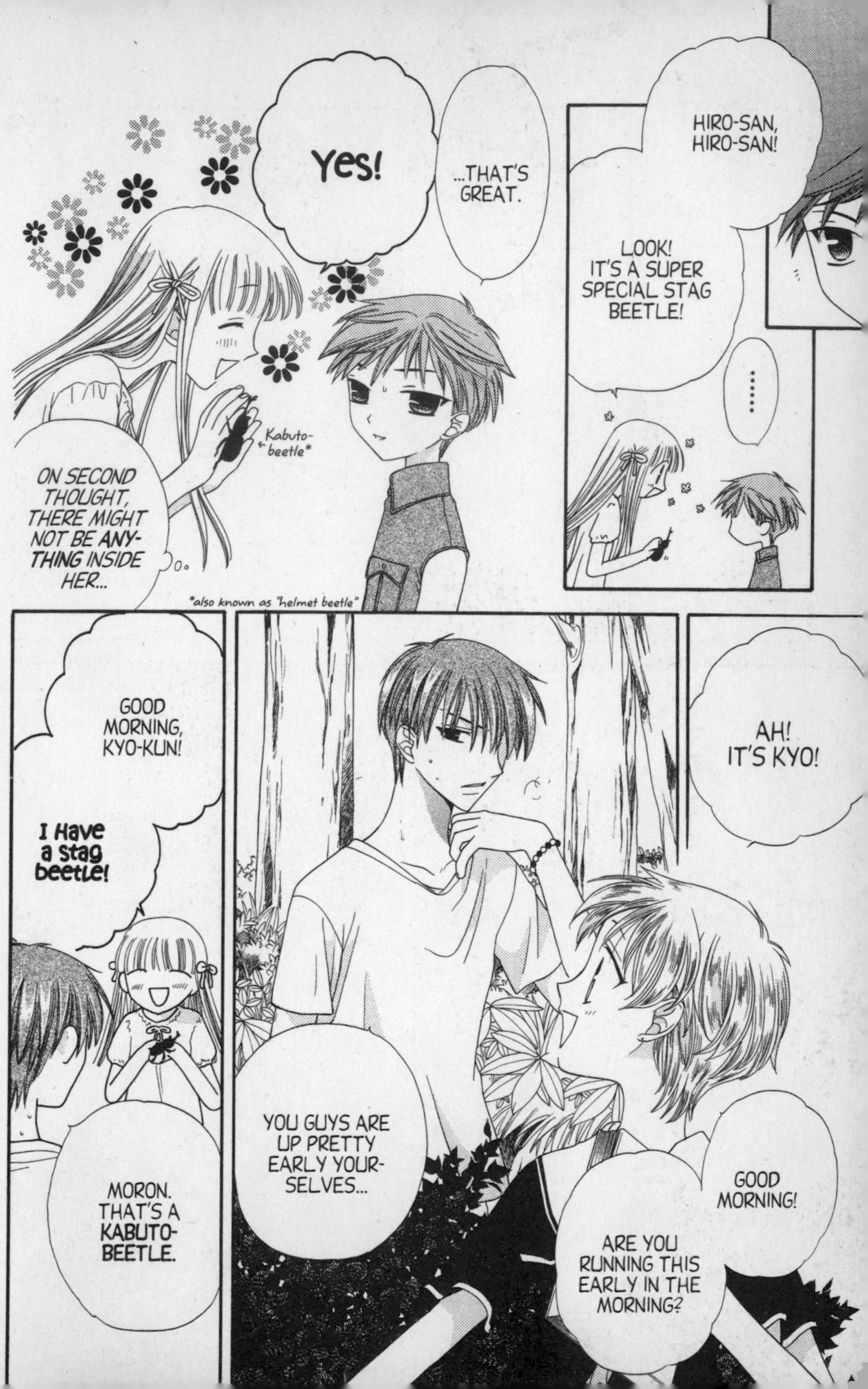
HIRO-SAN, HIRO-SAN!
LOOK! IT'S A SUPER SPECIAL STAG BEETLE!
......
...THAT'S GREAT.
Yes!
Kabuto-beetle*
ON SECOND THOUGHT, THERE MIGHT NOT BE ANY-THING INSIDE HER...
*also known as "helmet beetle"
AH! IT'S KYO!
GOOD MORNING!
ARE YOU RUNNING THIS EARLY IN THE MORNING?
YOU GUYS ARE UP PRETTY EARLY YOUR-SELVES...
GOOD MORNING, KYO-KUN!
I Have a stag beetle!
MORON. THAT'S A KABUTO-BEETLE.

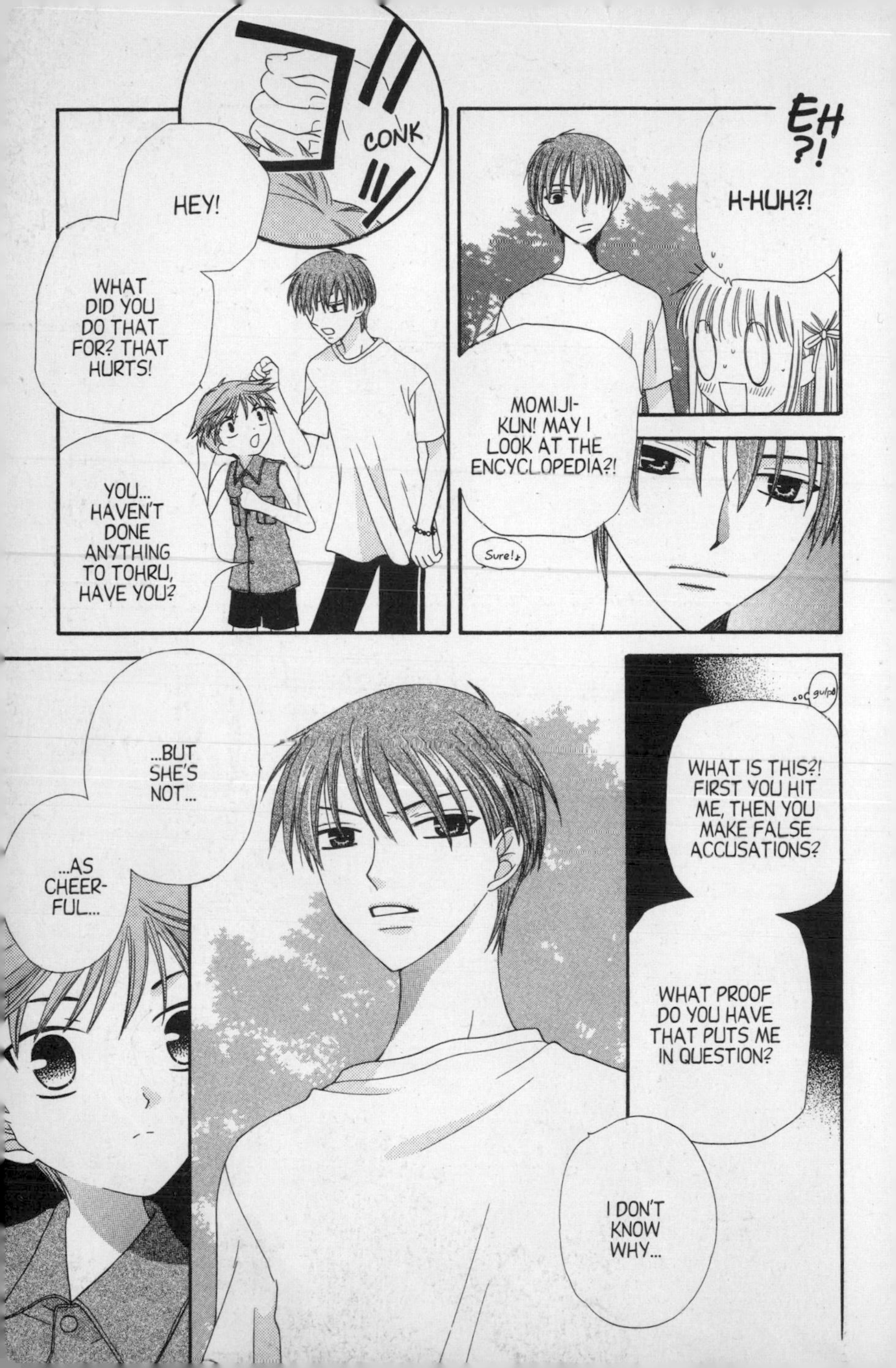
CONK
HEY!
WHAT DID YOU DO THAT FOR? THAT HURTS!
YOU... HAVEN'T DONE ANYTHING TO TOHRU, HAVE YOU?
EH?!
H-HUH?!
MOMIJI-KUN! MAY I LOOK AT THE ENCYCLOPEDIA?!
Sure!♪
gulp
WHAT IS THIS?! FIRST YOU HIT ME, THEN YOU MAKE FALSE ACCUSATIONS?
WHAT PROOF DO YOU HAVE THAT PUTS ME IN QUESTION?
I DON'T KNOW WHY...
...BUT SHE'S NOT...
...AS CHEERFUL...

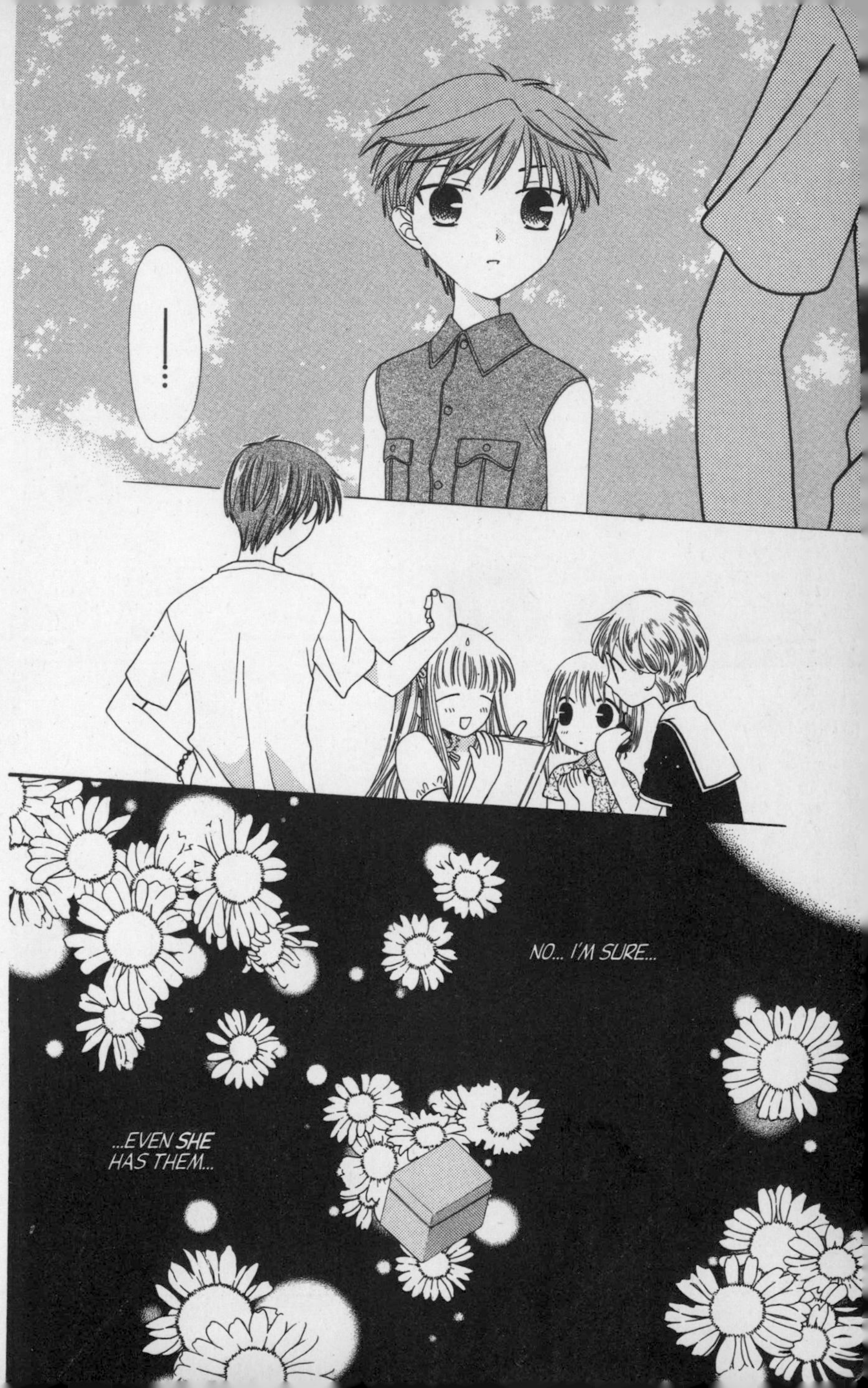

!...
NO... I'M SURE...
...EVEN SHE HAS THEM...

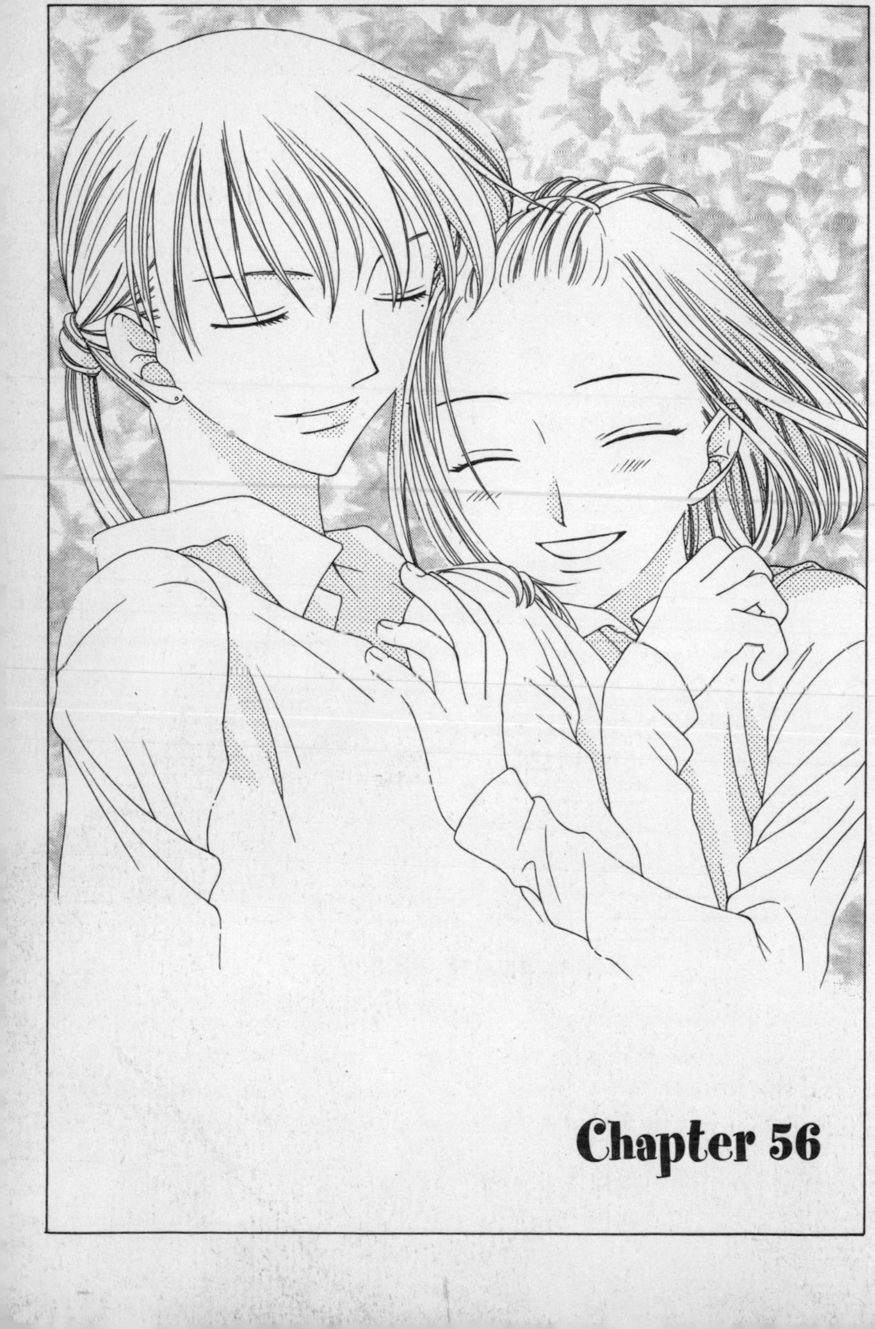

# Chapter 56

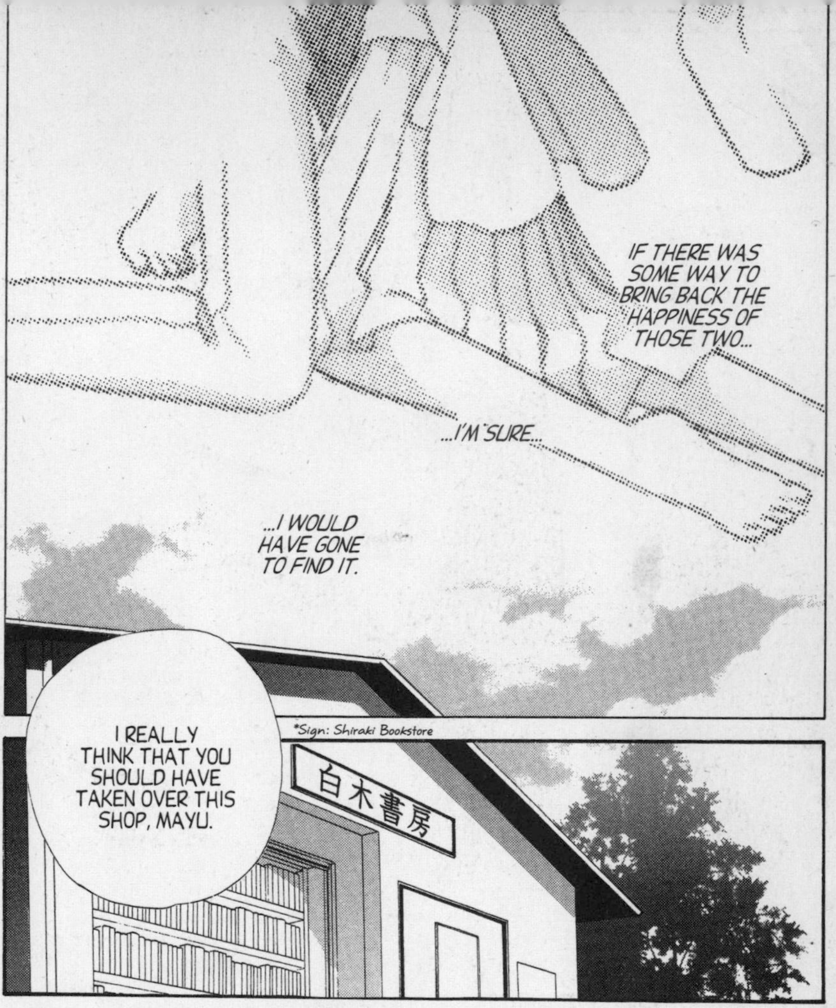
IF THERE WAS SOME WAY TO BRING BACK THE HAPPINESS OF THOSE TWO...
...I'M SURE...
...I WOULD HAVE GONE TO FIND IT.
I REALLY THINK THAT YOU SHOULD HAVE TAKEN OVER THIS SHOP, MAYU.
白木書房
*Sign: Shiraki Bookstore

## BLAH, BLAH, BLAH 3

Mayu-chan has shown her head before (Has her name come up?), as the homeroom teacher for Tohru and the others, but I don't think I ever figured out what it is that she teaches. I think she kind of fits the image of a classic lit teacher.

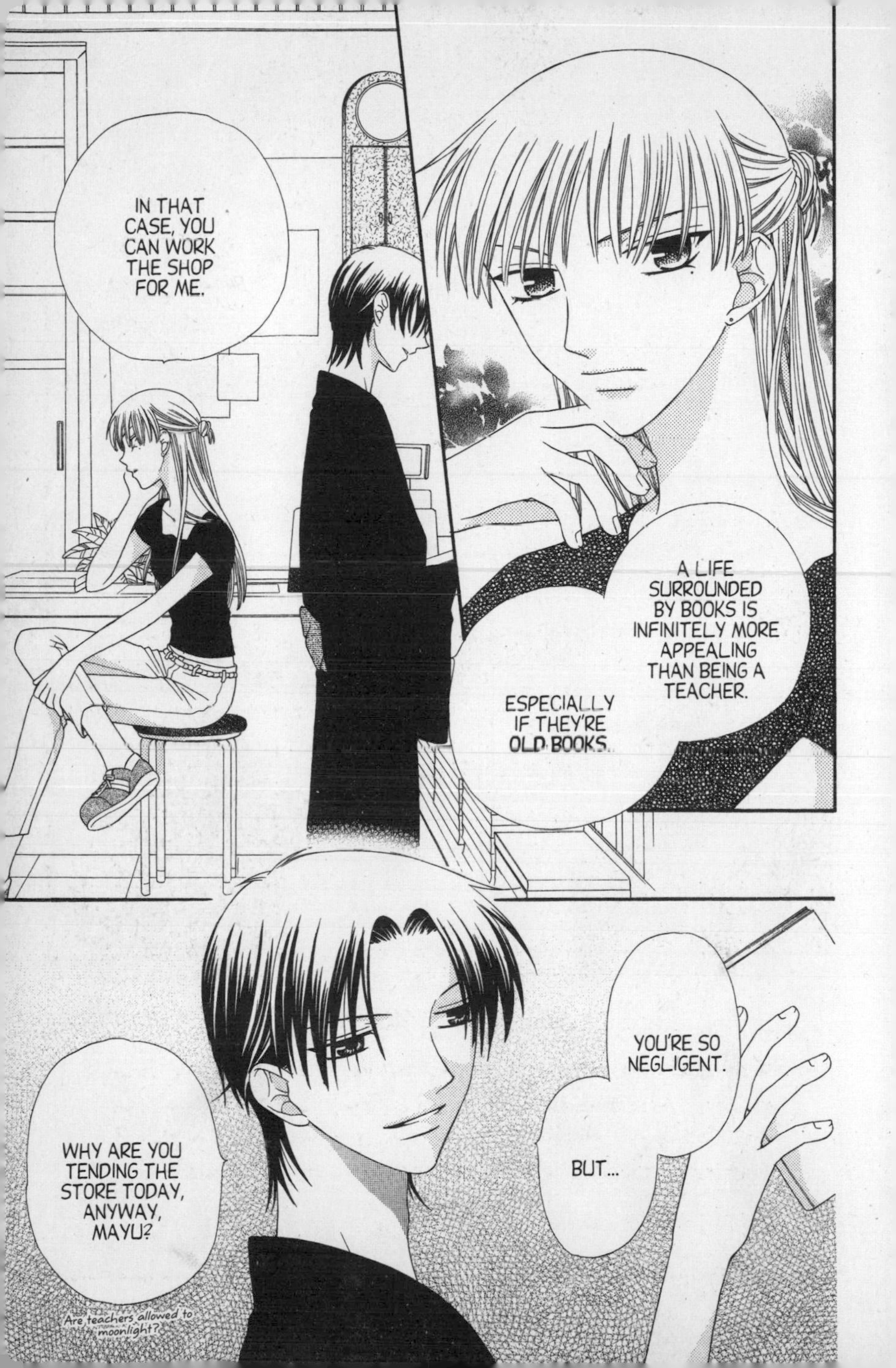
A LIFE SURROUNDED BY BOOKS IS INFINITELY MORE APPEALING THAN BEING A TEACHER.
ESPECIALLY IF THEY'RE OLD BOOKS.
IN THAT CASE, YOU CAN WORK THE SHOP FOR ME.
YOU'RE SO NEGLIGENT.
BUT...
WHY ARE YOU TENDING THE STORE TODAY, ANYWAY, MAYU?
Are teachers allowed to moonlight?

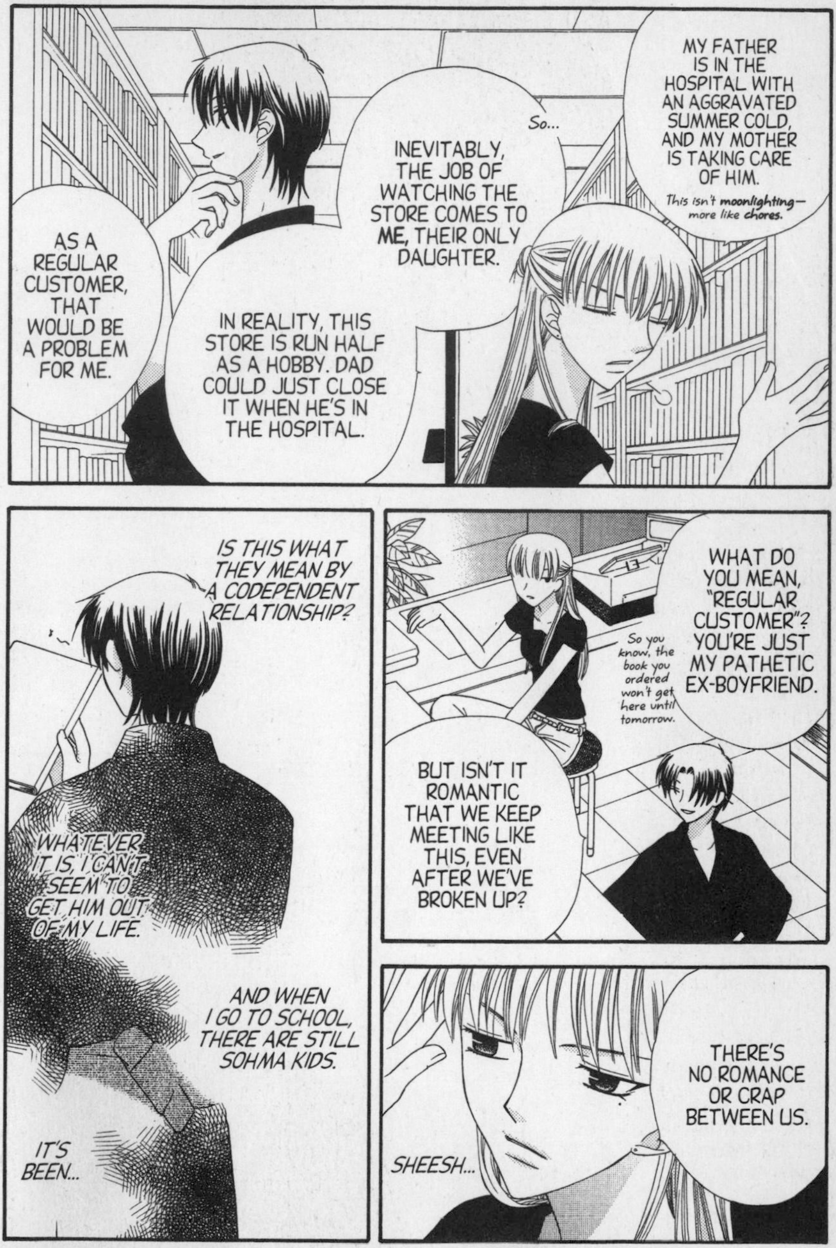
MY FATHER IS IN THE HOSPITAL WITH AN AGGRAVATED SUMMER COLD, AND MY MOTHER IS TAKING CARE OF HIM.
This isn't **moonlighting**—more like **chores**.
So...
INEVITABLY, THE JOB OF WATCHING THE STORE COMES TO **ME**, THEIR ONLY DAUGHTER.
IN REALITY, THIS STORE IS RUN HALF AS A HOBBY. DAD COULD JUST CLOSE IT WHEN HE'S IN THE HOSPITAL.
AS A REGULAR CUSTOMER, THAT WOULD BE A PROBLEM FOR ME.
WHAT DO YOU MEAN, "REGULAR CUSTOMER"? YOU'RE JUST MY PATHETIC EX-BOYFRIEND.
So you know, the book you ordered won't get here until tomorrow.
BUT ISN'T IT ROMANTIC THAT WE KEEP MEETING LIKE THIS, EVEN AFTER WE'VE BROKEN UP?
THERE'S NO ROMANCE OR CRAP BETWEEN US.
SHEESH...
IS THIS WHAT THEY MEAN BY A CODEPENDENT RELATIONSHIP?
WHATEVER IT IS, I CAN'T SEEM TO GET HIM OUT OF MY LIFE.
AND WHEN I GO TO SCHOOL, THERE ARE STILL SOHMA KIDS.
IT'S BEEN...

## Mogeta and his pal Ari

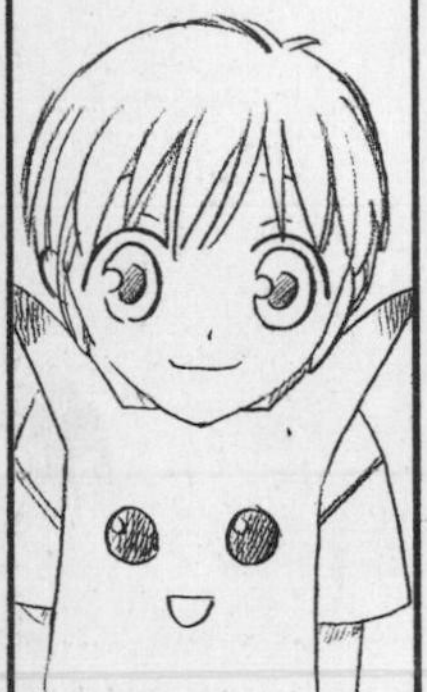

Mogeta?!! Of all things, I start with Mogeta?!! (Let's dig right in...) What volume did they first appear in? Was it four? Ah, it was three. I just looked it up. I think I drew them before, too, but they're characters I drew without thinking too deeply about them. It's been decided that Mogeta is actually female (?), and Ari is a miser. What lousy decisions...

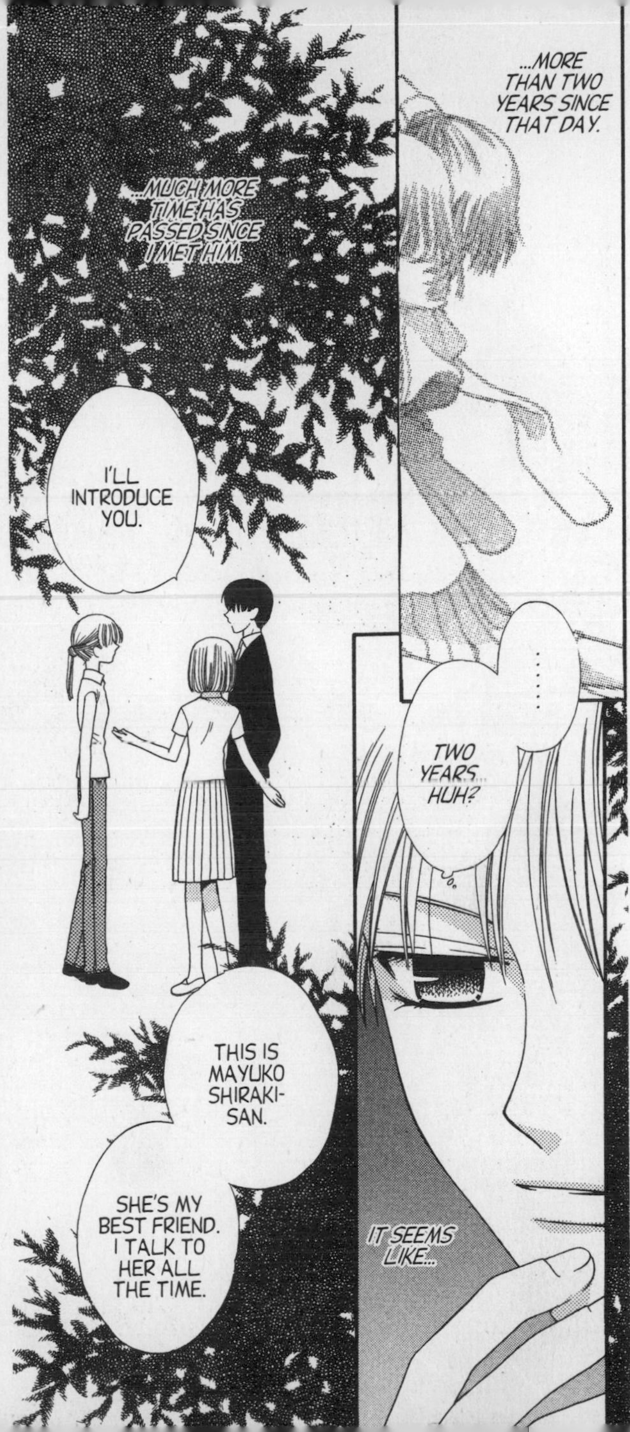
...MORE THAN TWO YEARS SINCE THAT DAY.
......
TWO YEARS, HUH?
IT SEEMS LIKE...
...MUCH MORE TIME HAS PASSED SINCE I MET HIM.
I'LL INTRODUCE YOU.
THIS IS MAYUKO SHIRAKI-SAN.
SHE'S MY BEST FRIEND. I TALK TO HER ALL THE TIME.

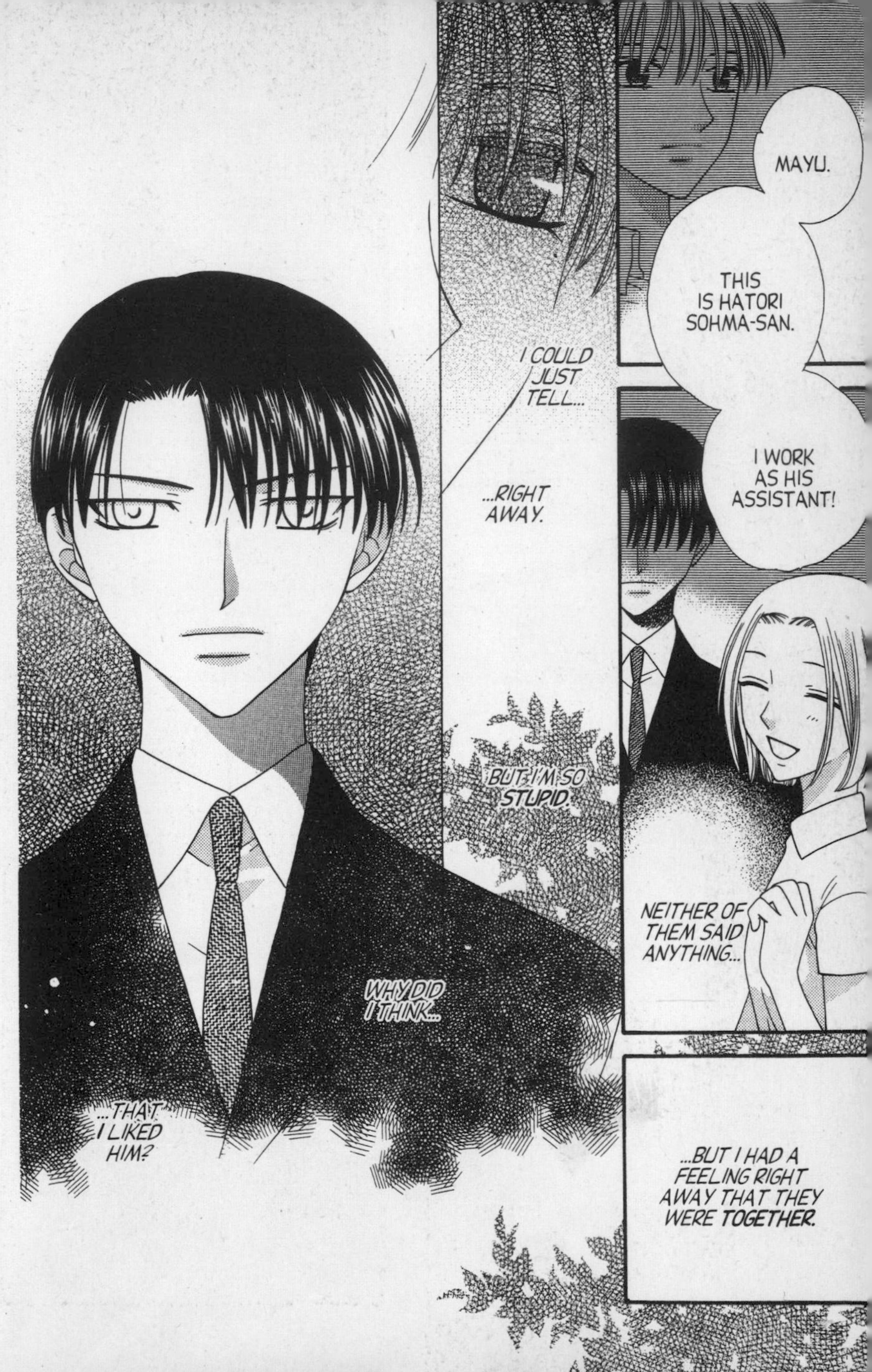

MAYU.
THIS IS HATORI SOHMA-SAN.
I WORK AS HIS ASSISTANT!
NEITHER OF THEM SAID ANYTHING...
...BUT I HAD A FEELING RIGHT AWAY THAT THEY WERE TOGETHER.
I COULD JUST TELL...
...RIGHT AWAY.
BUT I'M SO STUPID.
WHY DID I THINK...
...THAT I LIKED HIM?

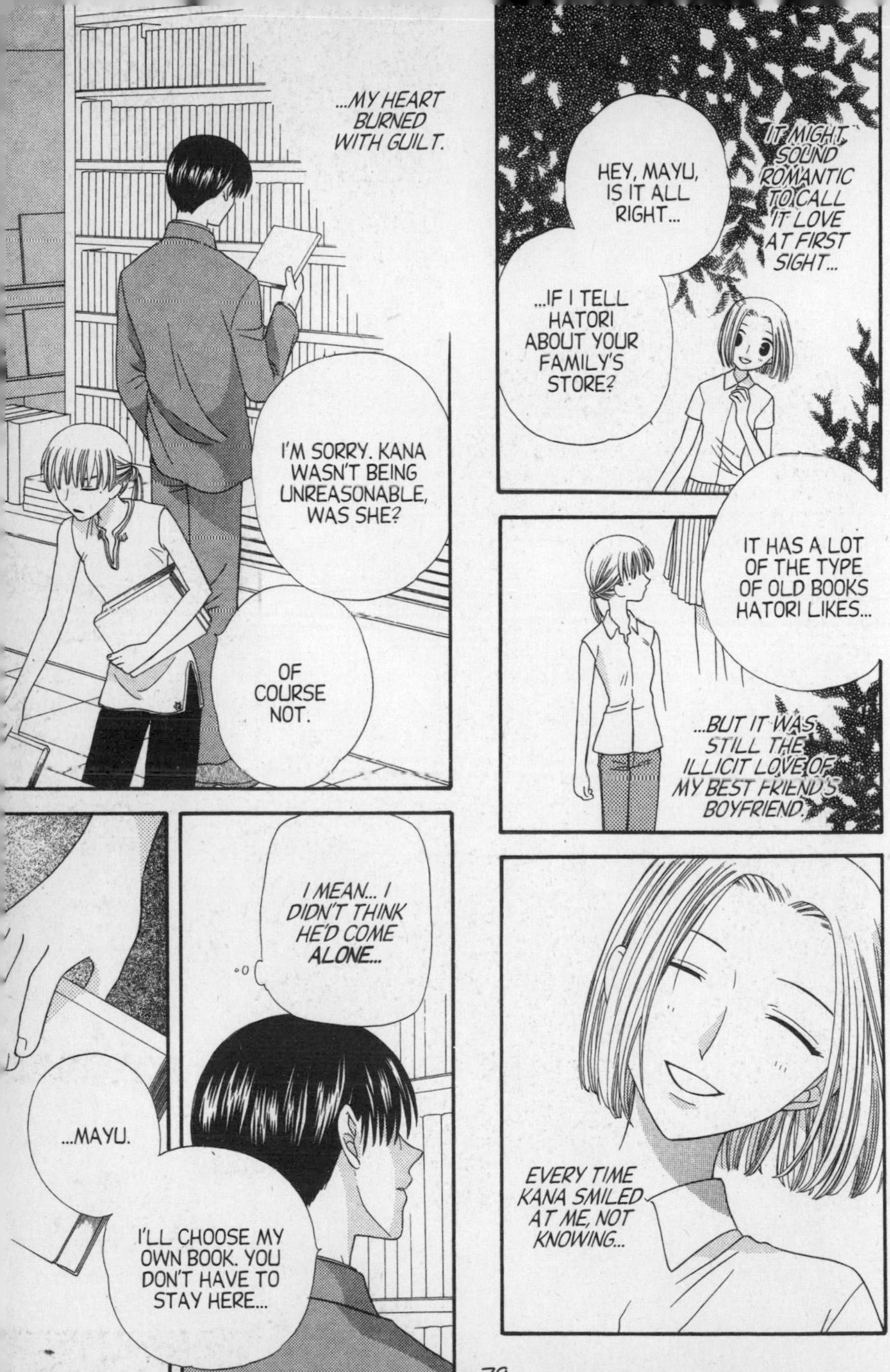

IT MIGHT SOUND ROMANTIC TO CALL IT LOVE AT FIRST SIGHT...
HEY, MAYU, IS IT ALL RIGHT...
...IF I TELL HATORI ABOUT YOUR FAMILY'S STORE?
IT HAS A LOT OF THE TYPE OF OLD BOOKS HATORI LIKES...
...BUT IT WAS STILL THE ILLICIT LOVE OF MY BEST FRIEND'S BOYFRIEND.
EVERY TIME KANA SMILED AT ME, NOT KNOWING...
...MY HEART BURNED WITH GUILT.
I'M SORRY. KANA WASN'T BEING UNREASONABLE, WAS SHE?
OF COURSE NOT.
I MEAN... I DIDN'T THINK HE'D COME ALONE...
...MAYU.
I'LL CHOOSE MY OWN BOOK. YOU DON'T HAVE TO STAY HERE...

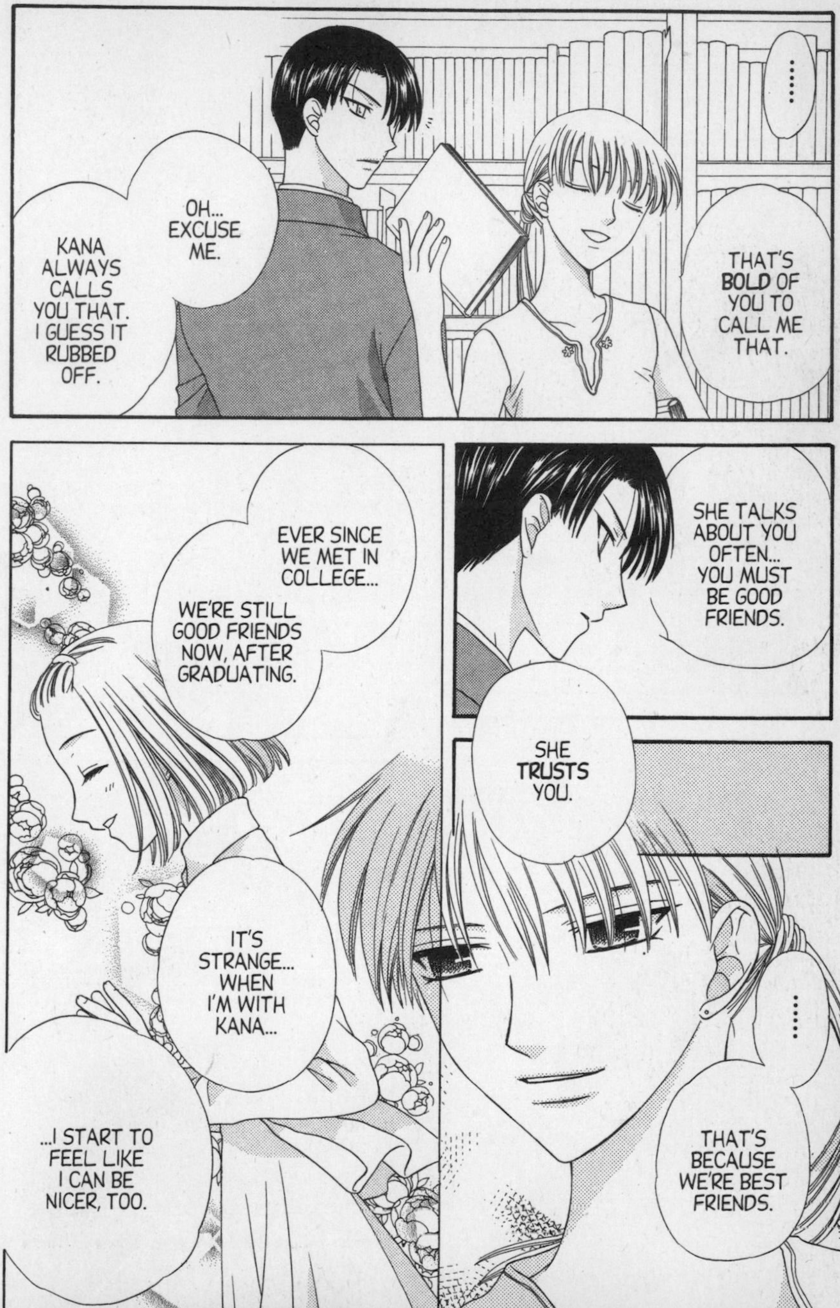
......
THAT'S BOLD OF YOU TO CALL ME THAT.
OH... EXCUSE ME.
KANA ALWAYS CALLS YOU THAT. I GUESS IT RUBBED OFF.
SHE TALKS ABOUT YOU OFTEN... YOU MUST BE GOOD FRIENDS.
SHE TRUSTS YOU.
......
THAT'S BECAUSE WE'RE BEST FRIENDS.
EVER SINCE WE MET IN COLLEGE...
WE'RE STILL GOOD FRIENDS NOW, AFTER GRADUATING.
IT'S STRANGE... WHEN I'M WITH KANA...
...I START TO FEEL LIKE I CAN BE NICER, TOO.

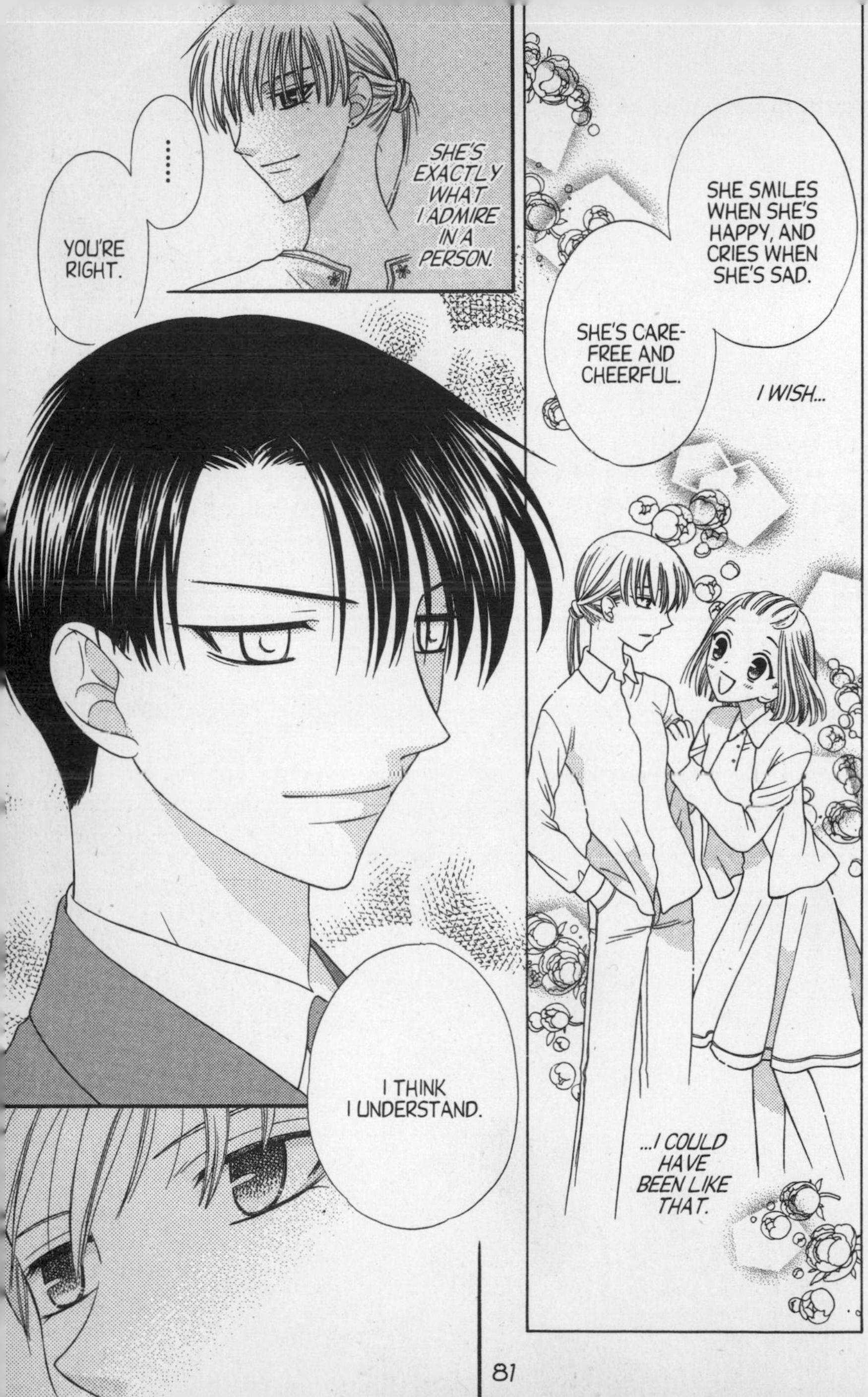
SHE SMILES WHEN SHE'S HAPPY, AND CRIES WHEN SHE'S SAD.
SHE'S CARE-FREE AND CHEERFUL.
SHE'S EXACTLY WHAT I ADMIRE IN A PERSON.
......
YOU'RE RIGHT.
I WISH...
I THINK I UNDERSTAND.
...I COULD HAVE BEEN LIKE THAT.

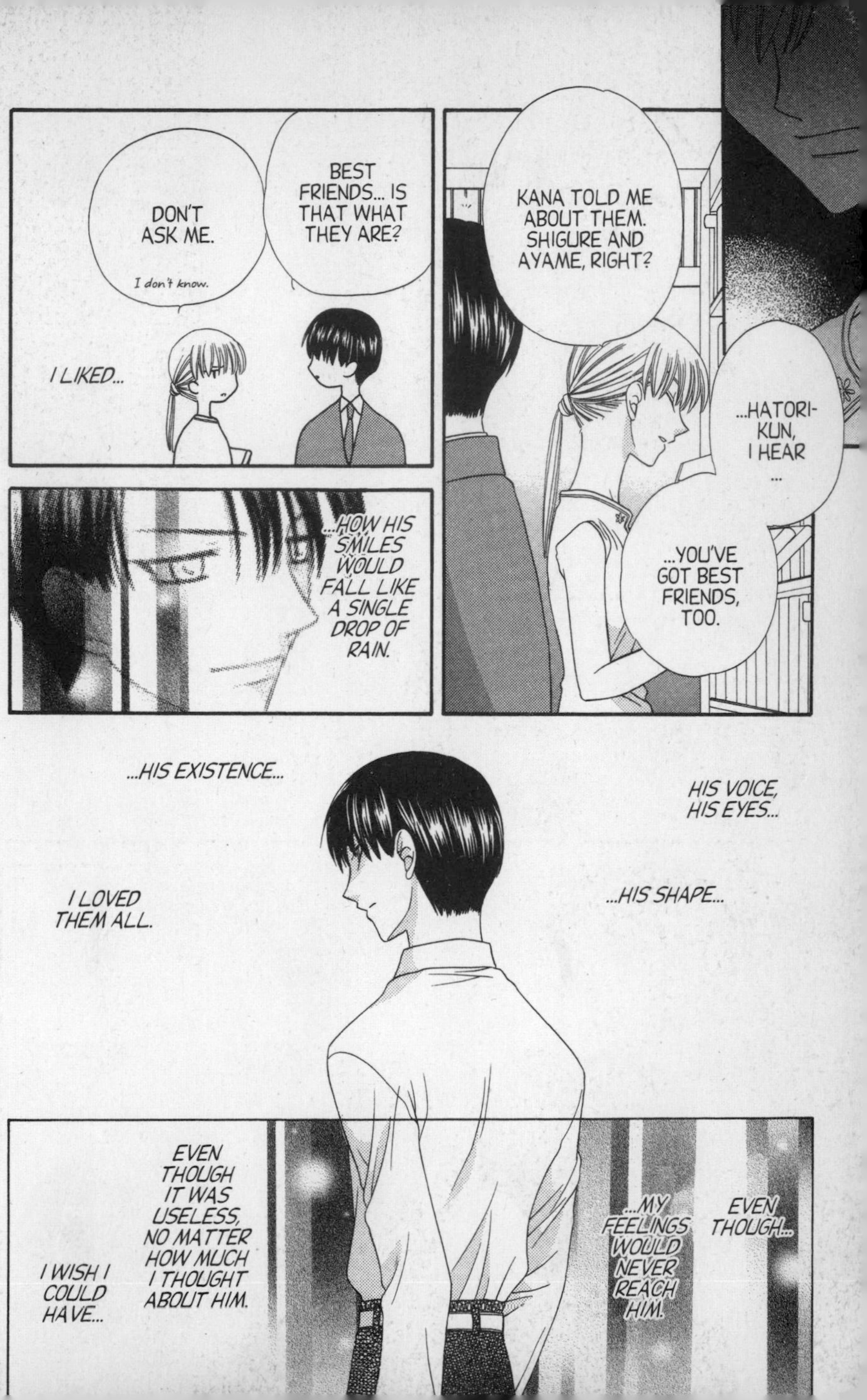
KANA TOLD ME ABOUT THEM. SHIGURE AND AYAME, RIGHT?
...HATORI-KUN, I HEAR ...
...YOU'VE GOT BEST FRIENDS, TOO.
BEST FRIENDS... IS THAT WHAT THEY ARE?
DON'T ASK ME.
I don't know.
I LIKED...
...HOW HIS SMILES WOULD FALL LIKE A SINGLE DROP OF RAIN.
HIS VOICE, HIS EYES...
...HIS SHAPE...
...HIS EXISTENCE...
I LOVED THEM ALL.
EVEN THOUGH...
...MY FEELINGS WOULD NEVER REACH HIM.
EVEN THOUGH IT WAS USELESS, NO MATTER HOW MUCH I THOUGHT ABOUT HIM.
I WISH I COULD HAVE...

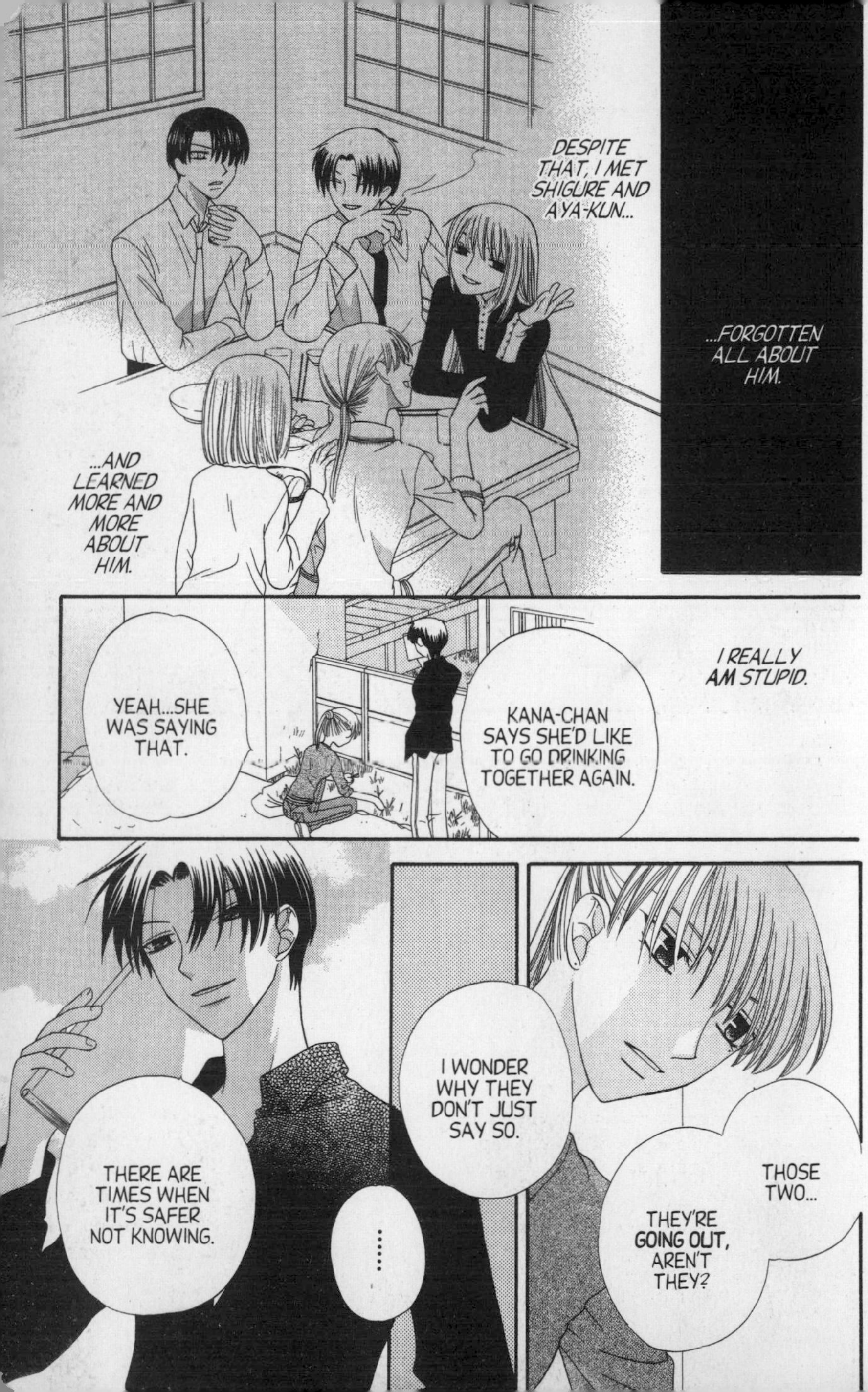
...FORGOTTEN ALL ABOUT HIM.
DESPITE THAT, I MET SHIGURE AND AYA-KUN...
...AND LEARNED MORE AND MORE ABOUT HIM.
I REALLY AM STUPID.
KANA-CHAN SAYS SHE'D LIKE TO GO DRINKING TOGETHER AGAIN.
YEAH...SHE WAS SAYING THAT.
THOSE TWO...
THEY'RE GOING OUT, AREN'T THEY?
I WONDER WHY THEY DON'T JUST SAY SO.
......
THERE ARE TIMES WHEN IT'S SAFER NOT KNOWING.

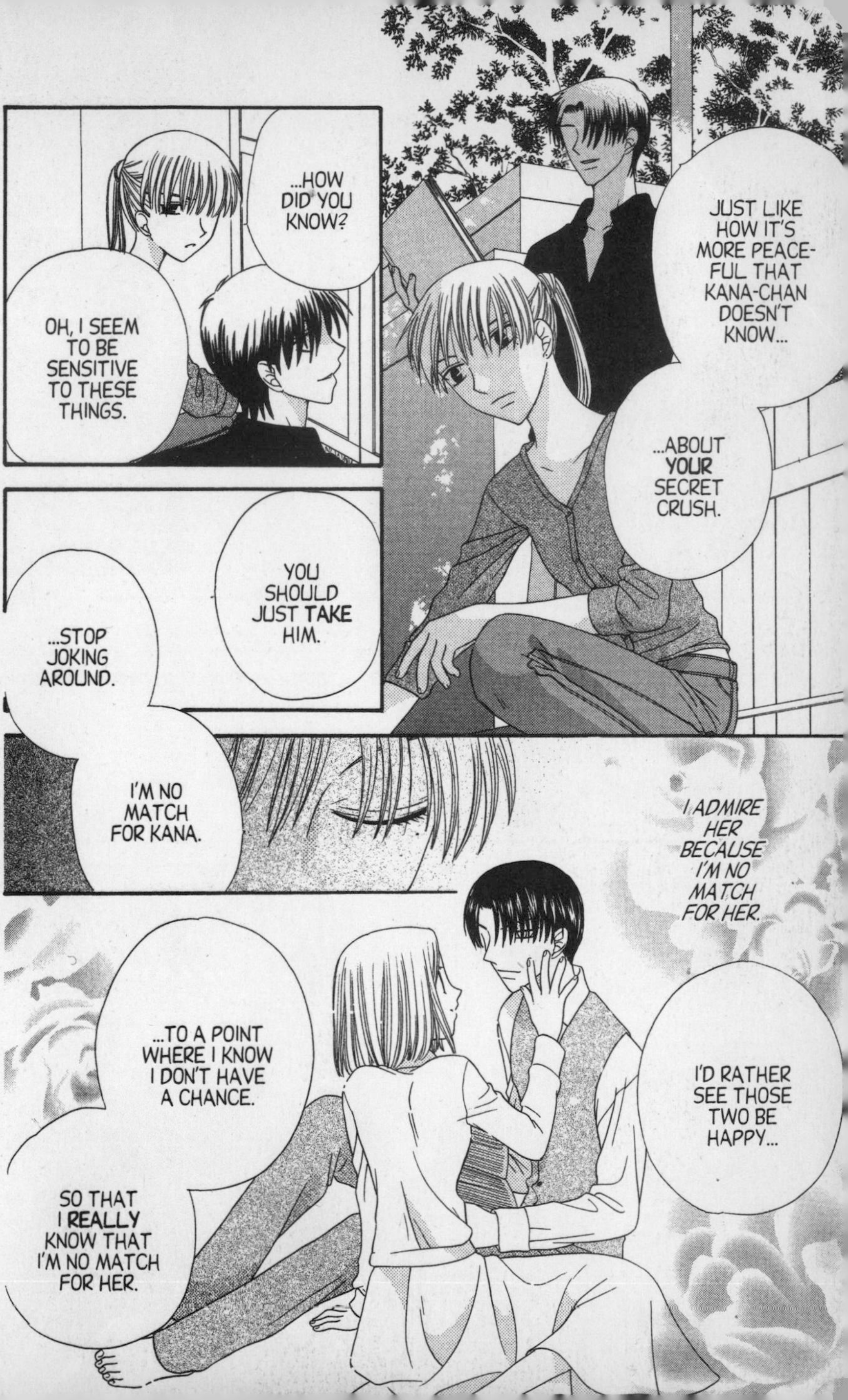
JUST LIKE HOW IT'S MORE PEACE-FUL THAT KANA-CHAN DOESN'T KNOW...
...ABOUT **YOUR** SECRET CRUSH.
...HOW DID YOU KNOW?
OH, I SEEM TO BE SENSITIVE TO THESE THINGS.
YOU SHOULD JUST **TAKE** HIM.
...STOP JOKING AROUND.
I'M NO MATCH FOR KANA.
I ADMIRE HER BECAUSE I'M NO MATCH FOR HER.
I'D RATHER SEE THOSE TWO BE HAPPY...
...TO A POINT WHERE I KNOW I DON'T HAVE A CHANCE.
SO THAT I **REALLY** KNOW THAT I'M NO MATCH FOR HER.

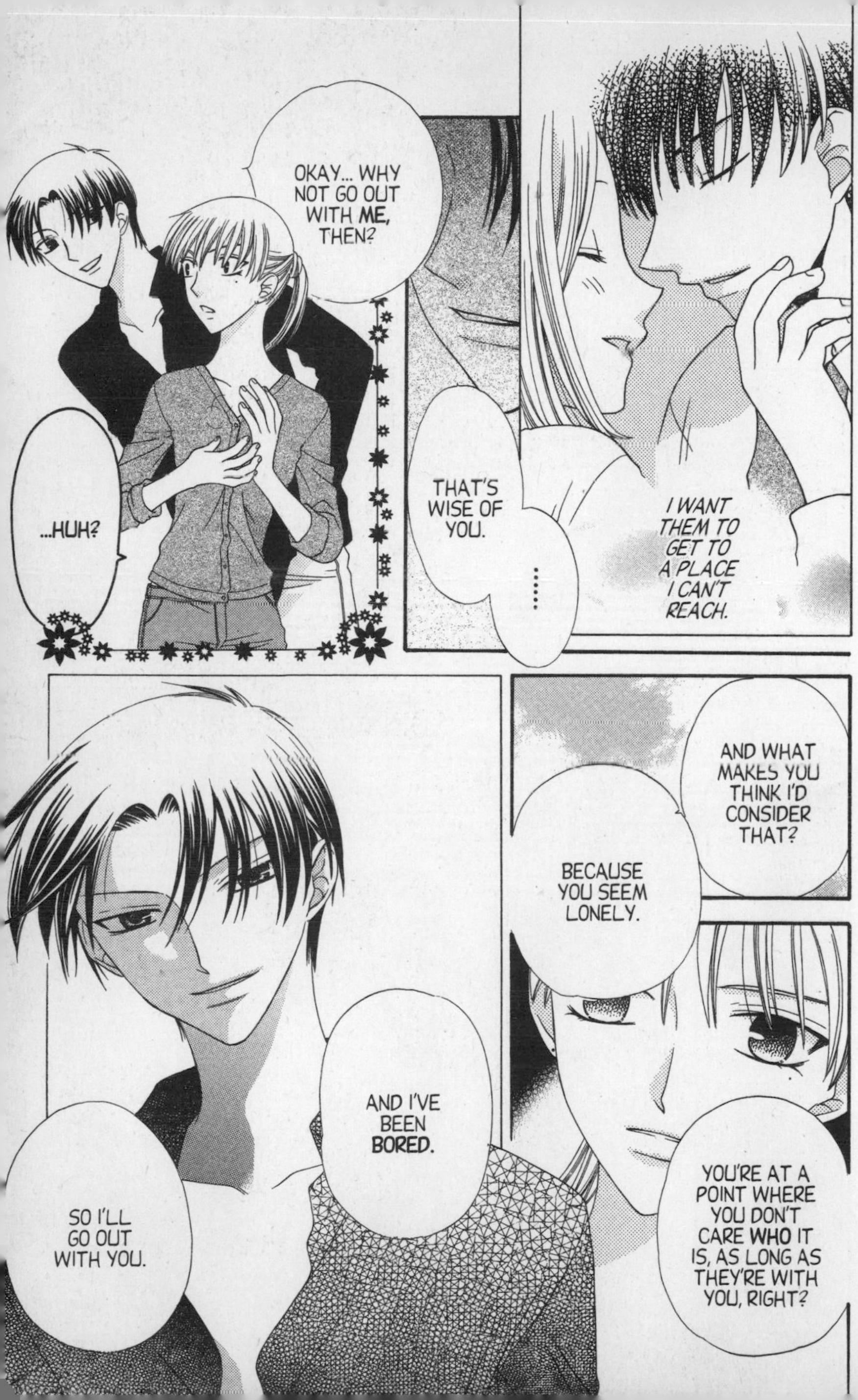
I WANT THEM TO GET TO A PLACE I CAN'T REACH.
THAT'S WISE OF YOU.
......
OKAY... WHY NOT GO OUT WITH ME, THEN?
...HUH?
AND WHAT MAKES YOU THINK I'D CONSIDER THAT?
BECAUSE YOU SEEM LONELY.
YOU'RE AT A POINT WHERE YOU DON'T CARE WHO IT IS, AS LONG AS THEY'RE WITH YOU, RIGHT?
AND I'VE BEEN BORED.
SO I'LL GO OUT WITH YOU.

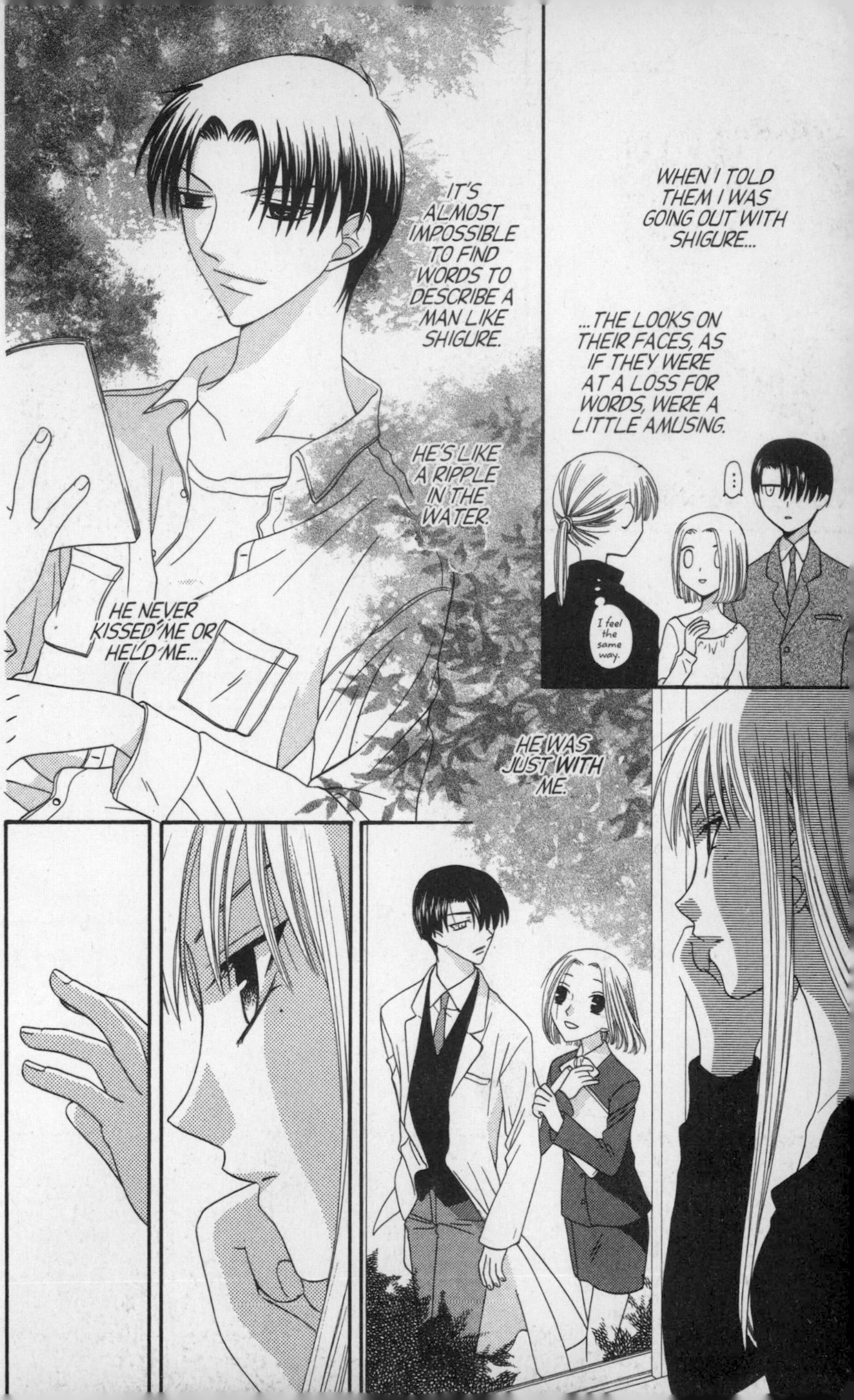
WHEN I TOLD THEM I WAS GOING OUT WITH SHIGURE...
...THE LOOKS ON THEIR FACES, AS IF THEY WERE AT A LOSS FOR WORDS, WERE A LITTLE AMUSING.
...
I feel the same way.
IT'S ALMOST IMPOSSIBLE TO FIND WORDS TO DESCRIBE A MAN LIKE SHIGURE.
HE'S LIKE A RIPPLE IN THE WATER.
HE NEVER KISSED ME OR HELD ME...
HE WAS JUST WITH ME.

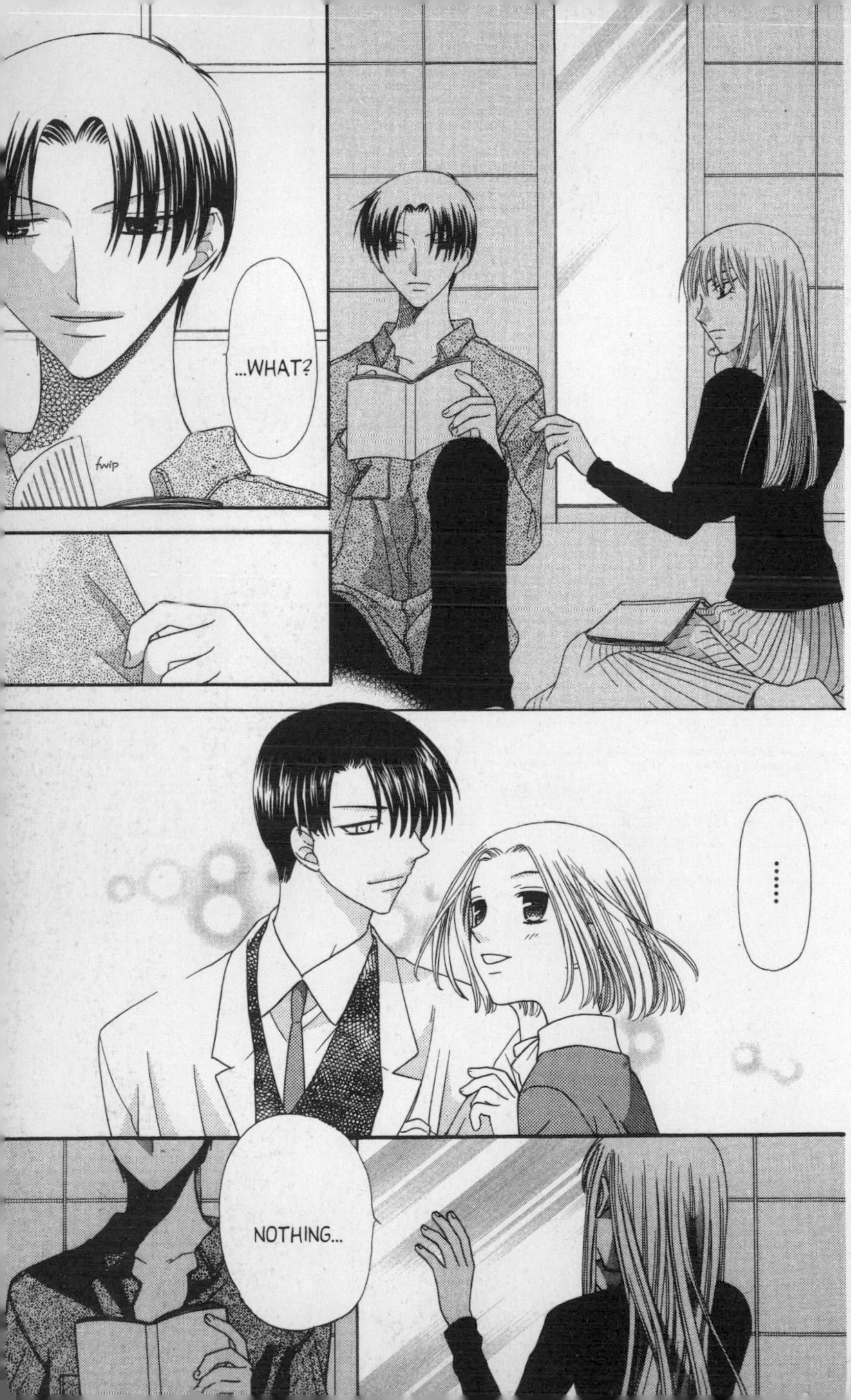
...WHAT?
fwip
......
NOTHING...

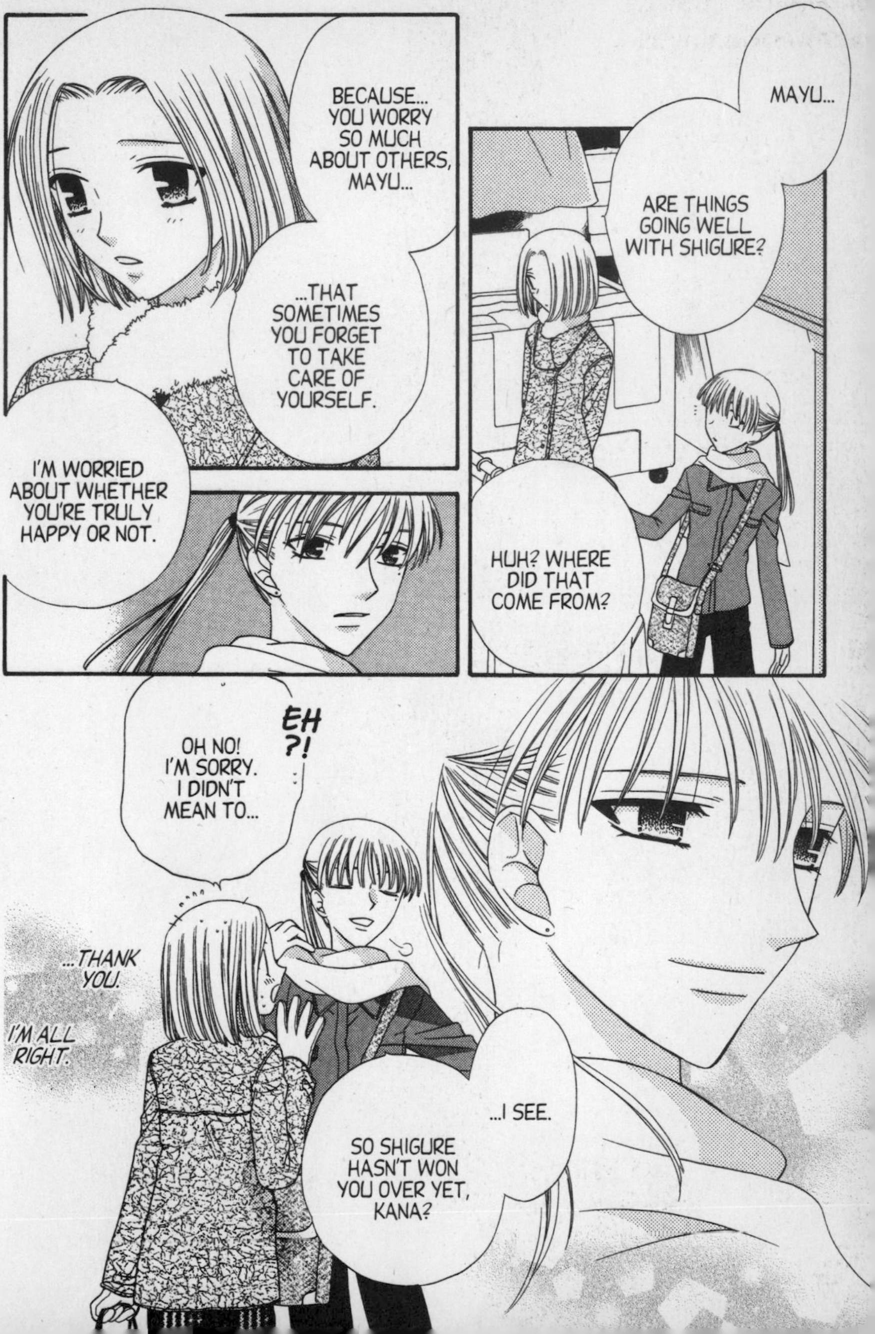
MAYU...
ARE THINGS GOING WELL WITH SHIGURE?
HUH? WHERE DID THAT COME FROM?
BECAUSE... YOU WORRY SO MUCH ABOUT OTHERS, MAYU...
...THAT SOMETIMES YOU FORGET TO TAKE CARE OF YOURSELF.
I'M WORRIED ABOUT WHETHER YOU'RE TRULY HAPPY OR NOT.
...I SEE.
SO SHIGURE HASN'T WON YOU OVER YET, KANA?
EH ?!
OH NO! I'M SORRY. I DIDN'T MEAN TO...
...THANK YOU.
I'M ALL RIGHT.

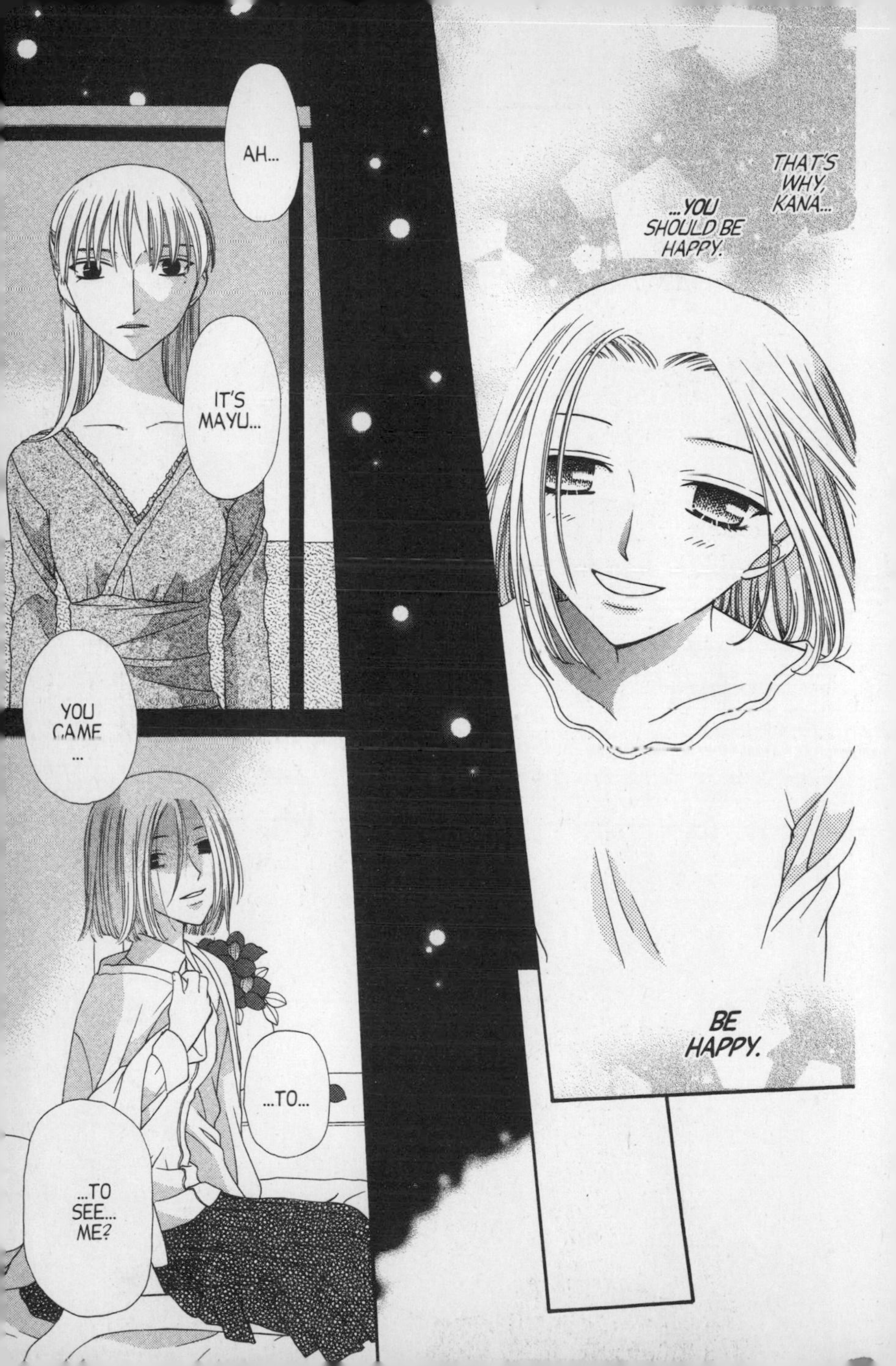
THAT'S WHY, KANA...
...YOU SHOULD BE HAPPY.
BE HAPPY.
AH...
IT'S MAYU...
YOU CAME ...
...TO...
...TO SEE... ME?

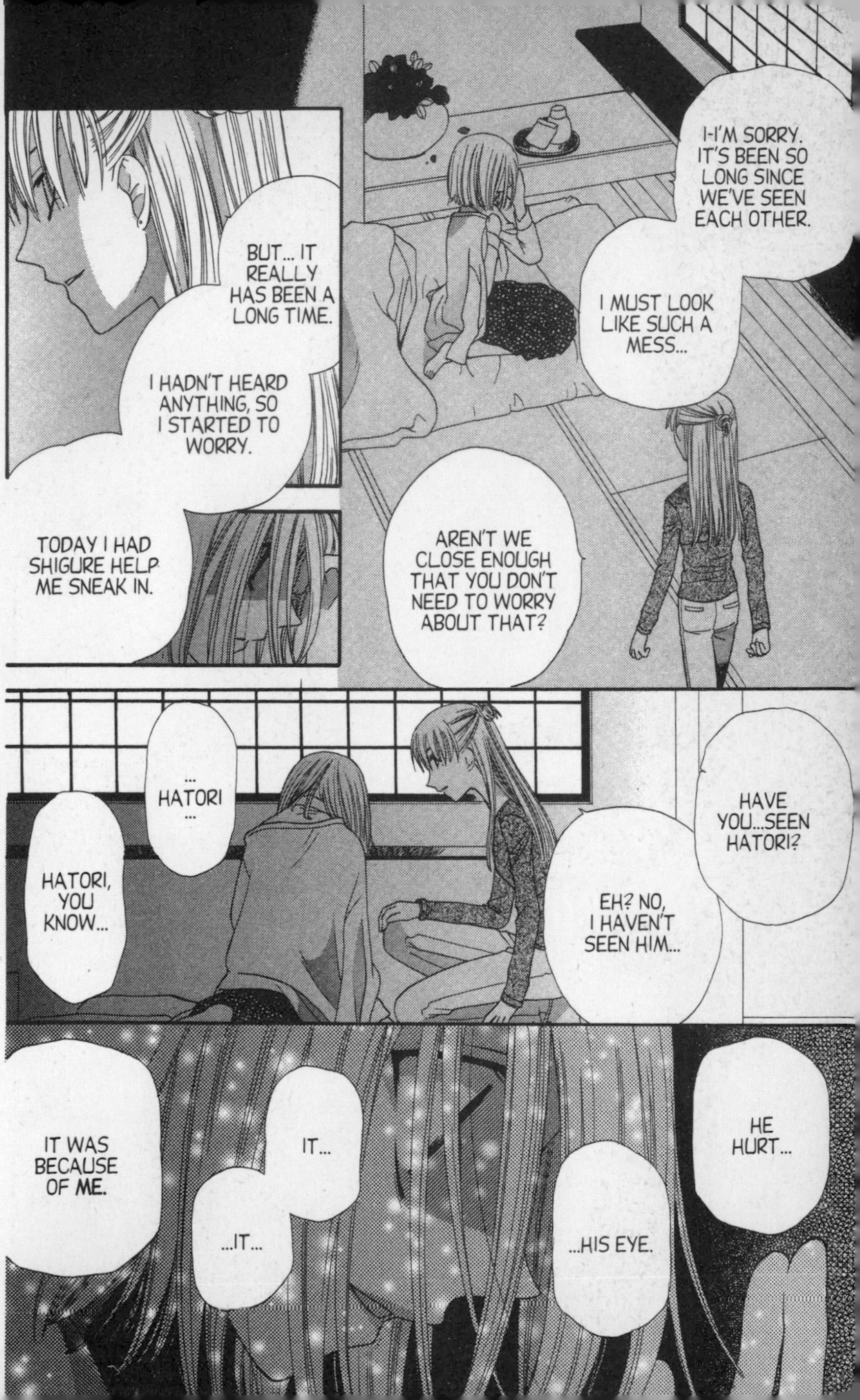
I-I'M SORRY. IT'S BEEN SO LONG SINCE WE'VE SEEN EACH OTHER.
I MUST LOOK LIKE SUCH A MESS...
AREN'T WE CLOSE ENOUGH THAT YOU DON'T NEED TO WORRY ABOUT THAT?
BUT... IT REALLY HAS BEEN A LONG TIME.
I HADN'T HEARD ANYTHING, SO I STARTED TO WORRY.
TODAY I HAD SHIGURE HELP ME SNEAK IN.
HAVE YOU...SEEN HATORI?
EH? NO, I HAVEN'T SEEN HIM...
... HATORI ...
HATORI, YOU KNOW...
HE HURT...
...HIS EYE.
IT...
...IT...
IT WAS BECAUSE OF ME.

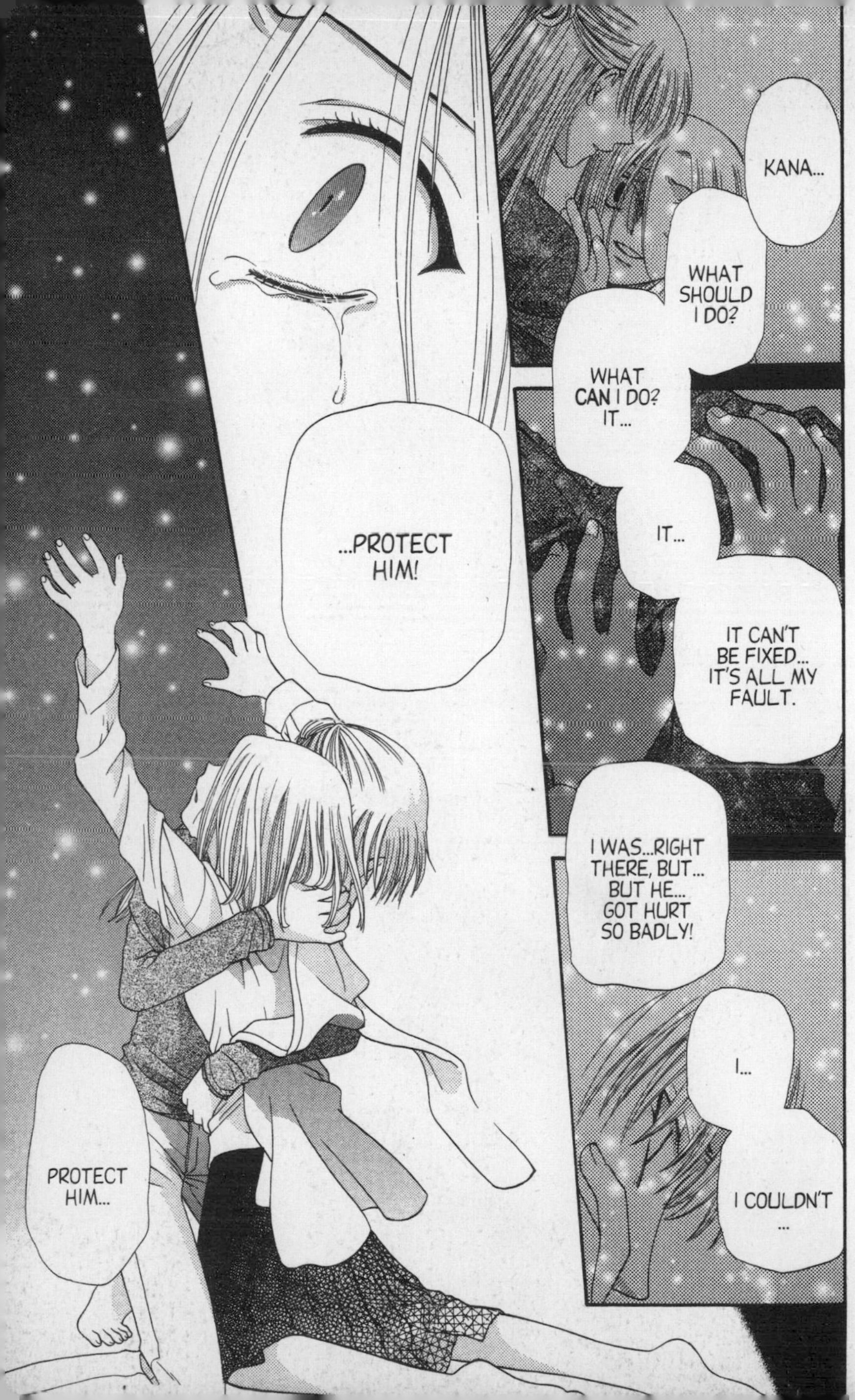

KANA...
WHAT SHOULD I DO?
WHAT CAN I DO? IT...
IT...
IT CAN'T BE FIXED... IT'S ALL MY FAULT.
I WAS...RIGHT THERE, BUT... BUT HE... GOT HURT SO BADLY!
I...
I COULDN'T ...
...PROTECT HIM!
PROTECT HIM...

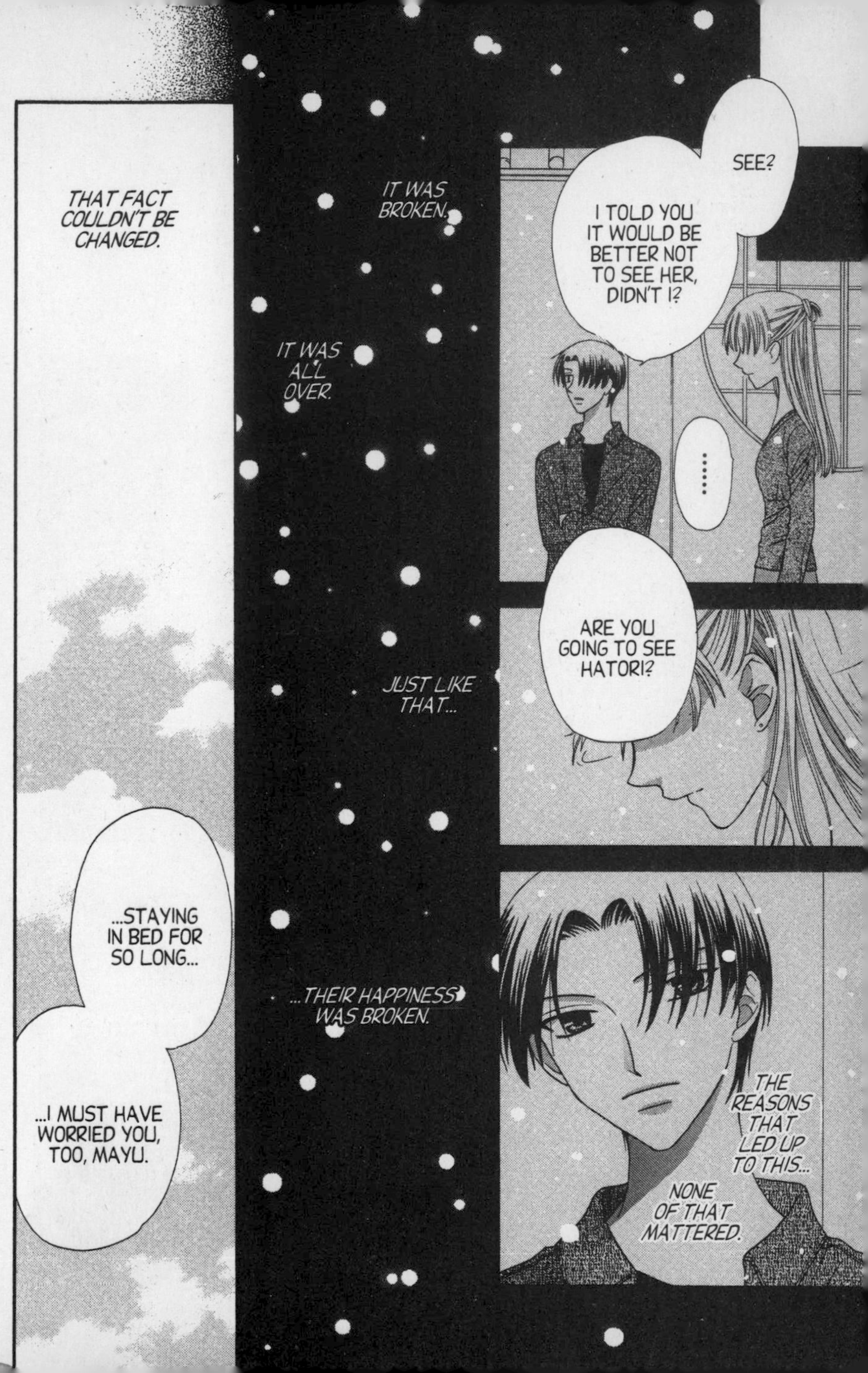
SEE?
I TOLD YOU IT WOULD BE BETTER NOT TO SEE HER, DIDN'T I?
......
ARE YOU GOING TO SEE HATORI?
THE REASONS THAT LED UP TO THIS...
NONE OF THAT MATTERED.
IT WAS BROKEN.
IT WAS ALL OVER.
JUST LIKE THAT...
...THEIR HAPPINESS WAS BROKEN.
THAT FACT COULDN'T BE CHANGED.
...STAYING IN BED FOR SO LONG...
...I MUST HAVE WORRIED YOU, TOO, MAYU.

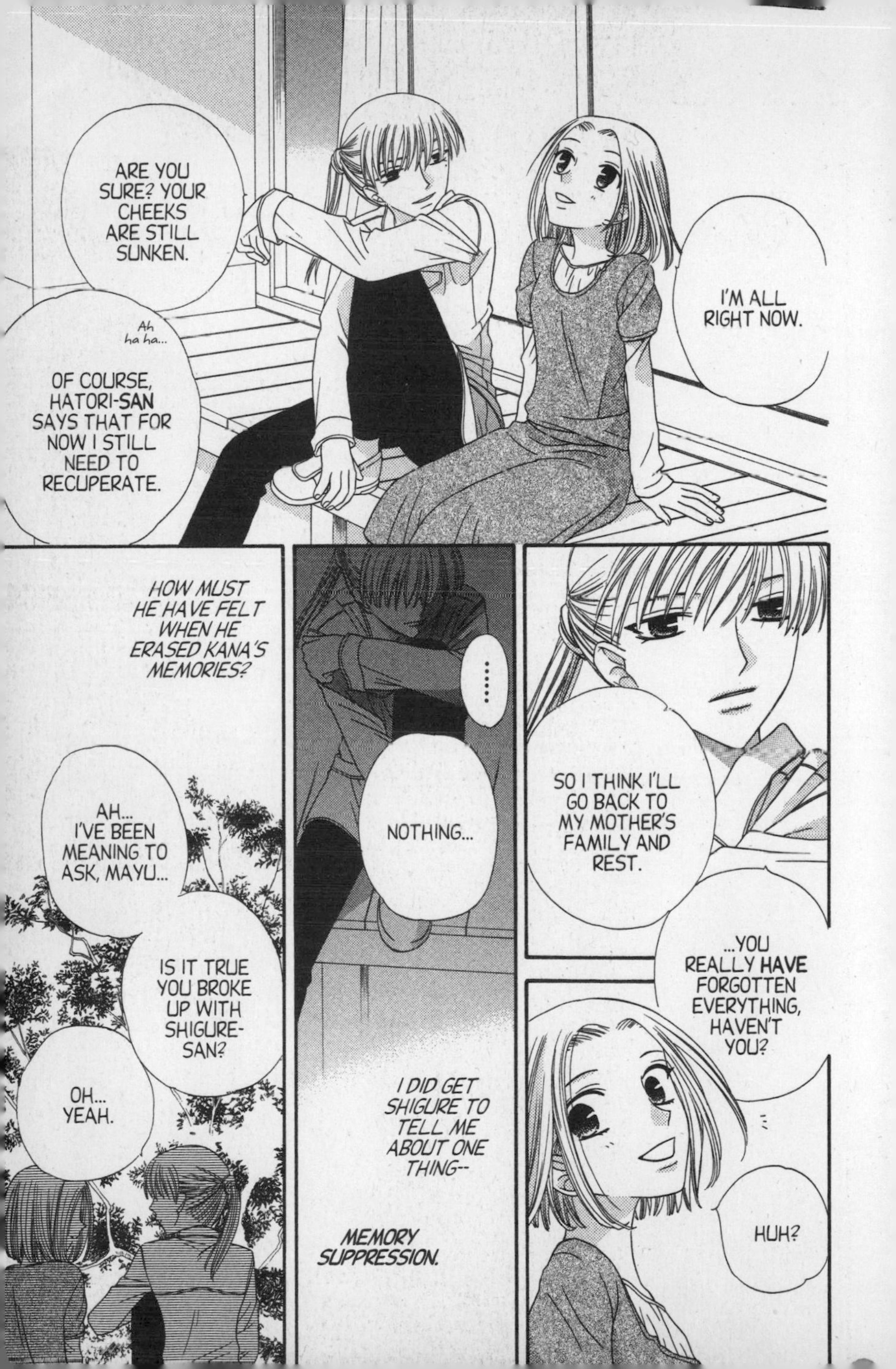
I'M ALL RIGHT NOW.
ARE YOU SURE? YOUR CHEEKS ARE STILL SUNKEN.
Ah ha ha...
OF COURSE, HATORI-SAN SAYS THAT FOR NOW I STILL NEED TO RECUPERATE.
SO I THINK I'LL GO BACK TO MY MOTHER'S FAMILY AND REST.
...YOU REALLY HAVE FORGOTTEN EVERYTHING, HAVEN'T YOU?
HUH?
......
NOTHING...
I DID GET SHIGURE TO TELL ME ABOUT ONE THING--
MEMORY SUPPRESSION.
HOW MUST HE HAVE FELT WHEN HE ERASED KANA'S MEMORIES?
AH... I'VE BEEN MEANING TO ASK, MAYU...
IS IT TRUE YOU BROKE UP WITH SHIGURE-SAN?
OH... YEAH.

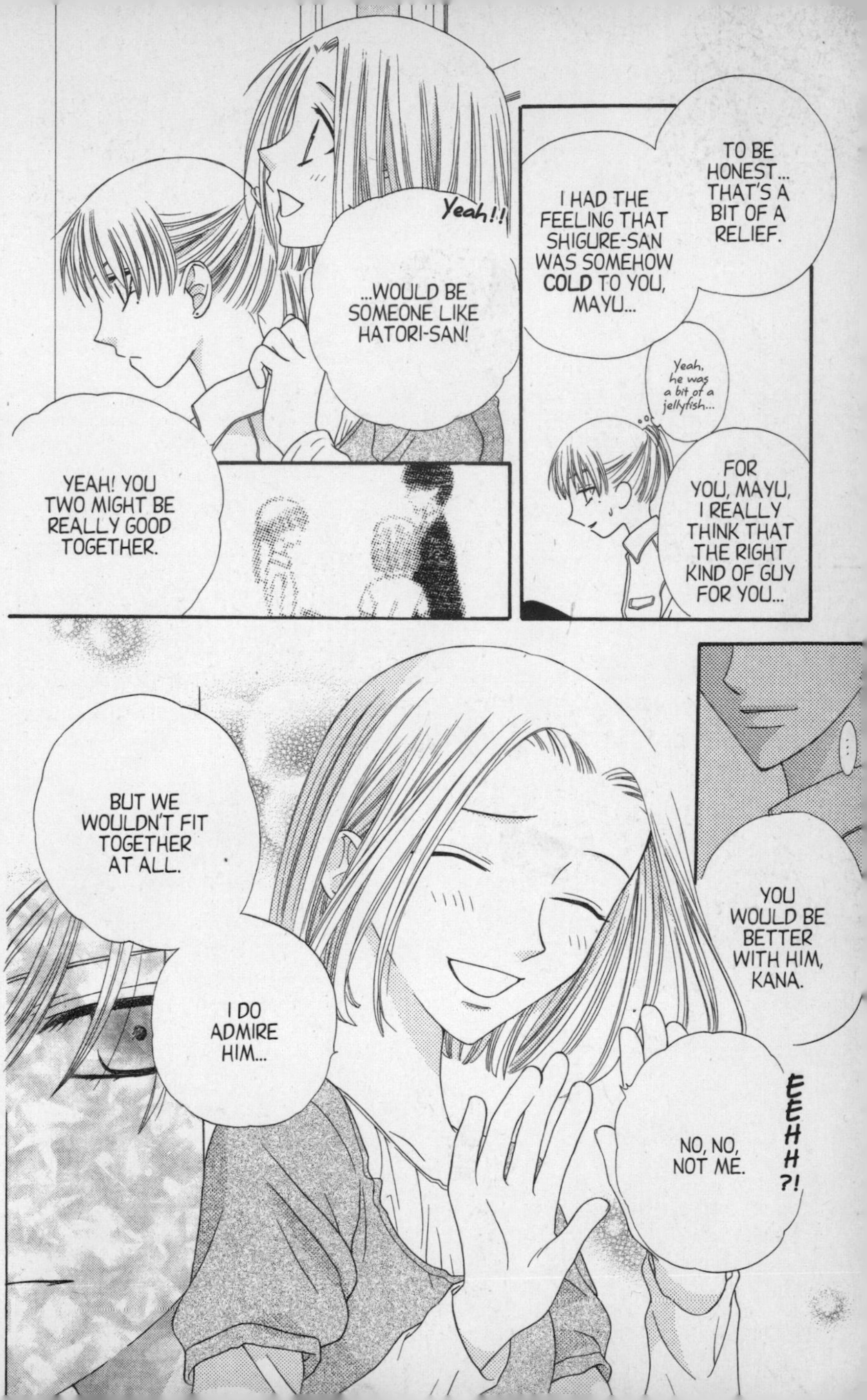
TO BE HONEST... THAT'S A BIT OF A RELIEF.
I HAD THE FEELING THAT SHIGURE-SAN WAS SOMEHOW COLD TO YOU, MAYU...
Yeah, he was a bit of a jellyfish...
FOR YOU, MAYU, I REALLY THINK THAT THE RIGHT KIND OF GUY FOR YOU...
...WOULD BE SOMEONE LIKE HATORI-SAN!
Yeah!!
YEAH! YOU TWO MIGHT BE REALLY GOOD TOGETHER.
...
YOU WOULD BE BETTER WITH HIM, KANA.
EEHH?!
NO, NO, NOT ME.
I DO ADMIRE HIM...
BUT WE WOULDN'T FIT TOGETHER AT ALL.

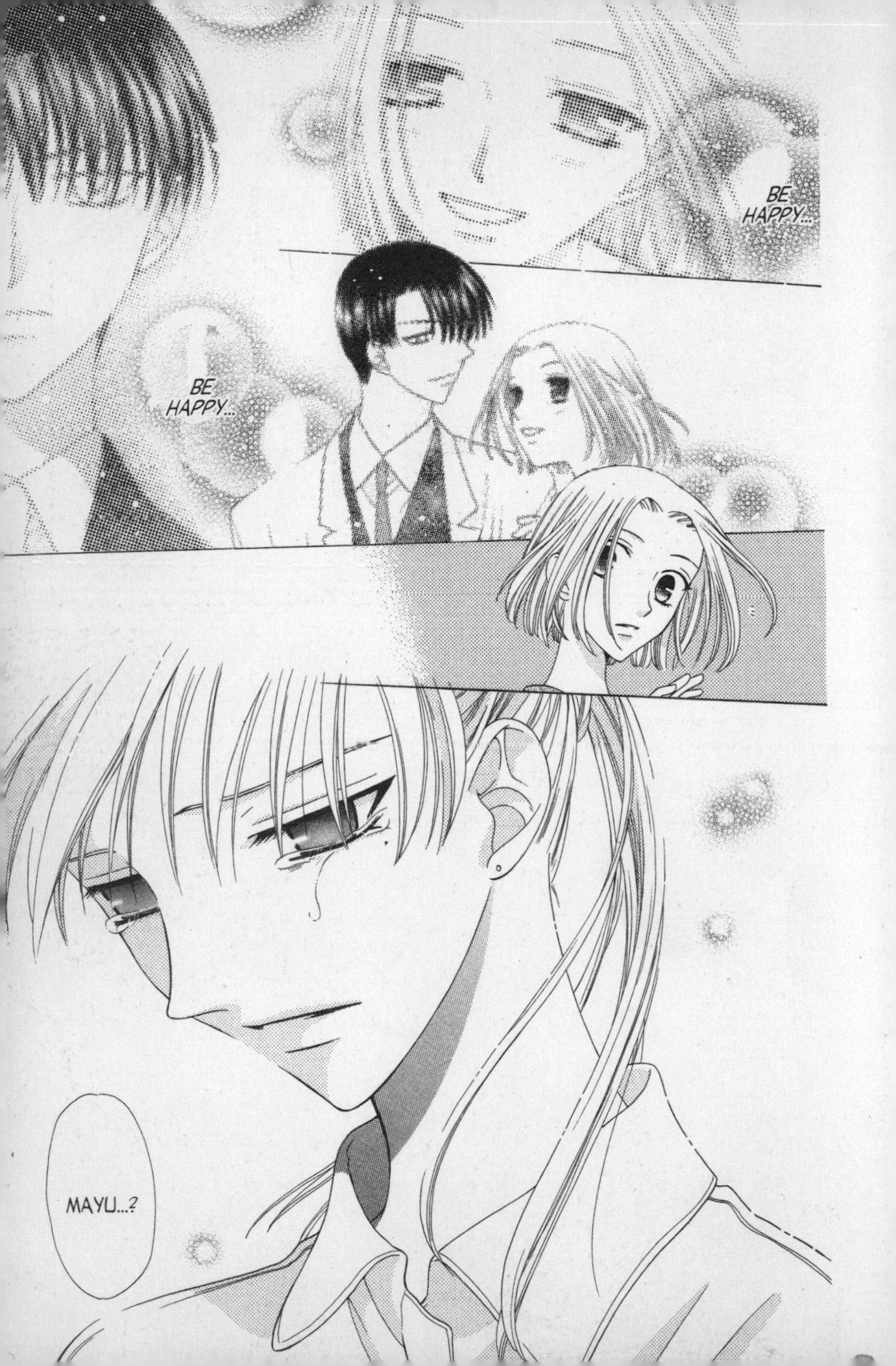
BE HAPPY...
BE HAPPY...
MAYU...?

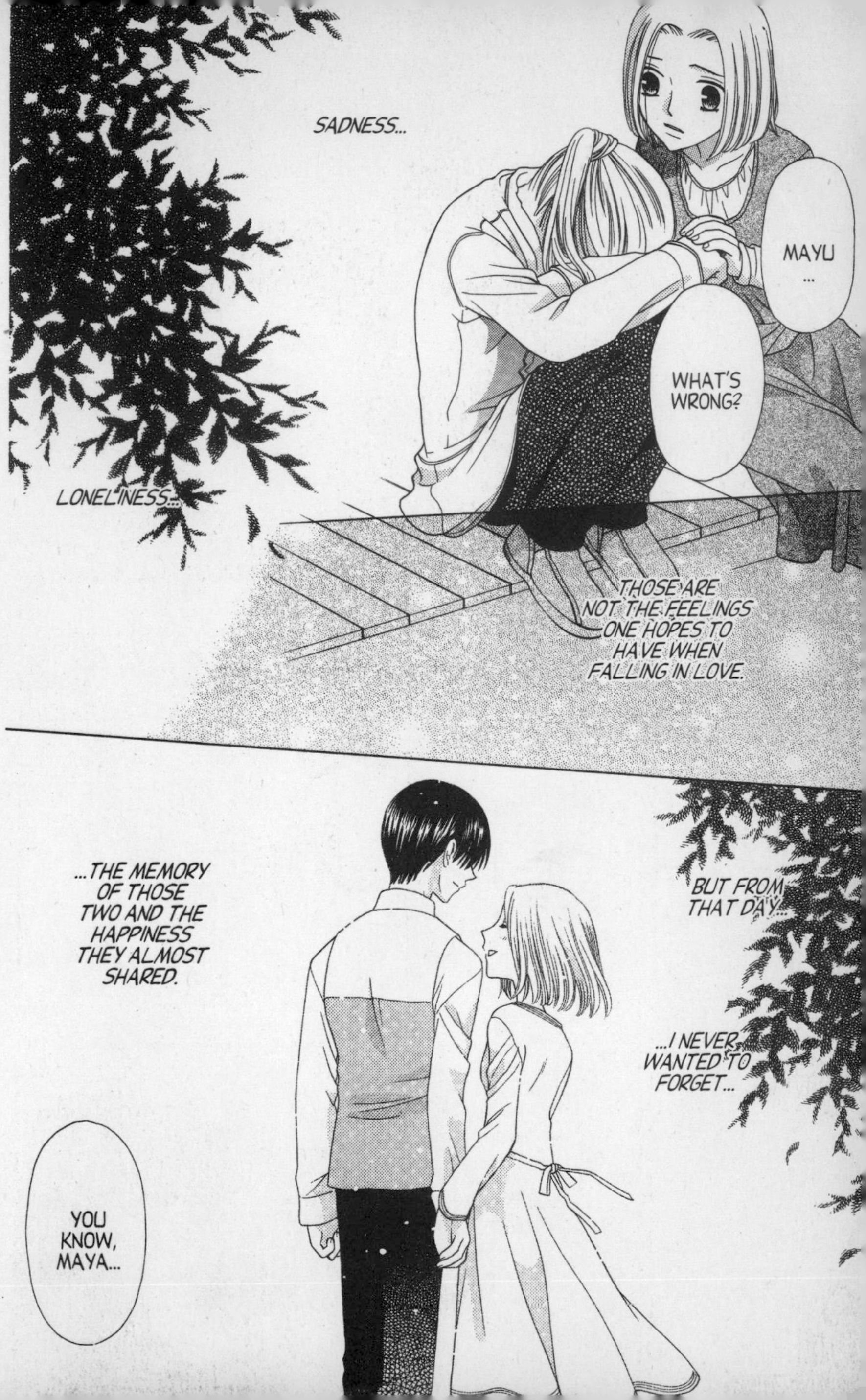
SADNESS...
MAYU...
WHAT'S WRONG?
LONELINESS...
THOSE ARE NOT THE FEELINGS ONE HOPES TO HAVE WHEN FALLING IN LOVE.
BUT FROM THAT DAY...
...I NEVER WANTED TO FORGET...
...THE MEMORY OF THOSE TWO AND THE HAPPINESS THEY ALMOST SHARED.
YOU KNOW, MAYA...

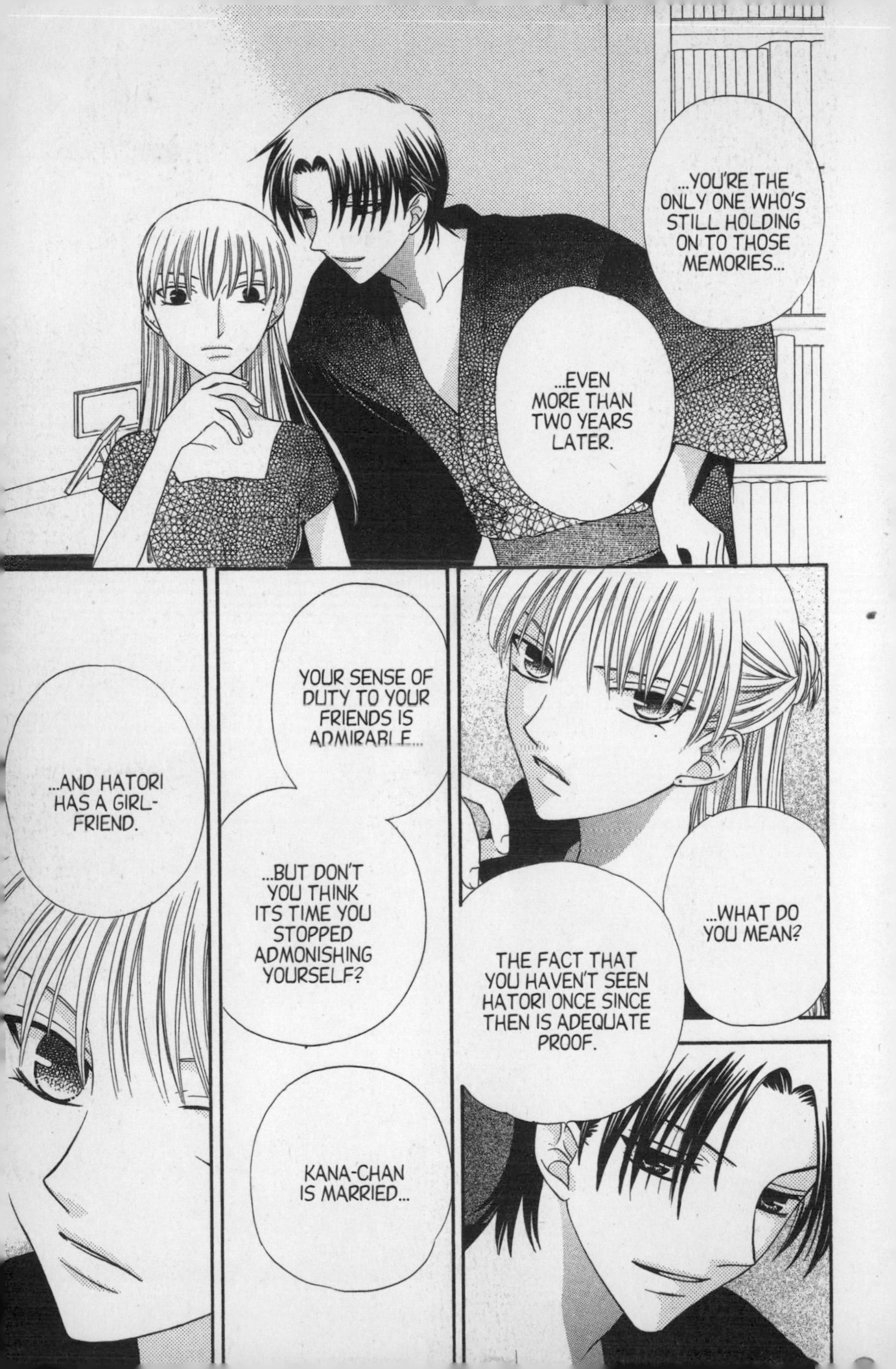
...YOU'RE THE ONLY ONE WHO'S STILL HOLDING ON TO THOSE MEMORIES...
...EVEN MORE THAN TWO YEARS LATER.
...WHAT DO YOU MEAN?
THE FACT THAT YOU HAVEN'T SEEN HATORI ONCE SINCE THEN IS ADEQUATE PROOF.
YOUR SENSE OF DUTY TO YOUR FRIENDS IS ADMIRABLE...
...BUT DON'T YOU THINK ITS TIME YOU STOPPED ADMONISHING YOURSELF?
KANA-CHAN IS MARRIED...
...AND HATORI HAS A GIRL-FRIEND.

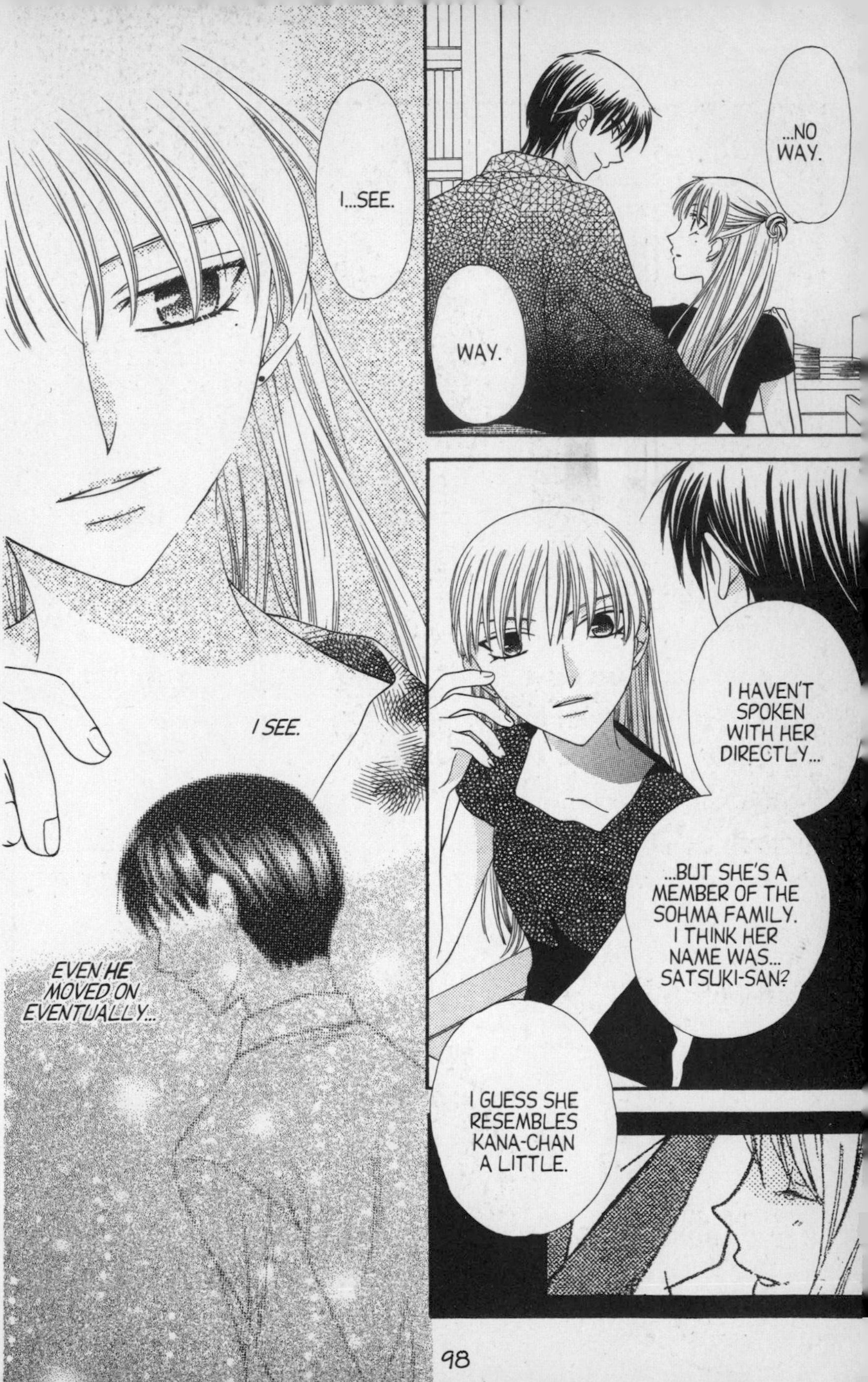

...NO WAY.
WAY.
I HAVEN'T SPOKEN WITH HER DIRECTLY...
...BUT SHE'S A MEMBER OF THE SOHMA FAMILY. I THINK HER NAME WAS... SATSUKI-SAN?
I GUESS SHE RESEMBLES KANA-CHAN A LITTLE.
I...SEE.
I SEE.
EVEN HE MOVED ON EVENTUALLY...

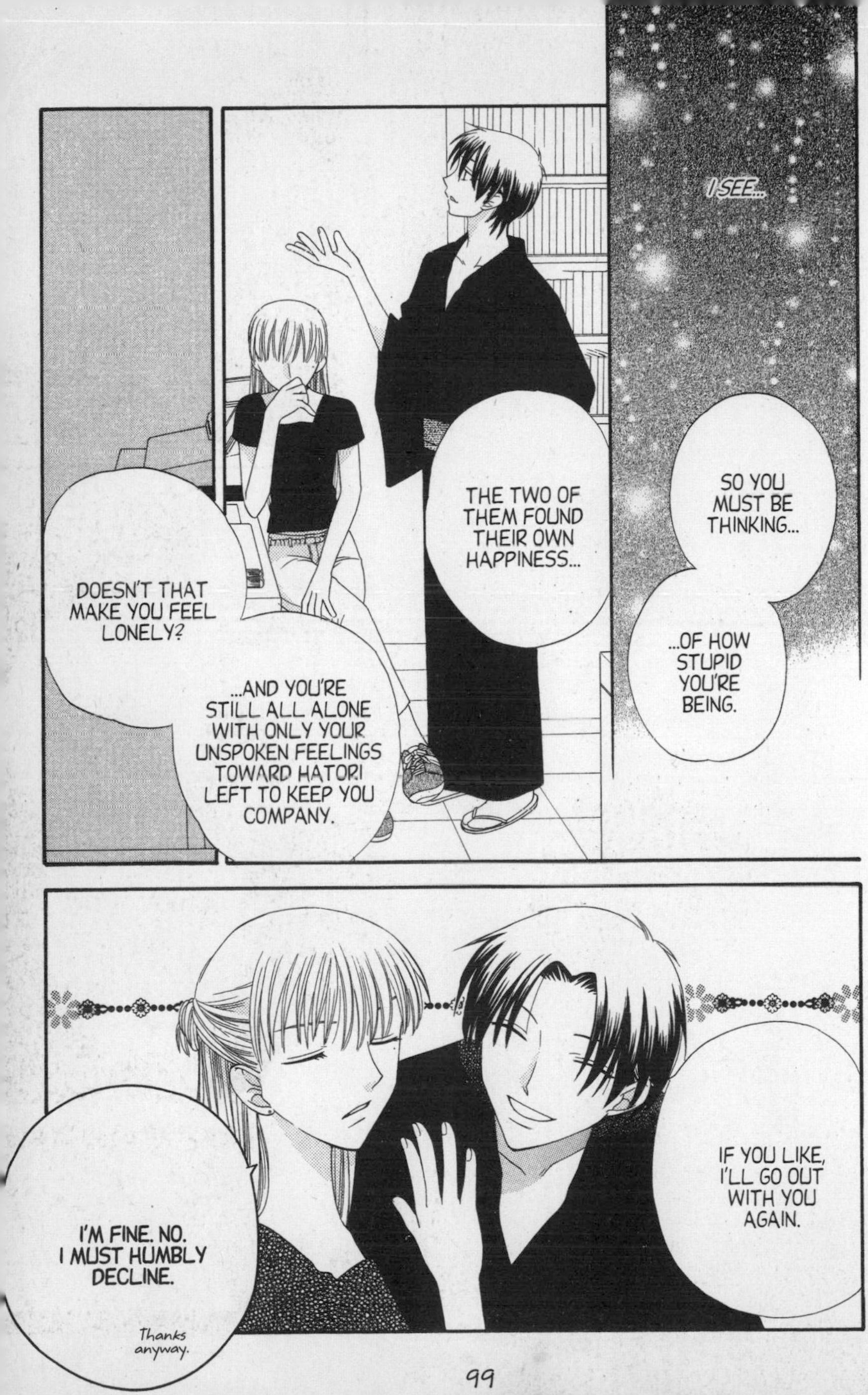
I SEE...
SO YOU MUST BE THINKING...
...OF HOW STUPID YOU'RE BEING.
THE TWO OF THEM FOUND THEIR OWN HAPPINESS...
...AND YOU'RE STILL ALL ALONE WITH ONLY YOUR UNSPOKEN FEELINGS TOWARD HATORI LEFT TO KEEP YOU COMPANY.
DOESN'T THAT MAKE YOU FEEL LONELY?
IF YOU LIKE, I'LL GO OUT WITH YOU AGAIN.
I'M FINE. NO. I MUST HUMBLY DECLINE.
Thanks anyway.

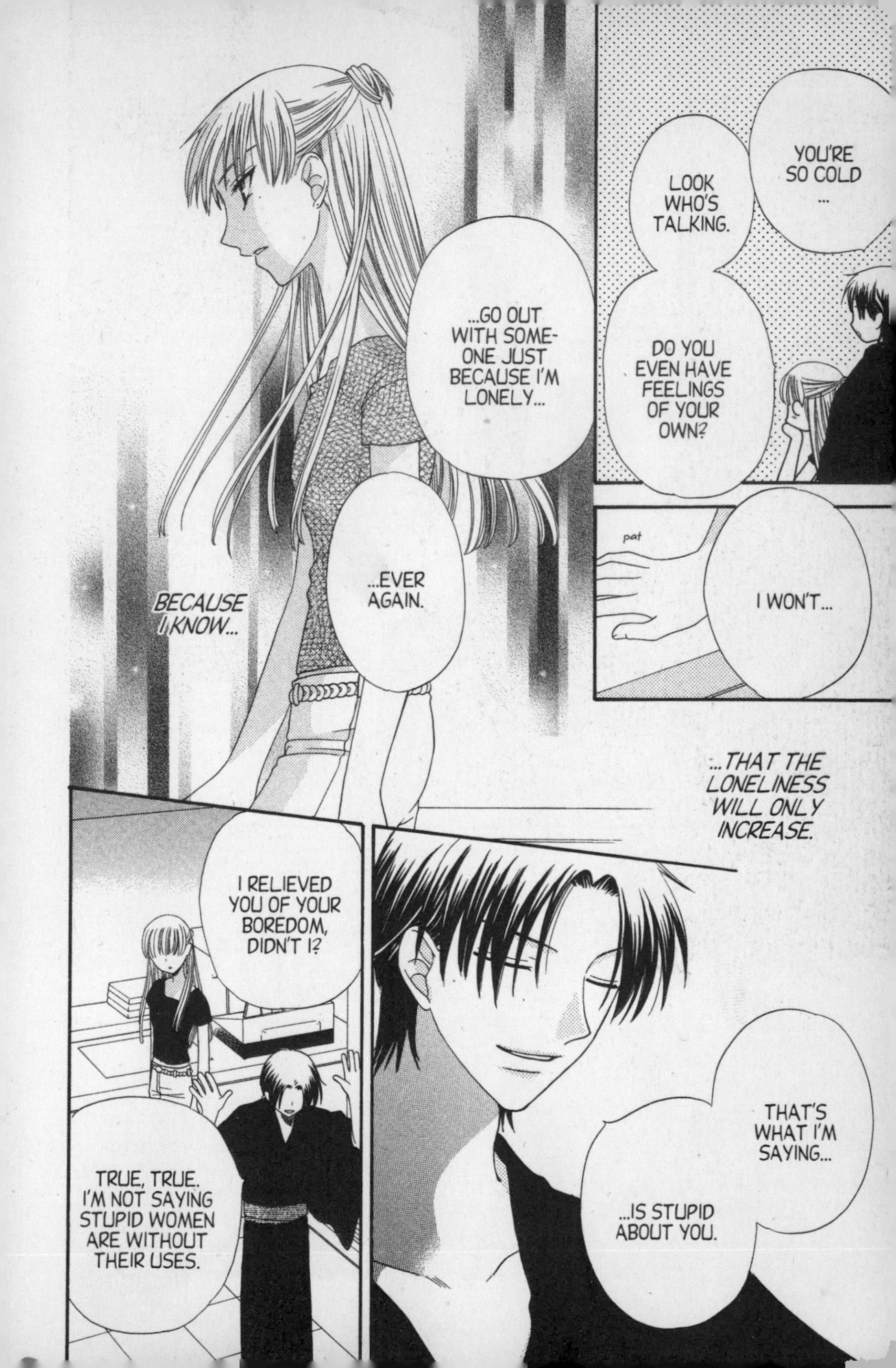
YOU'RE SO COLD ...
LOOK WHO'S TALKING.
DO YOU EVEN HAVE FEELINGS OF YOUR OWN?
pat
I WON'T...
...GO OUT WITH SOME-ONE JUST BECAUSE I'M LONELY...
...EVER AGAIN.
BECAUSE I KNOW...
...THAT THE LONELINESS WILL ONLY INCREASE.
THAT'S WHAT I'M SAYING...
...IS STUPID ABOUT YOU.
I RELIEVED YOU OF YOUR BOREDOM, DIDN'T I?
TRUE, TRUE. I'M NOT SAYING STUPID WOMEN ARE WITHOUT THEIR USES.

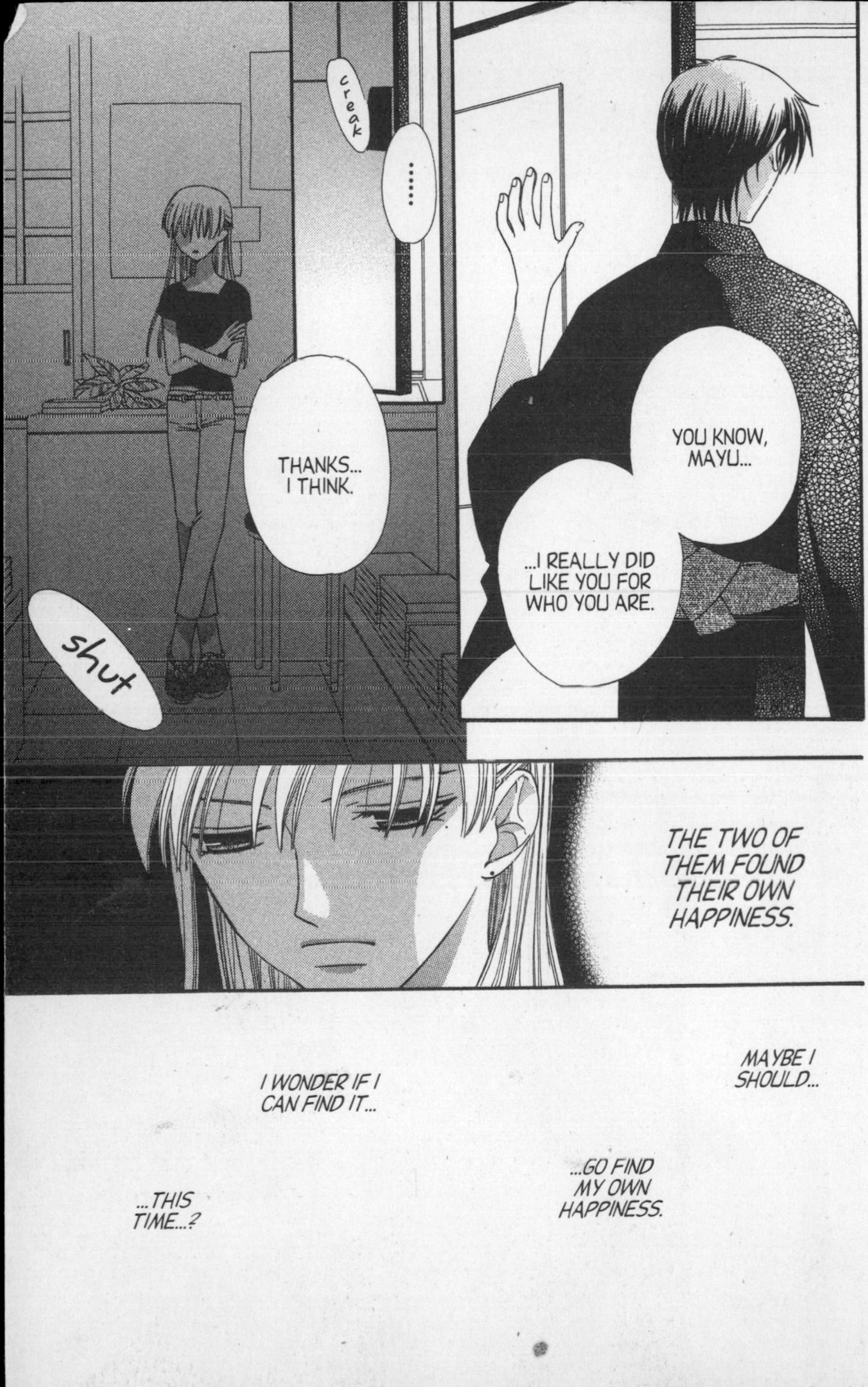
YOU KNOW, MAYU...
...I REALLY DID LIKE YOU FOR WHO YOU ARE.
creak
......
THANKS... I THINK.
shut
THE TWO OF THEM FOUND THEIR OWN HAPPINESS.
MAYBE I SHOULD...
...GO FIND MY OWN HAPPINESS.
I WONDER IF I CAN FIND IT...
...THIS TIME...?

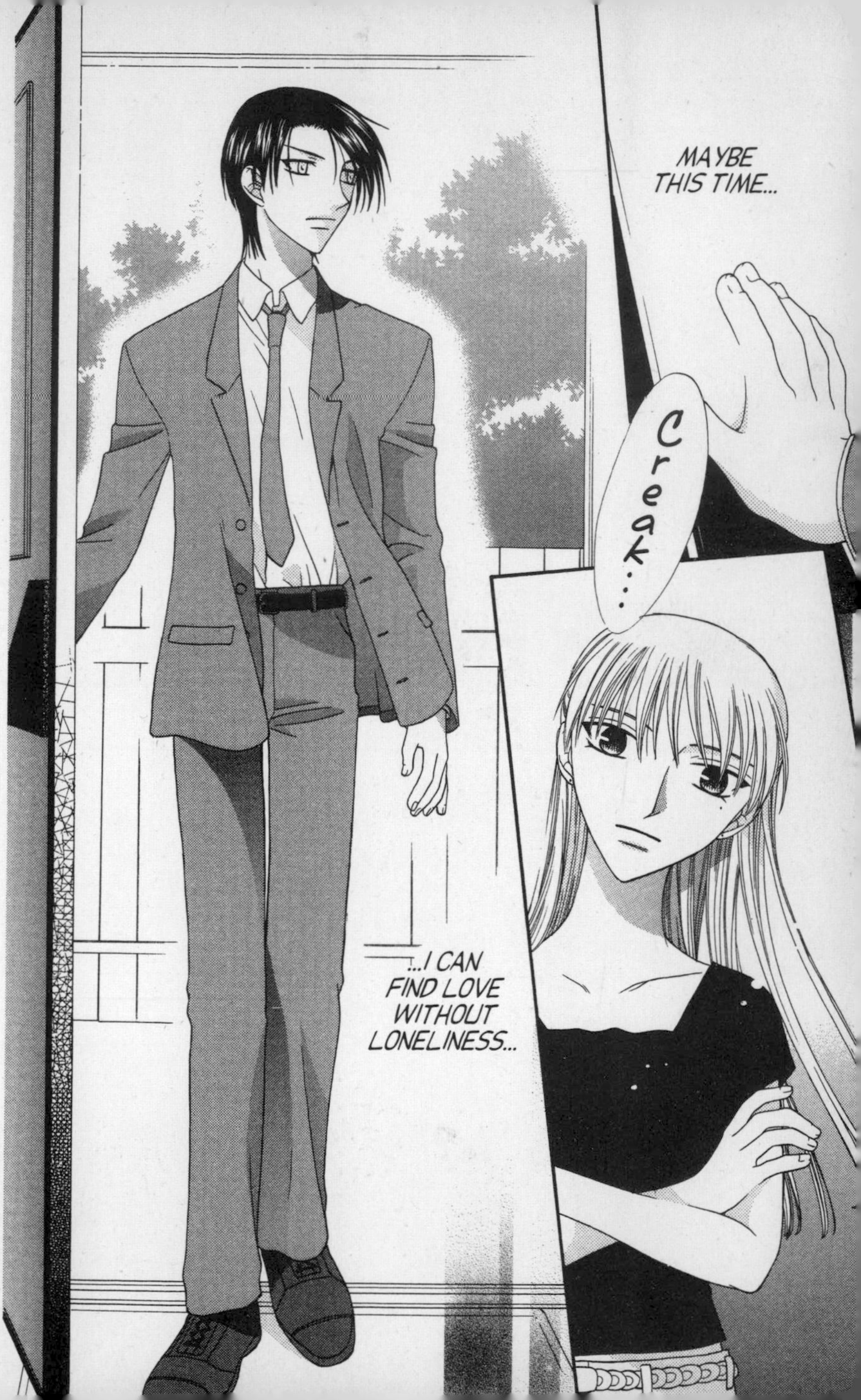
MAYBE THIS TIME...
Creak...
...I CAN FIND LOVE WITHOUT LONELINESS...

Filler Sketch

Not near. Not far. Someday.

# Chapter 57

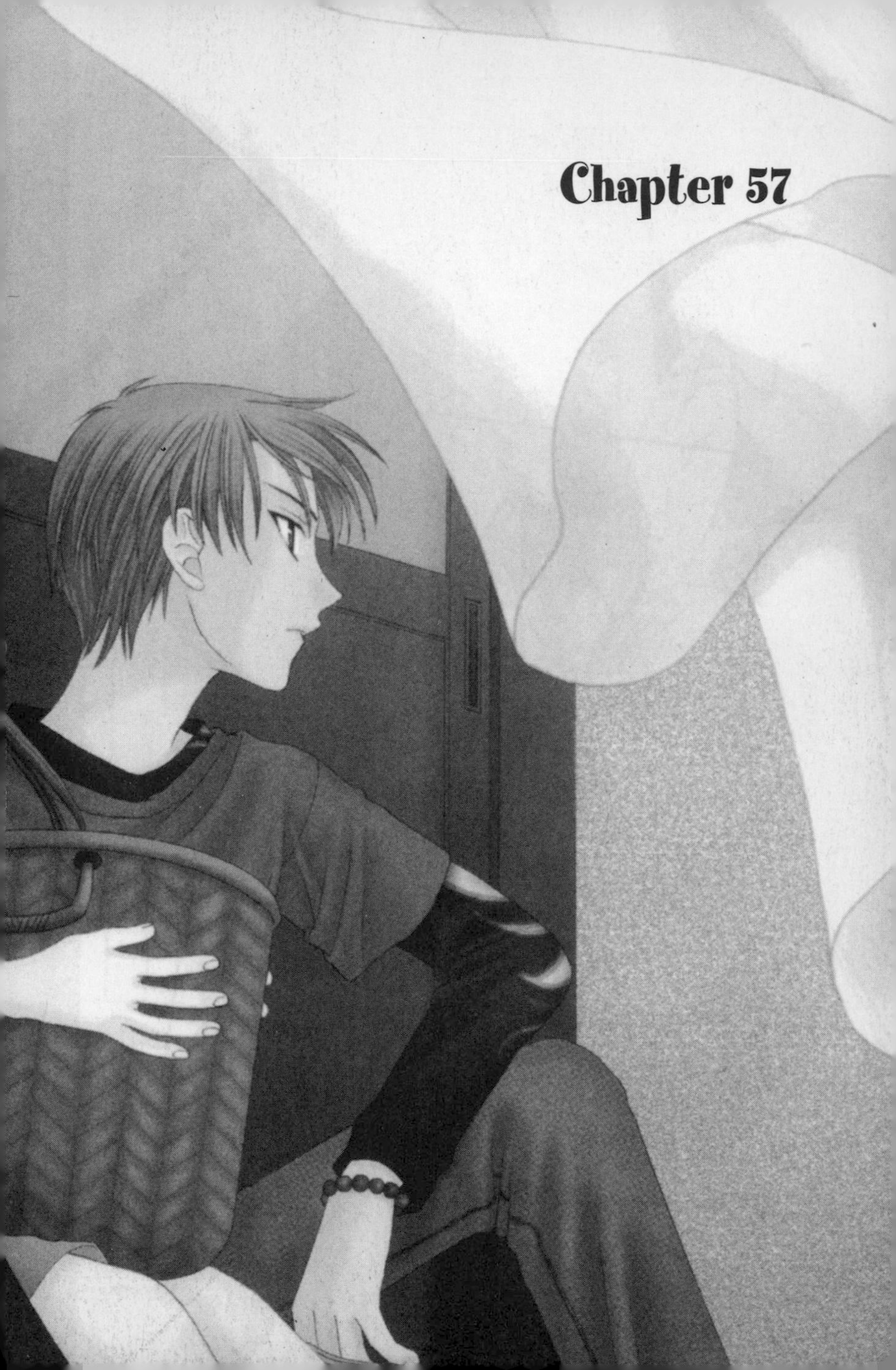

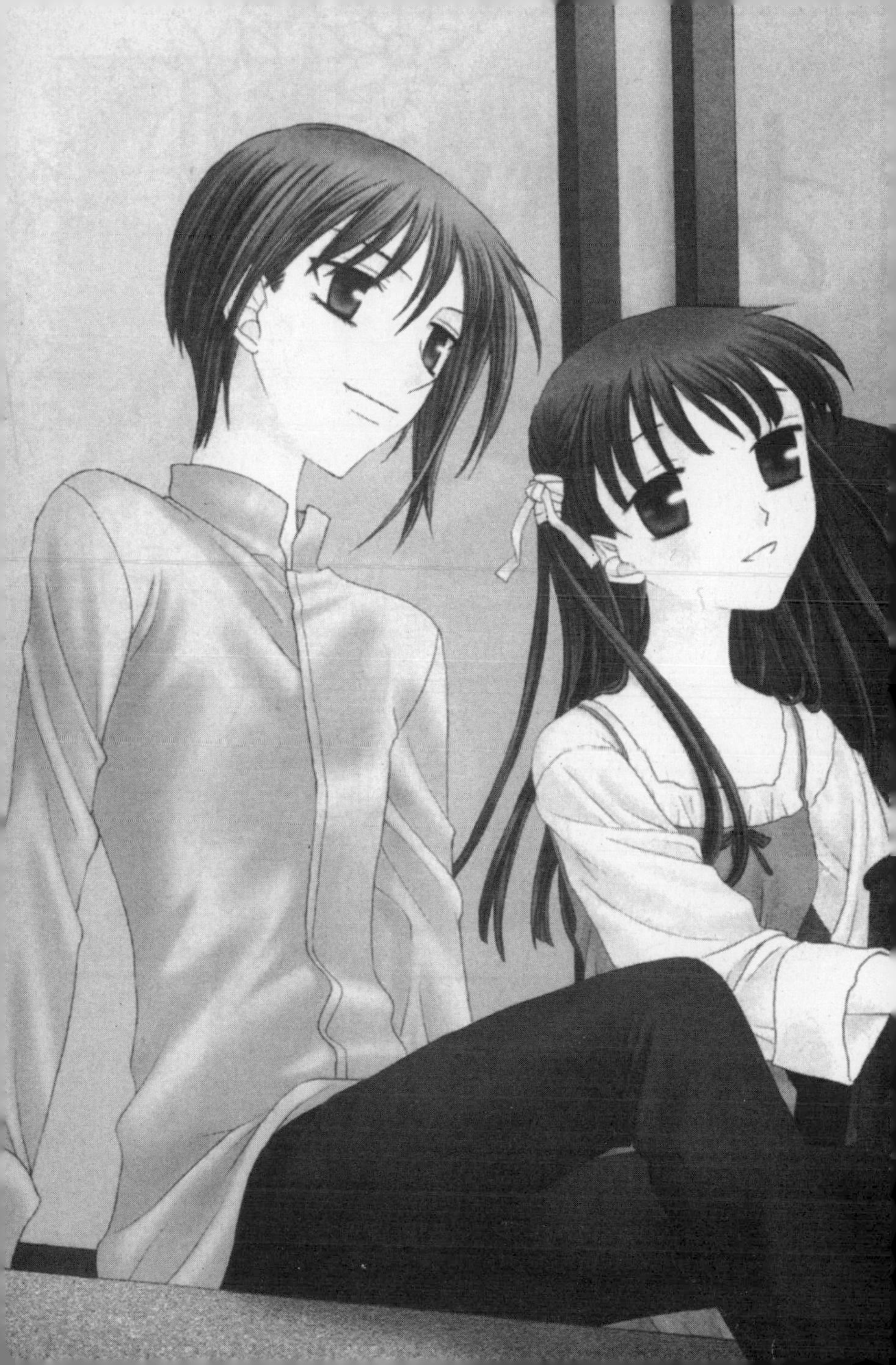

# I feel so grateful!

...desu...

Harada-sama, Araki-sama, mother, father, and everyone who reads and supports this manga...thank you so much!

(And thank you for the presents!)

Next time is... Ah! good for you, Hiro. You're next to Kisa.

—Natsuki Takaya

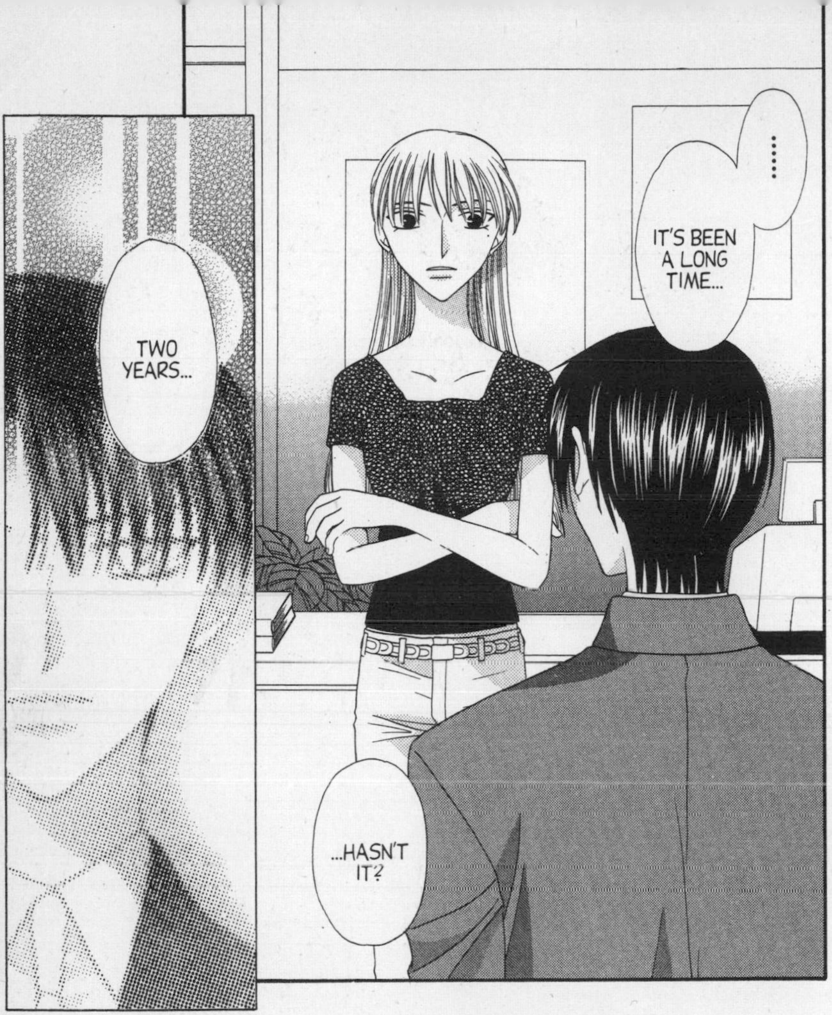
......
IT'S BEEN A LONG TIME...
TWO YEARS...
...HASN'T IT?

## BLAH, BLAH, BLAH 4

Anyway, it doesn't really matter what I write here, so— There are times when I cry suddenly, like turning on the lights, without caring what's around me, and times when I can't do anything but cry. Afterwards, I like to happily eat rice.

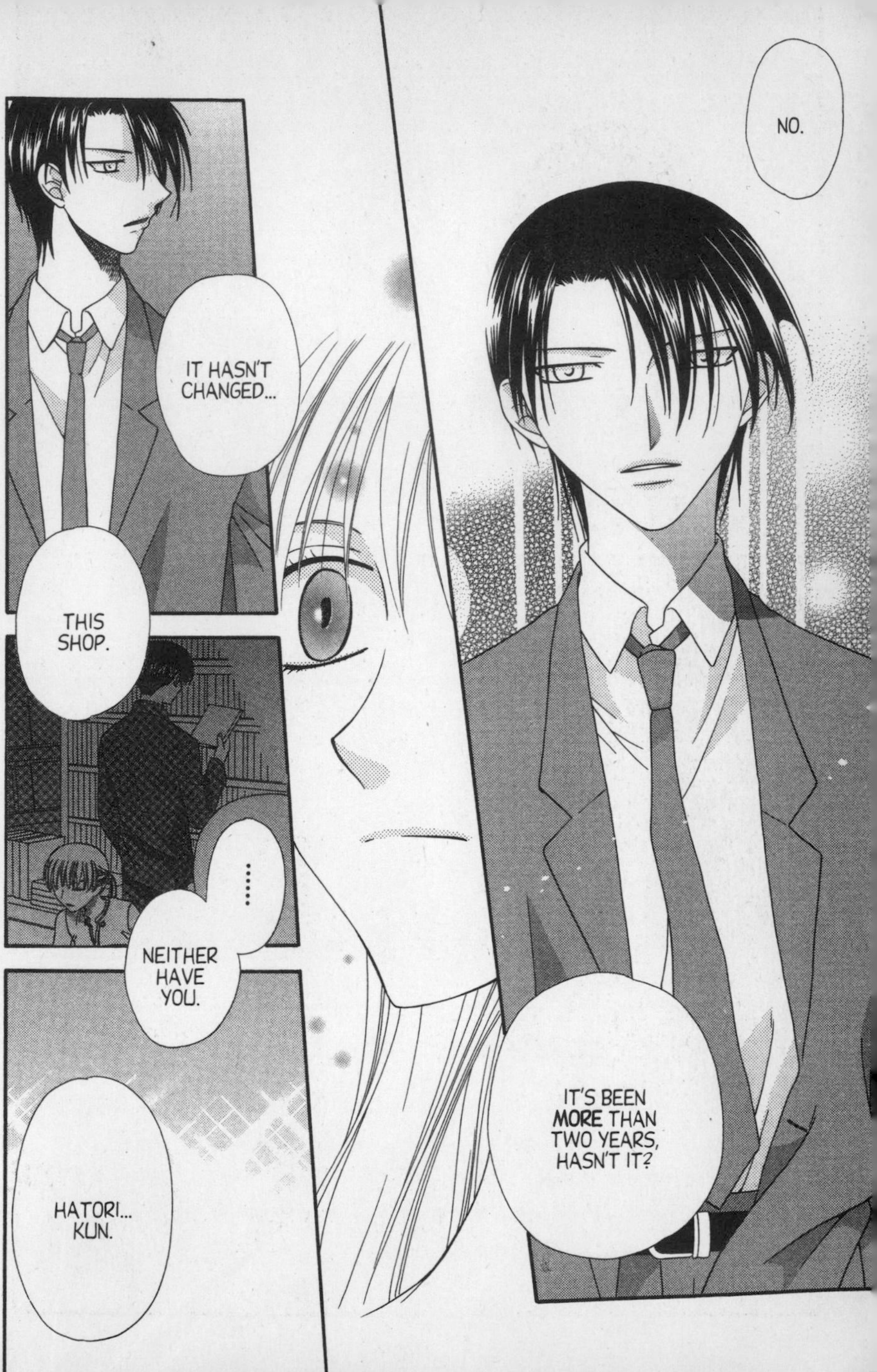
NO.
IT'S BEEN **MORE** THAN TWO YEARS, HASN'T IT?
IT HASN'T CHANGED...
THIS SHOP.
......
NEITHER HAVE YOU.
HATORI... KUN.

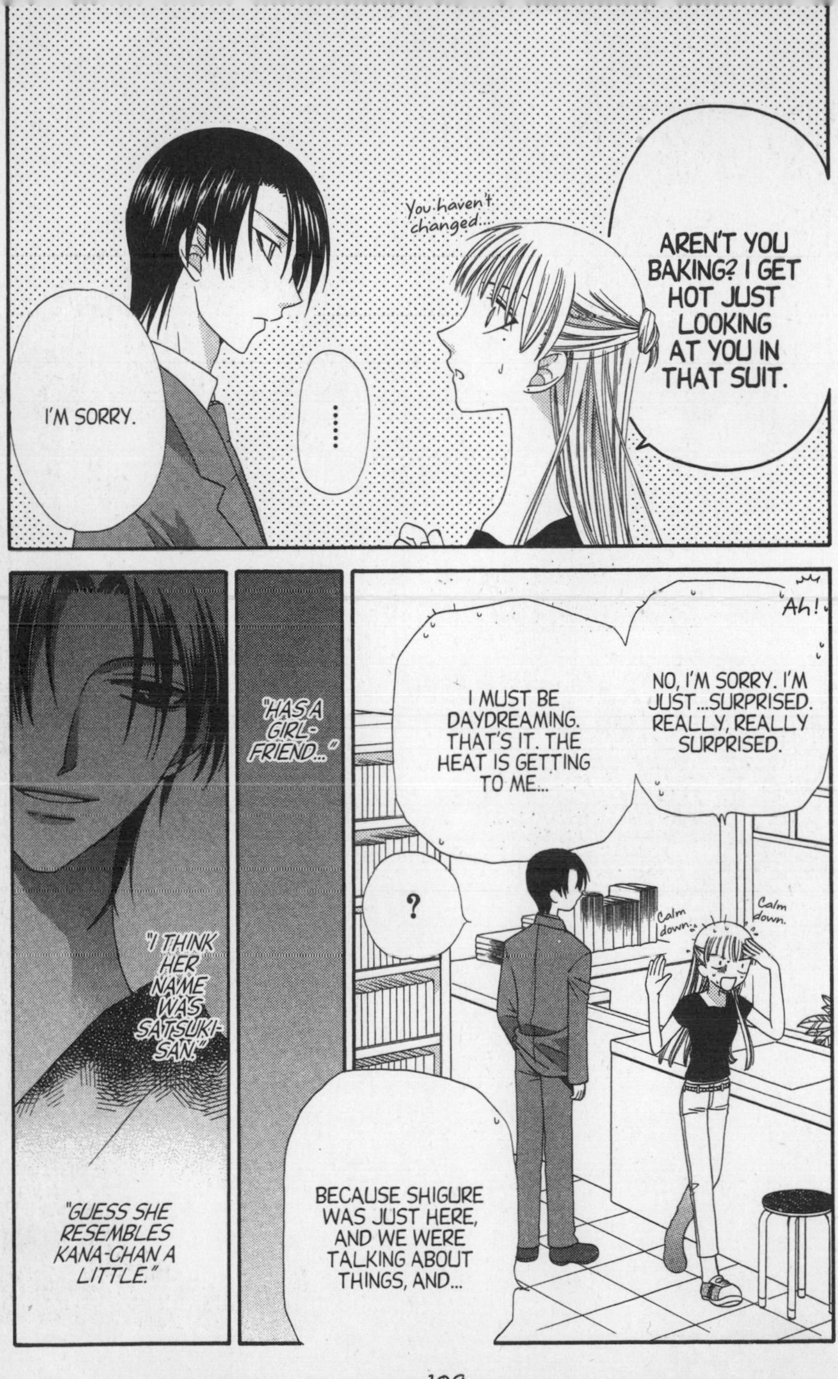
AREN'T YOU BAKING? I GET HOT JUST LOOKING AT YOU IN THAT SUIT.
You haven't changed...
......
I'M SORRY.
Ah!
NO, I'M SORRY. I'M JUST...SURPRISED. REALLY, REALLY SURPRISED.
I MUST BE DAYDREAMING. THAT'S IT. THE HEAT IS GETTING TO ME...
?
Calm down.
Calm down.
BECAUSE SHIGURE WAS JUST HERE, AND WE WERE TALKING ABOUT THINGS, AND...
"HAS A GIRL-FRIEND..."
"I THINK HER NAME WAS SATSUKI-SAN."
"GUESS SHE RESEMBLES KANA-CHAN A LITTLE."

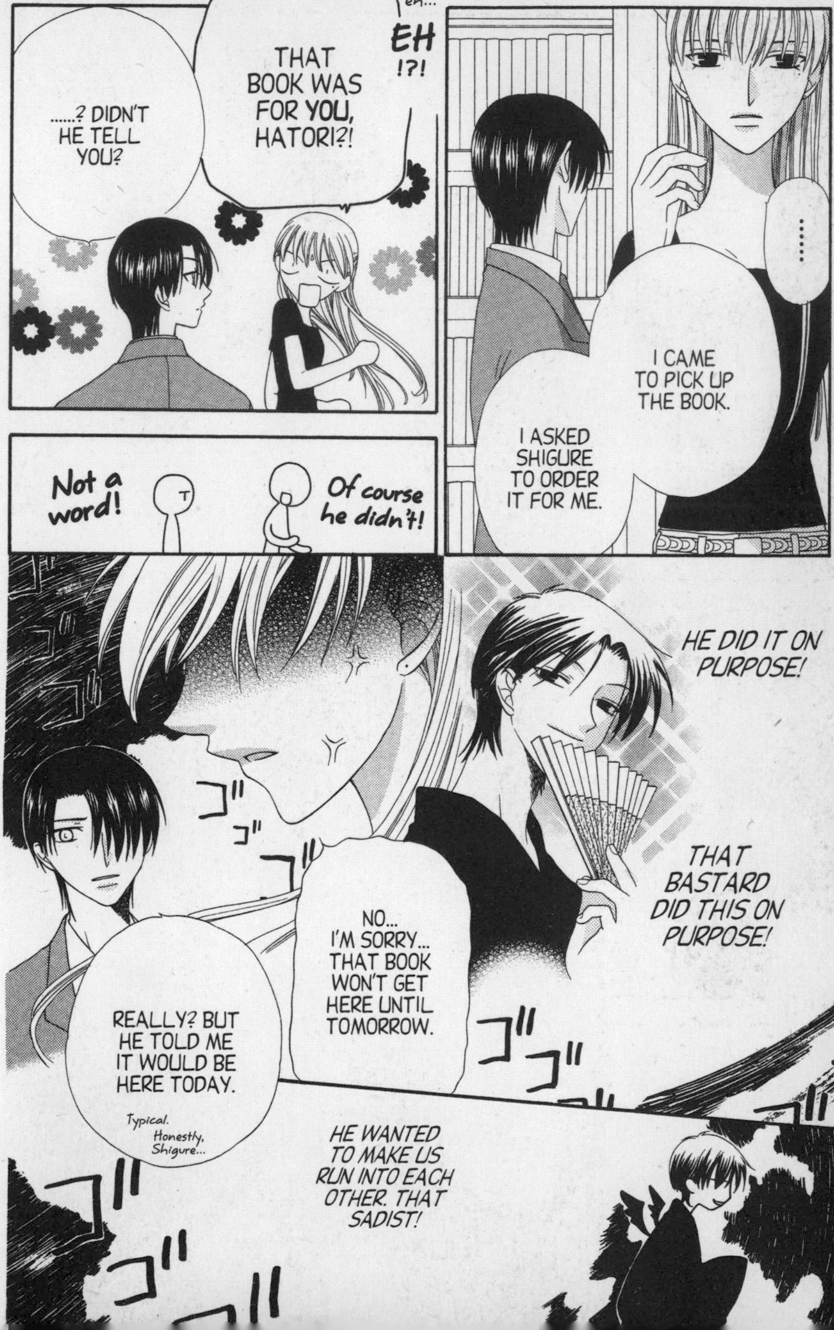
......
I CAME TO PICK UP THE BOOK.
I ASKED SHIGURE TO ORDER IT FOR ME.
eh...
EH !?!
THAT BOOK WAS FOR YOU, HATORI?!
......? DIDN'T HE TELL YOU?
Of course he didn't!
Not a word!
HE DID IT ON PURPOSE!
THAT BASTARD DID THIS ON PURPOSE!
NO... I'M SORRY... THAT BOOK WON'T GET HERE UNTIL TOMORROW.
REALLY? BUT HE TOLD ME IT WOULD BE HERE TODAY.
Typical. Honestly, Shigure...
HE WANTED TO MAKE US RUN INTO EACH OTHER. THAT SADIST!

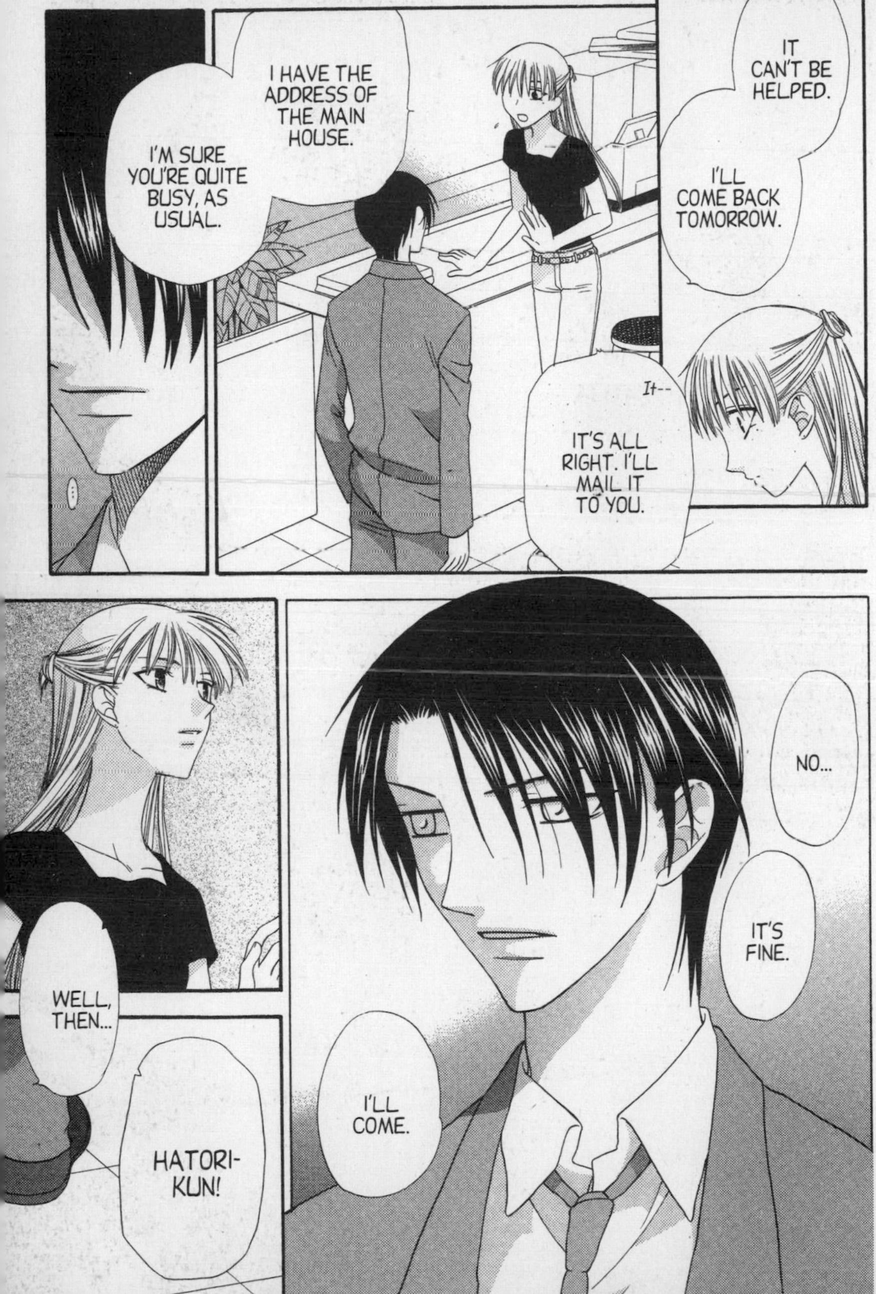
IT CAN'T BE HELPED.
I'LL COME BACK TOMORROW.
It--
IT'S ALL RIGHT. I'LL MAIL IT TO YOU.
I HAVE THE ADDRESS OF THE MAIN HOUSE.
I'M SURE YOU'RE QUITE BUSY, AS USUAL.
...
NO...
IT'S FINE.
I'LL COME.
WELL, THEN...
HATORI-KUN!

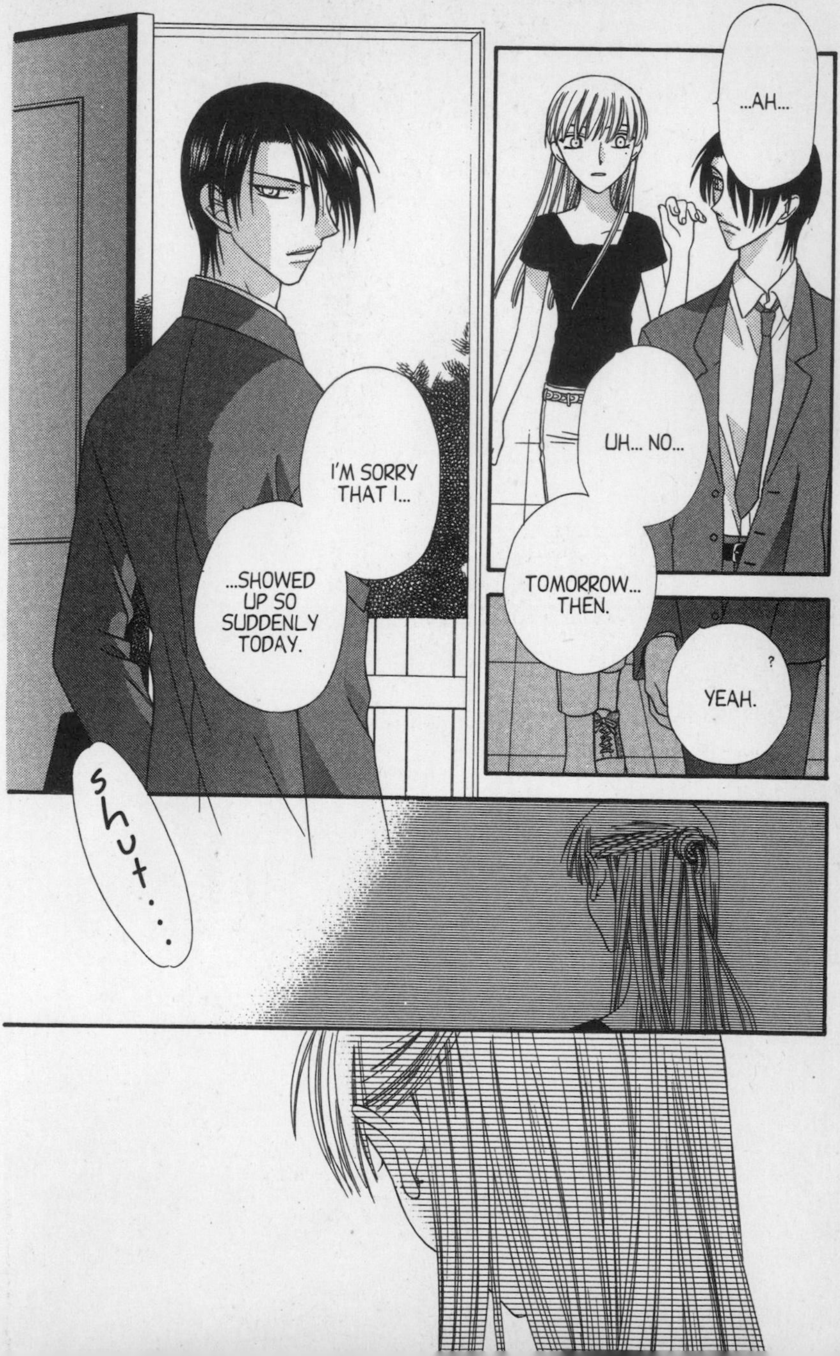
...AH...
UH... NO...
TOMORROW... THEN.
?
YEAH.
I'M SORRY THAT I...
...SHOWED UP SO SUDDENLY TODAY.
shut...

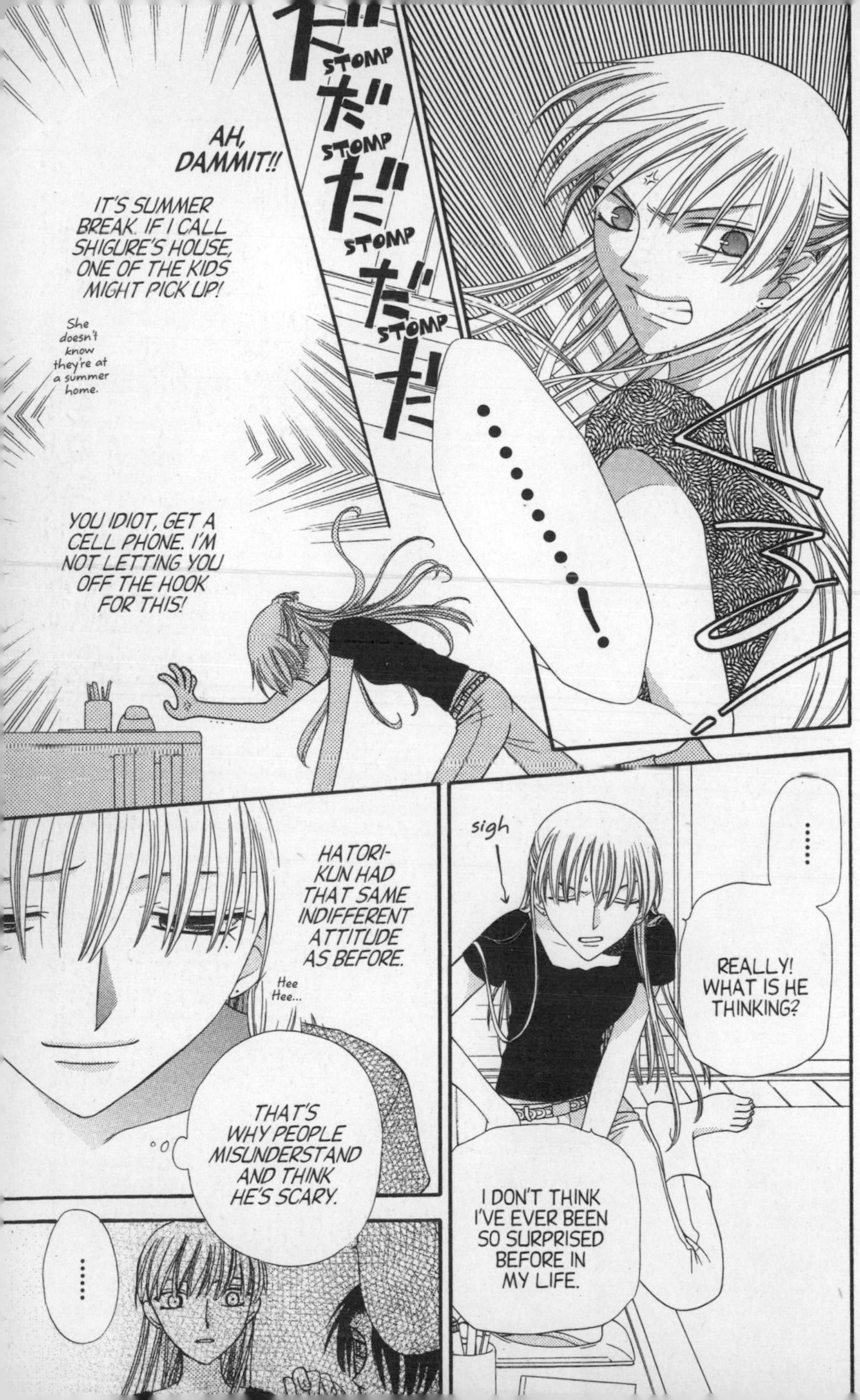
ド
STOMP
だ
STOMP
だ
STOMP
だ
STOMP
だ
......!
AH, DAMMIT!!
IT'S SUMMER BREAK. IF I CALL SHIGURE'S HOUSE, ONE OF THE KIDS MIGHT PICK UP!
She doesn't know they're at a summer home.
YOU IDIOT, GET A CELL PHONE. I'M NOT LETTING YOU OFF THE HOOK FOR THIS!
......
REALLY! WHAT IS HE THINKING?
sigh
I DON'T THINK I'VE EVER BEEN SO SURPRISED BEFORE IN MY LIFE.
HATORI-KUN HAD THAT SAME INDIFFERENT ATTITUDE AS BEFORE.
Hee Hee...
THAT'S WHY PEOPLE MISUNDERSTAND AND THINK HE'S SCARY.
......

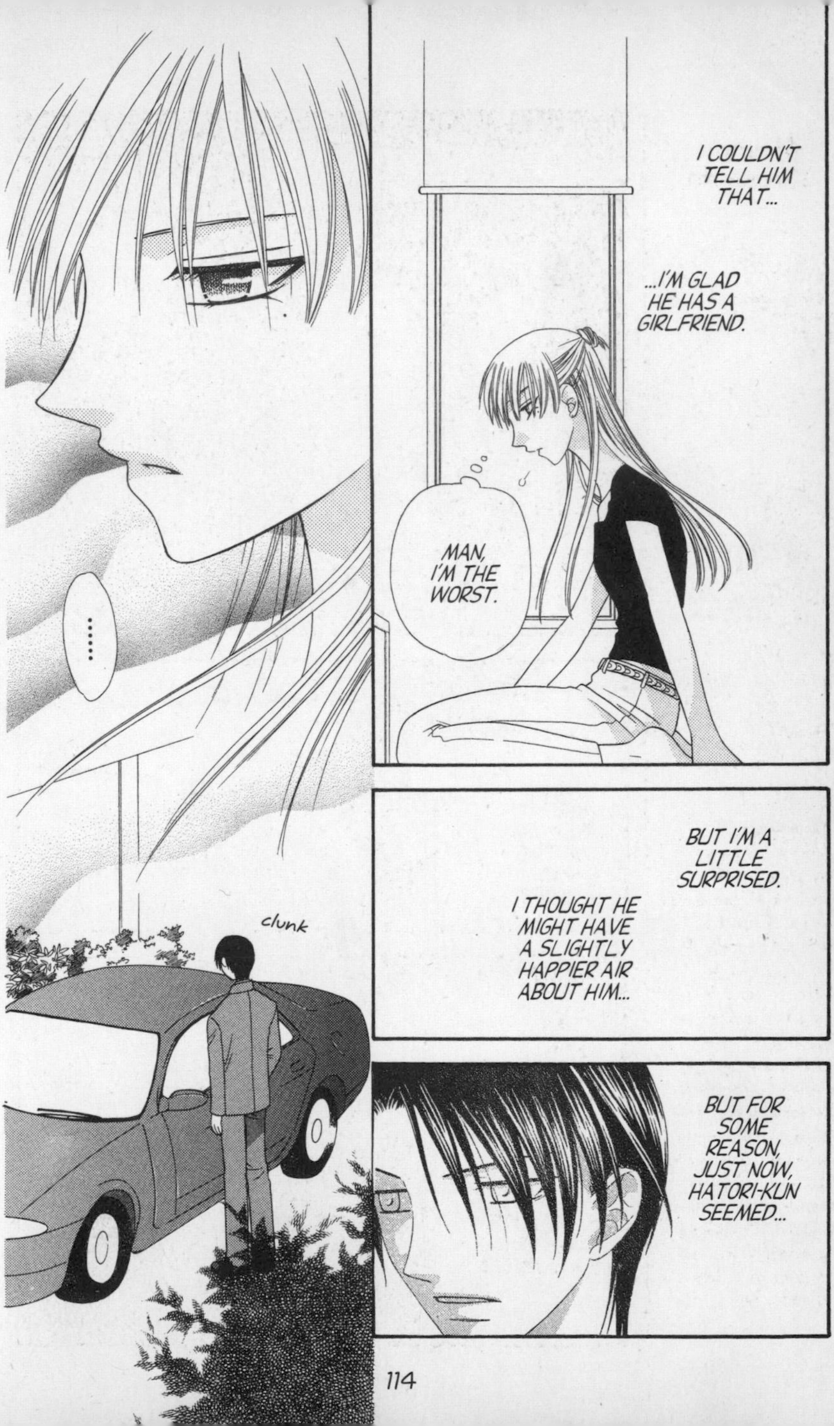
I COULDN'T TELL HIM THAT...
...I'M GLAD HE HAS A GIRLFRIEND.
MAN, I'M THE WORST.
......
BUT I'M A LITTLE SURPRISED.
I THOUGHT HE MIGHT HAVE A SLIGHTLY HAPPIER AIR ABOUT HIM...
BUT FOR SOME REASON, JUST NOW, HATORI-KUN SEEMED...
clunk

## Minami Kinoshita

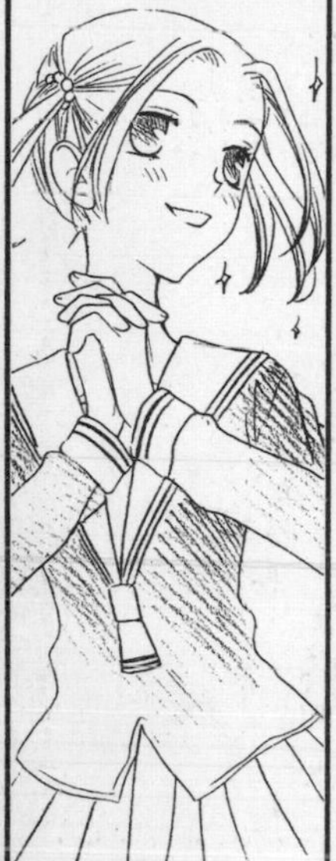

She started appearing in the first chapter. If you were to say she's an old character, you'd be correct! A youth that never stops... a youth that plunges ever forward! She doesn't worry about what's going on around her (let's try doing that). But it's good that she's energetic. She really does love Yuki, but doesn't seem to think of actually touching the real thing. That, too, is youth. Motoko's like that, too.

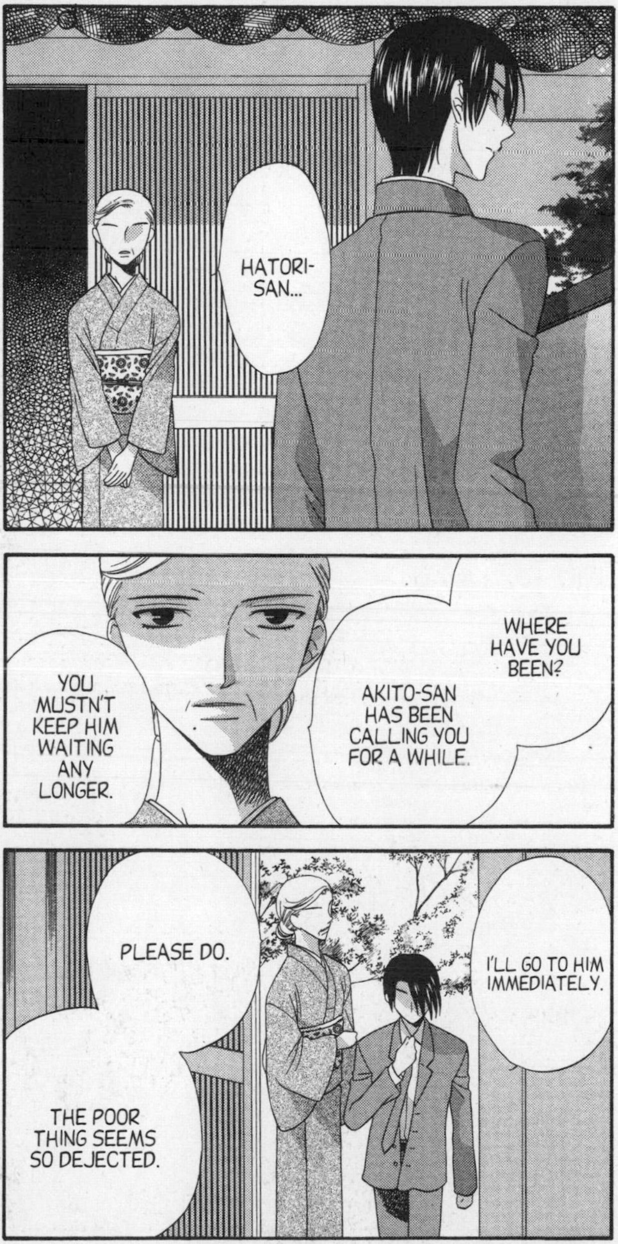

HATORI-SAN...
WHERE HAVE YOU BEEN?
AKITO-SAN HAS BEEN CALLING YOU FOR A WHILE.
YOU MUSTN'T KEEP HIM WAITING ANY LONGER.
I'LL GO TO HIM IMMEDIATELY.
PLEASE DO.
THE POOR THING SEEMS SO DEJECTED.

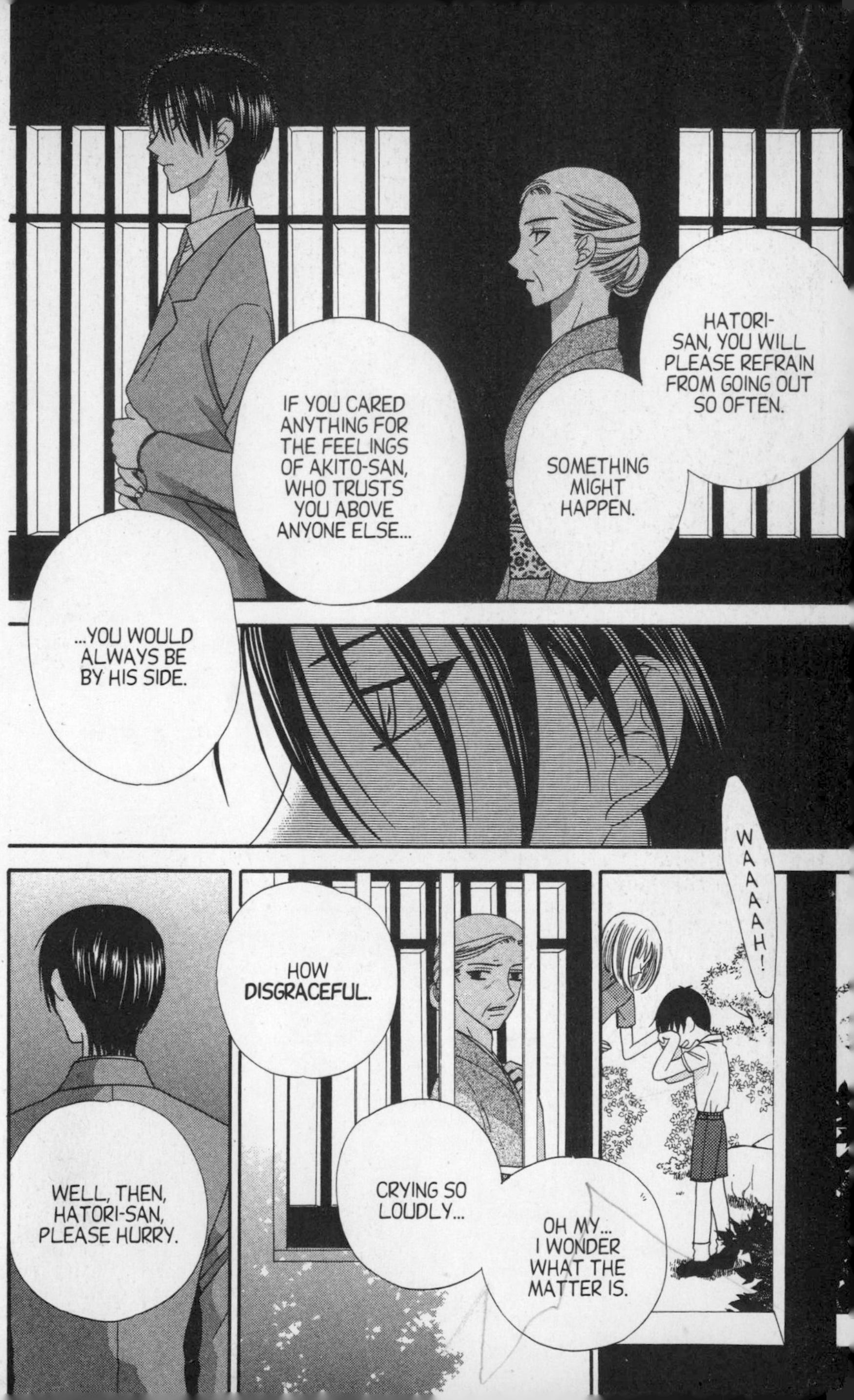
HATORI-SAN, YOU WILL PLEASE REFRAIN FROM GOING OUT SO OFTEN.
SOMETHING MIGHT HAPPEN.
IF YOU CARED ANYTHING FOR THE FEELINGS OF AKITO-SAN, WHO TRUSTS YOU ABOVE ANYONE ELSE...
...YOU WOULD ALWAYS BE BY HIS SIDE.
WAAAAH!
OH MY... I WONDER WHAT THE MATTER IS.
CRYING SO LOUDLY...
HOW **DISGRACEFUL.**
WELL, THEN, HATORI-SAN, PLEASE HURRY.

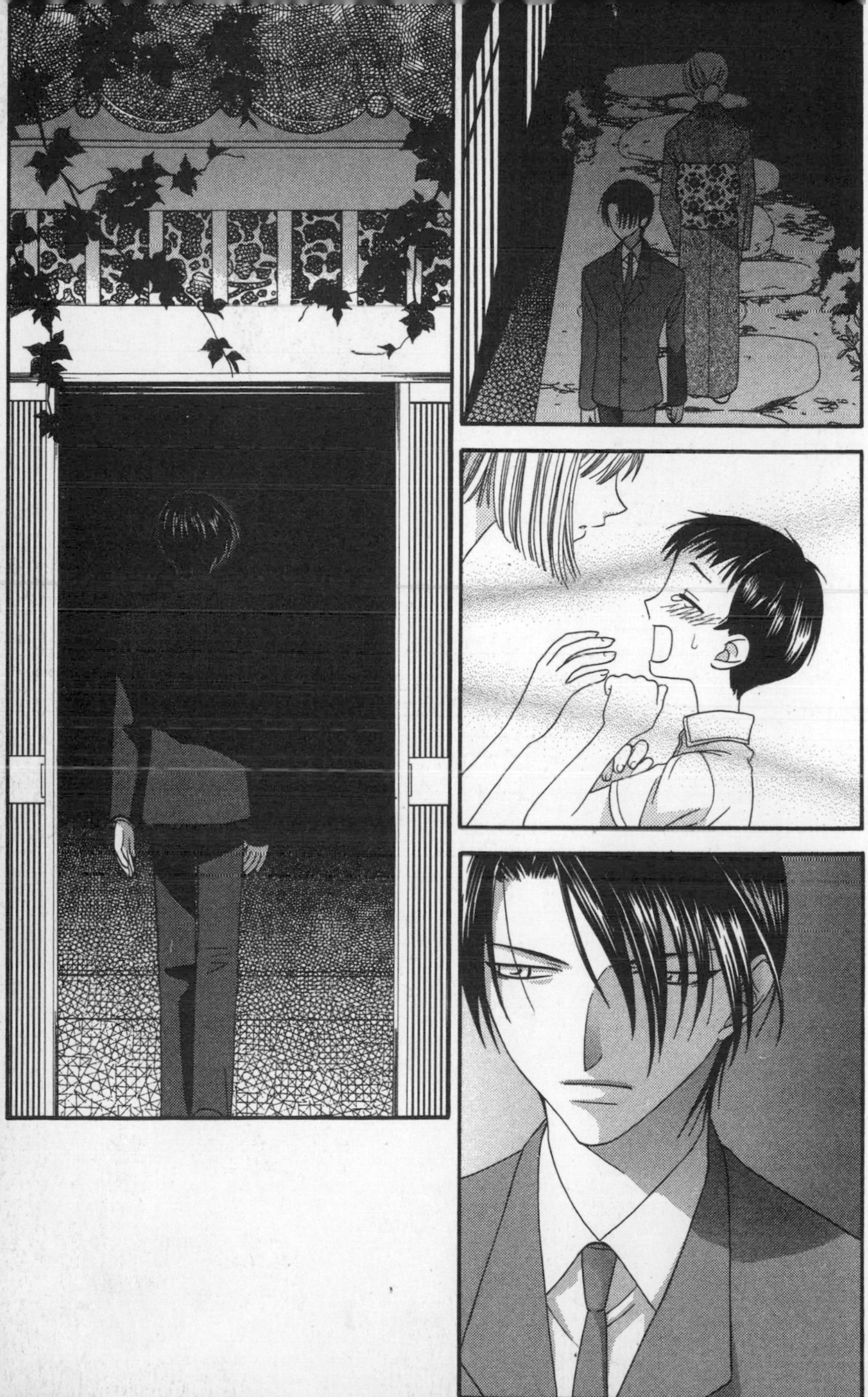

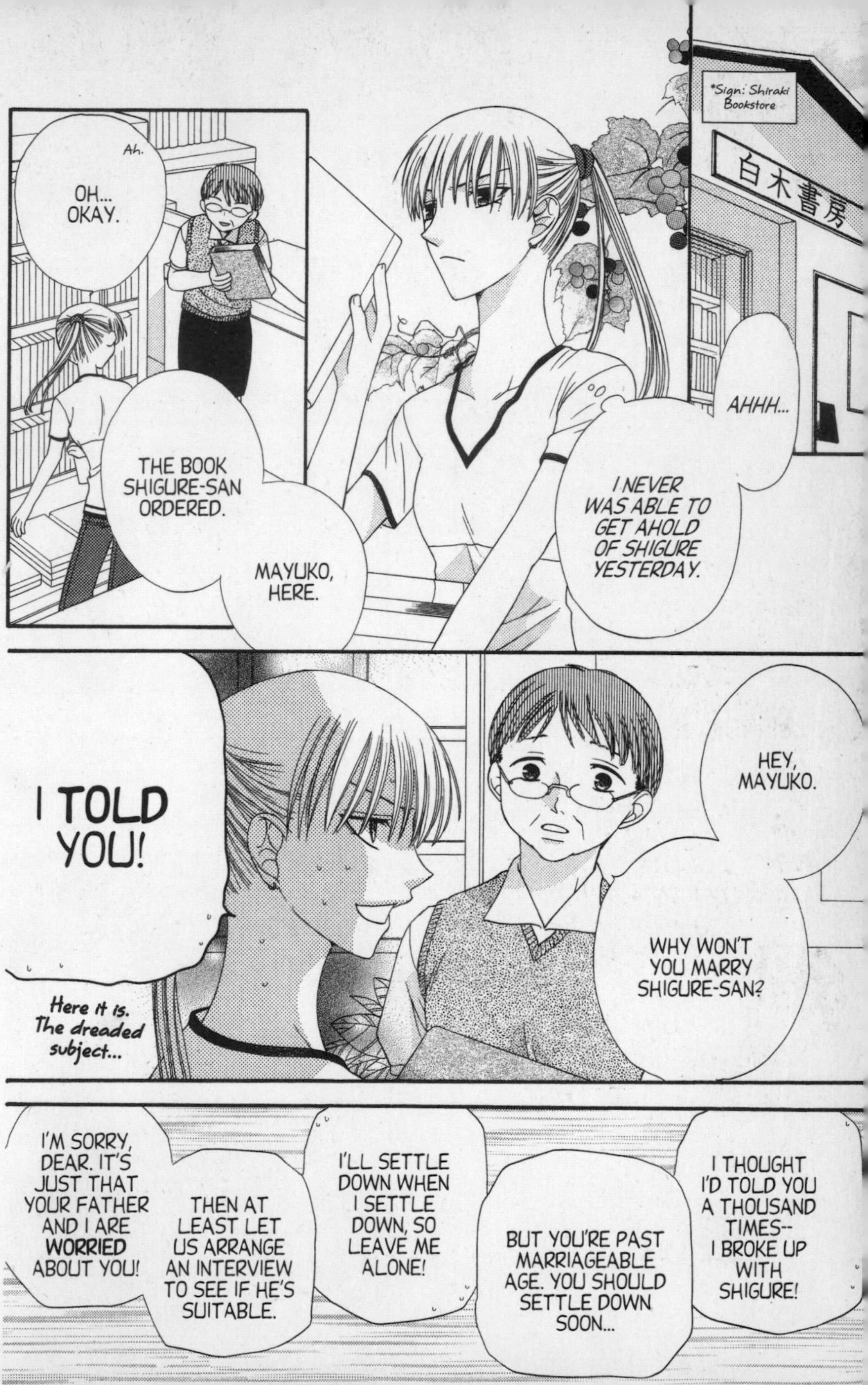
*Sign: Shiraki Bookstore
白木書房
AHHH...
I NEVER WAS ABLE TO GET AHOLD OF SHIGURE YESTERDAY.
MAYUKO, HERE.
THE BOOK SHIGURE-SAN ORDERED.
Ah.
OH... OKAY.
HEY, MAYUKO.
WHY WON'T YOU MARRY SHIGURE-SAN?
I TOLD YOU!
Here it is. The dreaded subject...
I THOUGHT I'D TOLD YOU A THOUSAND TIMES-- I BROKE UP WITH SHIGURE!
BUT YOU'RE PAST MARRIAGEABLE AGE. YOU SHOULD SETTLE DOWN SOON...
I'LL SETTLE DOWN WHEN I SETTLE DOWN, SO LEAVE ME ALONE!
THEN AT LEAST LET US ARRANGE AN INTERVIEW TO SEE IF HE'S SUITABLE.
I'M SORRY, DEAR. IT'S JUST THAT YOUR FATHER AND I ARE **WORRIED** ABOUT YOU!

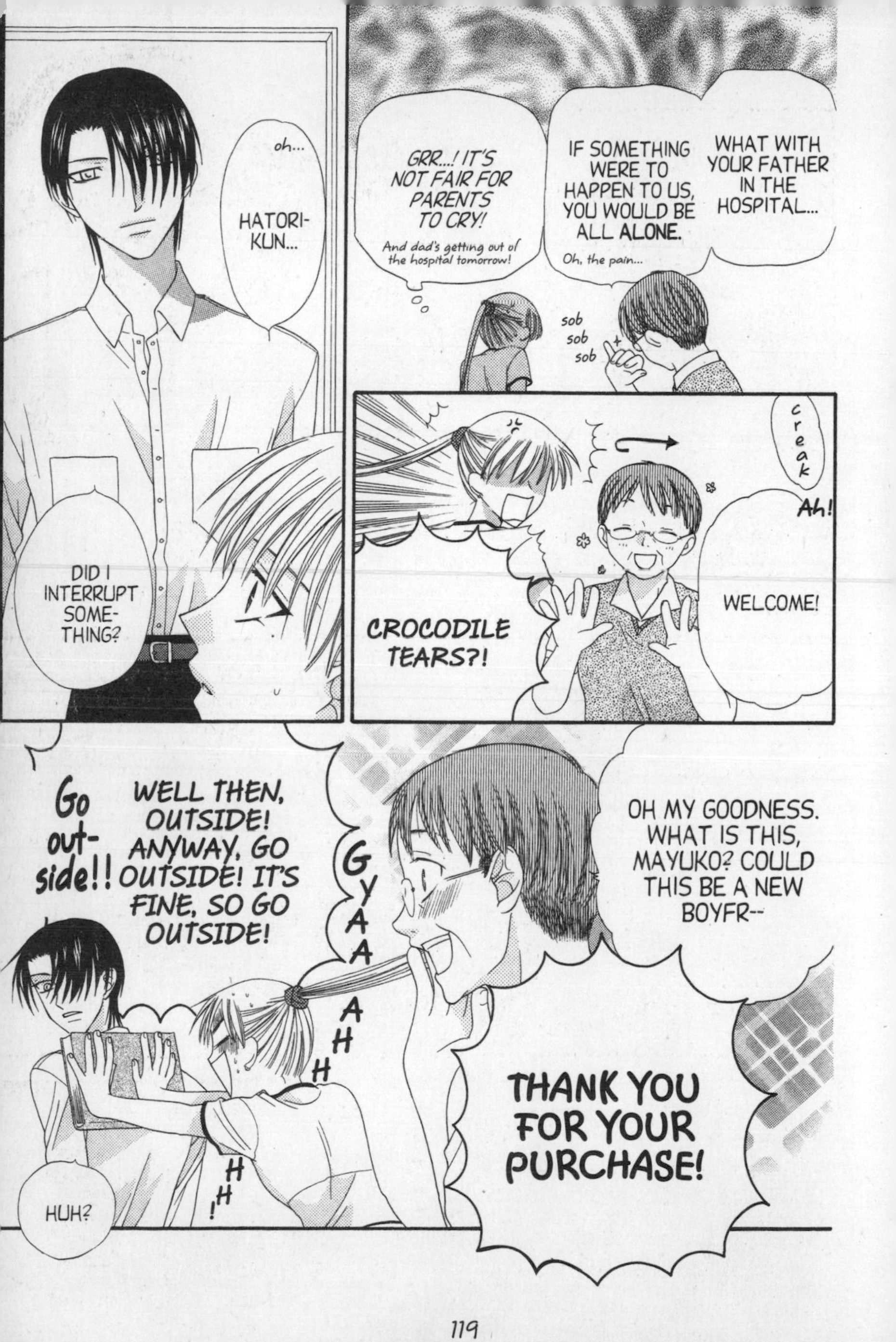
WHAT WITH YOUR FATHER IN THE HOSPITAL...
IF SOMETHING WERE TO HAPPEN TO US, YOU WOULD BE ALL ALONE.
Oh, the pain...
GRR...! IT'S NOT FAIR FOR PARENTS TO CRY!
And dad's getting out of the hospital tomorrow!
sob sob sob
creak
Ah!
WELCOME!
CROCODILE TEARS?!
oh...
HATORI-KUN...
DID I INTERRUPT SOMETHING?
OH MY GOODNESS. WHAT IS THIS, MAYUKO? COULD THIS BE A NEW BOYFR--
GYAAAAHHHH!
WELL THEN, OUTSIDE! ANYWAY, GO OUTSIDE! IT'S FINE, SO GO OUTSIDE!
Go out-side!!
THANK YOU FOR YOUR PURCHASE!
HUH?

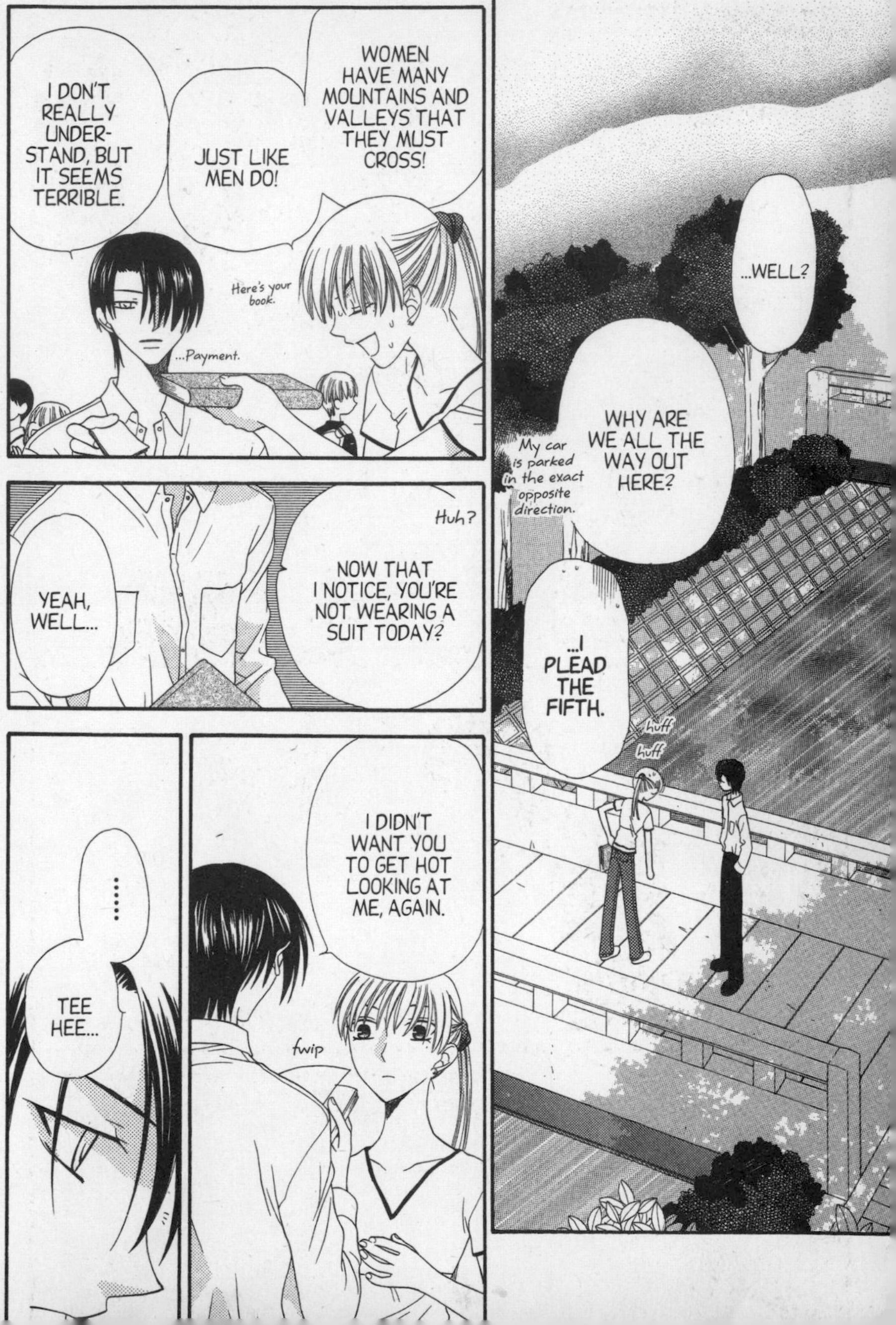
...WELL?
WHY ARE WE ALL THE WAY OUT HERE?
My car is parked in the exact opposite direction.
...I PLEAD THE FIFTH.
huff huff
WOMEN HAVE MANY MOUNTAINS AND VALLEYS THAT THEY MUST CROSS!
JUST LIKE MEN DO!
I DON'T REALLY UNDER-STAND, BUT IT SEEMS TERRIBLE.
Here's your book.
...Payment.
Huh?
NOW THAT I NOTICE, YOU'RE NOT WEARING A SUIT TODAY?
YEAH, WELL...
I DIDN'T WANT YOU TO GET HOT LOOKING AT ME, AGAIN.
fwip
......
TEE HEE...

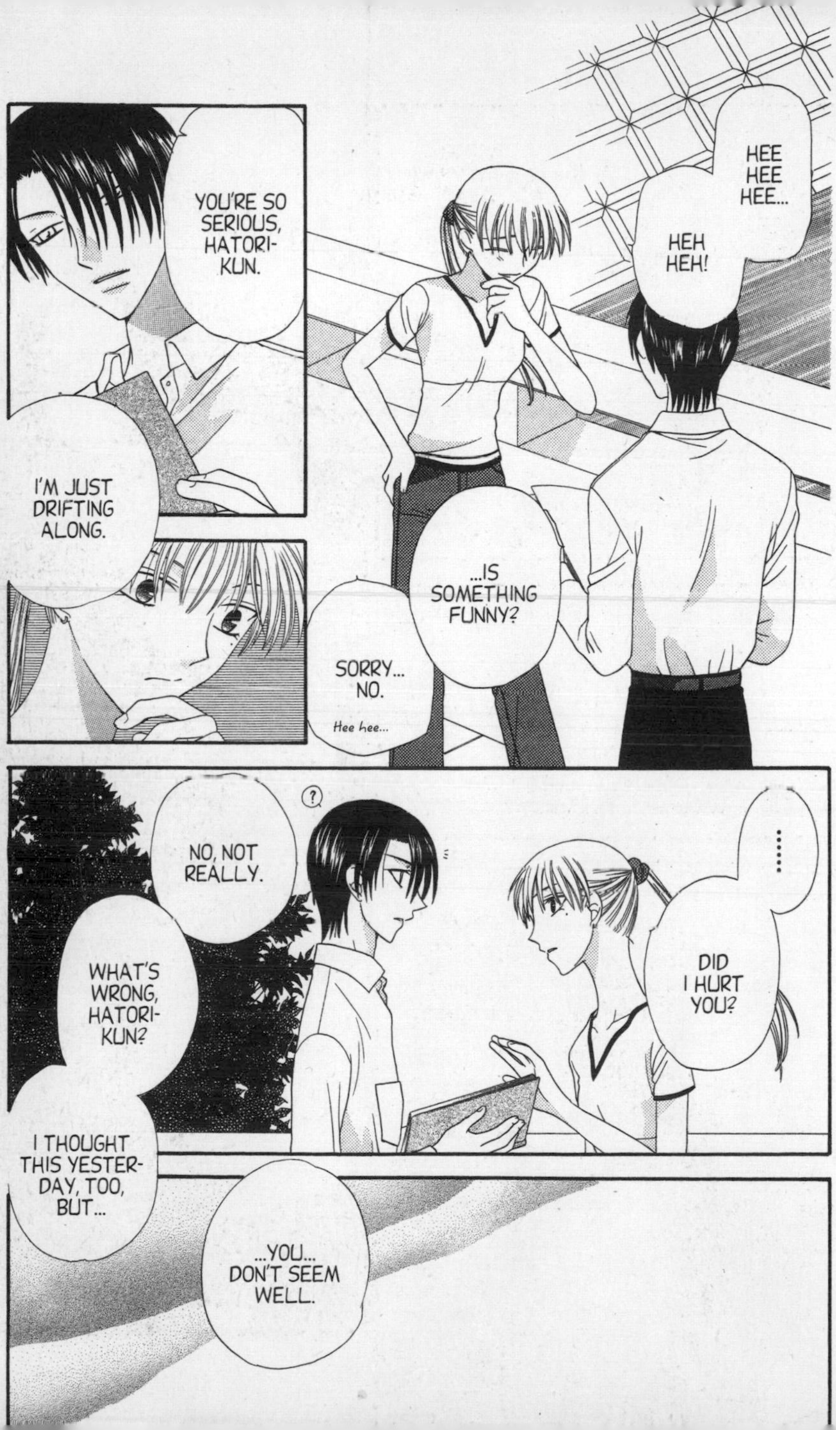
HEE HEE HEE...
HEH HEH!
...IS SOMETHING FUNNY?
SORRY... NO.
Hee hee...
YOU'RE SO SERIOUS, HATORI-KUN.
I'M JUST DRIFTING ALONG.
......
DID I HURT YOU?
?
NO, NOT REALLY.
WHAT'S WRONG, HATORI-KUN?
I THOUGHT THIS YESTER-DAY, TOO, BUT...
...YOU... DON'T SEEM WELL.

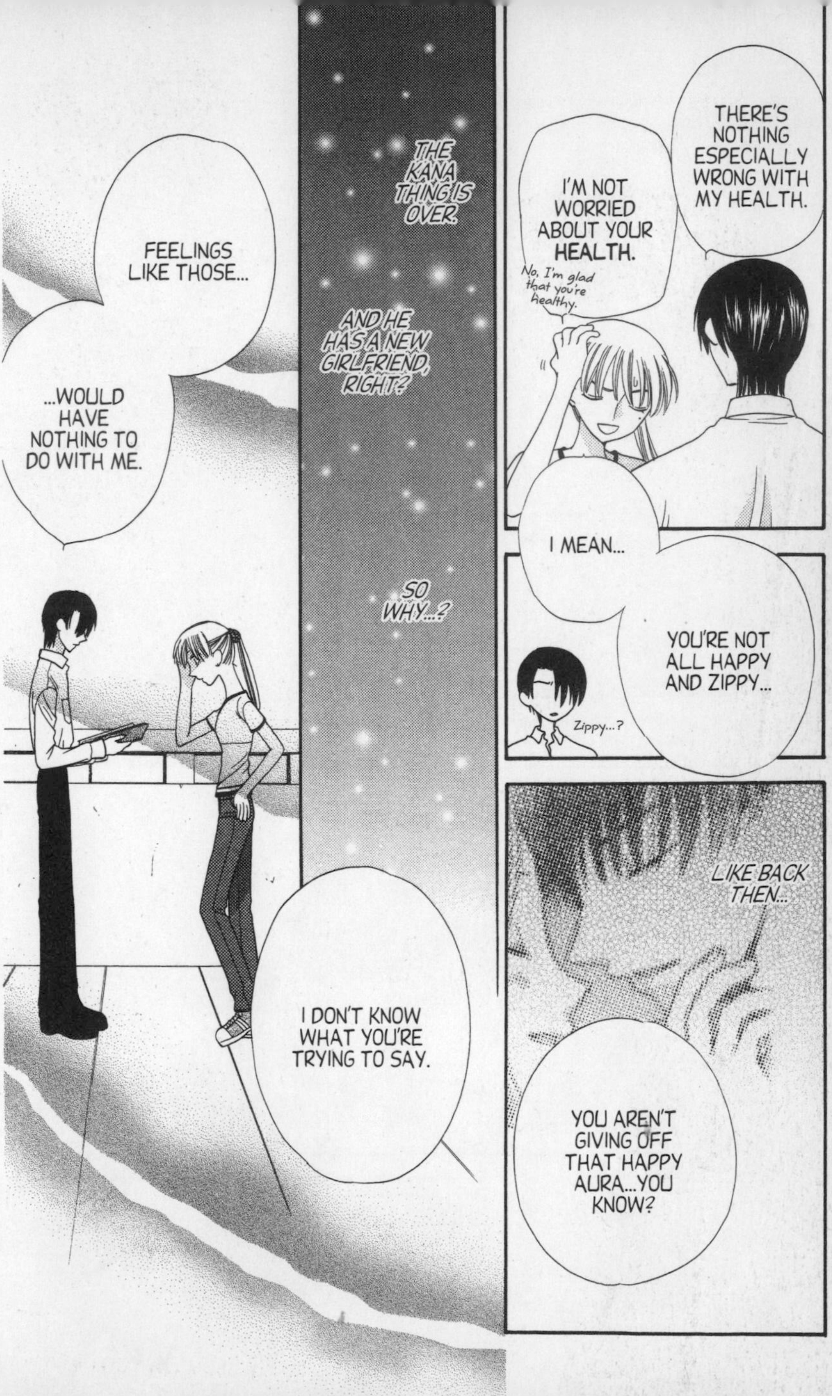
THERE'S NOTHING ESPECIALLY WRONG WITH MY HEALTH.
I'M NOT WORRIED ABOUT YOUR **HEALTH**.
No, I'm glad that you're healthy.
I MEAN...
YOU'RE NOT ALL HAPPY AND ZIPPY...
Zippy...?
LIKE BACK THEN...
YOU AREN'T GIVING OFF THAT HAPPY AURA...YOU KNOW?
THE KANA THING IS OVER.
AND HE HAS A NEW GIRLFRIEND, RIGHT?
SO WHY...?
I DON'T KNOW WHAT YOU'RE TRYING TO SAY.
FEELINGS LIKE THOSE...
...WOULD HAVE NOTHING TO DO WITH ME.

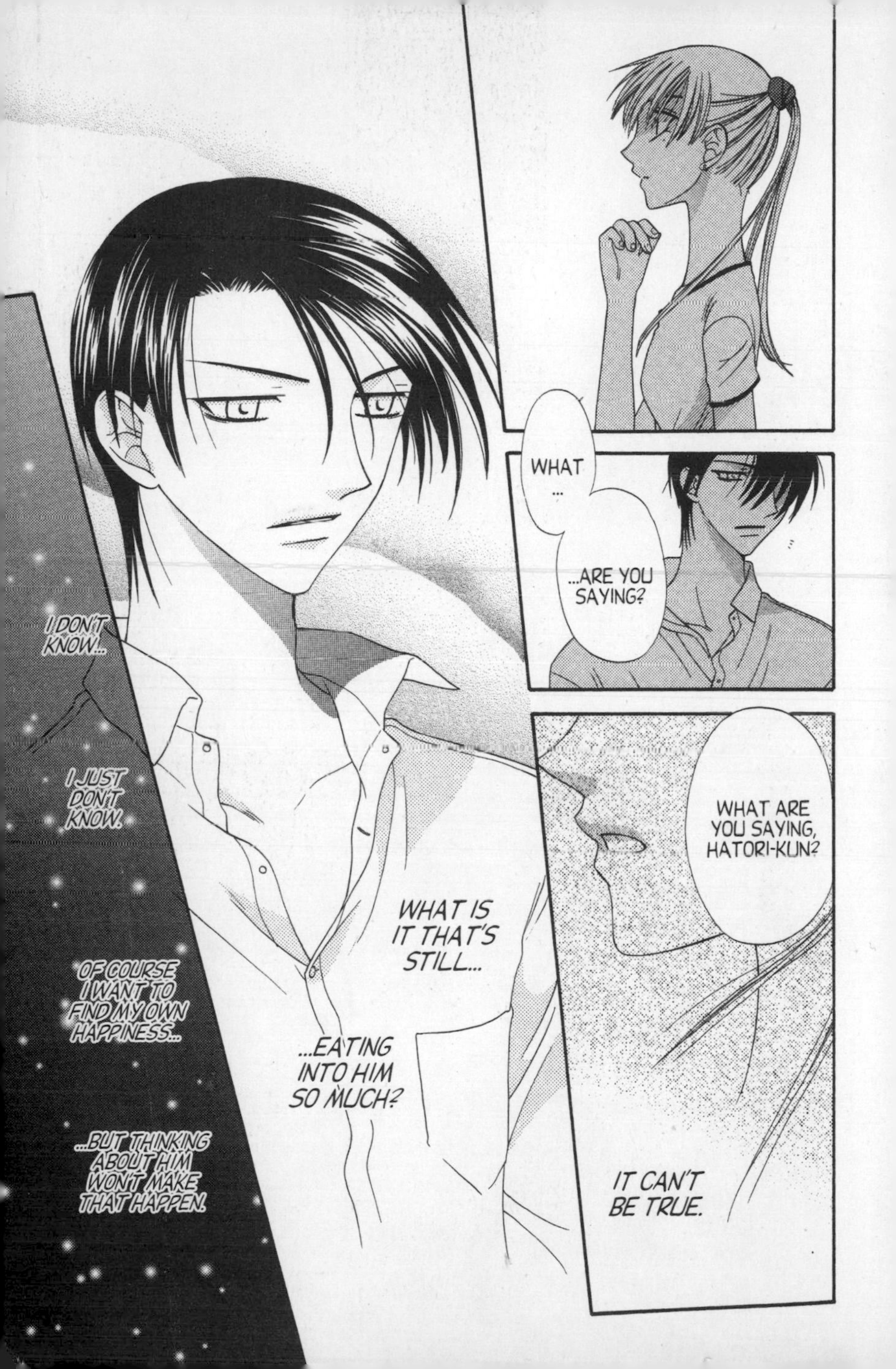
WHAT ...
...ARE YOU SAYING?
WHAT ARE YOU SAYING, HATORI-KUN?
IT CAN'T BE TRUE.
WHAT IS IT THAT'S STILL...
...EATING INTO HIM SO MUCH?
I DON'T KNOW...
I JUST DON'T KNOW.
OF COURSE I WANT TO FIND MY OWN HAPPINESS...
...BUT THINKING ABOUT HIM WON'T MAKE THAT HAPPEN.

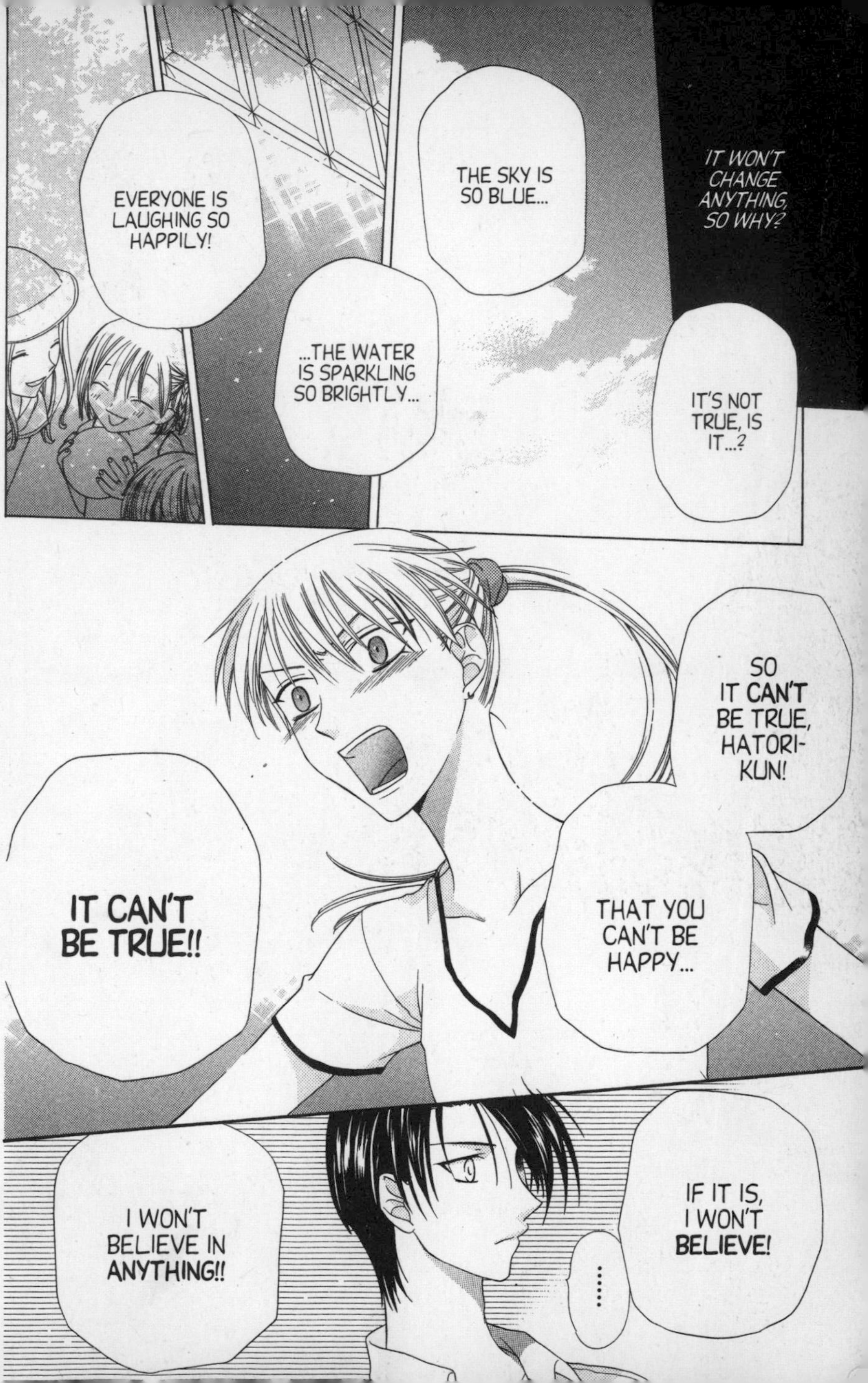
IT WON'T CHANGE ANYTHING, SO WHY?
THE SKY IS SO BLUE...
...THE WATER IS SPARKLING SO BRIGHTLY...
EVERYONE IS LAUGHING SO HAPPILY!
IT'S NOT TRUE, IS IT...?
SO IT CAN'T BE TRUE, HATORI-KUN!
THAT YOU CAN'T BE HAPPY...
IT CAN'T BE TRUE!!
IF IT IS, I WON'T BELIEVE!
......
I WON'T BELIEVE IN ANYTHING!!

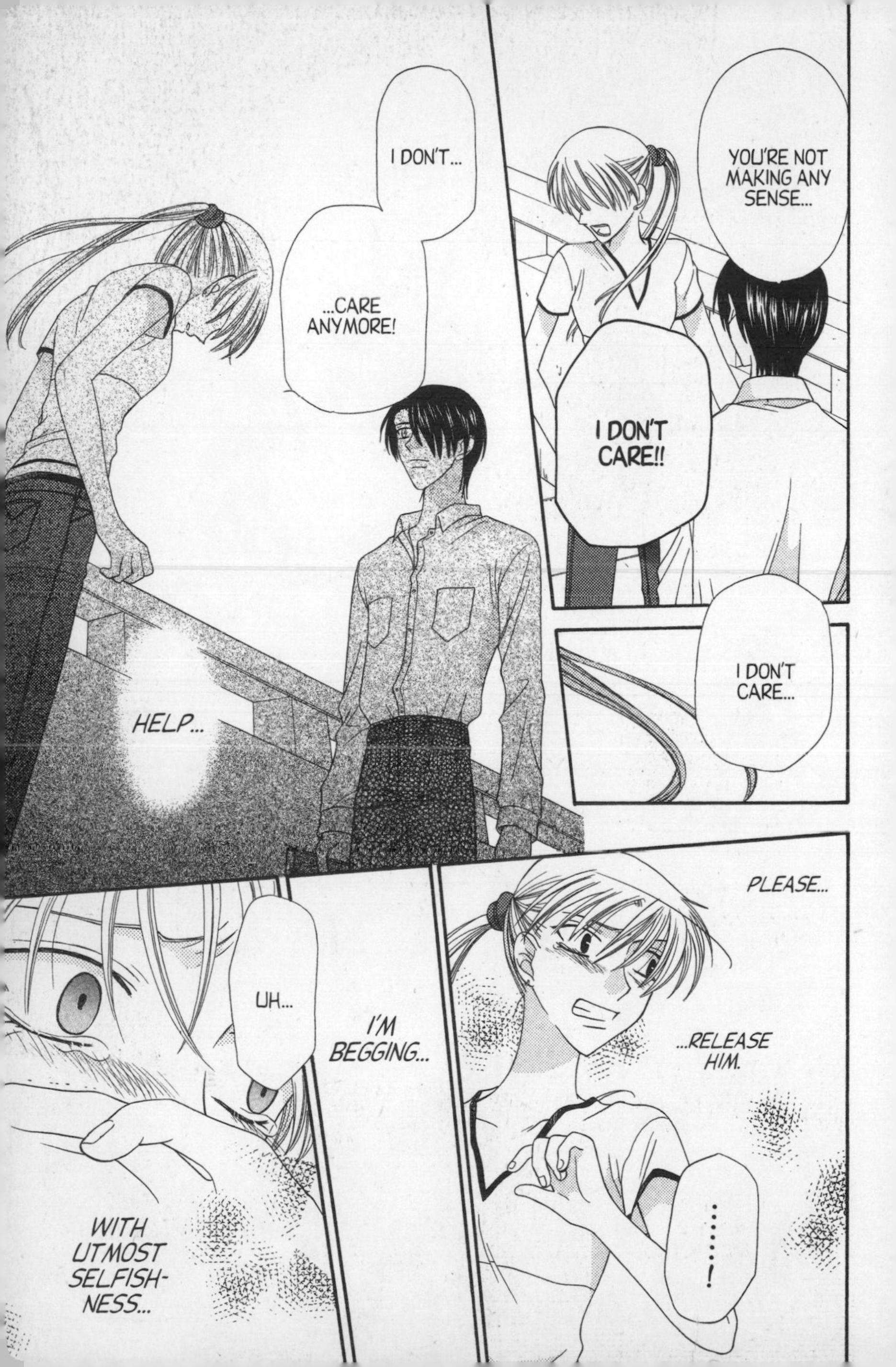
YOU'RE NOT MAKING ANY SENSE...
I DON'T CARE!!
I DON'T CARE...
I DON'T...
...CARE ANYMORE!
HELP...
PLEASE...
...RELEASE HIM.
......!
I'M BEGGING...
UH...
WITH UTMOST SELFISH-NESS...

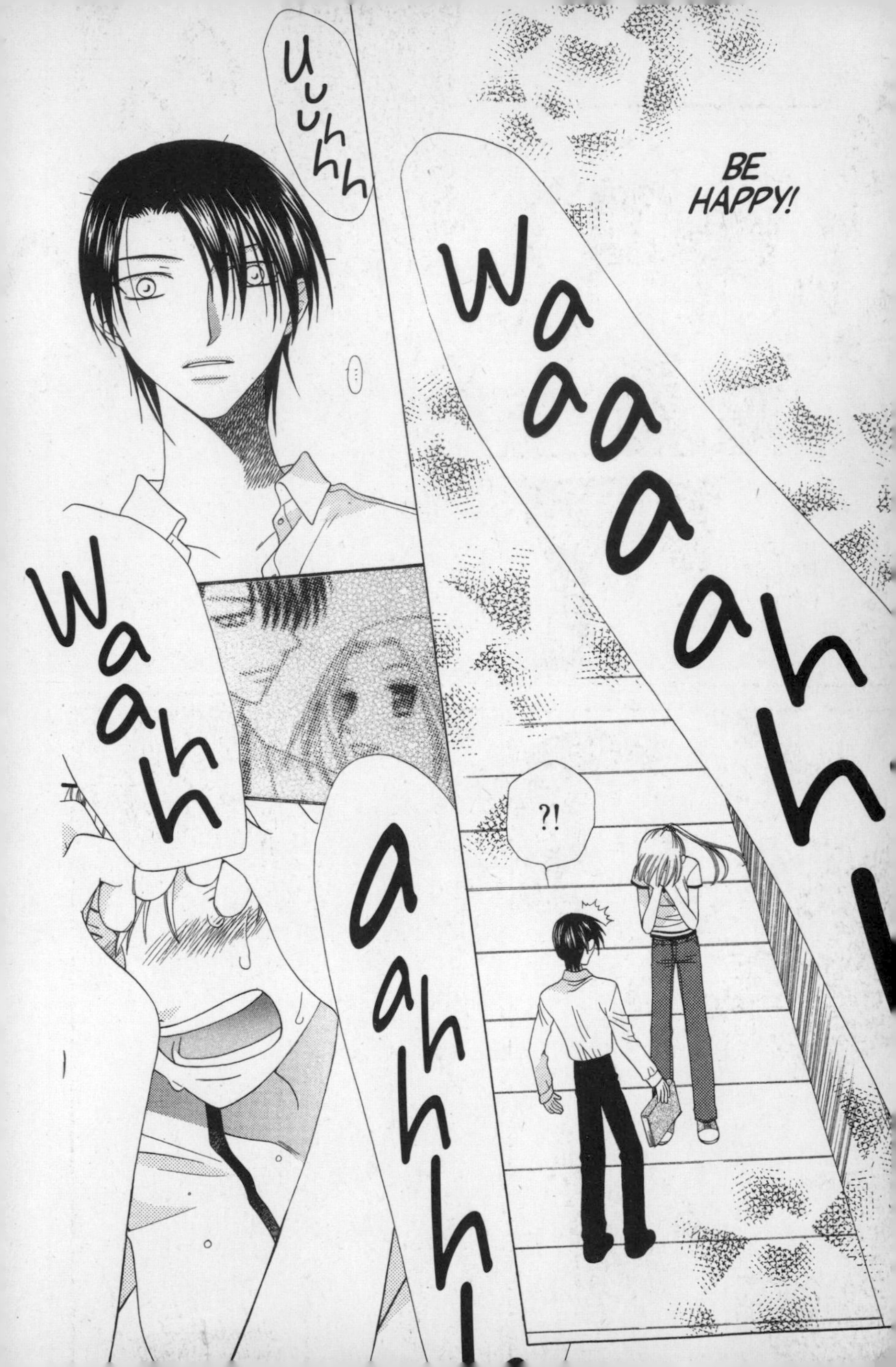

BE HAPPY!
Waaaaahh
Uuhhh
...
?!
Waahh
aahh

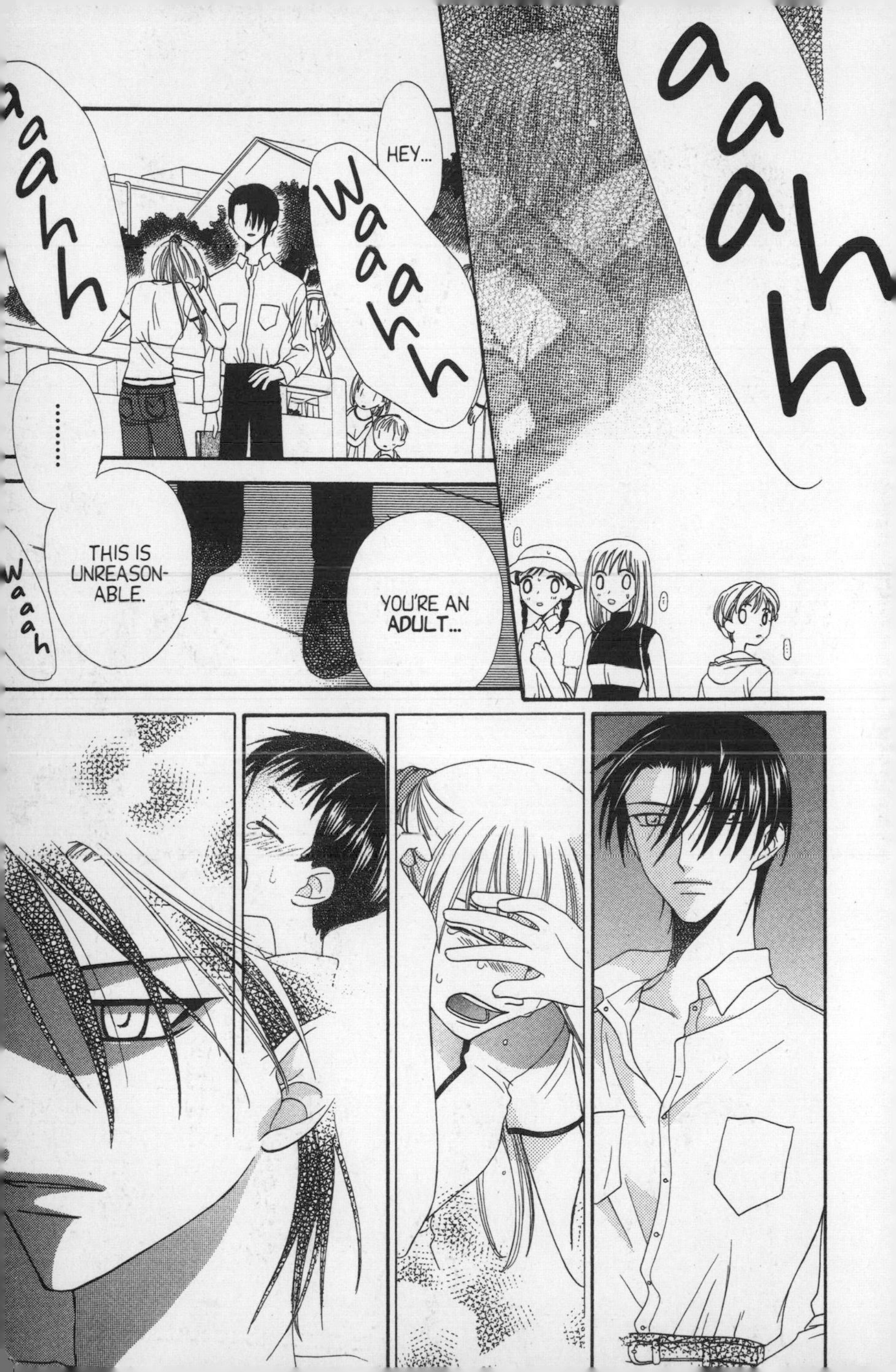
aaahh
HEY...
Waaahh
aaahh
......
YOU'RE AN ADULT...
THIS IS UNREASON-ABLE.
Waaah

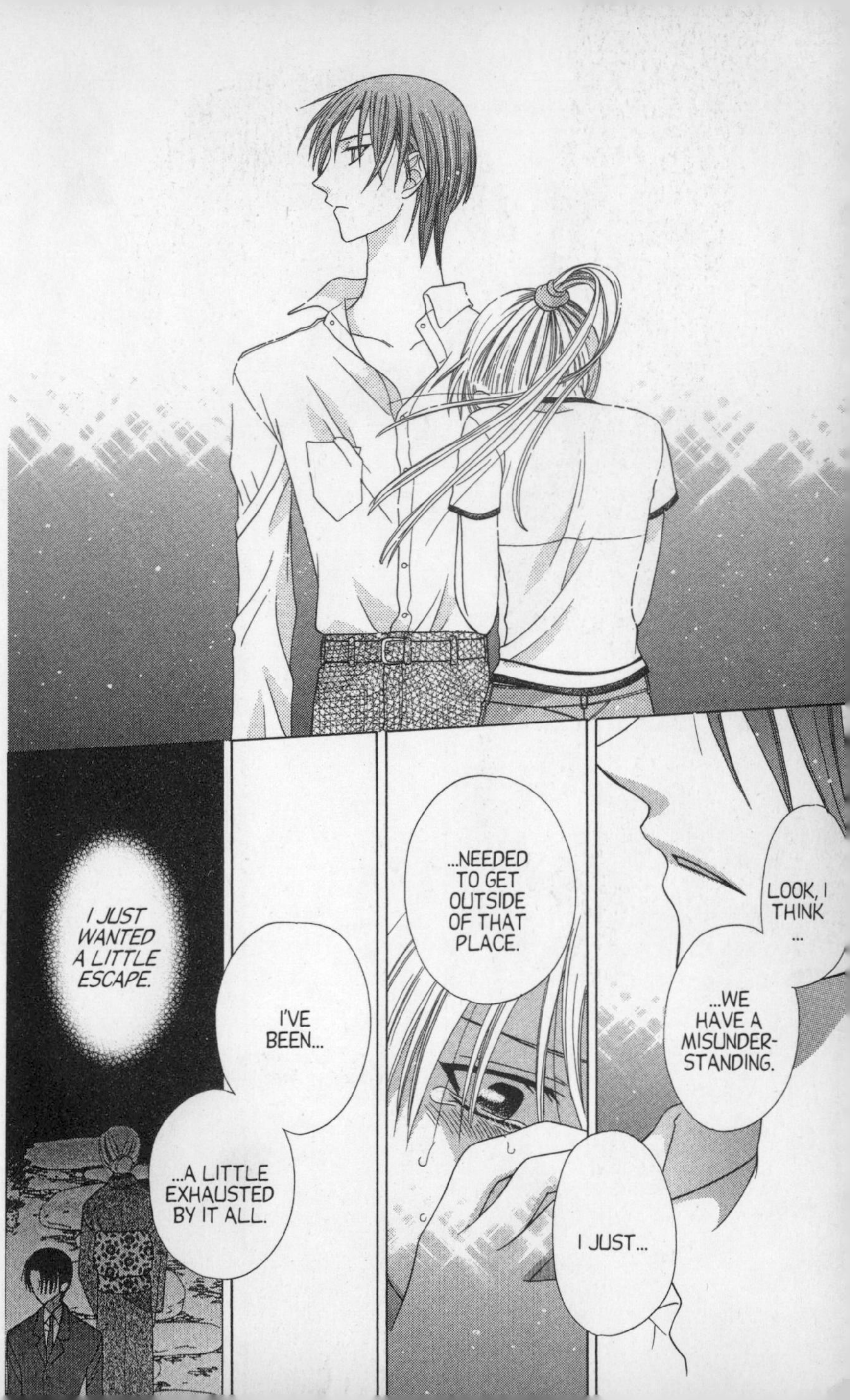
LOOK, I THINK ...
...WE HAVE A MISUNDERSTANDING.
I JUST...
...NEEDED TO GET OUTSIDE OF THAT PLACE.
I'VE BEEN...
...A LITTLE EXHAUSTED BY IT ALL.
I JUST WANTED A LITTLE ESCAPE.

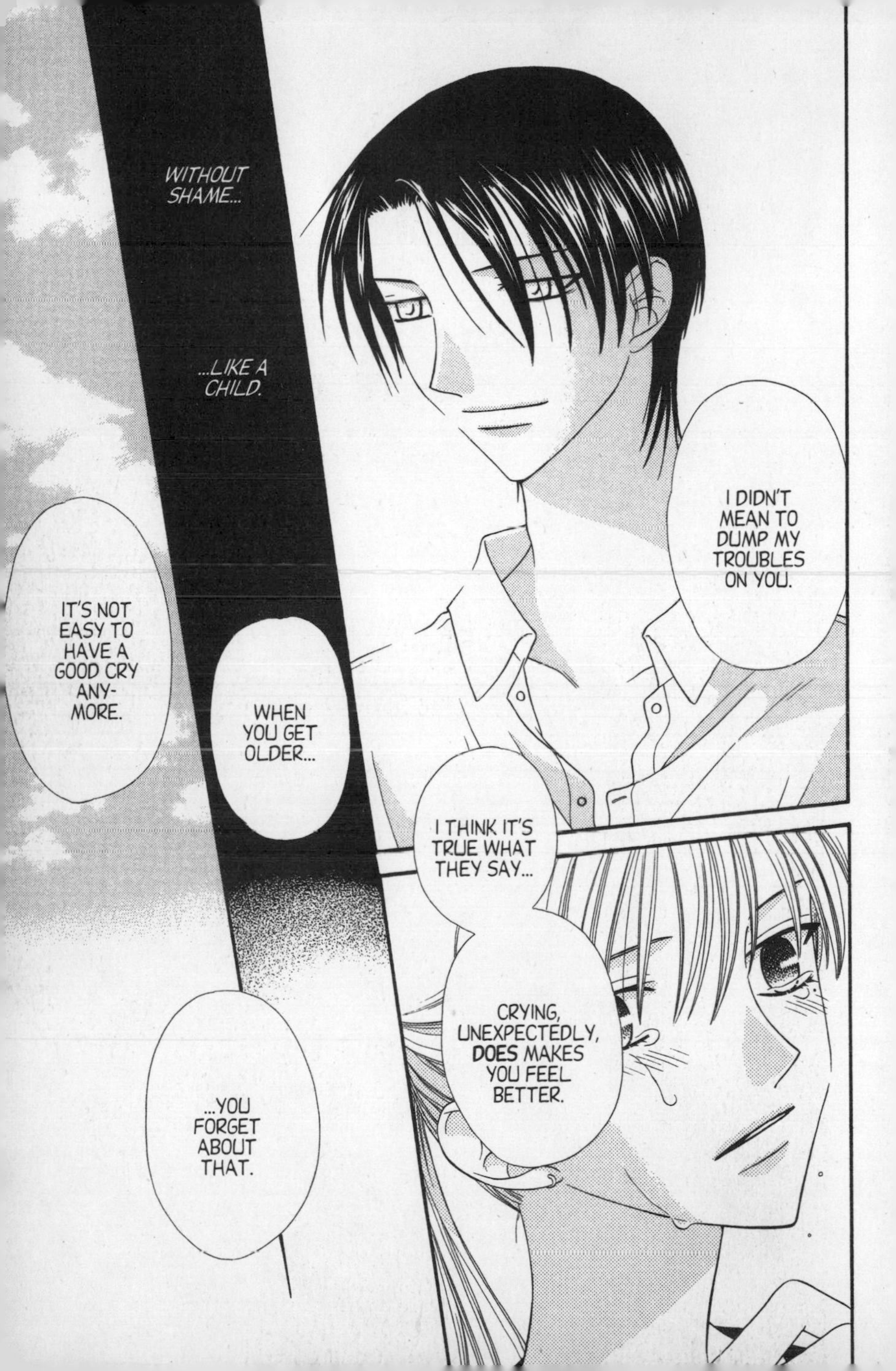
I DIDN'T MEAN TO DUMP MY TROUBLES ON YOU.
I THINK IT'S TRUE WHAT THEY SAY...
CRYING, UNEXPECTEDLY, **DOES** MAKES YOU FEEL BETTER.
WITHOUT SHAME...
...LIKE A CHILD.
WHEN YOU GET OLDER...
...YOU FORGET ABOUT THAT.
IT'S NOT EASY TO HAVE A GOOD CRY ANY-MORE.

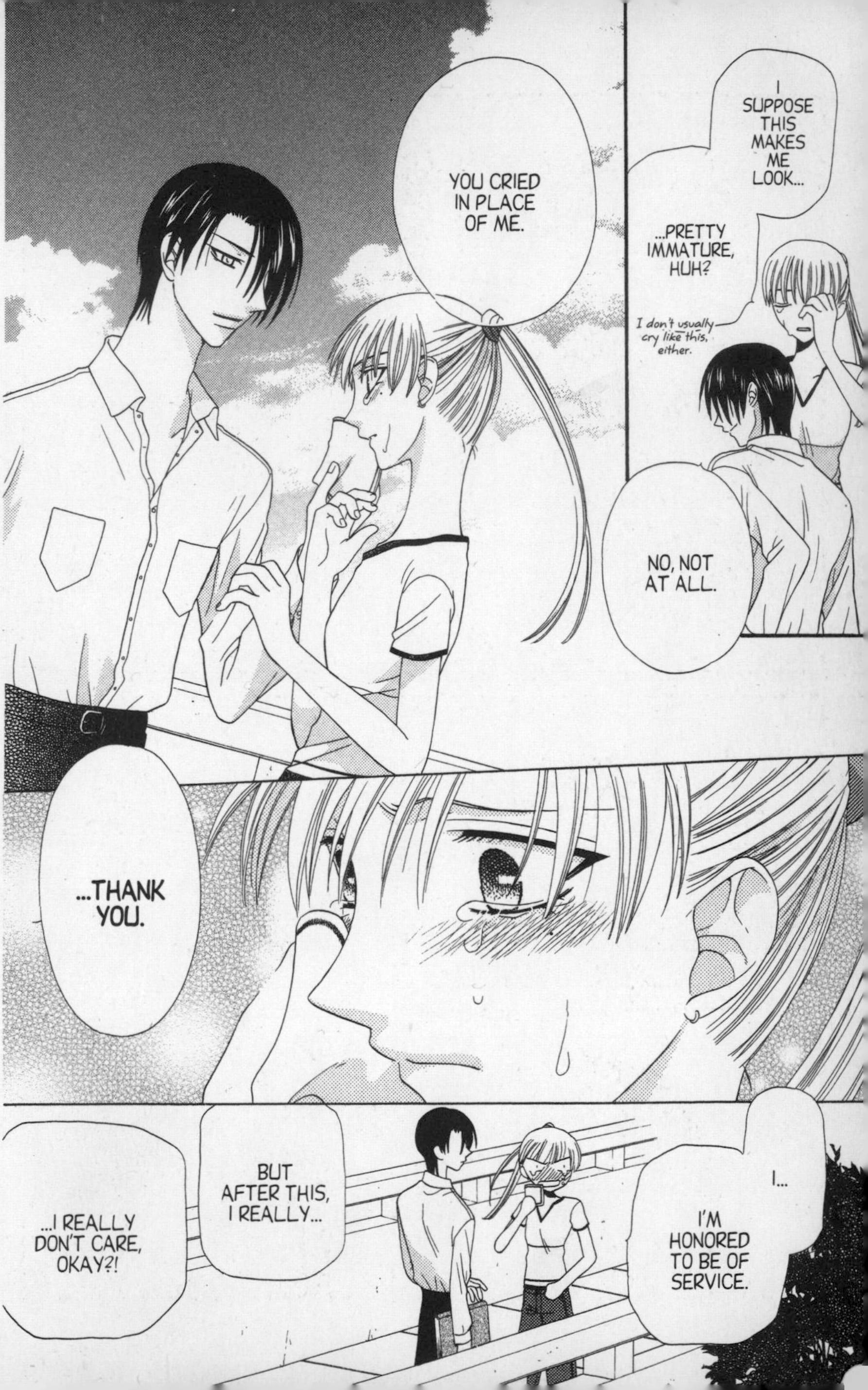
I SUPPOSE THIS MAKES ME LOOK...
...PRETTY IMMATURE, HUH?
I don't usually cry like this, either.
NO, NOT AT ALL.
YOU CRIED IN PLACE OF ME.
...THANK YOU.
I...
I'M HONORED TO BE OF SERVICE.
BUT AFTER THIS, I REALLY...
...I REALLY DON'T CARE, OKAY?!

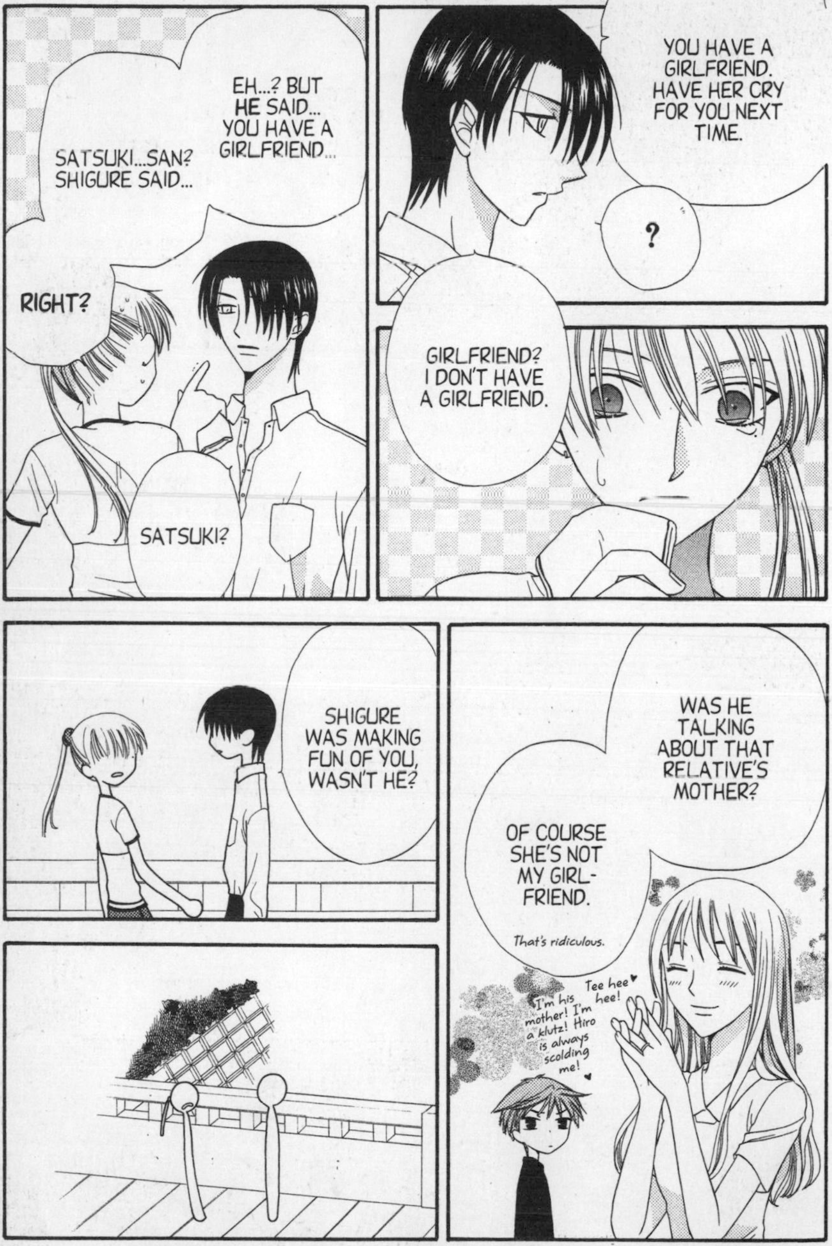
YOU HAVE A GIRLFRIEND. HAVE HER CRY FOR YOU NEXT TIME.
?
GIRLFRIEND? I DON'T HAVE A GIRLFRIEND.
EH...? BUT HE SAID... YOU HAVE A GIRLFRIEND...
SATSUKI...SAN? SHIGURE SAID...
RIGHT?
SATSUKI?
WAS HE TALKING ABOUT THAT RELATIVE'S MOTHER?
OF COURSE SHE'S NOT MY GIRL-FRIEND.
That's ridiculous.
Tee hee hee!
I'm his mother! I'm a klutz! Hiro is always scolding me!
SHIGURE WAS MAKING FUN OF YOU, WASN'T HE?

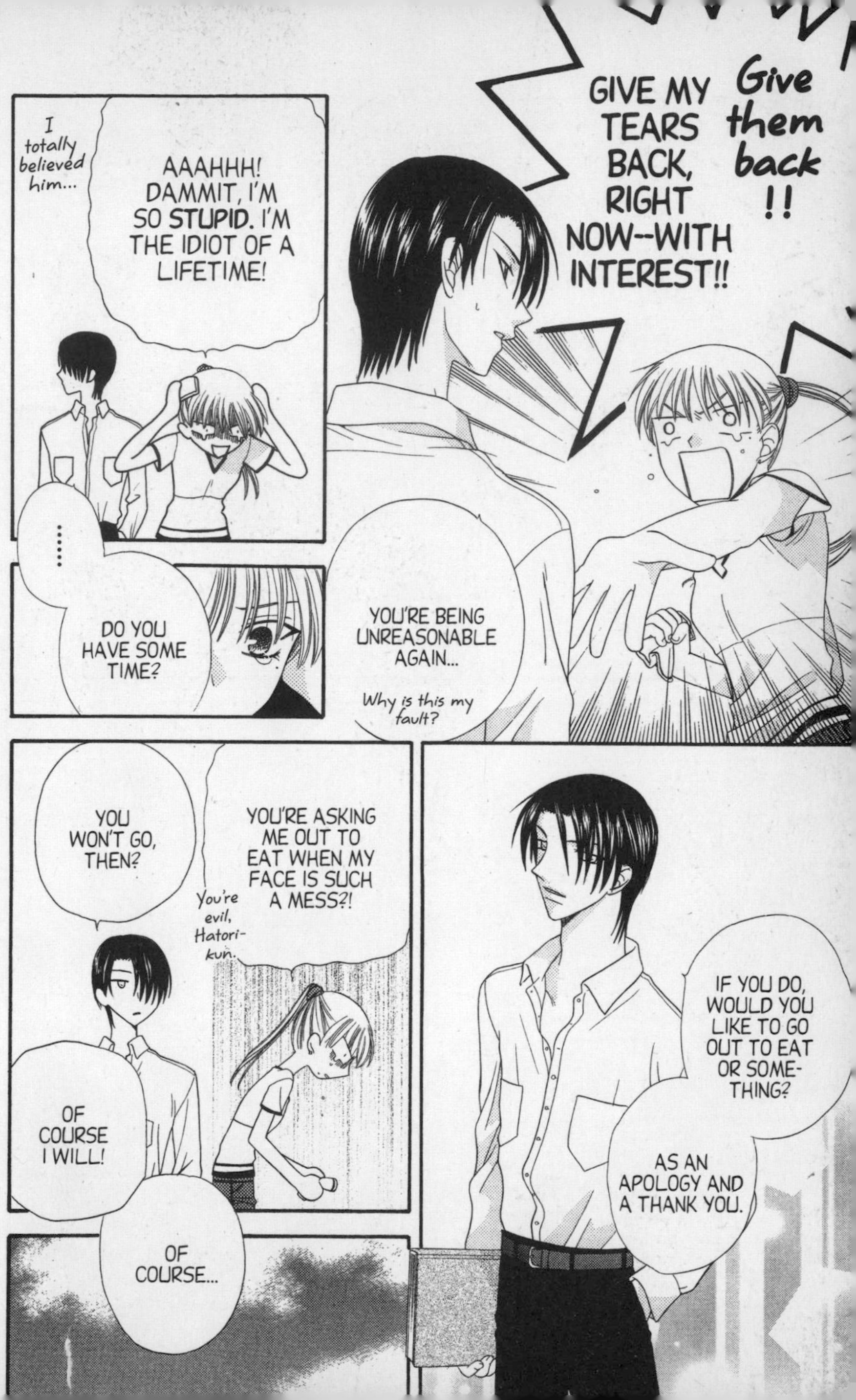
GIVE MY TEARS BACK, RIGHT NOW--WITH INTEREST!!
Give them back!!
YOU'RE BEING UNREASONABLE AGAIN...
Why is this my fault?
AAAHHH! DAMMIT, I'M SO **STUPID.** I'M THE IDIOT OF A LIFETIME!
I totally believed him...
......
DO YOU HAVE SOME TIME?
IF YOU DO, WOULD YOU LIKE TO GO OUT TO EAT OR SOME-THING?
AS AN APOLOGY AND A THANK YOU.
YOU'RE ASKING ME OUT TO EAT WHEN MY FACE IS SUCH A MESS?!
You're evil, Hatori-kun.
YOU WON'T GO, THEN?
OF COURSE I WILL!
OF COURSE...

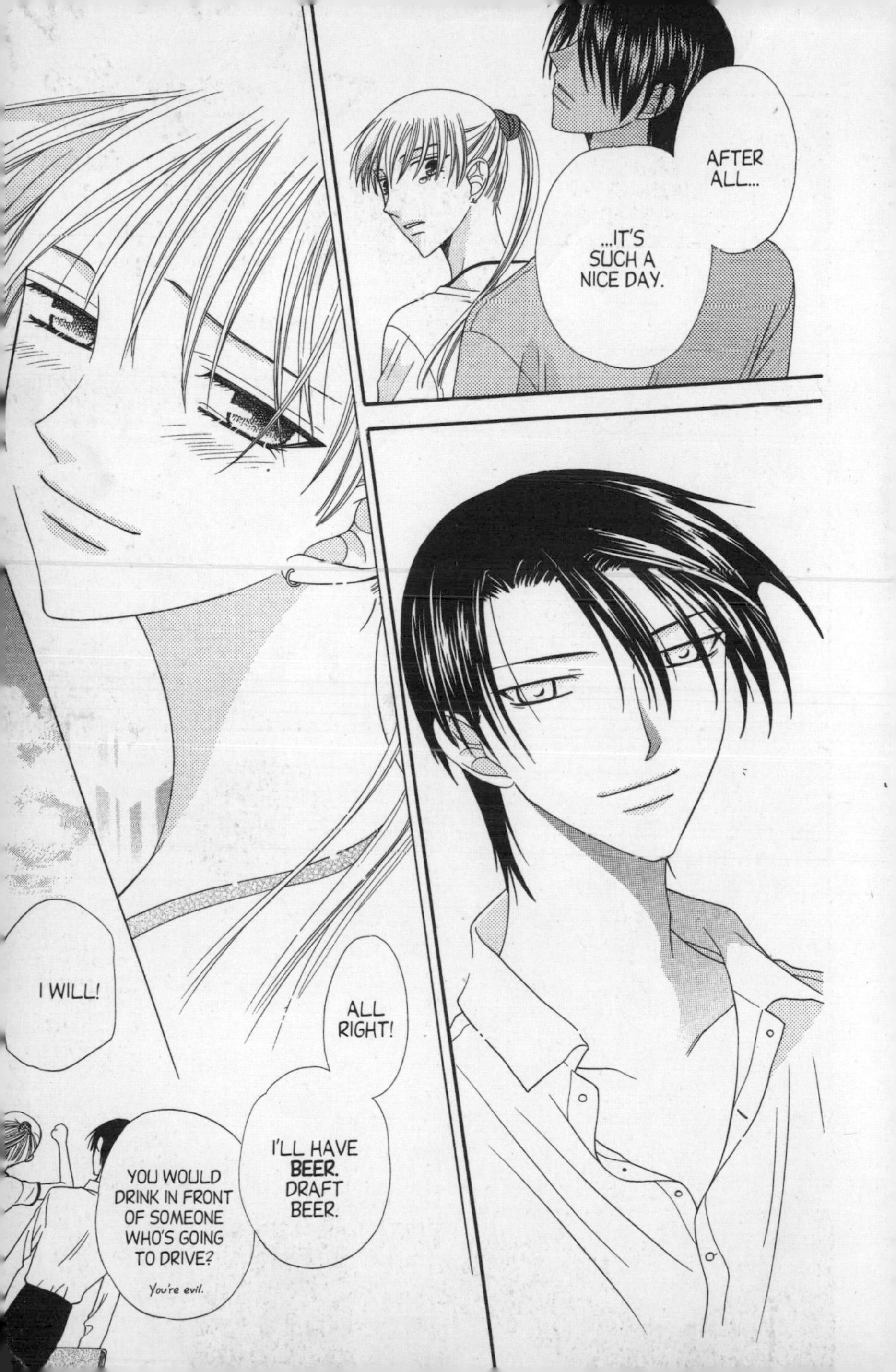

AFTER ALL...
...IT'S SUCH A NICE DAY.
ALL RIGHT!
I WILL!
I'LL HAVE BEER. DRAFT BEER.
YOU WOULD DRINK IN FRONT OF SOMEONE WHO'S GOING TO DRIVE?
You're evil.

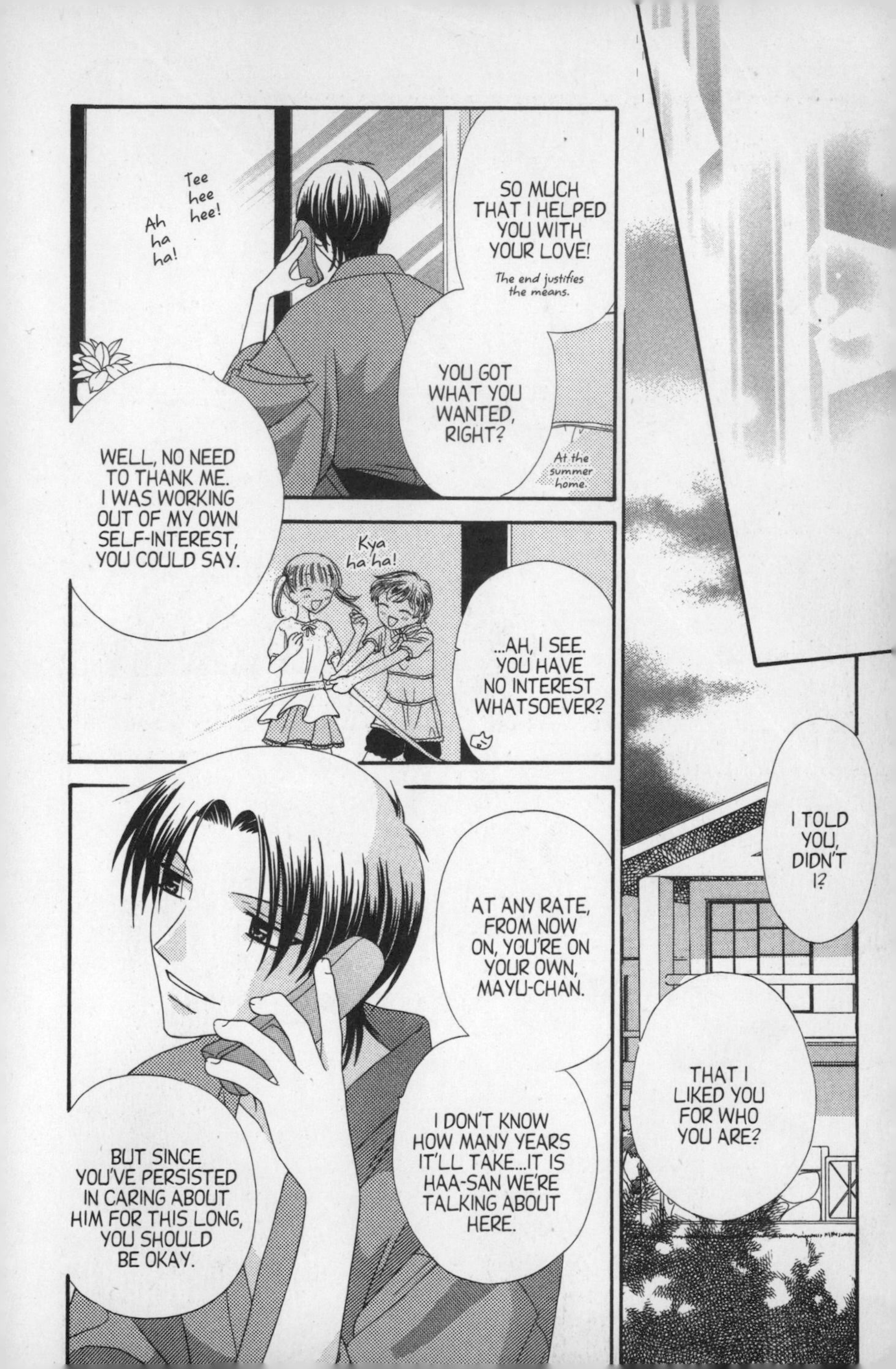

SO MUCH THAT I HELPED YOU WITH YOUR LOVE!
The end justifies the means.
Tee hee hee!
Ah ha ha!
YOU GOT WHAT YOU WANTED, RIGHT?
At the summer home.
WELL, NO NEED TO THANK ME. I WAS WORKING OUT OF MY OWN SELF-INTEREST, YOU COULD SAY.
...AH, I SEE. YOU HAVE NO INTEREST WHATSOEVER?
Kya ha ha!
AT ANY RATE, FROM NOW ON, YOU'RE ON YOUR OWN, MAYU-CHAN.
I DON'T KNOW HOW MANY YEARS IT'LL TAKE...IT IS HAA-SAN WE'RE TALKING ABOUT HERE.
BUT SINCE YOU'VE PERSISTED IN CARING ABOUT HIM FOR THIS LONG, YOU SHOULD BE OKAY.
I TOLD YOU, DIDN'T I?
THAT I LIKED YOU FOR WHO YOU ARE?

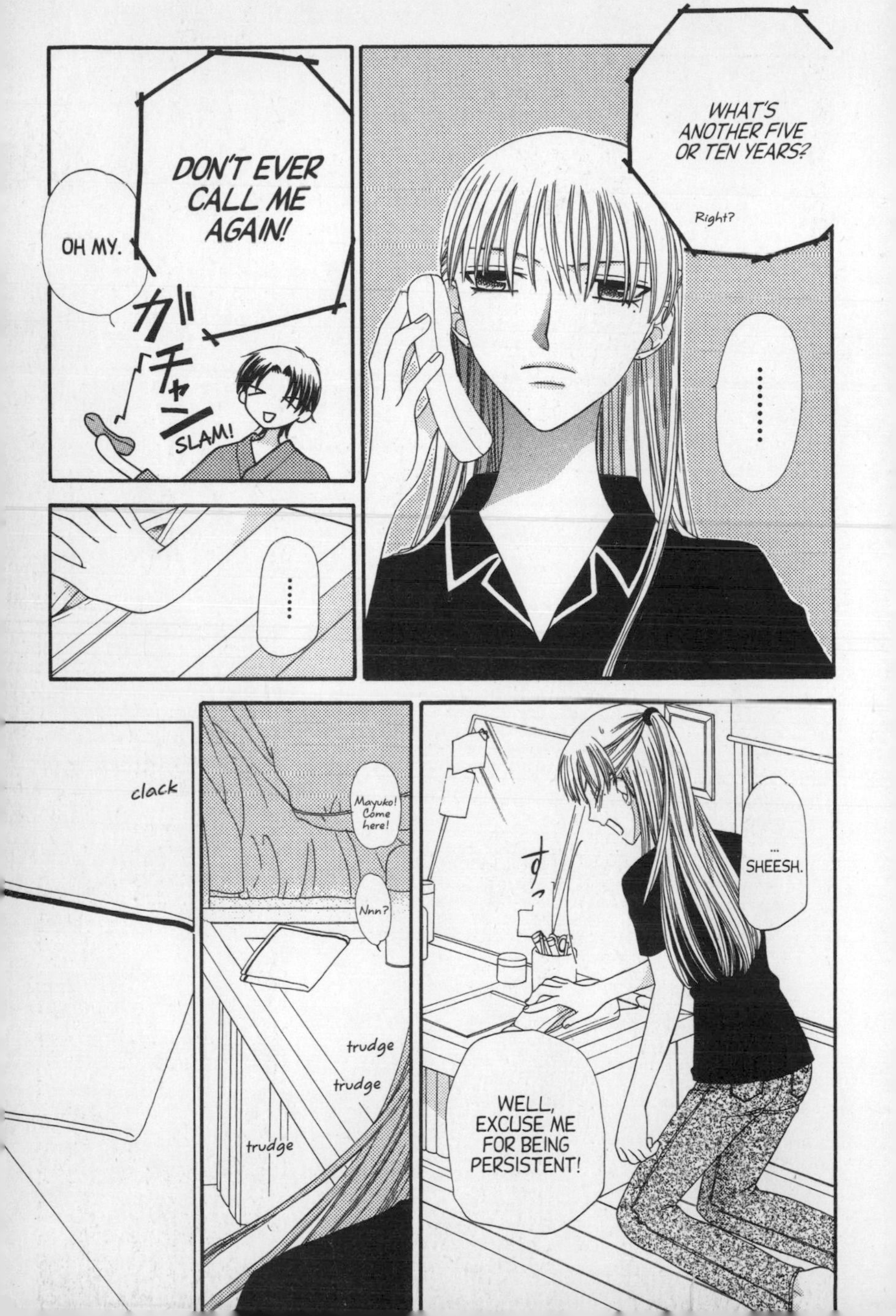
WHAT'S ANOTHER FIVE OR TEN YEARS?
Right?
......
DON'T EVER CALL ME AGAIN!
OH MY.
ガチャン
SLAM!
......
...SHEESH.
すっ
WELL, EXCUSE ME FOR BEING PERSISTENT!
Mayuko! Come here!
Nnn?
trudge
trudge
trudge
clack

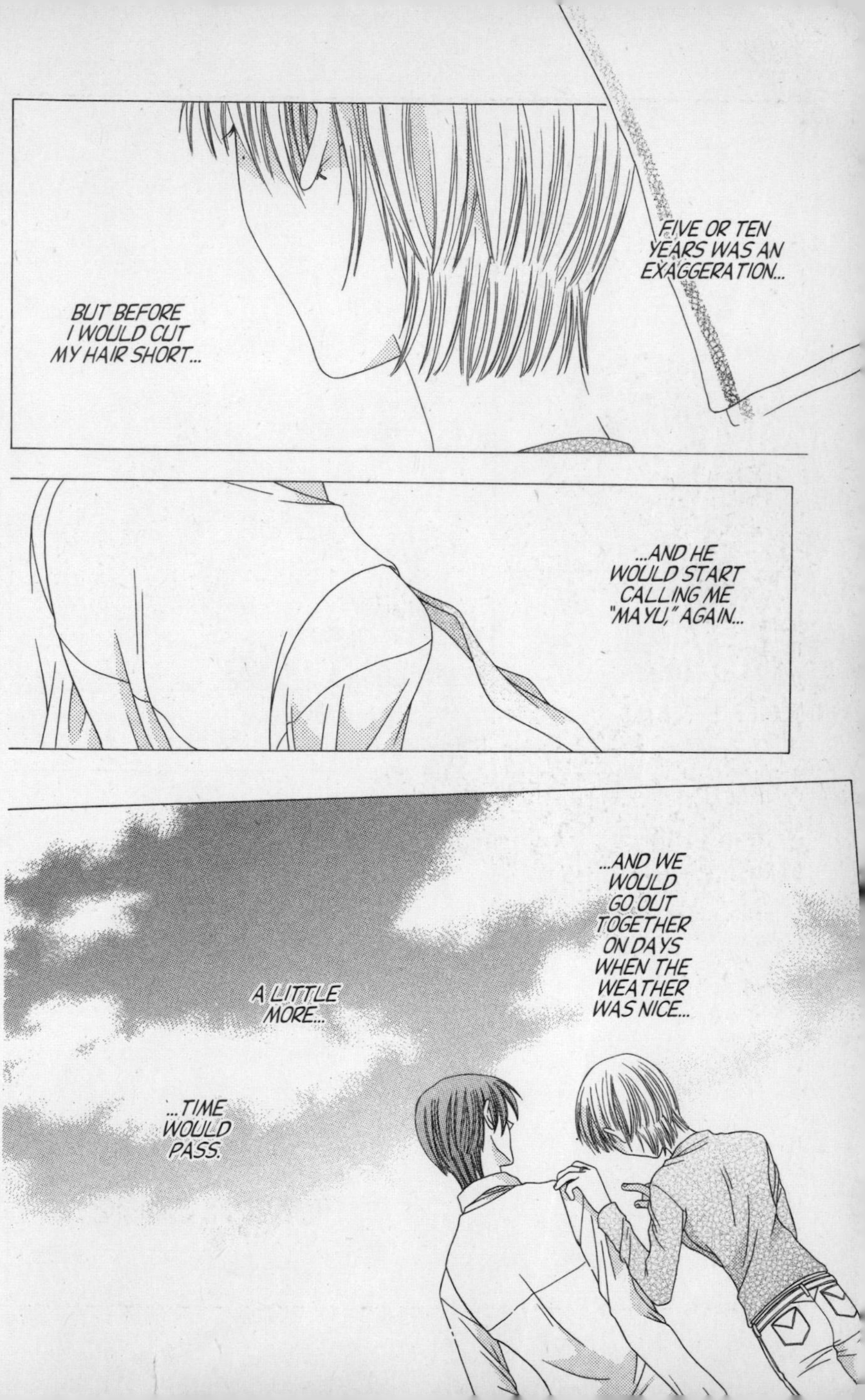
FIVE OR TEN YEARS WAS AN EXAGGERATION...
BUT BEFORE I WOULD CUT MY HAIR SHORT...
...AND HE WOULD START CALLING ME "MAYU," AGAIN...
...AND WE WOULD GO OUT TOGETHER ON DAYS WHEN THE WEATHER WAS NICE...
A LITTLE MORE...
...TIME WOULD PASS.

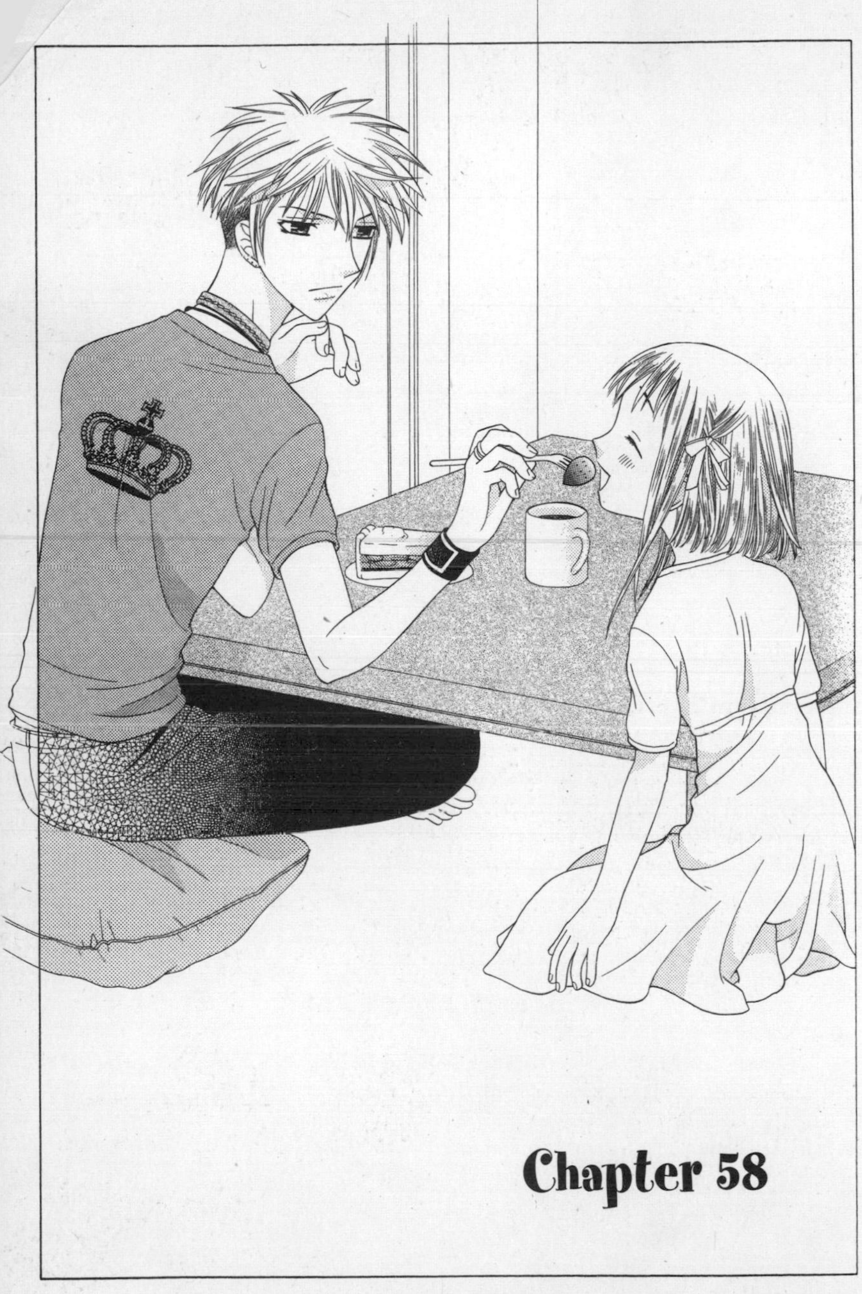

# Chapter 58

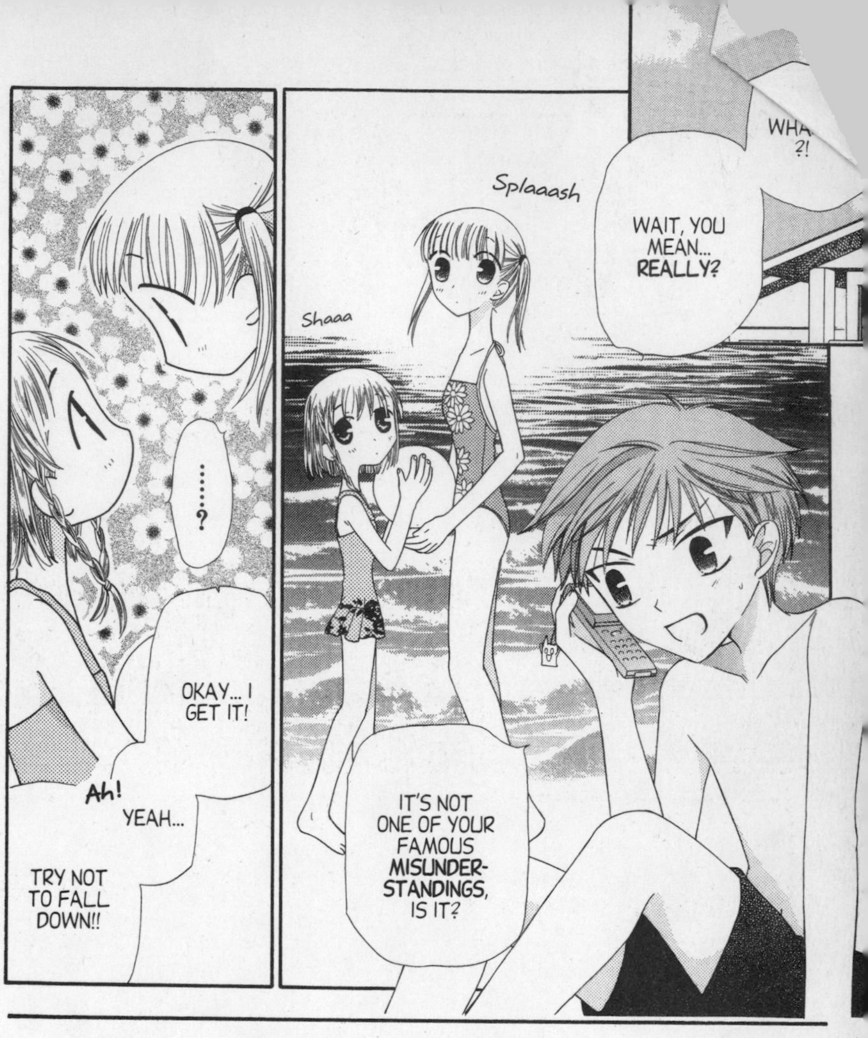
WHA
?!
WAIT, YOU MEAN... REALLY?
Splaaash
Shaaa
IT'S NOT ONE OF YOUR FAMOUS MISUNDER-STANDINGS, IS IT?
......?
OKAY... I GET IT!
Ah!
YEAH...
TRY NOT TO FALL DOWN!!

## BLAH, BLAH, BLAH 5

When I was little... I thought that if you swallowed the seeds, a watermelon **would** grow. I also worried that if I swallowed gum it would grow, too. Thinking about it now, I really wonder why...

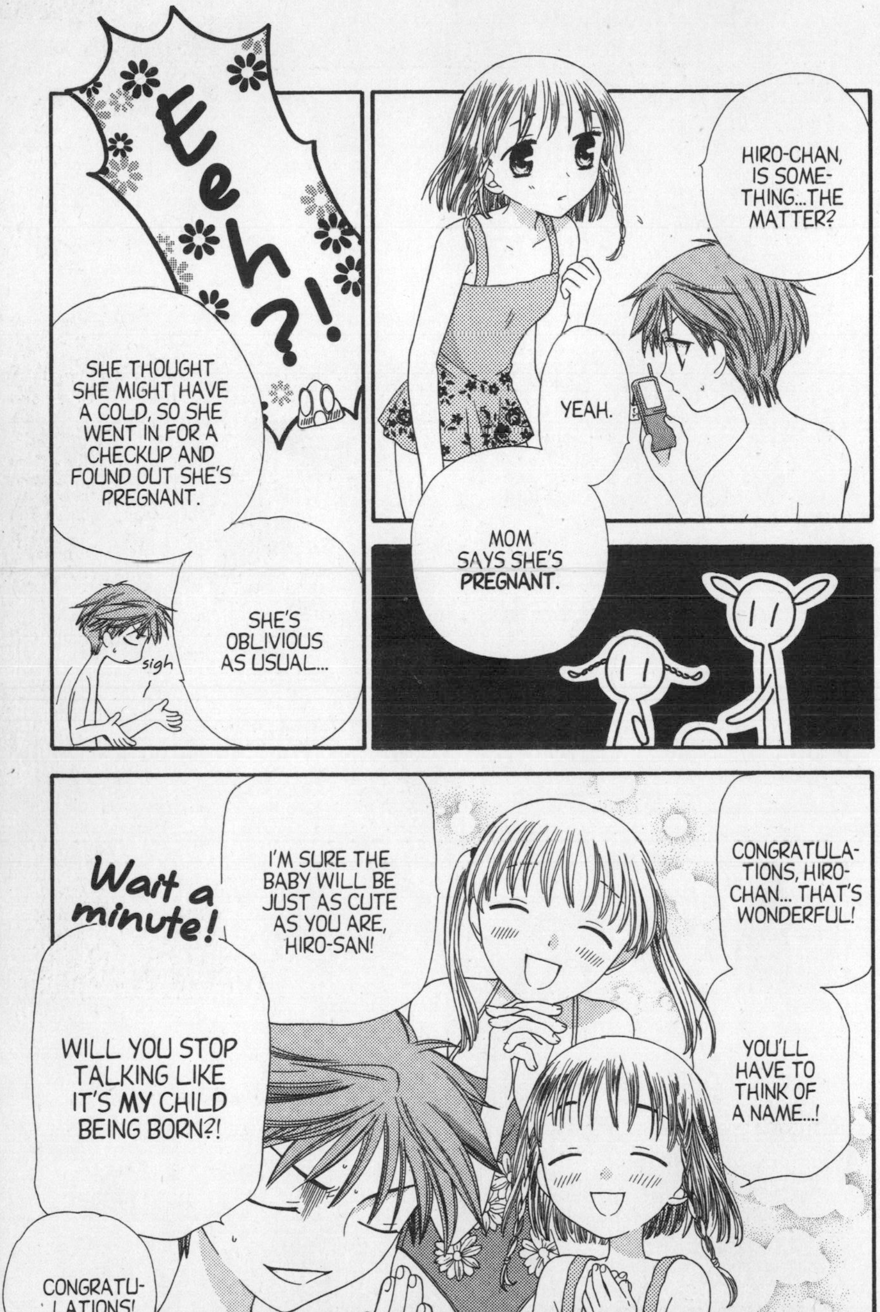

HIRO-CHAN, IS SOMETHING...THE MATTER?
YEAH.
MOM SAYS SHE'S PREGNANT.
Eeh?!
SHE THOUGHT SHE MIGHT HAVE A COLD, SO SHE WENT IN FOR A CHECKUP AND FOUND OUT SHE'S PREGNANT.
sigh
SHE'S OBLIVIOUS AS USUAL...
CONGRATULATIONS, HIRO-CHAN... THAT'S WONDERFUL!
YOU'LL HAVE TO THINK OF A NAME...!
I'M SURE THE BABY WILL BE JUST AS CUTE AS YOU ARE, HIRO-SAN!
Wait a minute!
WILL YOU STOP TALKING LIKE IT'S MY CHILD BEING BORN?!
CONGRATULATIONS!

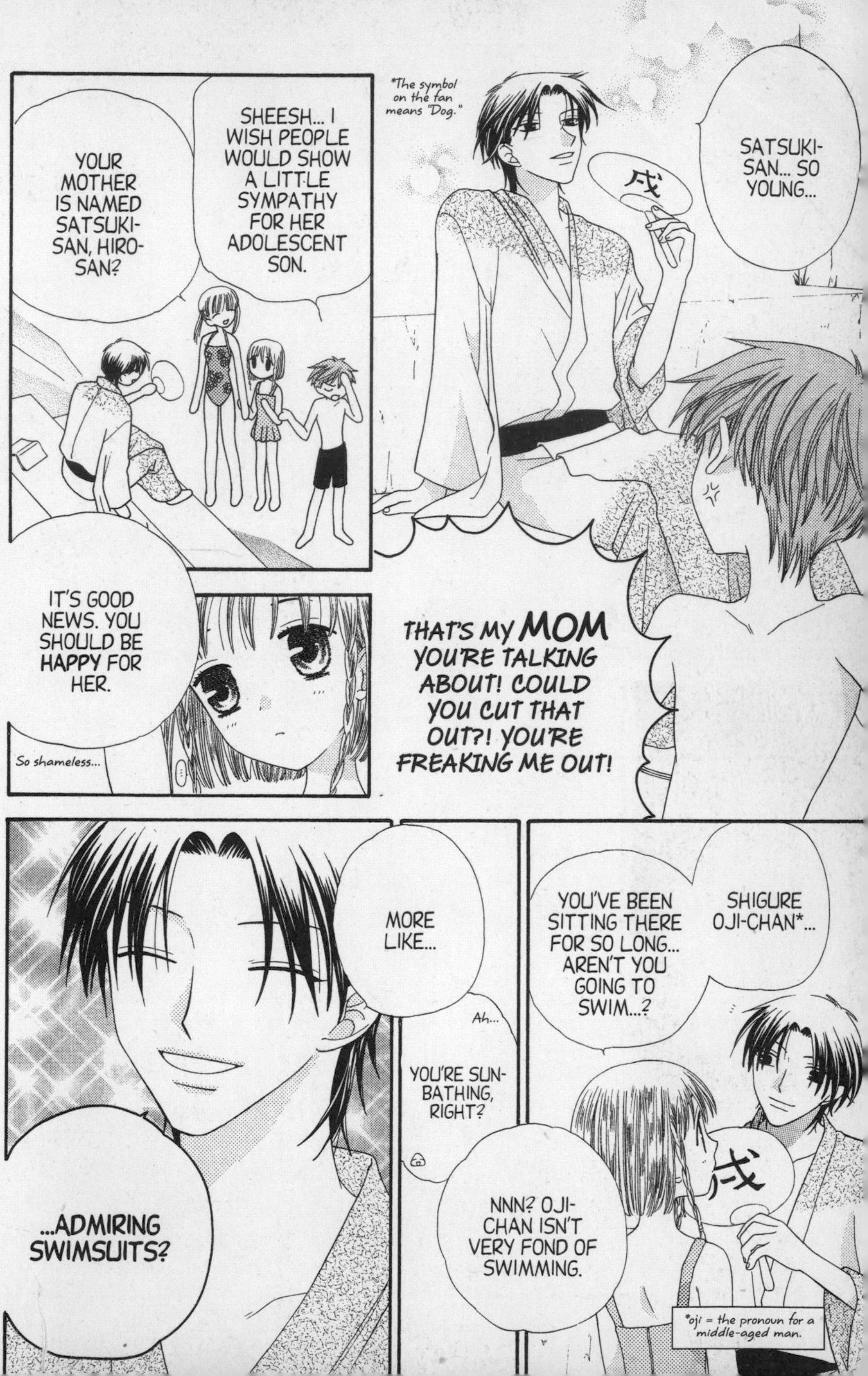
SATSUKI-SAN... SO YOUNG...
*The symbol on the fan means "Dog."
戌
SHEESH... I WISH PEOPLE WOULD SHOW A LITTLE SYMPATHY FOR HER ADOLESCENT SON.
YOUR MOTHER IS NAMED SATSUKI-SAN, HIRO-SAN?
THAT'S MY MOM YOU'RE TALKING ABOUT! COULD YOU CUT THAT OUT?! YOU'RE FREAKING ME OUT!
IT'S GOOD NEWS. YOU SHOULD BE HAPPY FOR HER.
So shameless...
SHIGURE OJI-CHAN*...
YOU'VE BEEN SITTING THERE FOR SO LONG... AREN'T YOU GOING TO SWIM...?
NNN? OJI-CHAN ISN'T VERY FOND OF SWIMMING.
戌
*oji = the pronoun for a middle-aged man.
Ah...
YOU'RE SUN-BATHING, RIGHT?
MORE LIKE...
...ADMIRING SWIMSUITS?

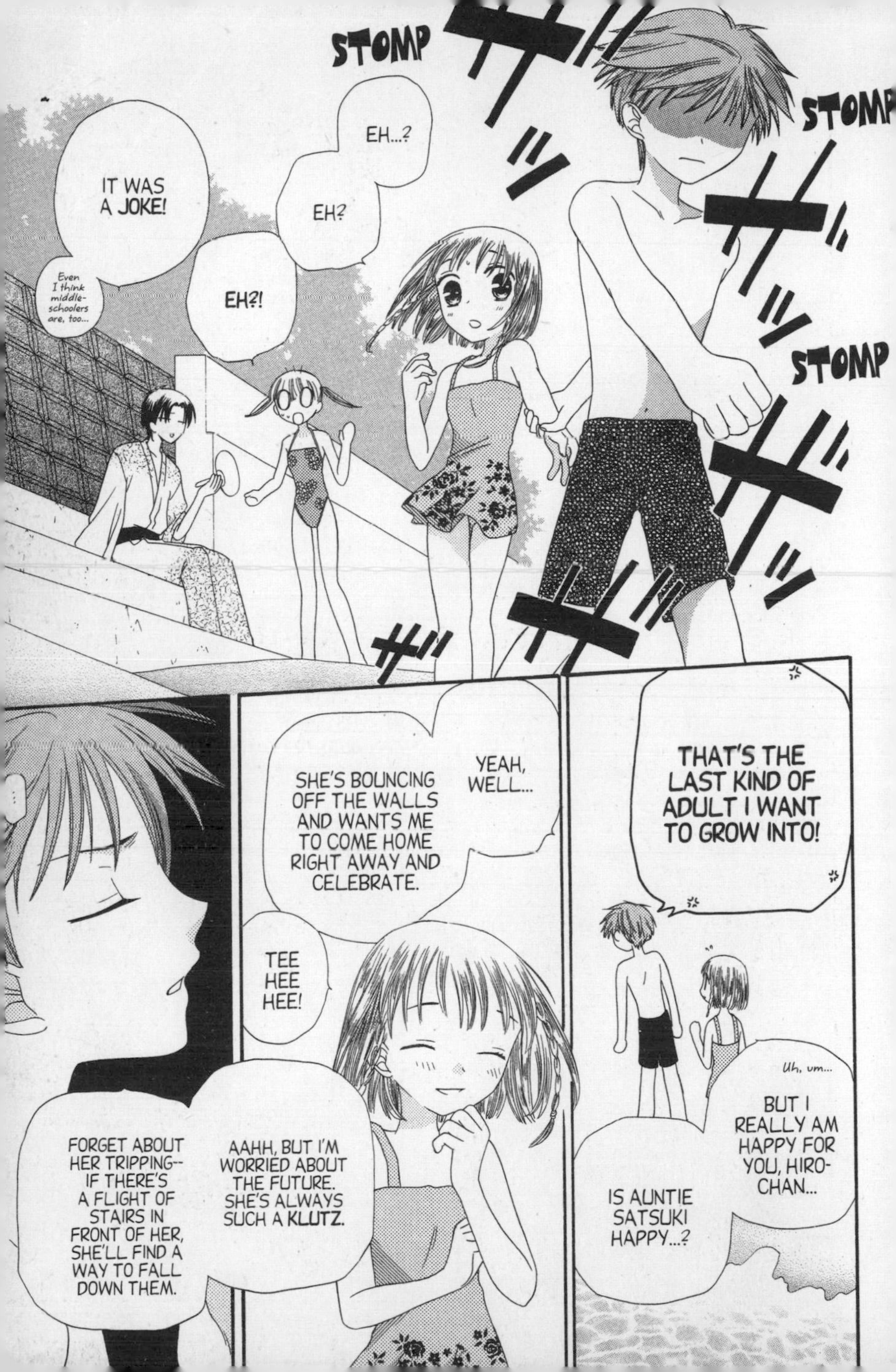
STOMP
STOMP
STOMP
EH...?
EH?
EH?!
IT WAS A JOKE!
Even I think middle-schoolers are, too...
THAT'S THE LAST KIND OF ADULT I WANT TO GROW INTO!
Uh, um...
BUT I REALLY AM HAPPY FOR YOU, HIRO-CHAN...
IS AUNTIE SATSUKI HAPPY...?
YEAH, WELL...
SHE'S BOUNCING OFF THE WALLS AND WANTS ME TO COME HOME RIGHT AWAY AND CELEBRATE.
TEE HEE HEE!
AAHH, BUT I'M WORRIED ABOUT THE FUTURE. SHE'S ALWAYS SUCH A KLUTZ.
FORGET ABOUT HER TRIPPING-- IF THERE'S A FLIGHT OF STAIRS IN FRONT OF HER, SHE'LL FIND A WAY TO FALL DOWN THEM.

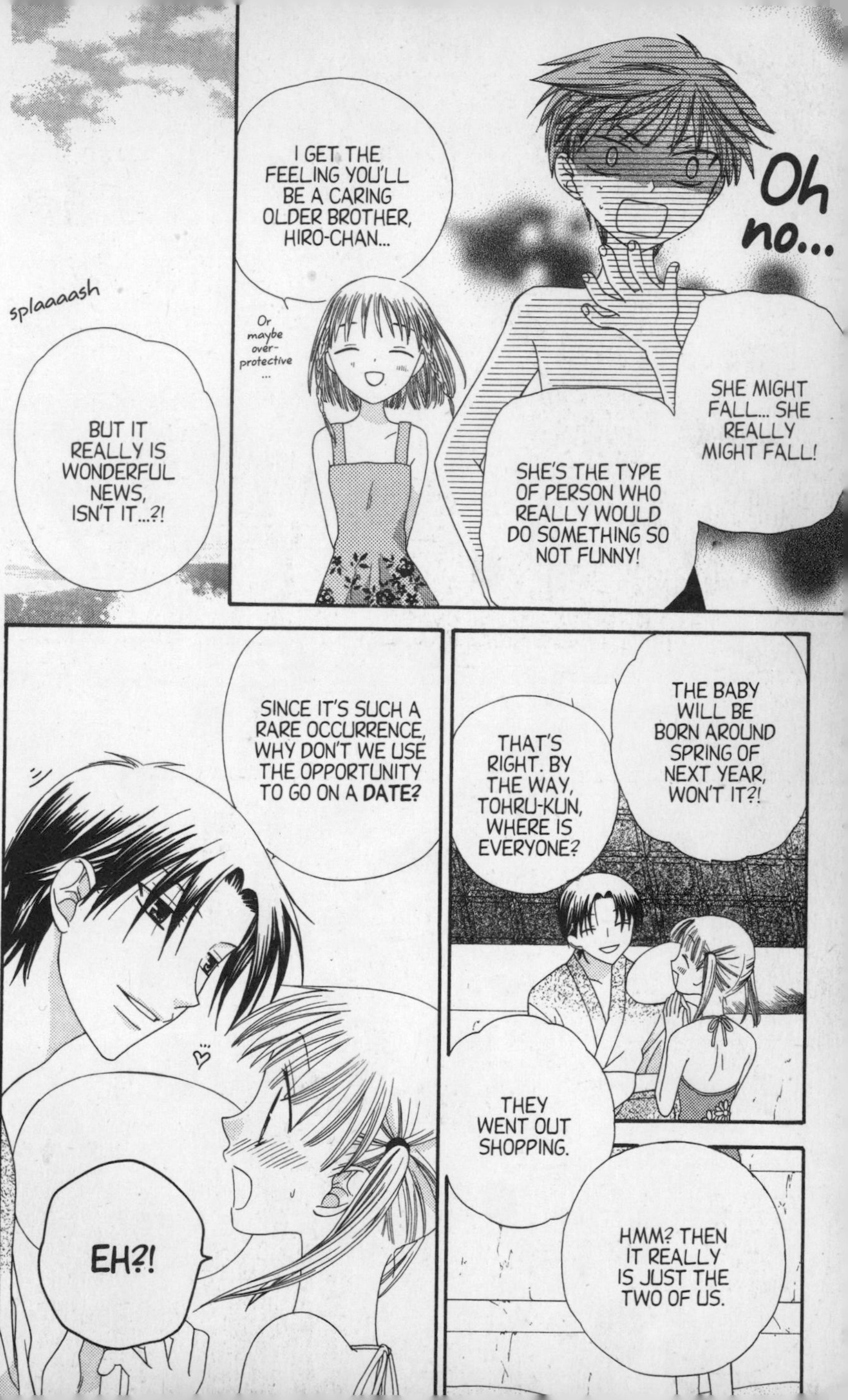
Oh no...
SHE MIGHT FALL... SHE REALLY MIGHT FALL!
SHE'S THE TYPE OF PERSON WHO REALLY WOULD DO SOMETHING SO NOT FUNNY!
I GET THE FEELING YOU'LL BE A CARING OLDER BROTHER, HIRO-CHAN...
Or maybe over-protective ...
splaaaash
BUT IT REALLY IS WONDERFUL NEWS, ISN'T IT...?!
THE BABY WILL BE BORN AROUND SPRING OF NEXT YEAR, WON'T IT?!
THAT'S RIGHT. BY THE WAY, TOHRU-KUN, WHERE IS EVERYONE?
THEY WENT OUT SHOPPING.
HMM? THEN IT REALLY IS JUST THE TWO OF US.
SINCE IT'S SUCH A RARE OCCURRENCE, WHY DON'T WE USE THE OPPORTUNITY TO GO ON A **DATE**?
EH?!

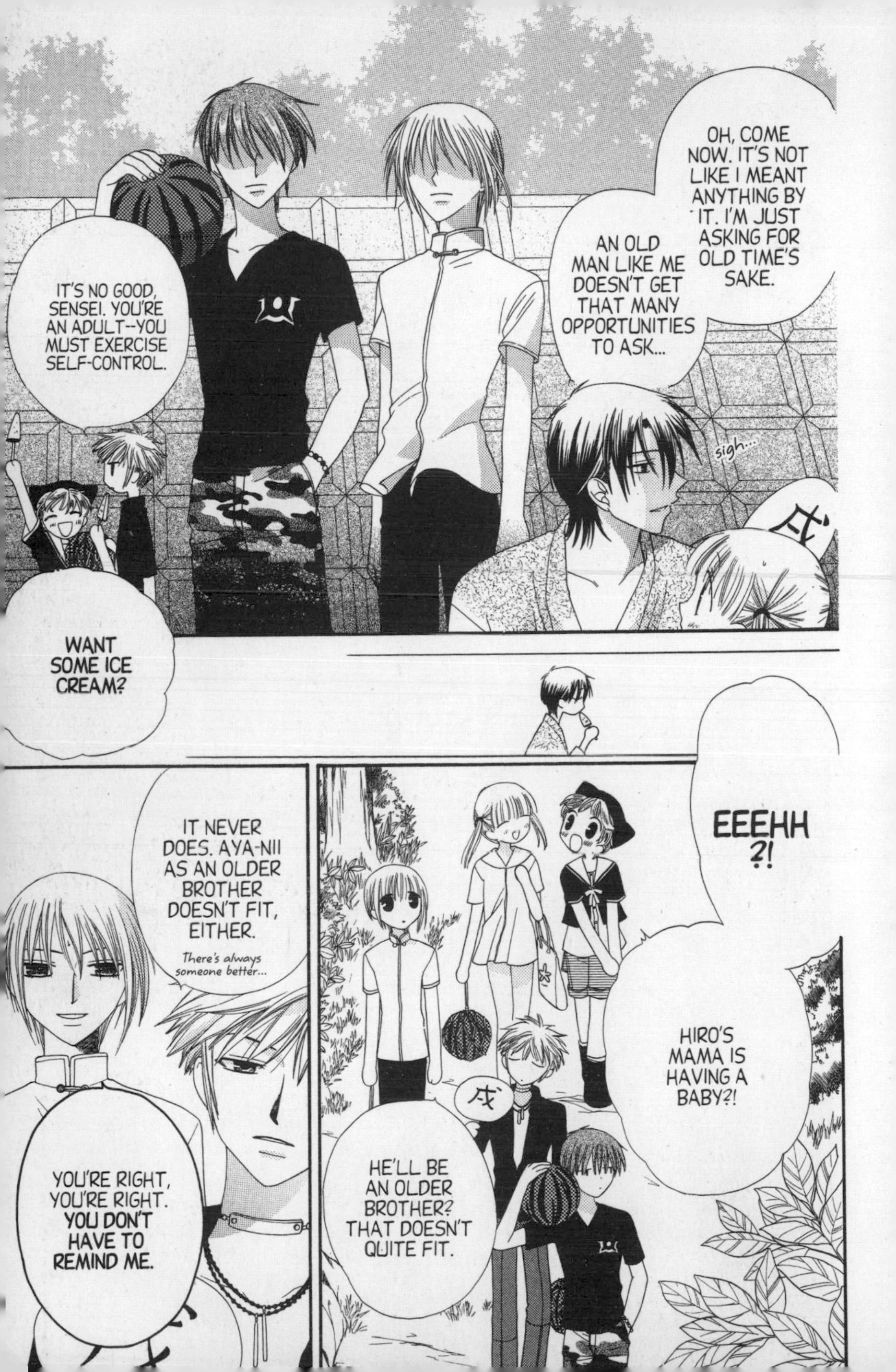
OH, COME NOW. IT'S NOT LIKE I MEANT ANYTHING BY IT. I'M JUST ASKING FOR OLD TIME'S SAKE.
AN OLD MAN LIKE ME DOESN'T GET THAT MANY OPPORTUNITIES TO ASK...
sigh...
戌
IT'S NO GOOD, SENSEI. YOU'RE AN ADULT--YOU MUST EXERCISE SELF-CONTROL.
WANT SOME ICE CREAM?
EEEHH ?!
HIRO'S MAMA IS HAVING A BABY?!
戌
HE'LL BE AN OLDER BROTHER? THAT DOESN'T QUITE FIT.
IT NEVER DOES. AYA-NII AS AN OLDER BROTHER DOESN'T FIT, EITHER.
There's always someone better...
YOU'RE RIGHT, YOU'RE RIGHT. **YOU DON'T HAVE TO REMIND ME.**

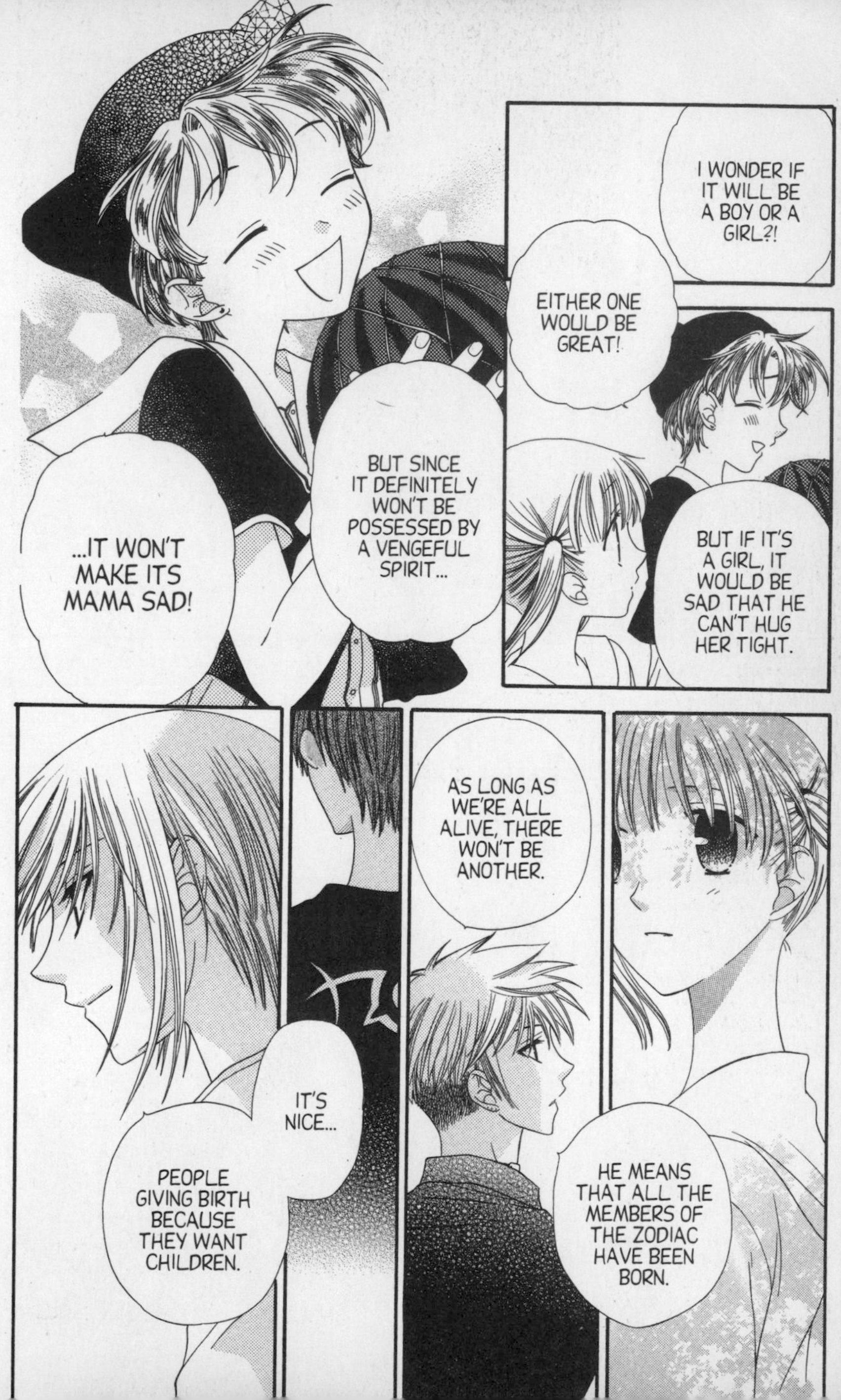
I WONDER IF IT WILL BE A BOY OR A GIRL?!
EITHER ONE WOULD BE GREAT!
BUT IF IT'S A GIRL, IT WOULD BE SAD THAT HE CAN'T HUG HER TIGHT.
BUT SINCE IT DEFINITELY WON'T BE POSSESSED BY A VENGEFUL SPIRIT...
...IT WON'T MAKE ITS MAMA SAD!
AS LONG AS WE'RE ALL ALIVE, THERE WON'T BE ANOTHER.
HE MEANS THAT ALL THE MEMBERS OF THE ZODIAC HAVE BEEN BORN.
IT'S NICE...
PEOPLE GIVING BIRTH BECAUSE THEY WANT CHILDREN.

## The Middle School Girl Who Wanted To Start a Gang

...One of them.

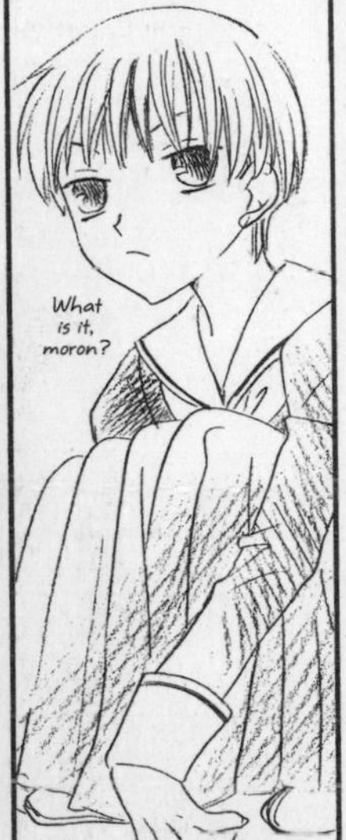
What is it, moron?

They're such minor characters that they don't have names, but they were fun girls to draw. Currently, they are attending school and keeping out of trouble. They're strictly following the teachings of their "Nee-san." I want to have them show up again, but there's no room for it, so I alone feel like saying, "Tch!" I guess I just like to draw high-spirited girls.

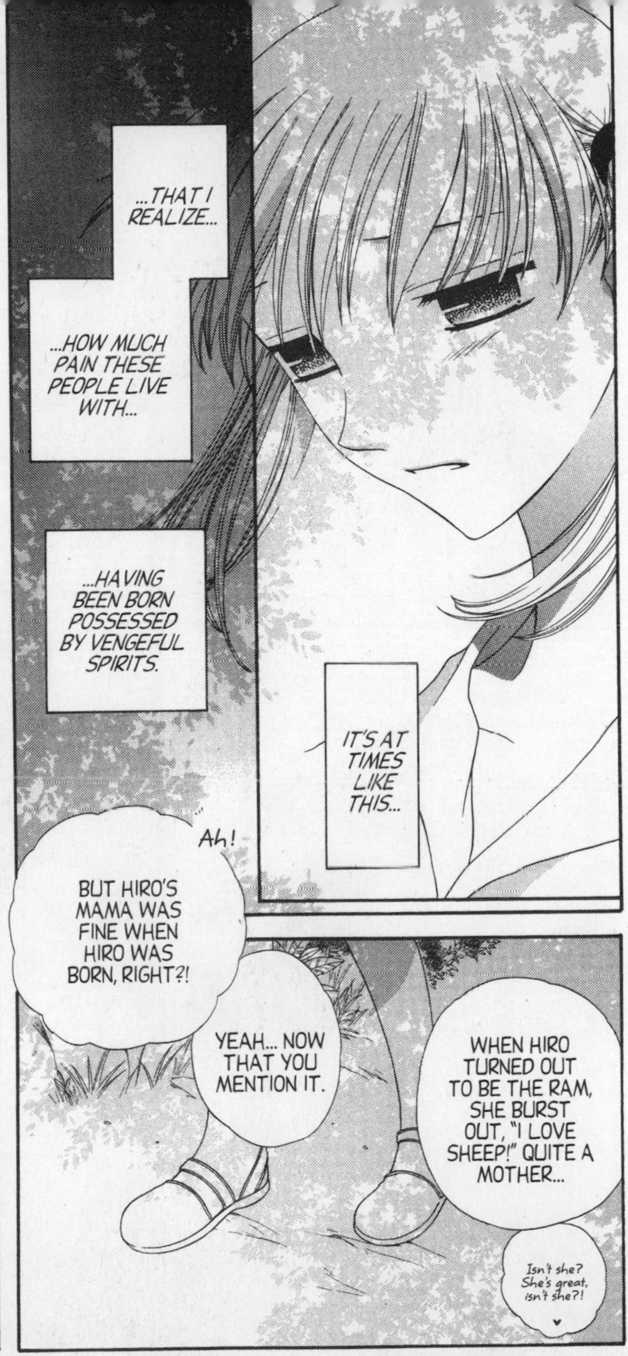
IT'S AT TIMES LIKE THIS...
...THAT I REALIZE...
...HOW MUCH PAIN THESE PEOPLE LIVE WITH...
...HAVING BEEN BORN POSSESSED BY VENGEFUL SPIRITS.
Ah!
BUT HIRO'S MAMA WAS FINE WHEN HIRO WAS BORN, RIGHT?!
YEAH... NOW THAT YOU MENTION IT.
WHEN HIRO TURNED OUT TO BE THE RAM, SHE BURST OUT, "I LOVE SHEEP!" QUITE A MOTHER...
Isn't she? She's great, isn't she?!

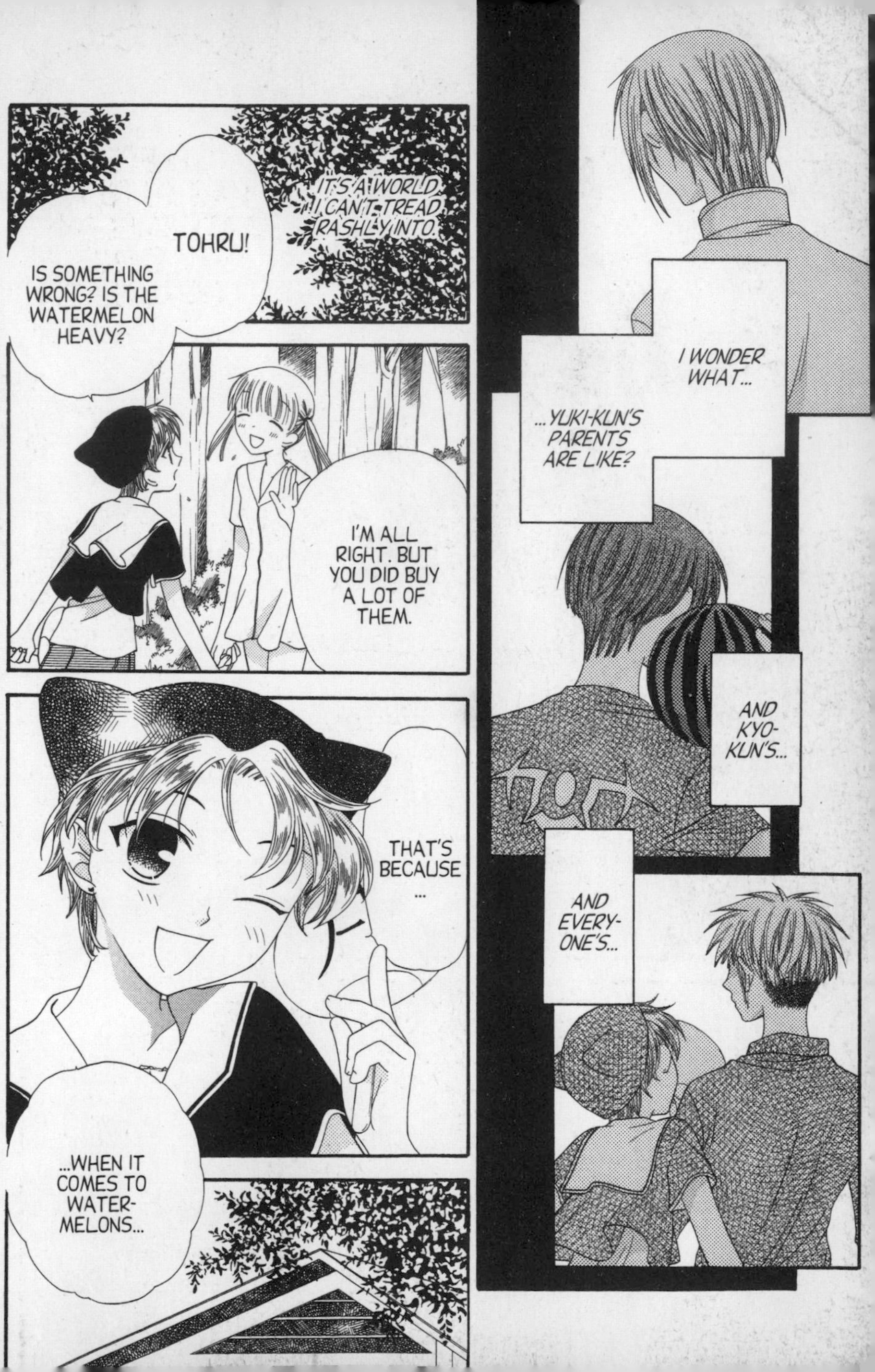
I WONDER WHAT...
...YUKI-KUN'S PARENTS ARE LIKE?
AND KYO-KUN'S...
AND EVERY-ONE'S...
IT'S A WORLD I CAN'T TREAD RASHLY INTO.
TOHRU!
IS SOMETHING WRONG? IS THE WATERMELON HEAVY?
I'M ALL RIGHT. BUT YOU DID BUY A LOT OF THEM.
THAT'S BECAUSE...
...WHEN IT COMES TO WATER-MELONS...

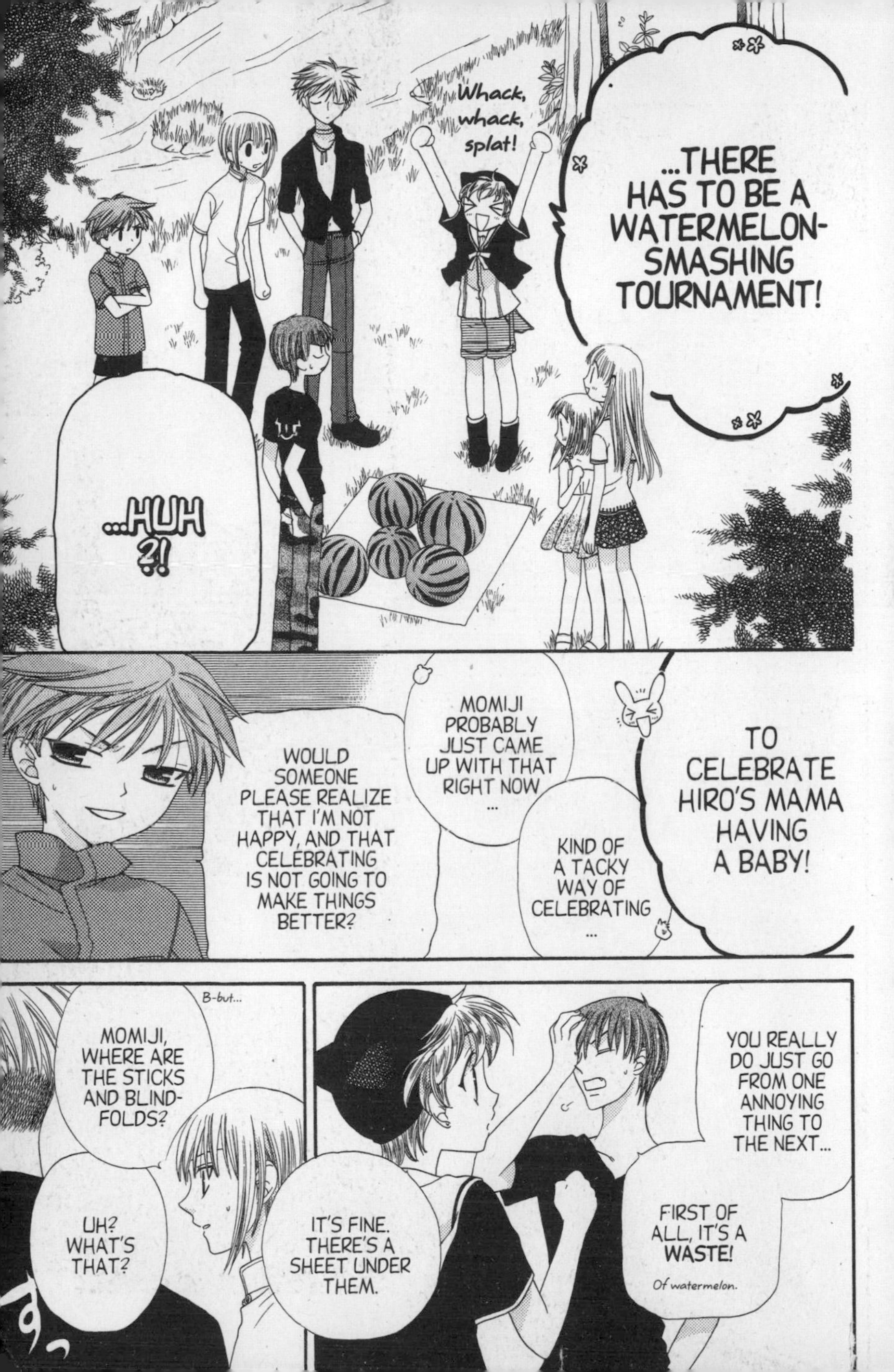
Whack, whack, splat!
...THERE HAS TO BE A WATERMELON-SMASHING TOURNAMENT!
...HUH?!
TO CELEBRATE HIRO'S MAMA HAVING A BABY!
MOMIJI PROBABLY JUST CAME UP WITH THAT RIGHT NOW ...
KIND OF A TACKY WAY OF CELEBRATING ...
WOULD SOMEONE PLEASE REALIZE THAT I'M NOT HAPPY, AND THAT CELEBRATING IS NOT GOING TO MAKE THINGS BETTER?
YOU REALLY DO JUST GO FROM ONE ANNOYING THING TO THE NEXT...
FIRST OF ALL, IT'S A WASTE!
Of watermelon.
IT'S FINE. THERE'S A SHEET UNDER THEM.
B-but...
MOMIJI, WHERE ARE THE STICKS AND BLIND-FOLDS?
UH? WHAT'S THAT?

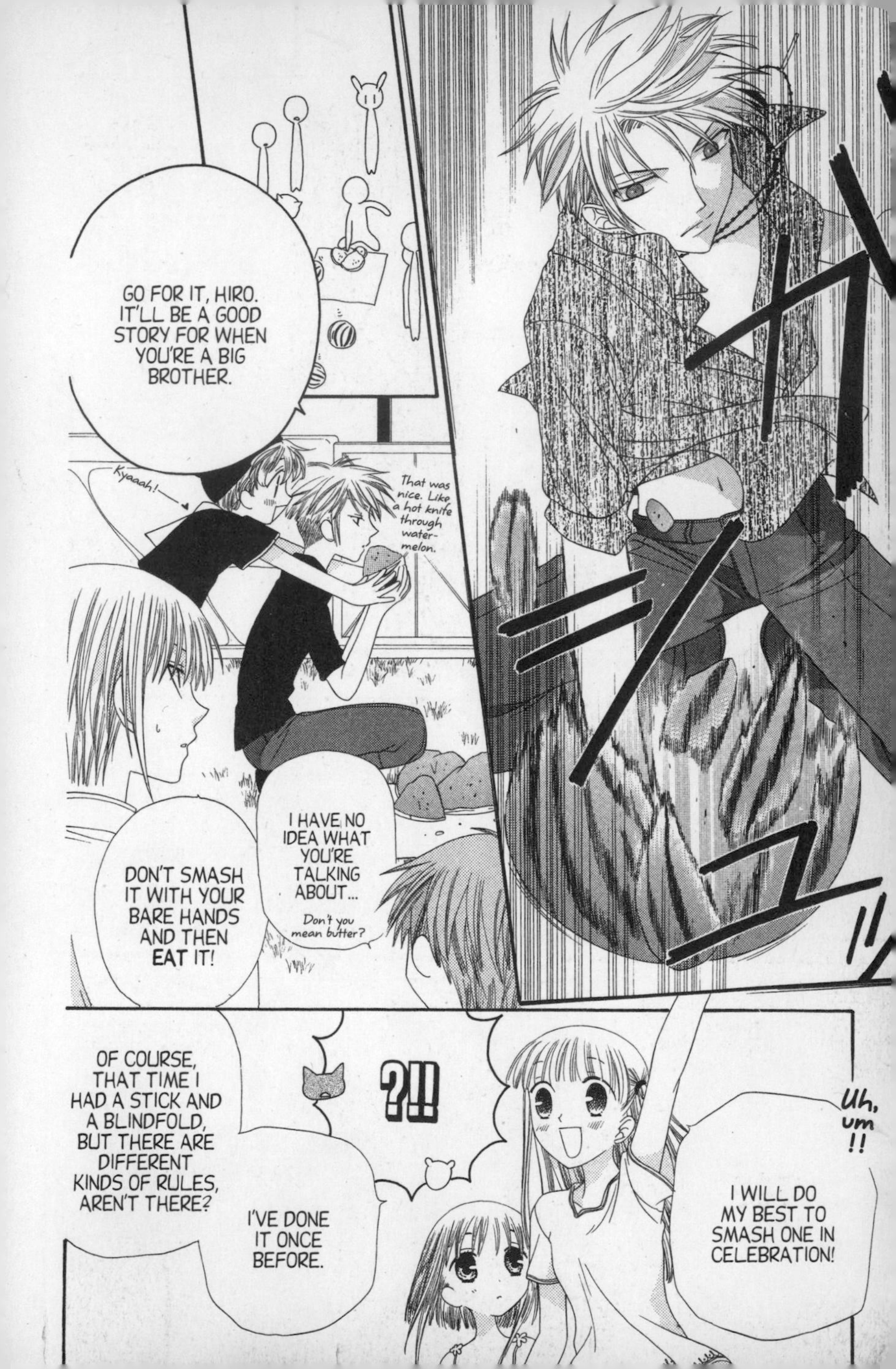
GO FOR IT, HIRO. IT'LL BE A GOOD STORY FOR WHEN YOU'RE A BIG BROTHER.
That was nice. Like a hot knife through water-melon.
Kyaaah!
DON'T SMASH IT WITH YOUR BARE HANDS AND THEN EAT IT!
I HAVE NO IDEA WHAT YOU'RE TALKING ABOUT...
Don't you mean butter?
Uh, um!!
I WILL DO MY BEST TO SMASH ONE IN CELEBRATION!
?!!
I'VE DONE IT ONCE BEFORE.
OF COURSE, THAT TIME I HAD A STICK AND A BLINDFOLD, BUT THERE ARE DIFFERENT KINDS OF RULES, AREN'T THERE?

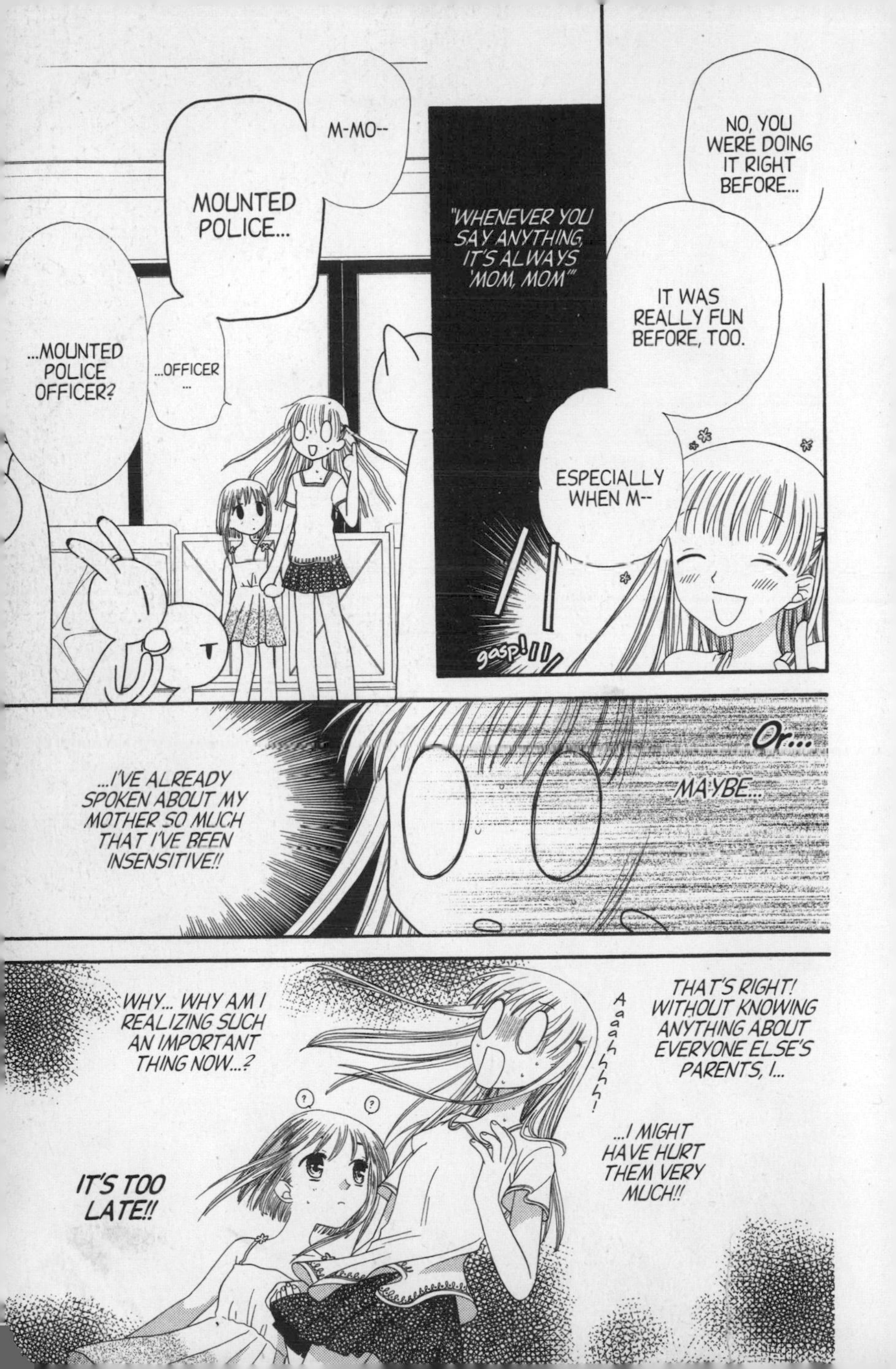

NO, YOU WERE DOING IT RIGHT BEFORE...
IT WAS REALLY FUN BEFORE, TOO.
ESPECIALLY WHEN M--
"WHENEVER YOU SAY ANYTHING, IT'S ALWAYS 'MOM, MOM'"
gasp!
M-MO--
MOUNTED POLICE...
...OFFICER ...
...MOUNTED POLICE OFFICER?
Or... MAYBE...
...I'VE ALREADY SPOKEN ABOUT MY MOTHER SO MUCH THAT I'VE BEEN INSENSITIVE!!
THAT'S RIGHT! WITHOUT KNOWING ANYTHING ABOUT EVERYONE ELSE'S PARENTS, I...
Aaaahhhh!
...I MIGHT HAVE HURT THEM VERY MUCH!!
WHY... WHY AM I REALIZING SUCH AN IMPORTANT THING NOW...?
IT'S TOO LATE!!

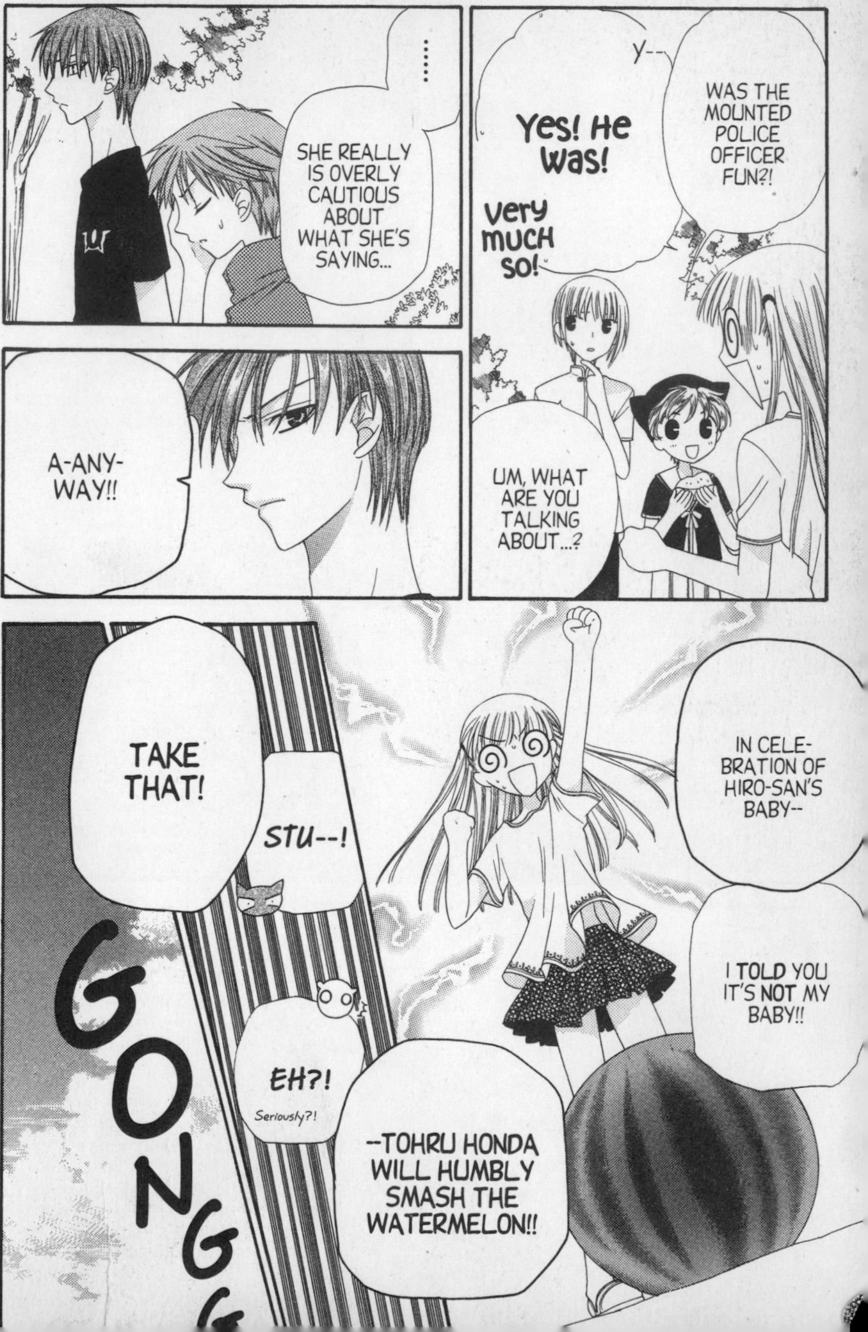
Y--
WAS THE MOUNTED POLICE OFFICER FUN?!
Yes! He was!
Very much so!
UM, WHAT ARE YOU TALKING ABOUT...?
......
SHE REALLY IS OVERLY CAUTIOUS ABOUT WHAT SHE'S SAYING...
A-ANY-WAY!!
IN CELE-BRATION OF HIRO-SAN'S BABY--
I TOLD YOU IT'S NOT MY BABY!!
--TOHRU HONDA WILL HUMBLY SMASH THE WATERMELON!!
TAKE THAT!
STU--!
EH?!
Seriously?!
GONG

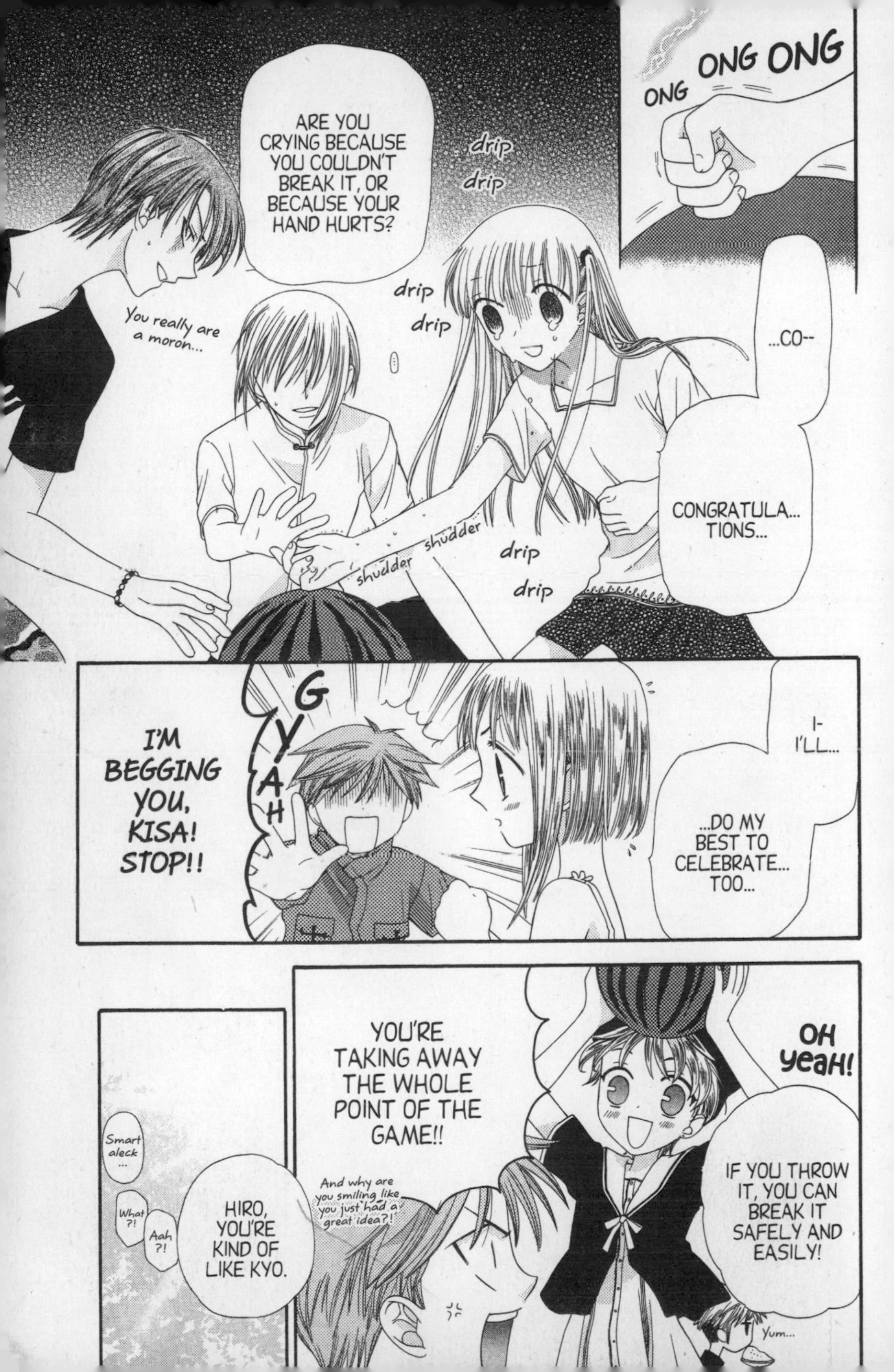

ONG ONG ONG
...CO--
CONGRATULA... TIONS...
drip drip
ARE YOU CRYING BECAUSE YOU COULDN'T BREAK IT, OR BECAUSE YOUR HAND HURTS?
drip drip
You really are a moron...
shudder shudder
drip drip
I- I'LL...
...DO MY BEST TO CELEBRATE... TOO...
GYAH
I'M BEGGING YOU, KISA! STOP!!
OH yeah!
IF YOU THROW IT, YOU CAN BREAK IT SAFELY AND EASILY!
Yum...
YOU'RE TAKING AWAY THE WHOLE POINT OF THE GAME!!
And why are you smiling like you just had a great idea?!
HIRO, YOU'RE KIND OF LIKE KYO.
Aah ?!
What ?!
Smart aleck ...

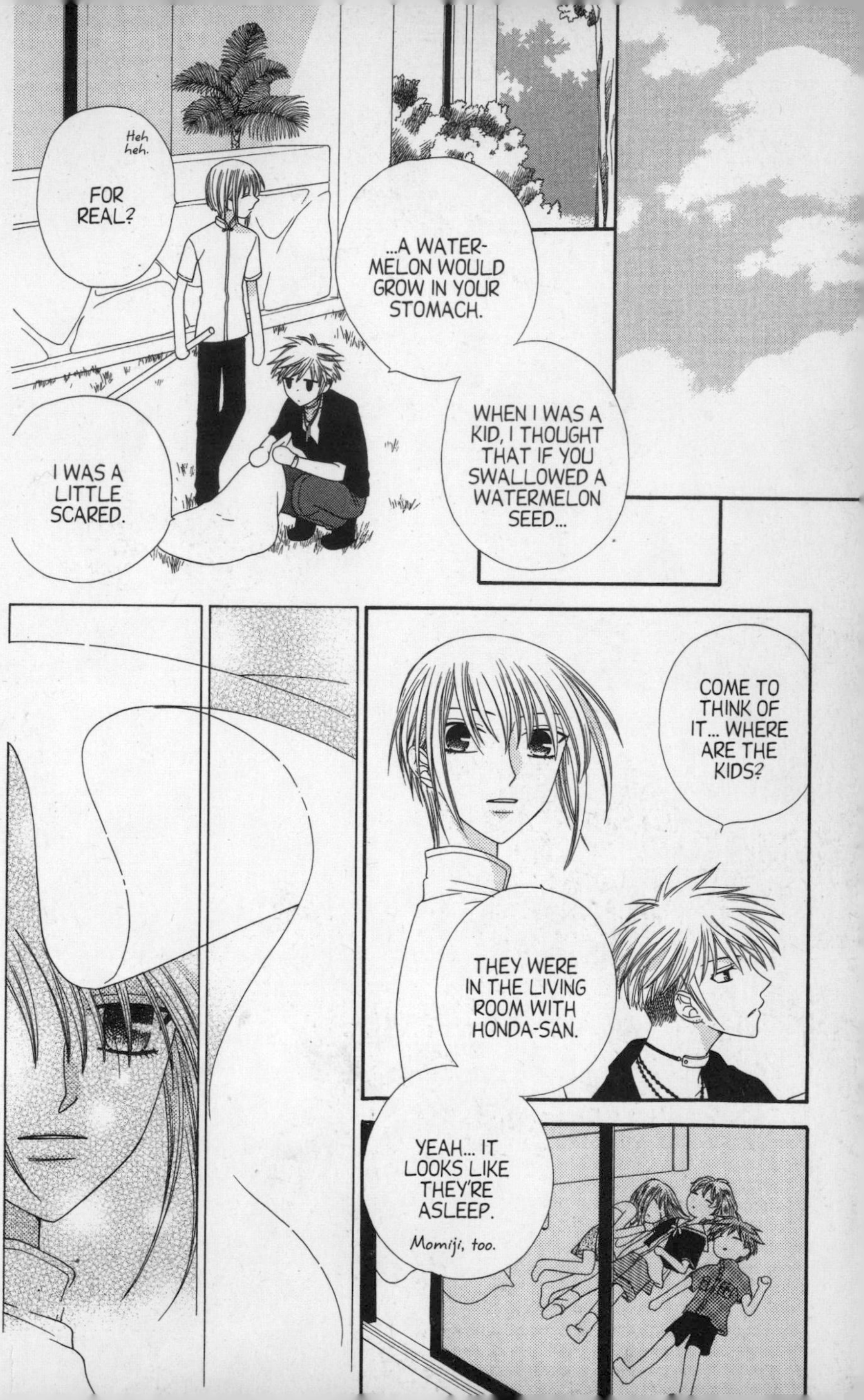
WHEN I WAS A KID, I THOUGHT THAT IF YOU SWALLOWED A WATERMELON SEED...
...A WATERMELON WOULD GROW IN YOUR STOMACH.
Heh heh.
FOR REAL?
I WAS A LITTLE SCARED.
COME TO THINK OF IT... WHERE ARE THE KIDS?
THEY WERE IN THE LIVING ROOM WITH HONDA-SAN.
YEAH... IT LOOKS LIKE THEY'RE ASLEEP.
Momiji, too.

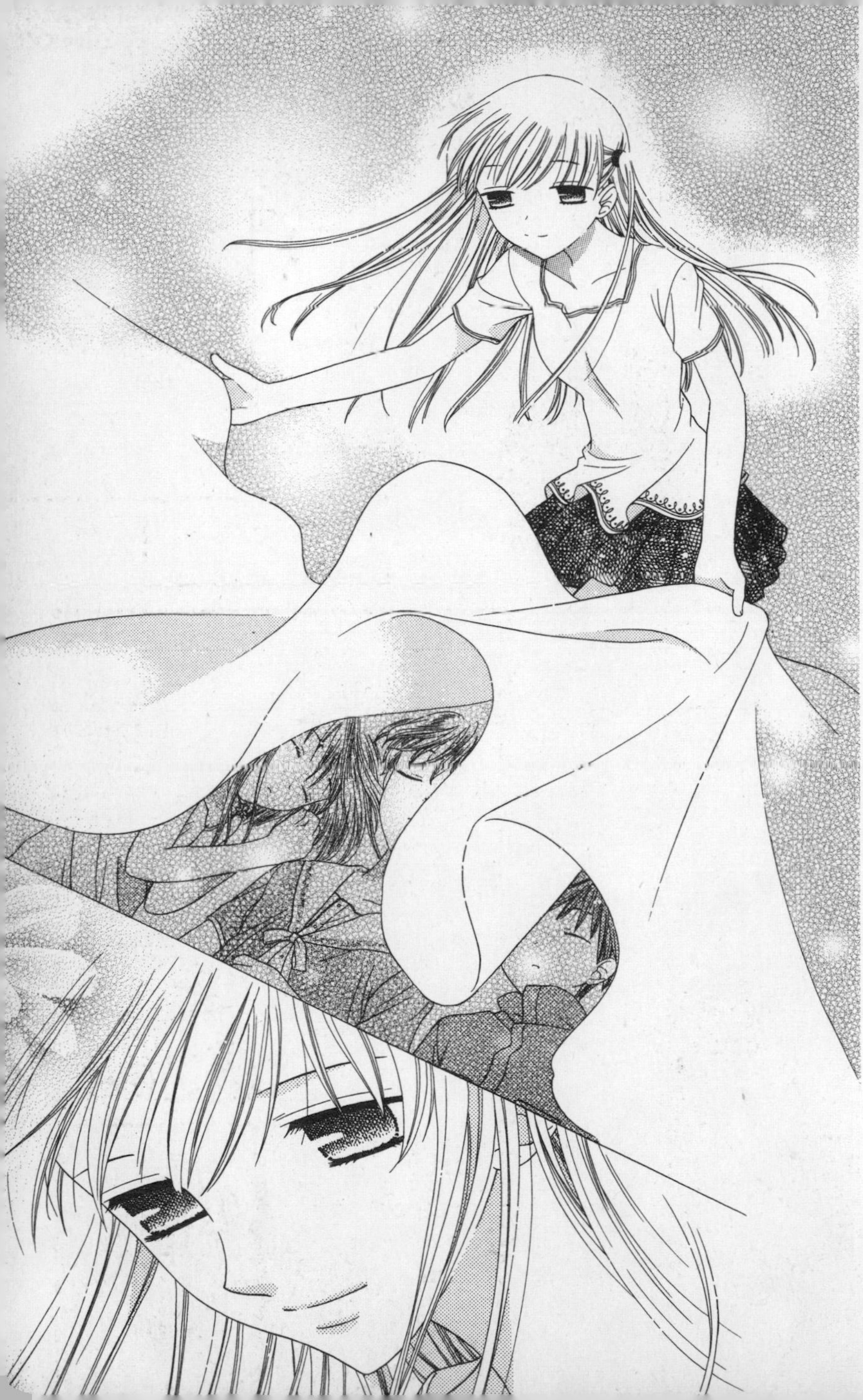

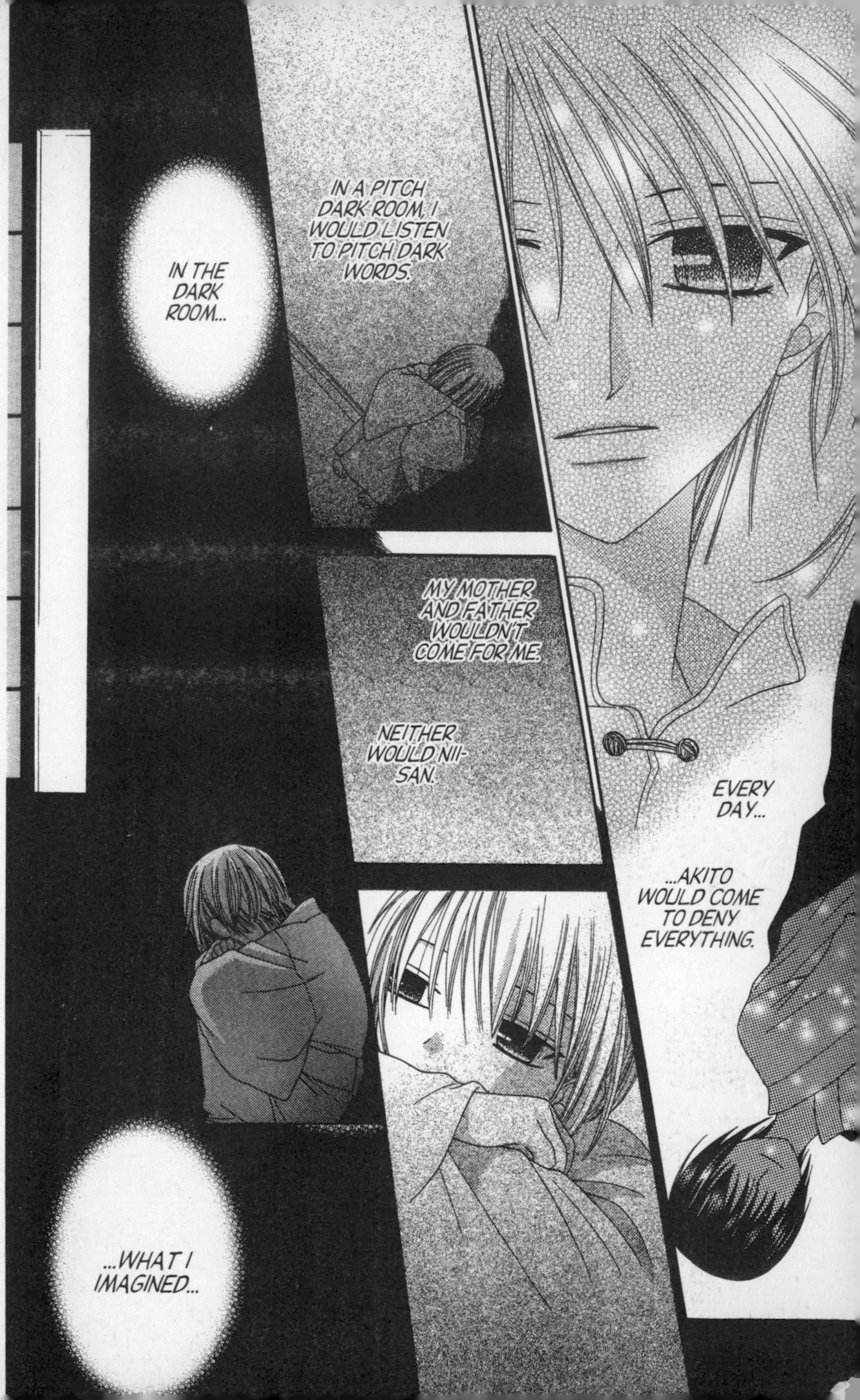
IN A PITCH DARK ROOM, I WOULD LISTEN TO PITCH DARK WORDS.
MY MOTHER AND FATHER WOULDN'T COME FOR ME.
NEITHER WOULD NII-SAN.
EVERY DAY...
...AKITO WOULD COME TO DENY EVERYTHING.
IN THE DARK ROOM...
...WHAT I IMAGINED...

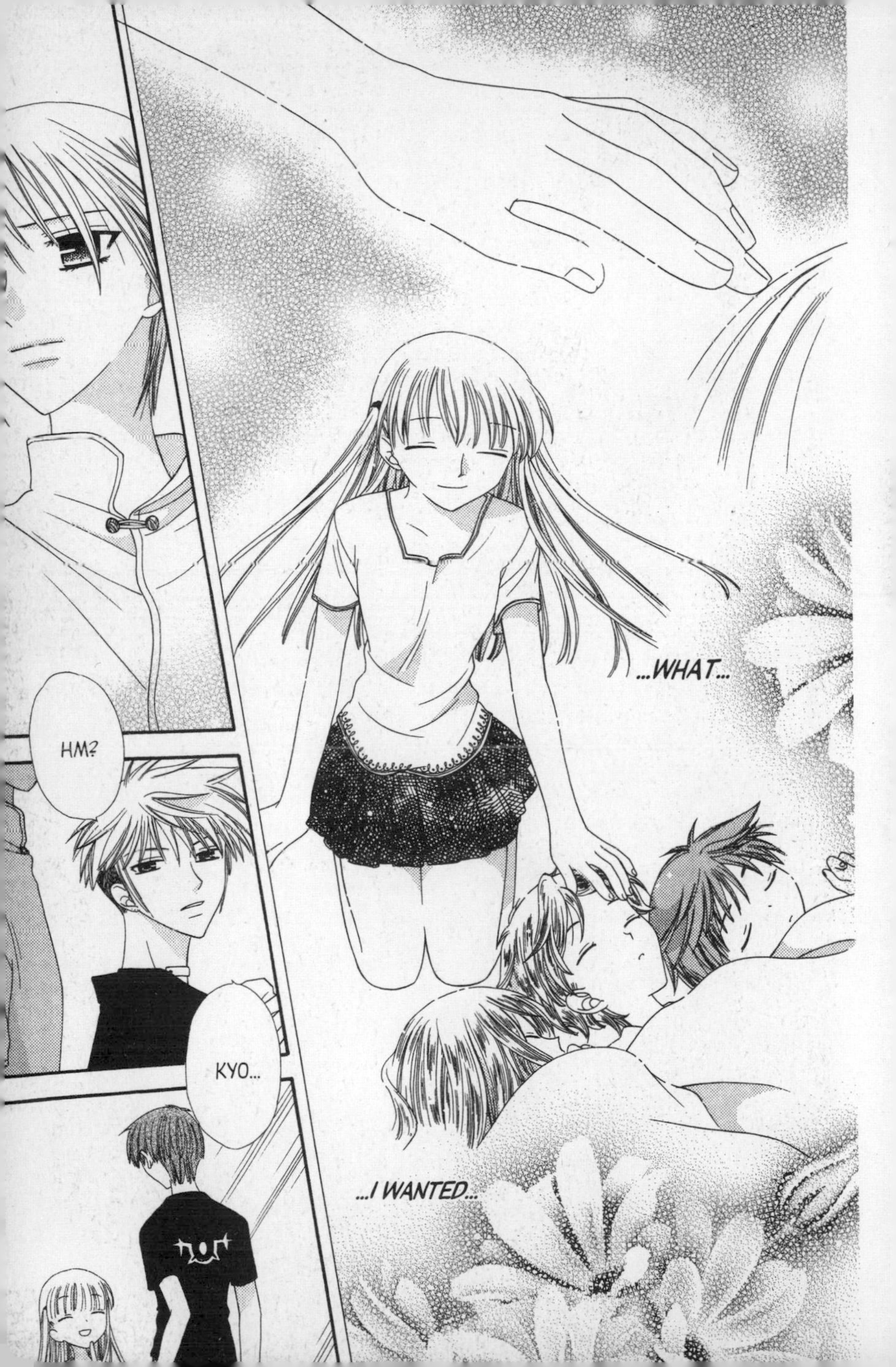
...WHAT...
...I WANTED...
HM?
KYO...

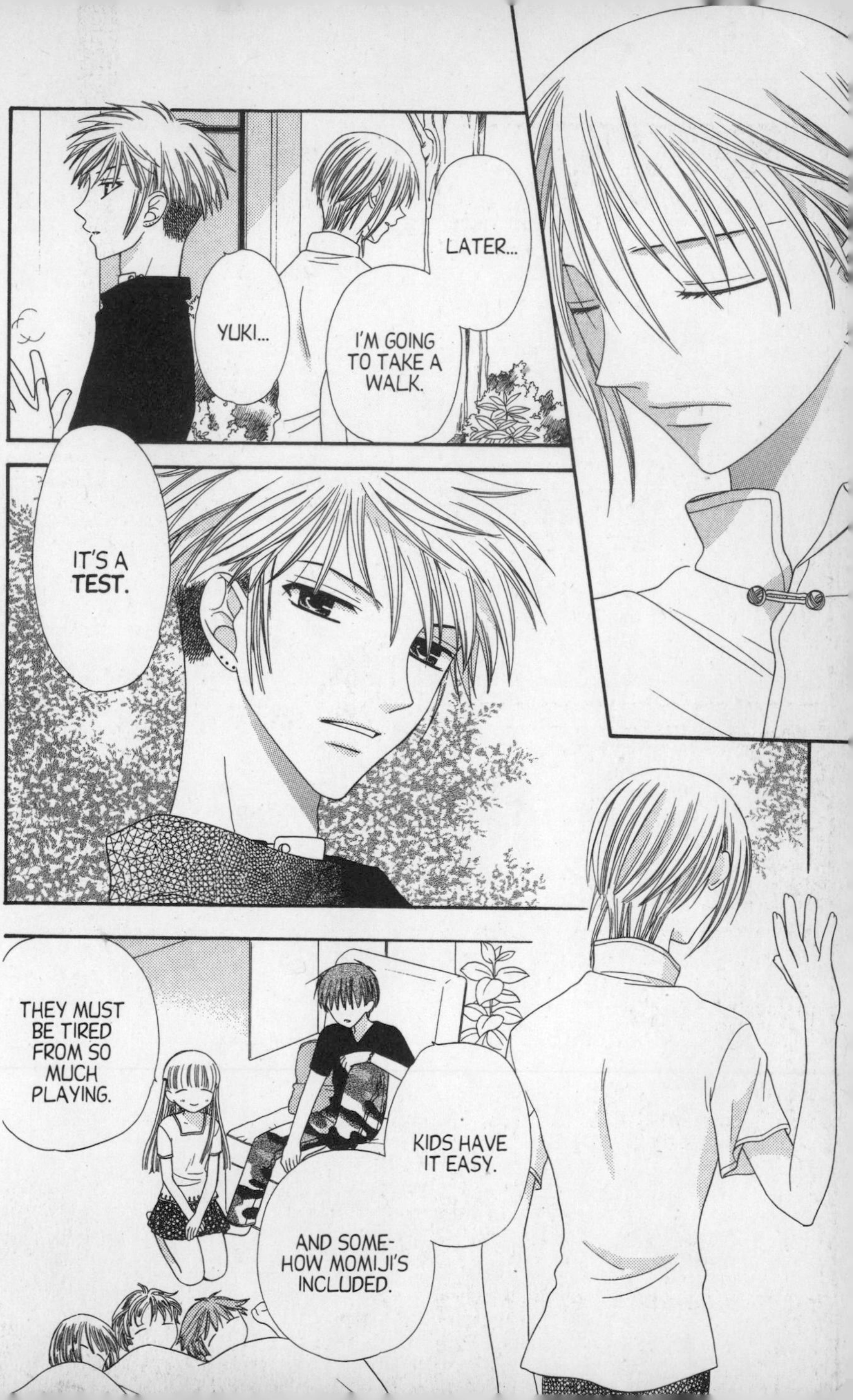
LATER...
I'M GOING TO TAKE A WALK.
YUKI...
IT'S A TEST.
KIDS HAVE IT EASY.
THEY MUST BE TIRED FROM SO MUCH PLAYING.
AND SOME-HOW MOMIJI'S INCLUDED.

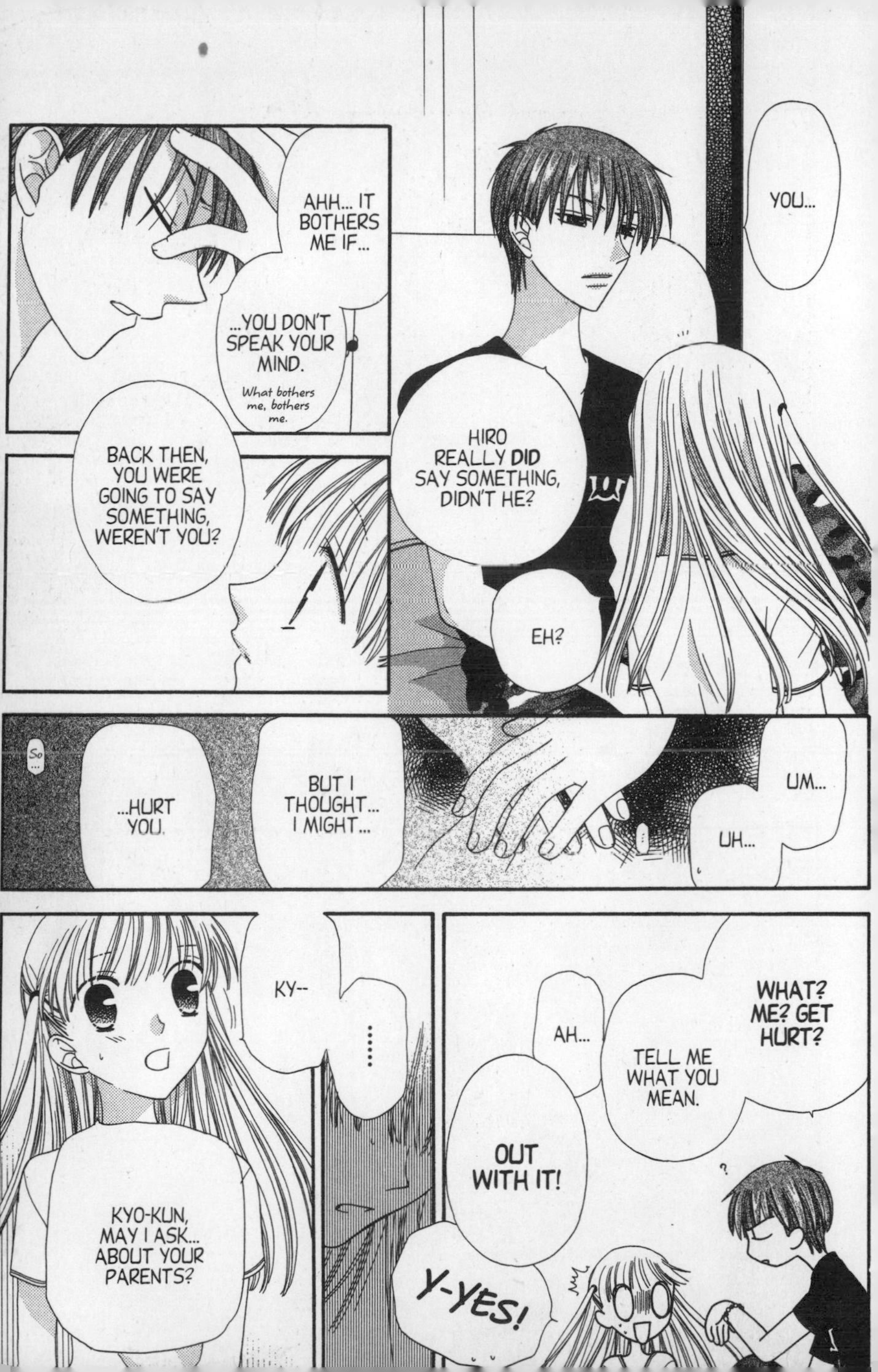
YOU...
HIRO REALLY DID SAY SOMETHING, DIDN'T HE?
EH?
AHH... IT BOTHERS ME IF...
...YOU DON'T SPEAK YOUR MIND.
What bothers me, bothers me.
BACK THEN, YOU WERE GOING TO SAY SOMETHING, WEREN'T YOU?
UM...
UH...
BUT I THOUGHT... I MIGHT...
...HURT YOU.
So ...
WHAT? ME? GET HURT?
TELL ME WHAT YOU MEAN.
AH...
OUT WITH IT!
Y-YES!
KY--
......
KYO-KUN, MAY I ASK... ABOUT YOUR PARENTS?

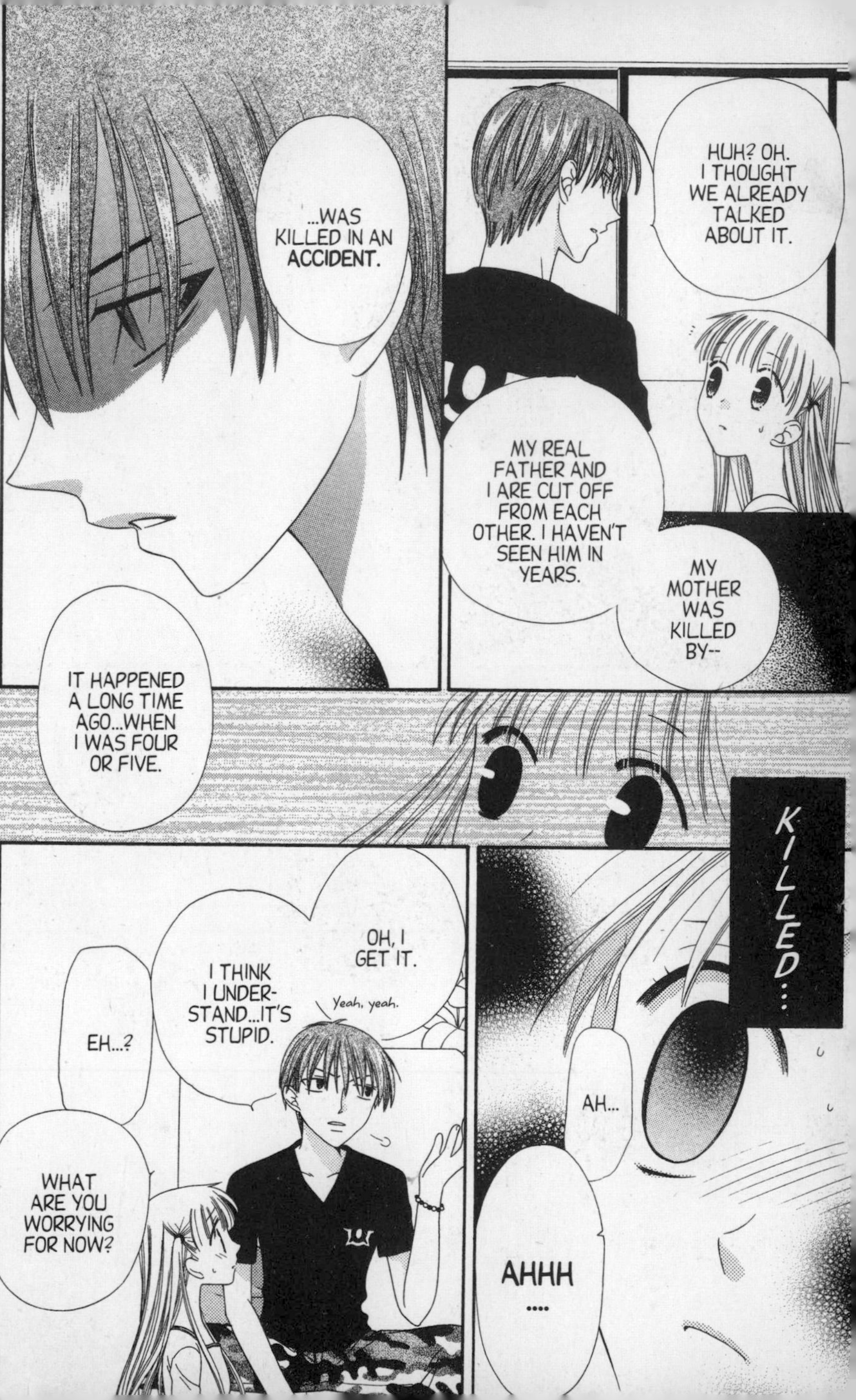
HUH? OH. I THOUGHT WE ALREADY TALKED ABOUT IT.
MY REAL FATHER AND I ARE CUT OFF FROM EACH OTHER. I HAVEN'T SEEN HIM IN YEARS.
MY MOTHER WAS KILLED BY--
...WAS KILLED IN AN ACCIDENT.
IT HAPPENED A LONG TIME AGO...WHEN I WAS FOUR OR FIVE.
KILLED...
AH...
AHHH ....
OH, I GET IT.
I THINK I UNDER-STAND...IT'S STUPID.
Yeah, yeah.
EH...?
WHAT ARE YOU WORRYING FOR NOW?

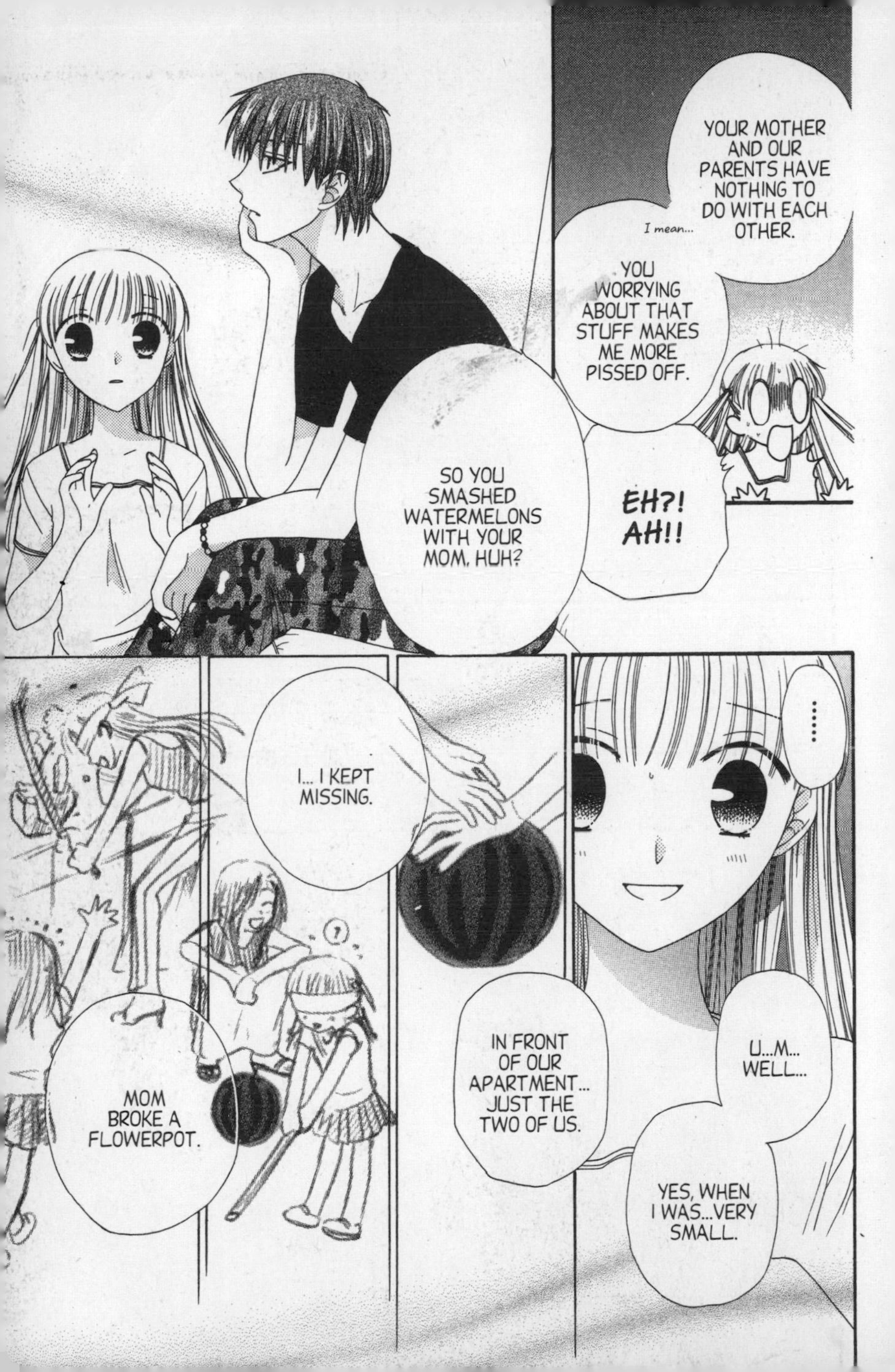

YOUR MOTHER AND OUR PARENTS HAVE NOTHING TO DO WITH EACH OTHER.
I mean...
YOU WORRYING ABOUT THAT STUFF MAKES ME MORE PISSED OFF.
EH?! AH!!
SO YOU SMASHED WATERMELONS WITH YOUR MOM, HUH?
......
U...M... WELL...
YES, WHEN I WAS...VERY SMALL.
IN FRONT OF OUR APARTMENT... JUST THE TWO OF US.
I... I KEPT MISSING.
MOM BROKE A FLOWERPOT.

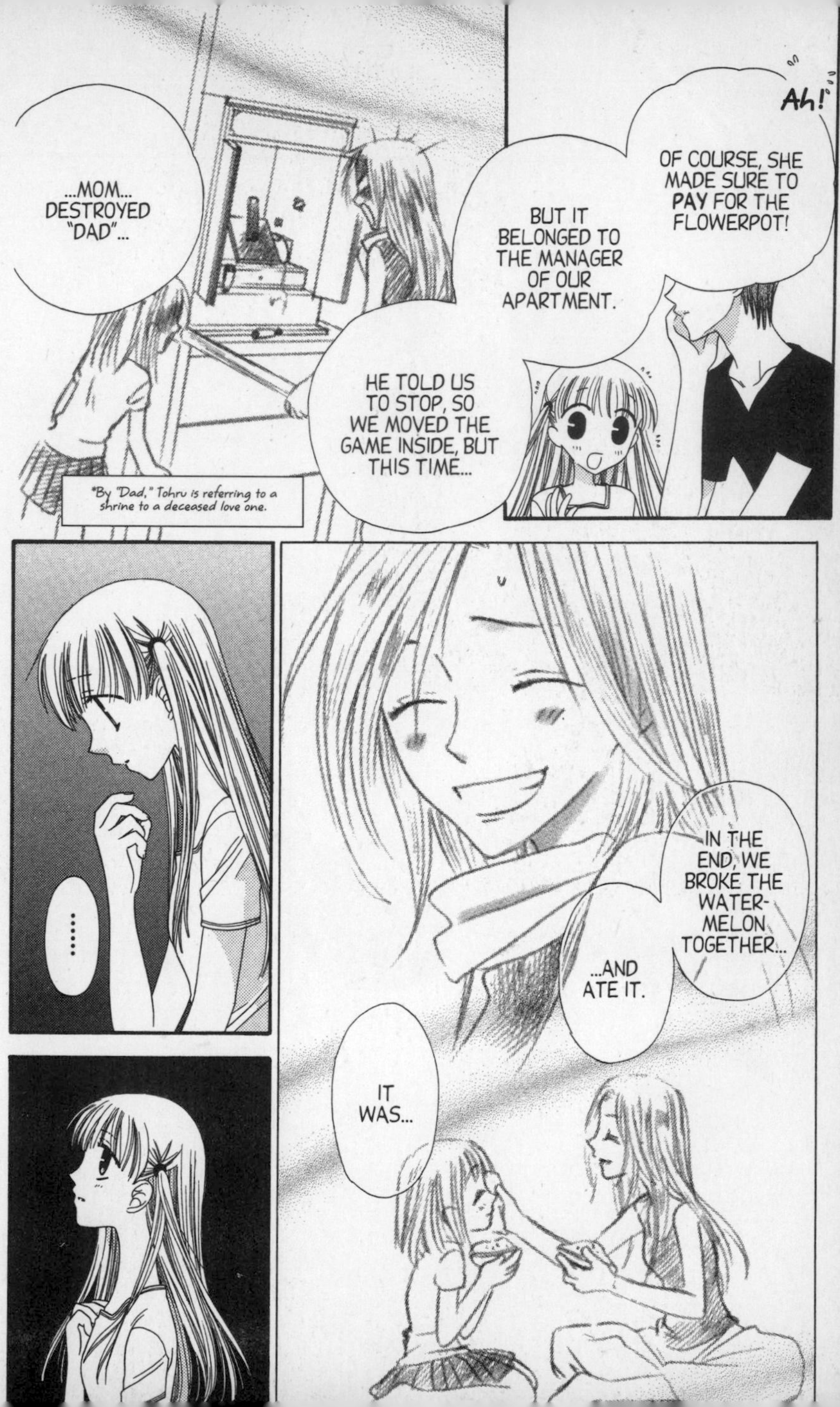
Ah!
OF COURSE, SHE MADE SURE TO PAY FOR THE FLOWERPOT!
BUT IT BELONGED TO THE MANAGER OF OUR APARTMENT.
HE TOLD US TO STOP, SO WE MOVED THE GAME INSIDE, BUT THIS TIME...
...MOM... DESTROYED "DAD"...
*By "Dad," Tohru is referring to a shrine to a deceased love one.
IN THE END, WE BROKE THE WATER-MELON TOGETHER...
...AND ATE IT.
IT WAS...
......

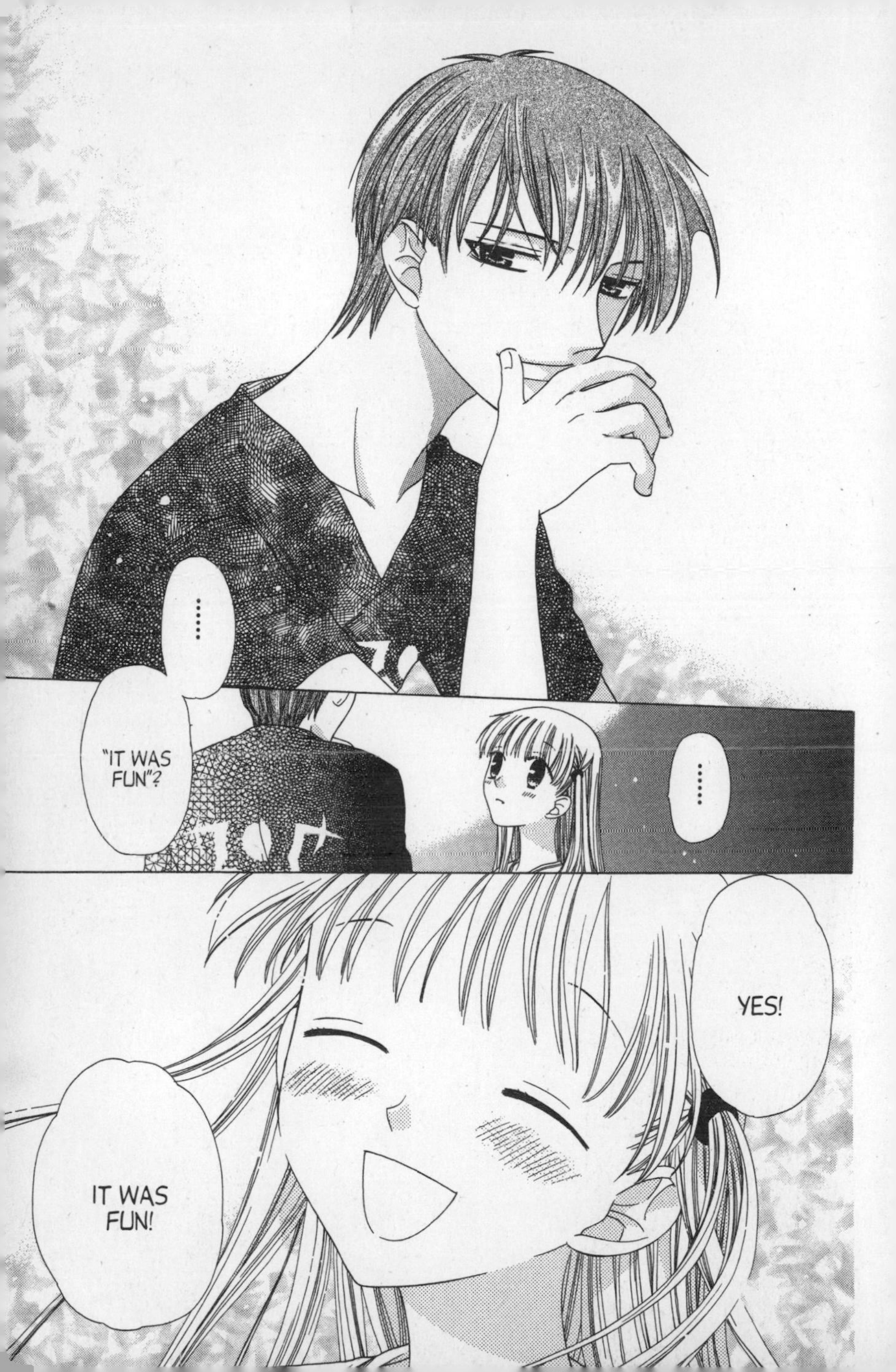
......
......
"IT WAS FUN"?
YES!
IT WAS FUN!

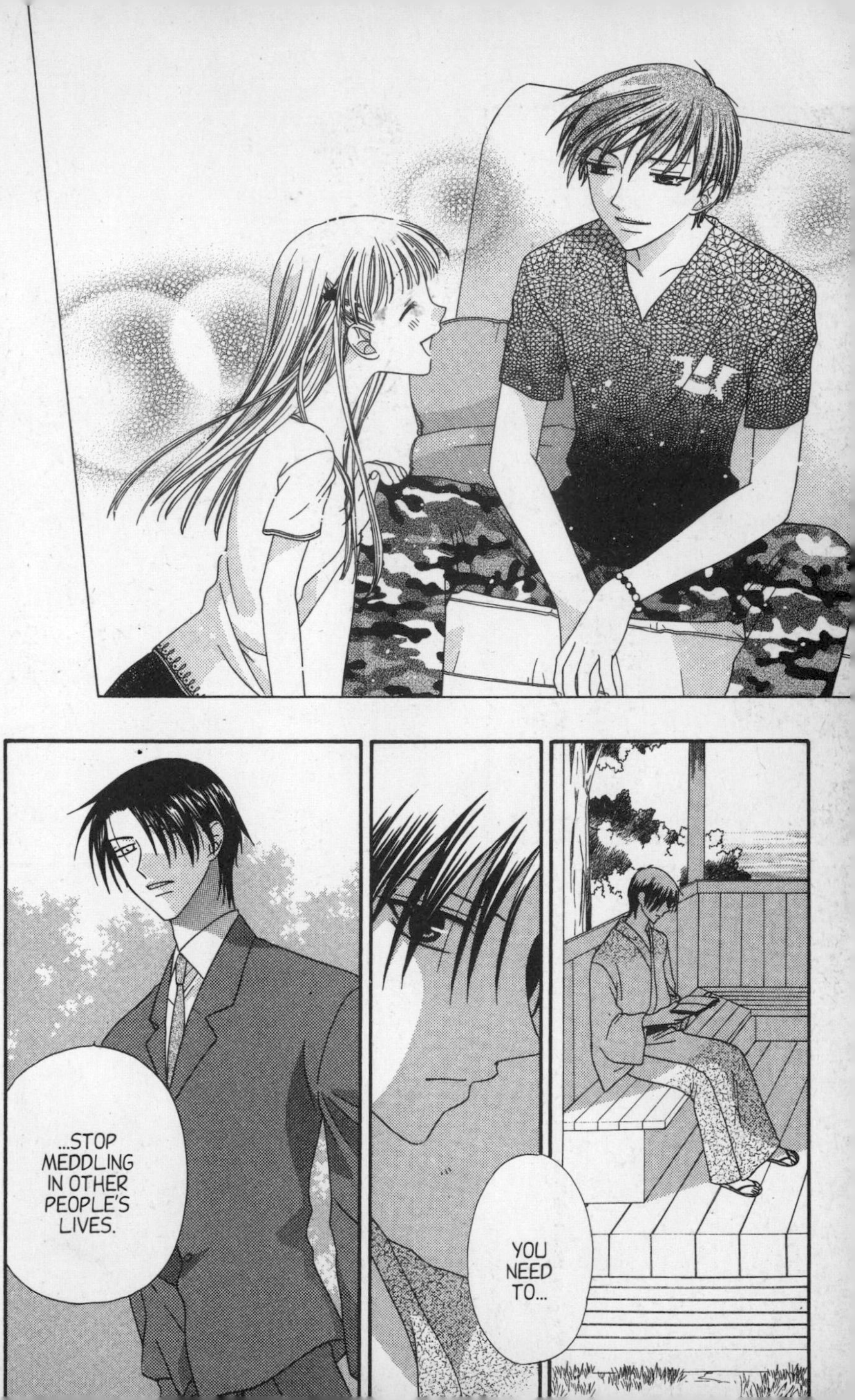
YOU NEED TO...
...STOP MEDDLING IN OTHER PEOPLE'S LIVES.

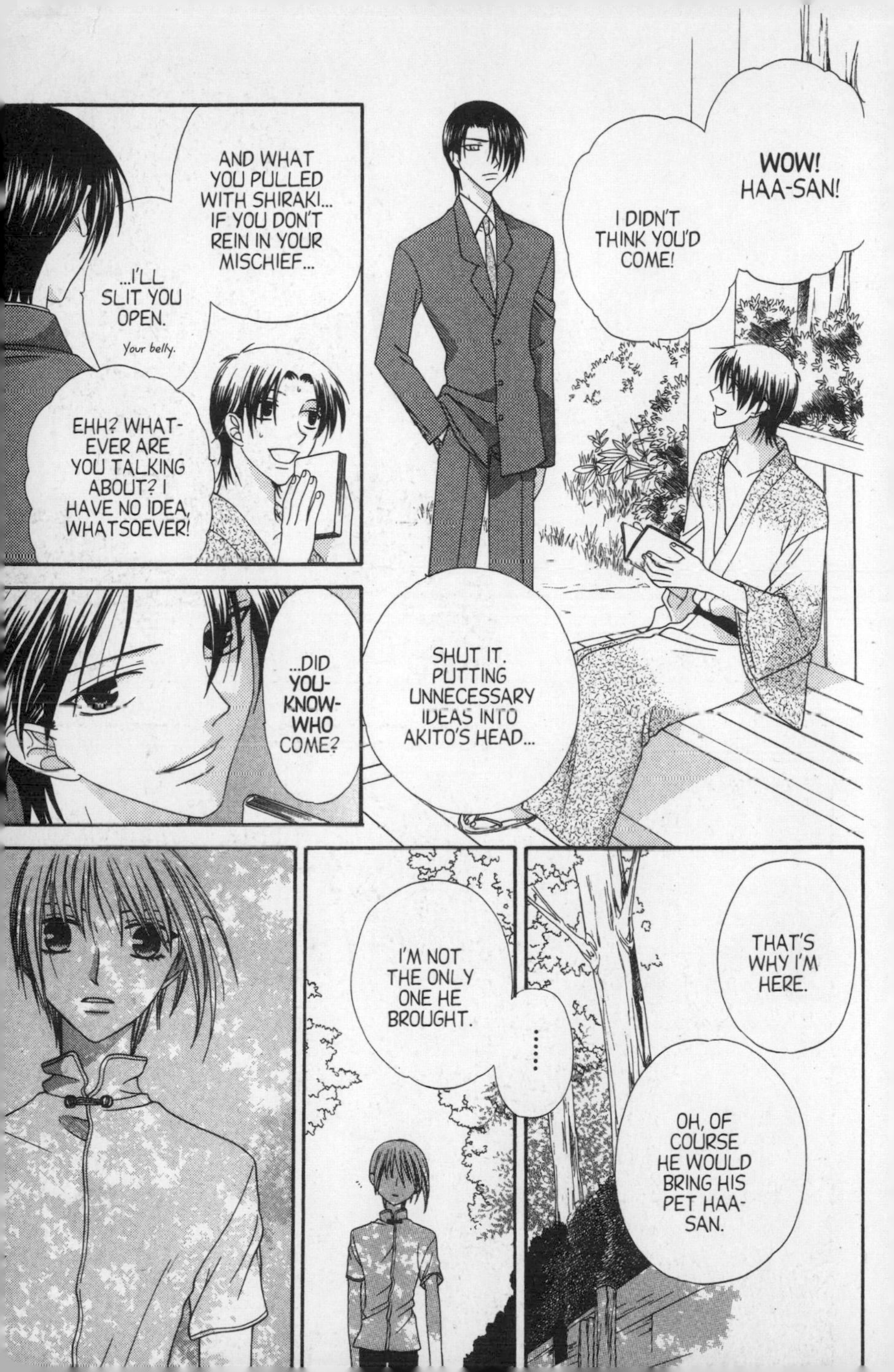
WOW! HAA-SAN!
I DIDN'T THINK YOU'D COME!
AND WHAT YOU PULLED WITH SHIRAKI... IF YOU DON'T REIN IN YOUR MISCHIEF...
...I'LL SLIT YOU OPEN.
Your belly.
EHH? WHATEVER ARE YOU TALKING ABOUT? I HAVE NO IDEA, WHATSOEVER!
SHUT IT. PUTTING UNNECESSARY IDEAS INTO AKITO'S HEAD...
...DID YOU-KNOW-WHO COME?
THAT'S WHY I'M HERE.
OH, OF COURSE HE WOULD BRING HIS PET HAA-SAN.
I'M NOT THE ONLY ONE HE BROUGHT.
......

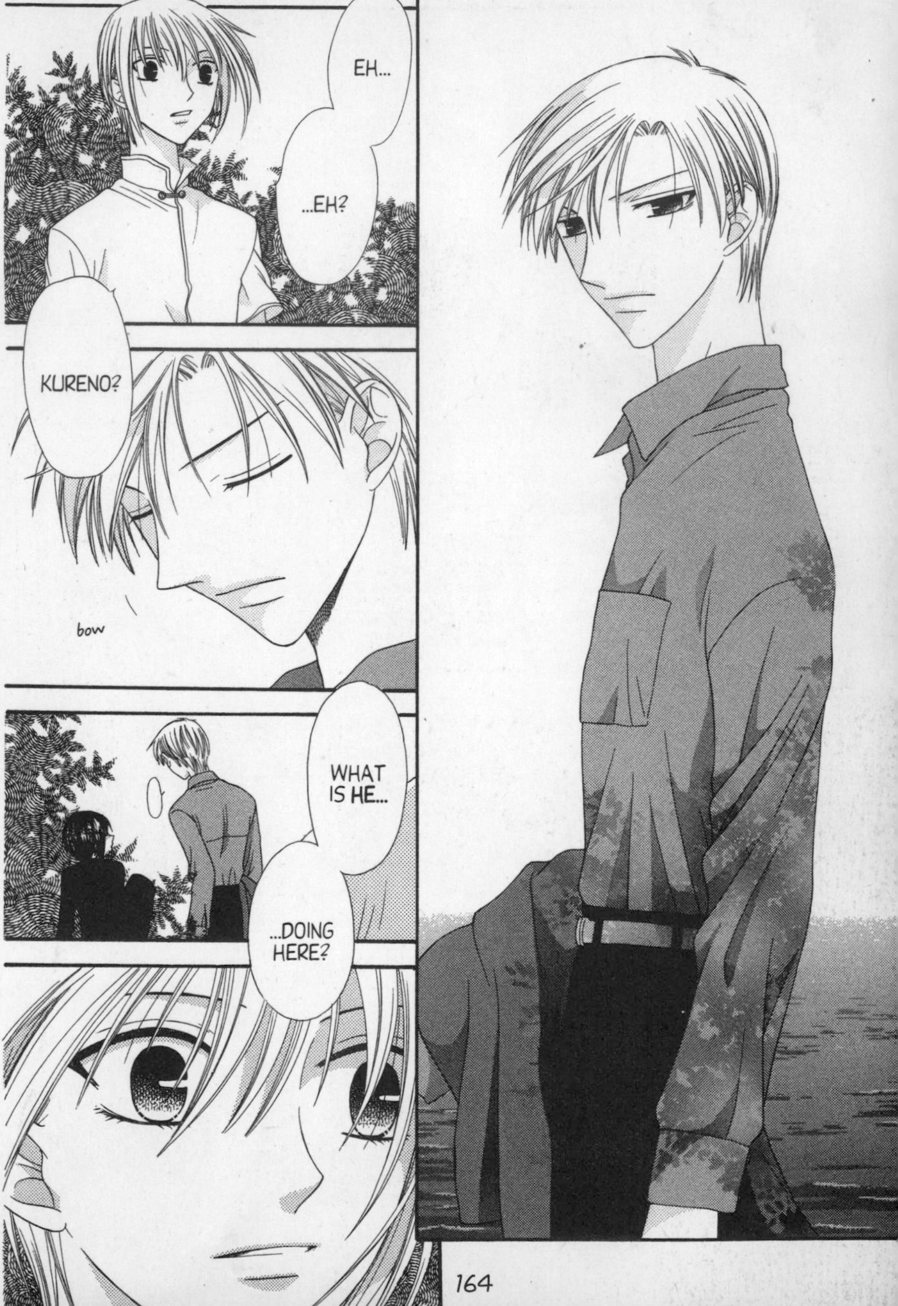
EH...
...EH?
KURENO?
bow
...
WHAT IS HE...
...DOING HERE?

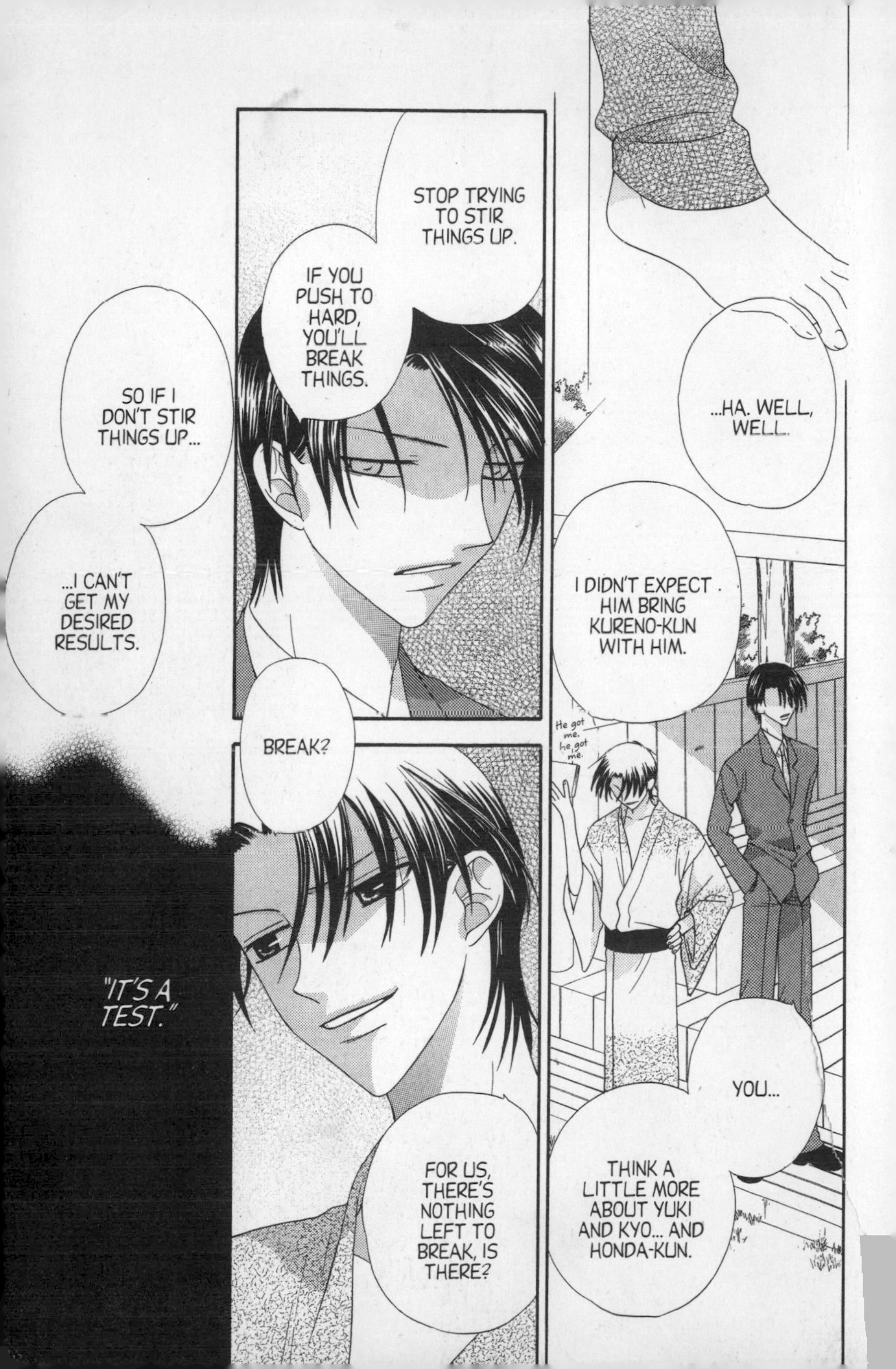
...HA. WELL, WELL.
I DIDN'T EXPECT HIM BRING KURENO-KUN WITH HIM.
He got me, he got me.
YOU...
THINK A LITTLE MORE ABOUT YUKI AND KYO... AND HONDA-KUN.
STOP TRYING TO STIR THINGS UP.
IF YOU PUSH TO HARD, YOU'LL BREAK THINGS.
SO IF I DON'T STIR THINGS UP...
...I CAN'T GET MY DESIRED RESULTS.
BREAK?
FOR US, THERE'S NOTHING LEFT TO BREAK, IS THERE?
"IT'S A TEST."

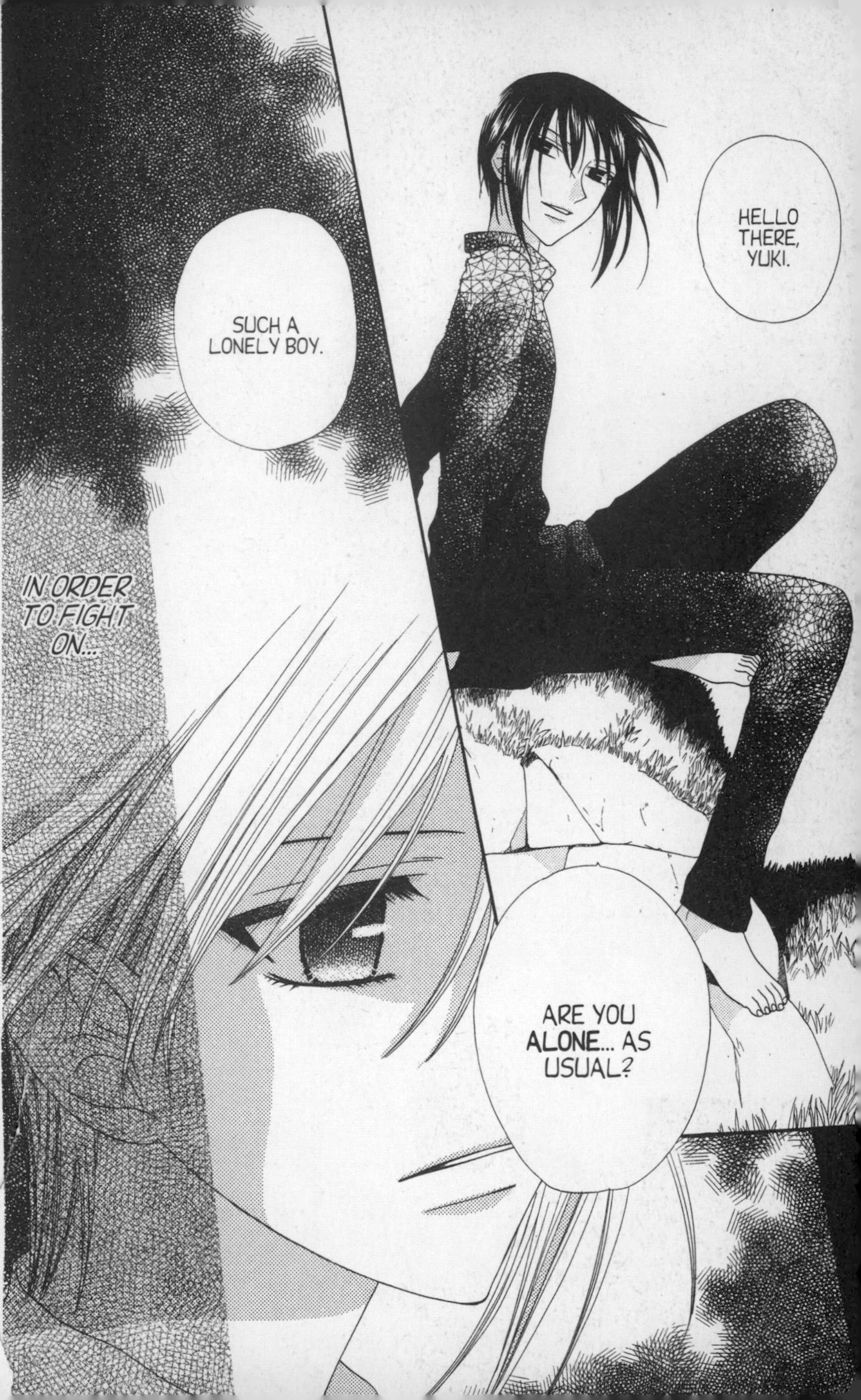
HELLO THERE, YUKI.
SUCH A LONELY BOY.
ARE YOU ALONE... AS USUAL?
IN ORDER TO FIGHT ON...

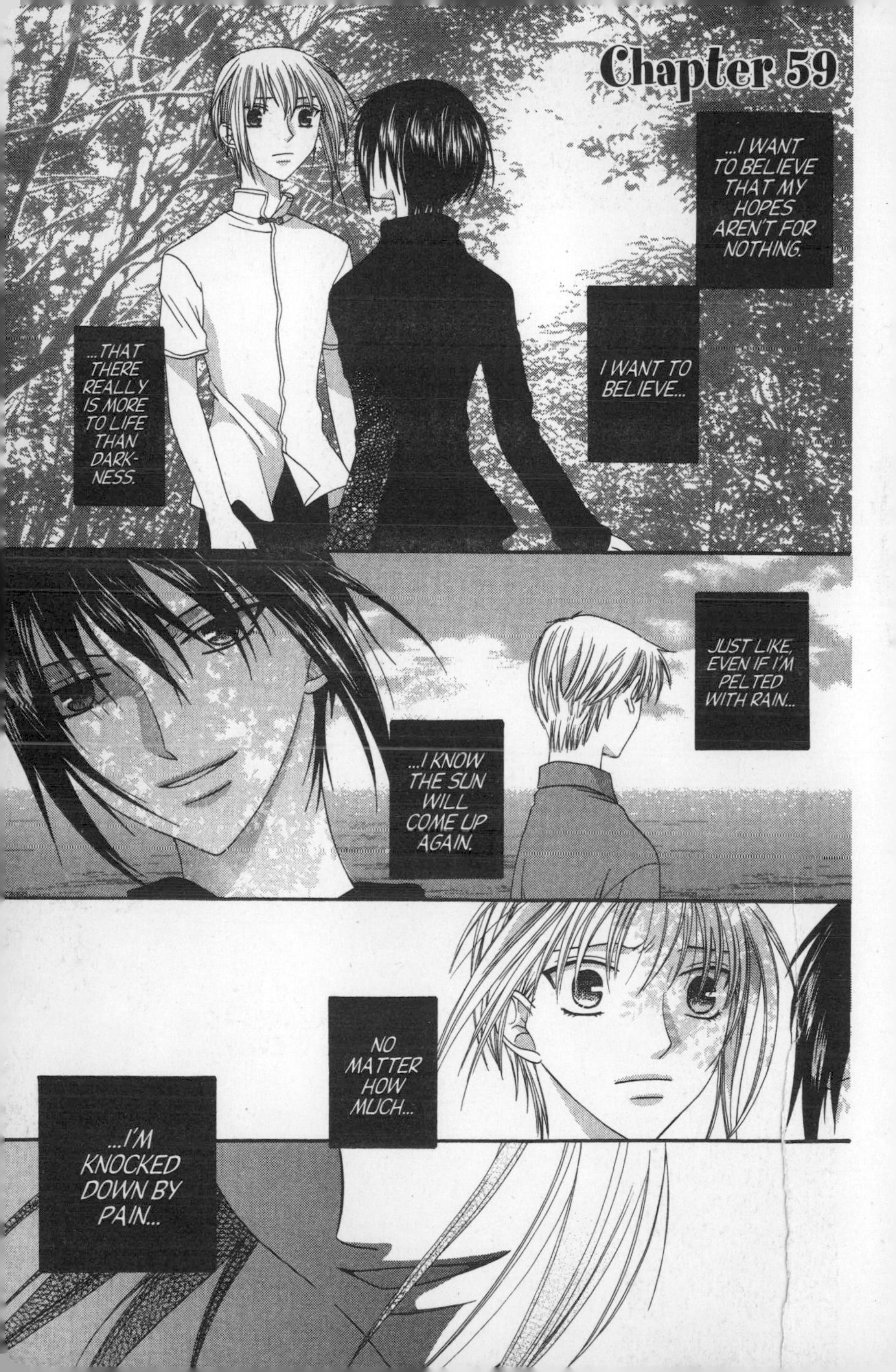
Chapter 59
...I WANT TO BELIEVE THAT MY HOPES AREN'T FOR NOTHING.
I WANT TO BELIEVE...
...THAT THERE REALLY IS MORE TO LIFE THAN DARK-NESS.
JUST LIKE, EVEN IF I'M PELTED WITH RAIN...
...I KNOW THE SUN WILL COME UP AGAIN.
NO MATTER HOW MUCH...
...I'M KNOCKED DOWN BY PAIN...

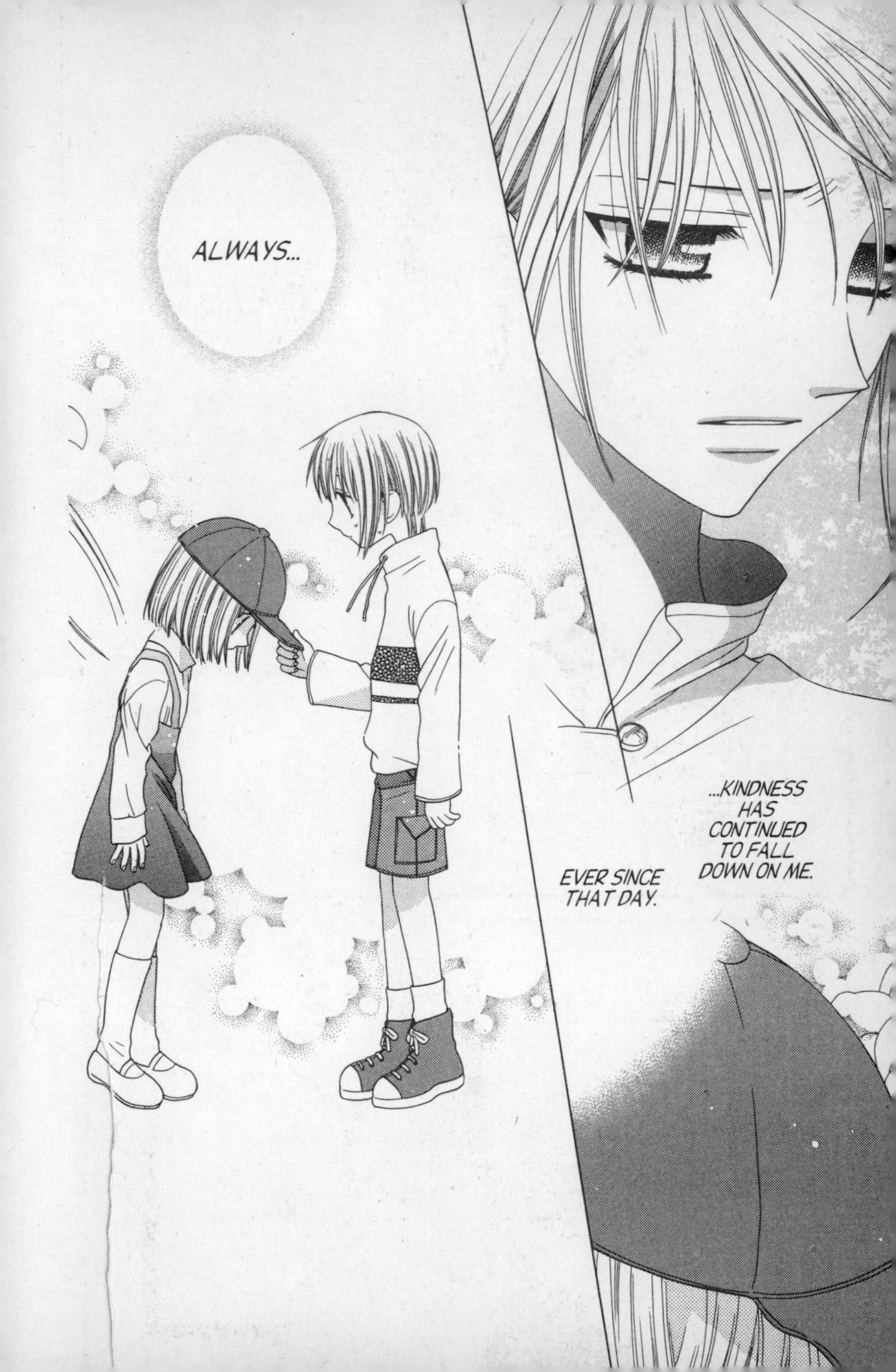
ALWAYS...
...KINDNESS HAS CONTINUED TO FALL DOWN ON ME.
EVER SINCE THAT DAY.

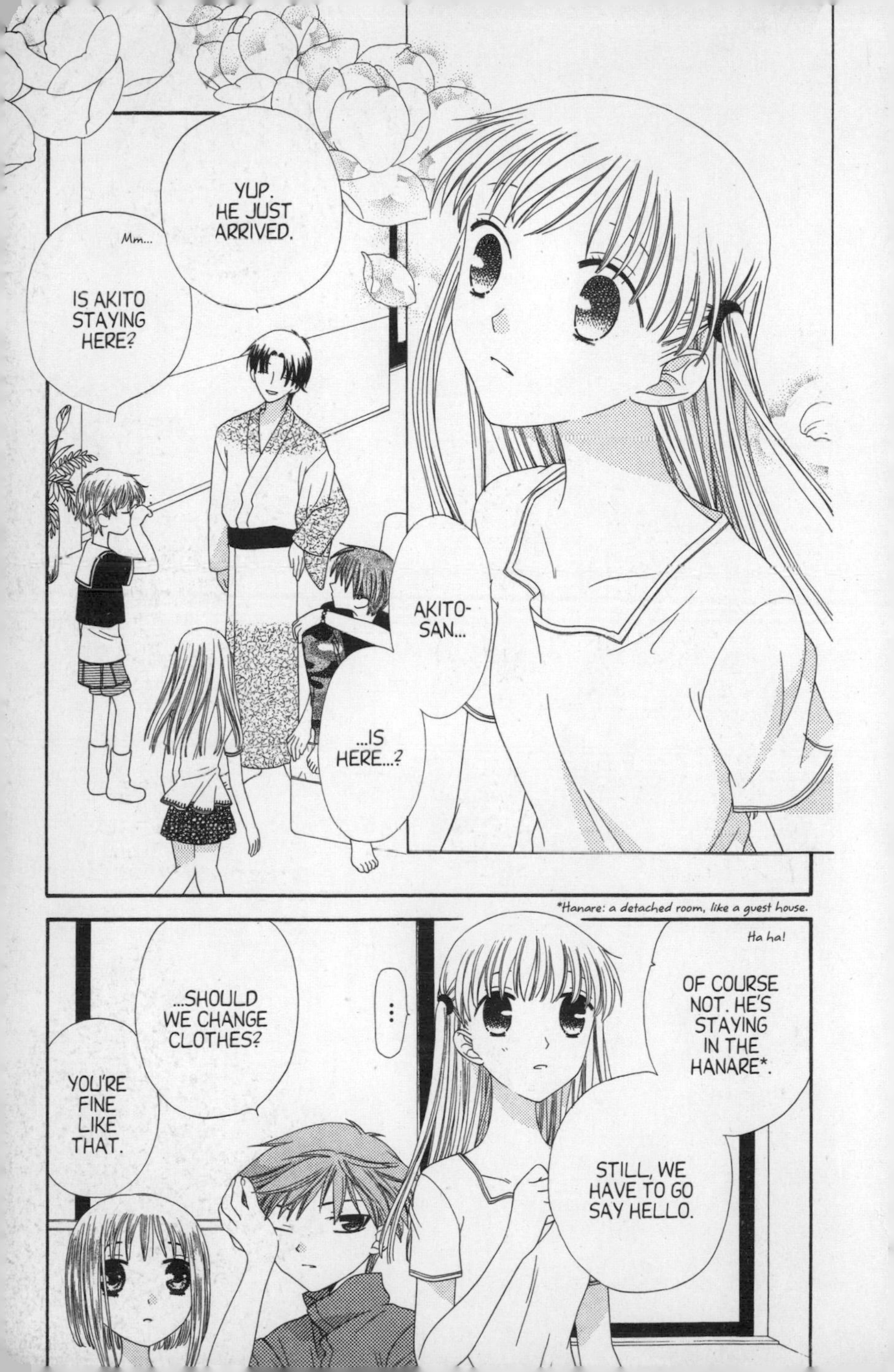
AKITO-SAN...
...IS HERE...?
YUP. HE JUST ARRIVED.
Mm...
IS AKITO STAYING HERE?
Ha ha!
OF COURSE NOT. HE'S STAYING IN THE HANARE*.
STILL, WE HAVE TO GO SAY HELLO.
...
...SHOULD WE CHANGE CLOTHES?
YOU'RE FINE LIKE THAT.

*Hanare: a detached room, like a guest house.

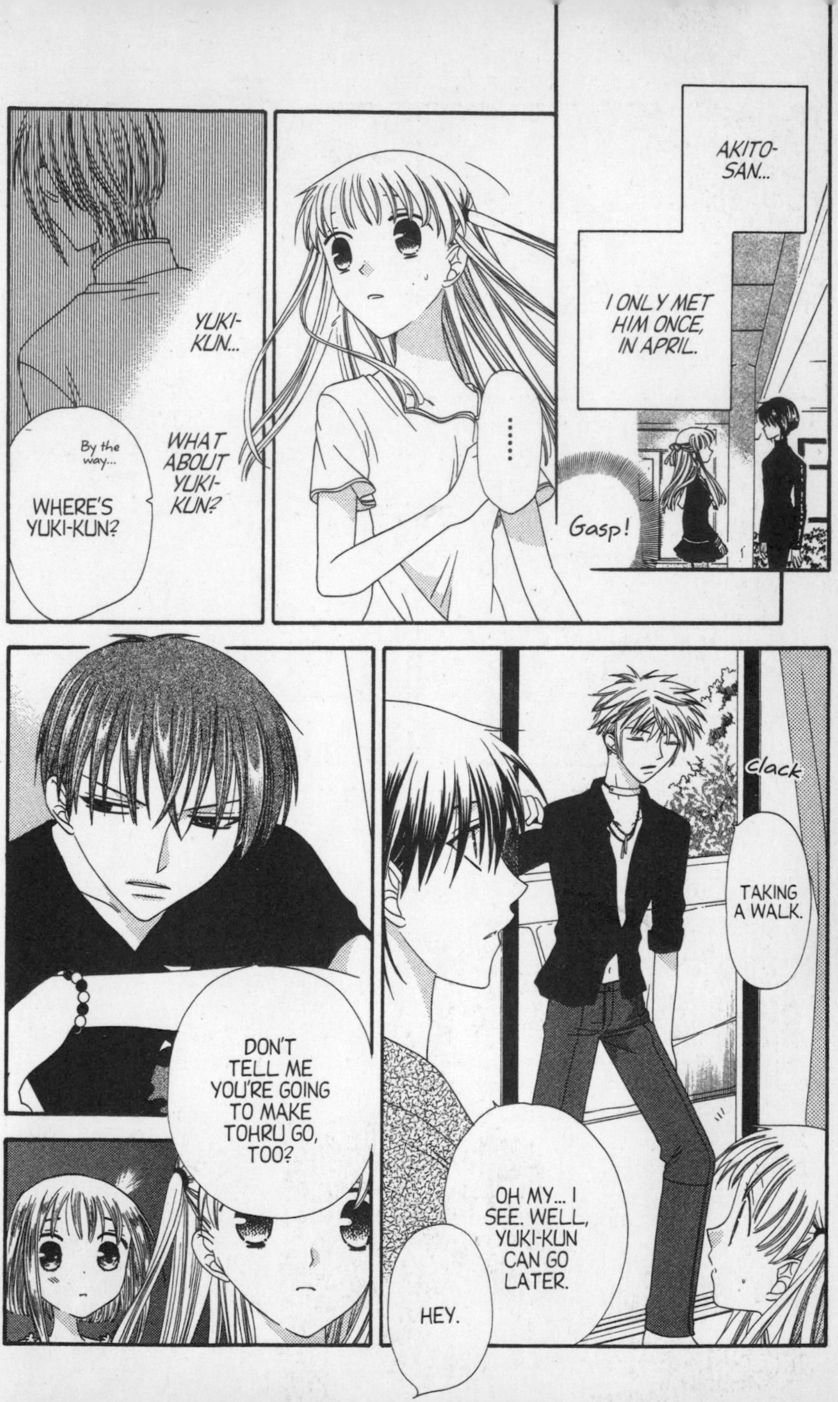
AKITO-SAN...
I ONLY MET HIM ONCE, IN APRIL.
Gasp!
......
YUKI-KUN...
WHAT ABOUT YUKI-KUN?
By the way...
WHERE'S YUKI-KUN?
Clack
TAKING A WALK.
OH MY... I SEE. WELL, YUKI-KUN CAN GO LATER.
HEY.
DON'T TELL ME YOU'RE GOING TO MAKE TOHRU GO, TOO?

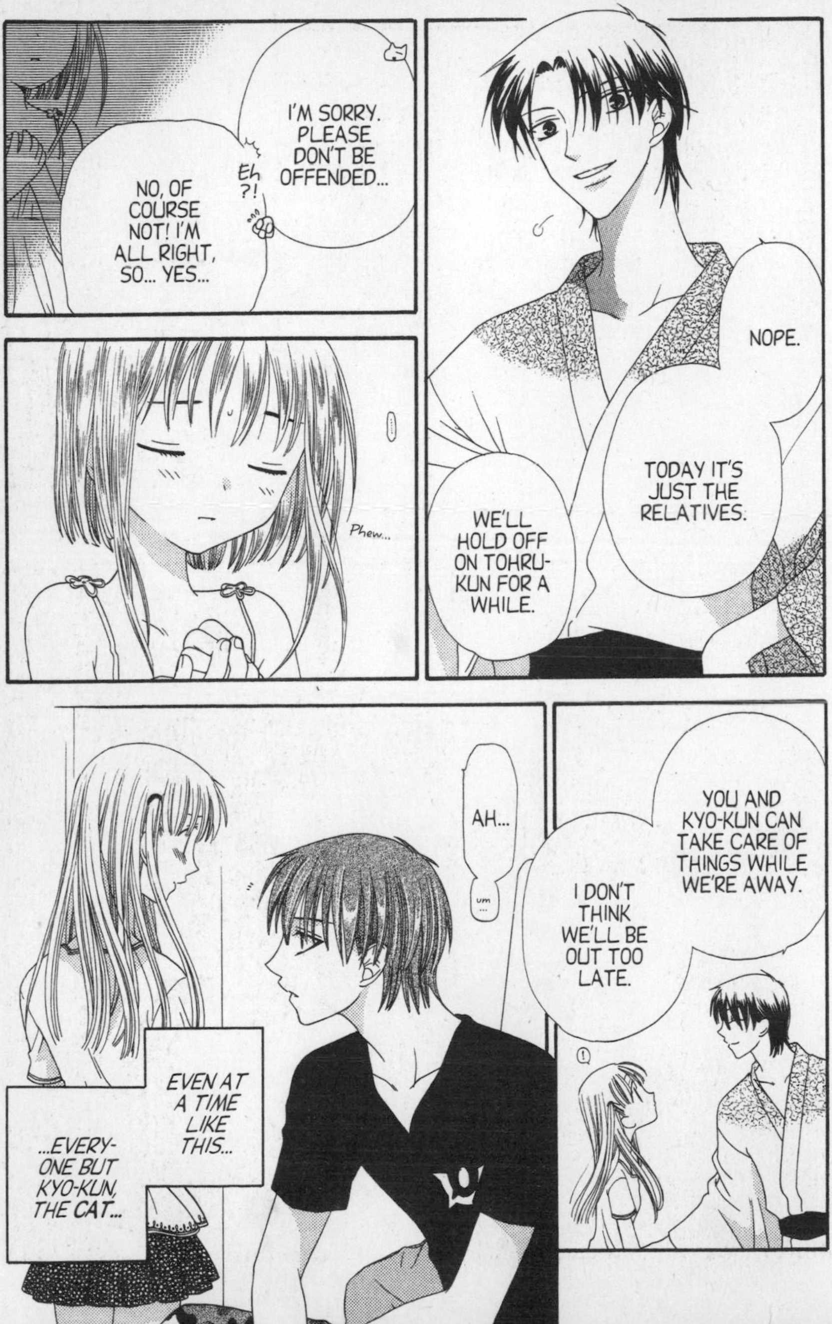
NOPE.
TODAY IT'S JUST THE RELATIVES.
WE'LL HOLD OFF ON TOHRU-KUN FOR A WHILE.
I'M SORRY. PLEASE DON'T BE OFFENDED...
Eh?!
NO, OF COURSE NOT! I'M ALL RIGHT, SO... YES...
Phew...
YOU AND KYO-KUN CAN TAKE CARE OF THINGS WHILE WE'RE AWAY.
I DON'T THINK WE'LL BE OUT TOO LATE.
AH...
um...
EVEN AT A TIME LIKE THIS...
...EVERY-ONE BUT KYO-KUN, THE CAT...

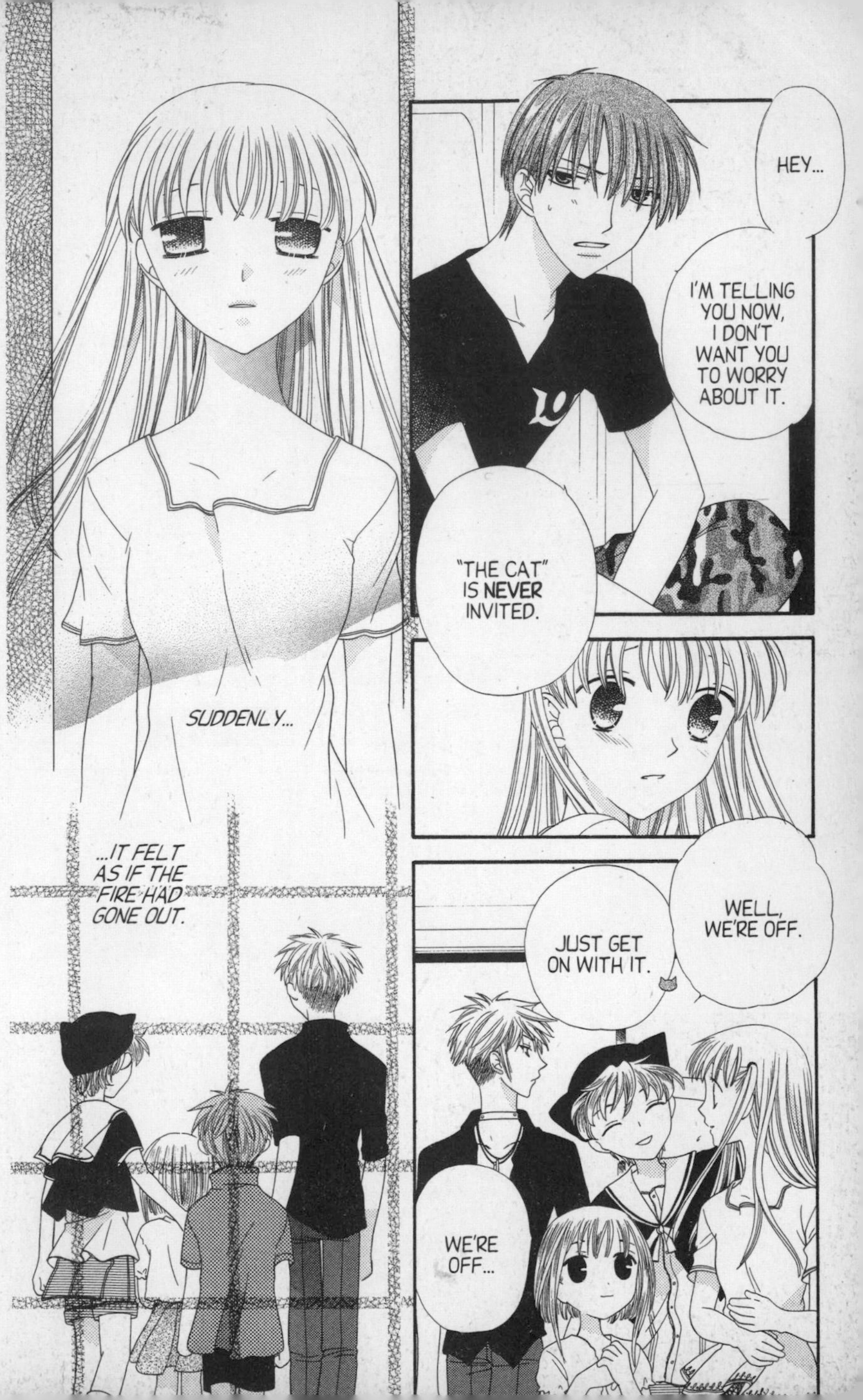
HEY...
I'M TELLING YOU NOW, I DON'T WANT YOU TO WORRY ABOUT IT.
"THE CAT" IS **NEVER** INVITED.
SUDDENLY...
WELL, WE'RE OFF.
JUST GET ON WITH IT.
WE'RE OFF...
...IT FELT AS IF THE FIRE HAD GONE OUT.

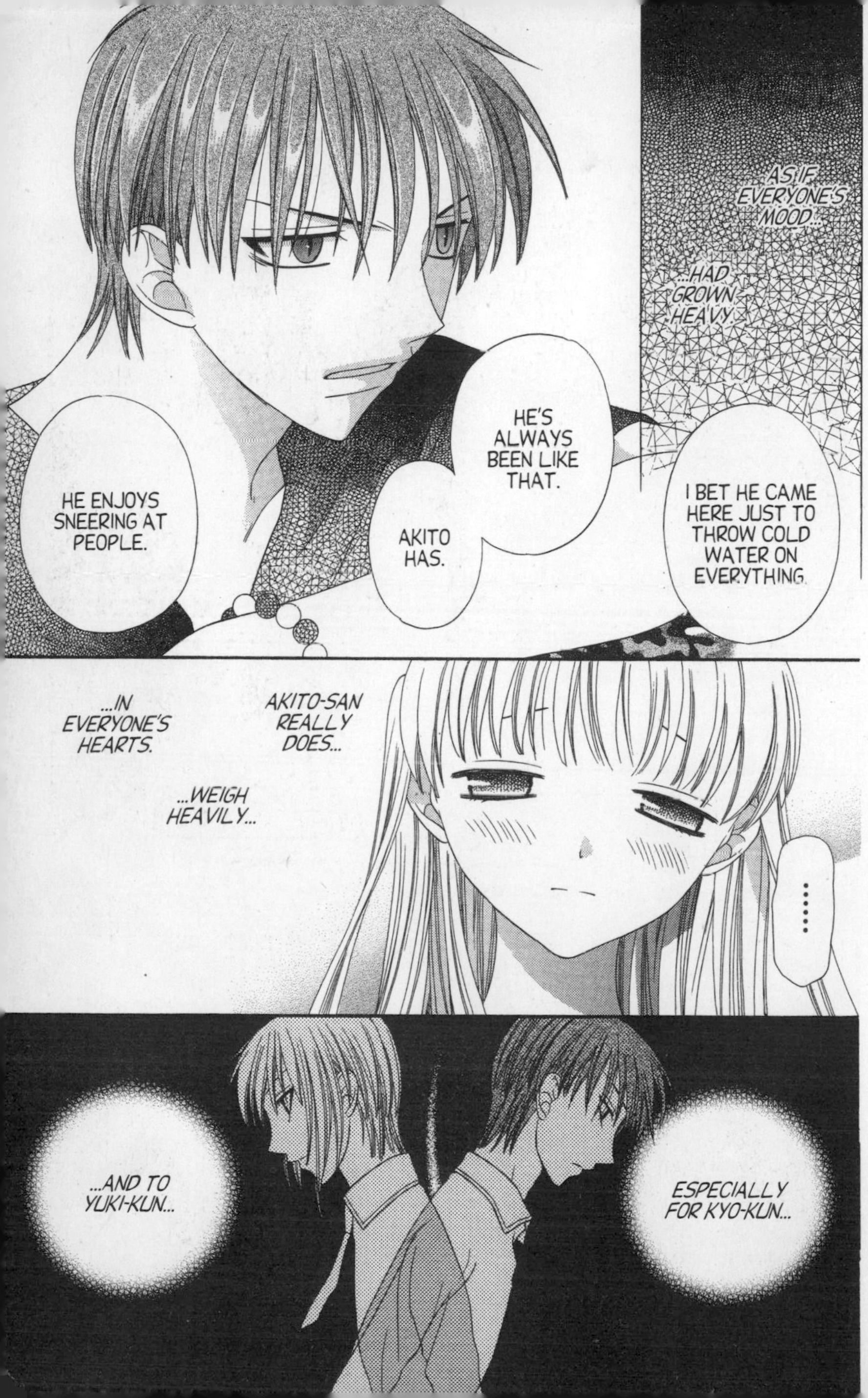
AS IF EVERYONE'S MOOD...
...HAD GROWN HEAVY.
I BET HE CAME HERE JUST TO THROW COLD WATER ON EVERYTHING.
HE'S ALWAYS BEEN LIKE THAT.
AKITO HAS.
HE ENJOYS SNEERING AT PEOPLE.
......
AKITO-SAN REALLY DOES...
...WEIGH HEAVILY...
...IN EVERYONE'S HEARTS.
ESPECIALLY FOR KYO-KUN...
...AND TO YUKI-KUN...

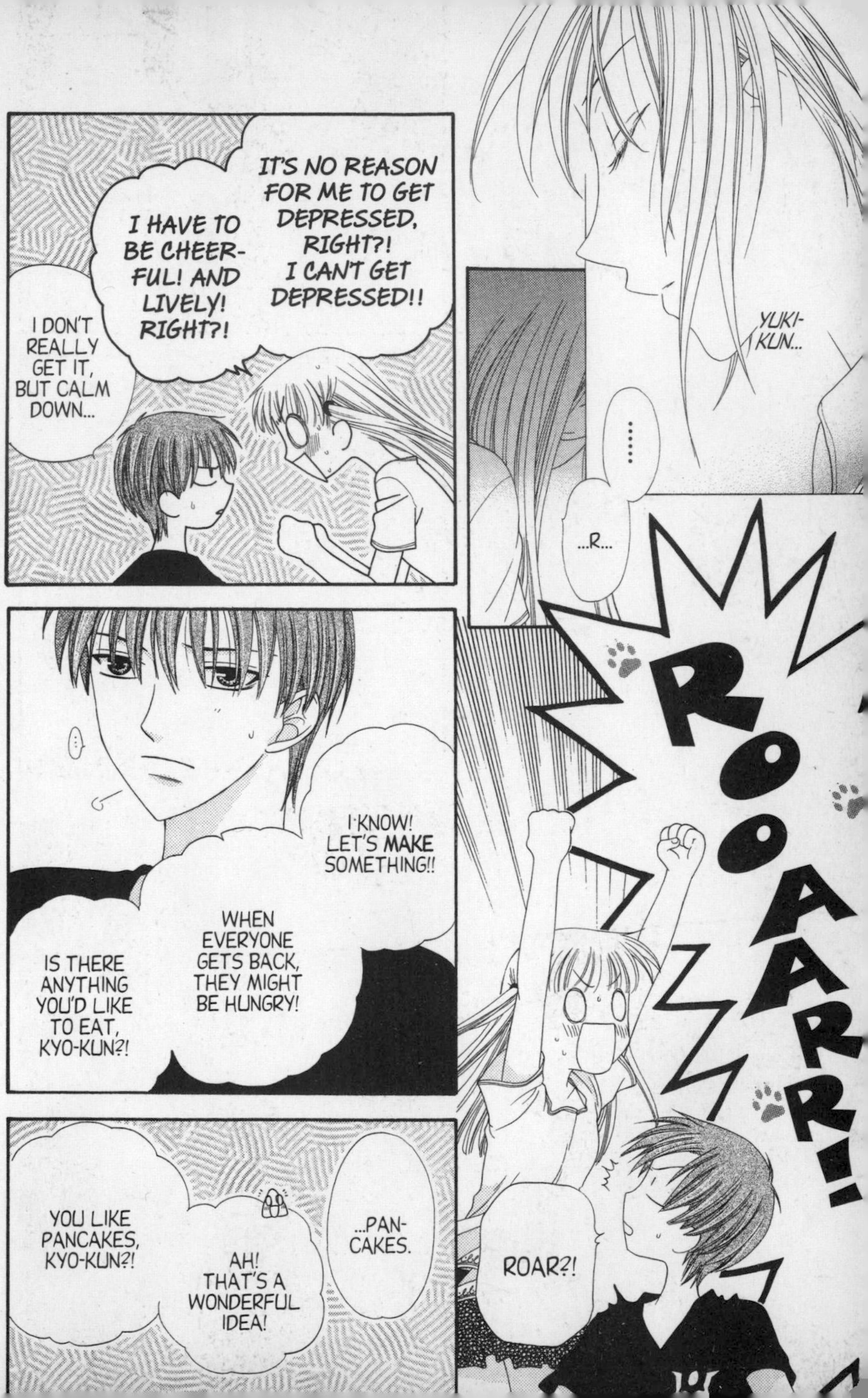
YUKI-KUN...
......
...R...
ROOOAARR!!
ROAR?!
IT'S NO REASON FOR ME TO GET DEPRESSED, RIGHT?! I CAN'T GET DEPRESSED!!
I HAVE TO BE CHEER-FUL! AND LIVELY! RIGHT?!
I DON'T REALLY GET IT, BUT CALM DOWN...
...
I KNOW! LET'S MAKE SOMETHING!!
WHEN EVERYONE GETS BACK, THEY MIGHT BE HUNGRY!
IS THERE ANYTHING YOU'D LIKE TO EAT, KYO-KUN?!
...PAN-CAKES.
AH! THAT'S A WONDERFUL IDEA!
YOU LIKE PANCAKES, KYO-KUN?!

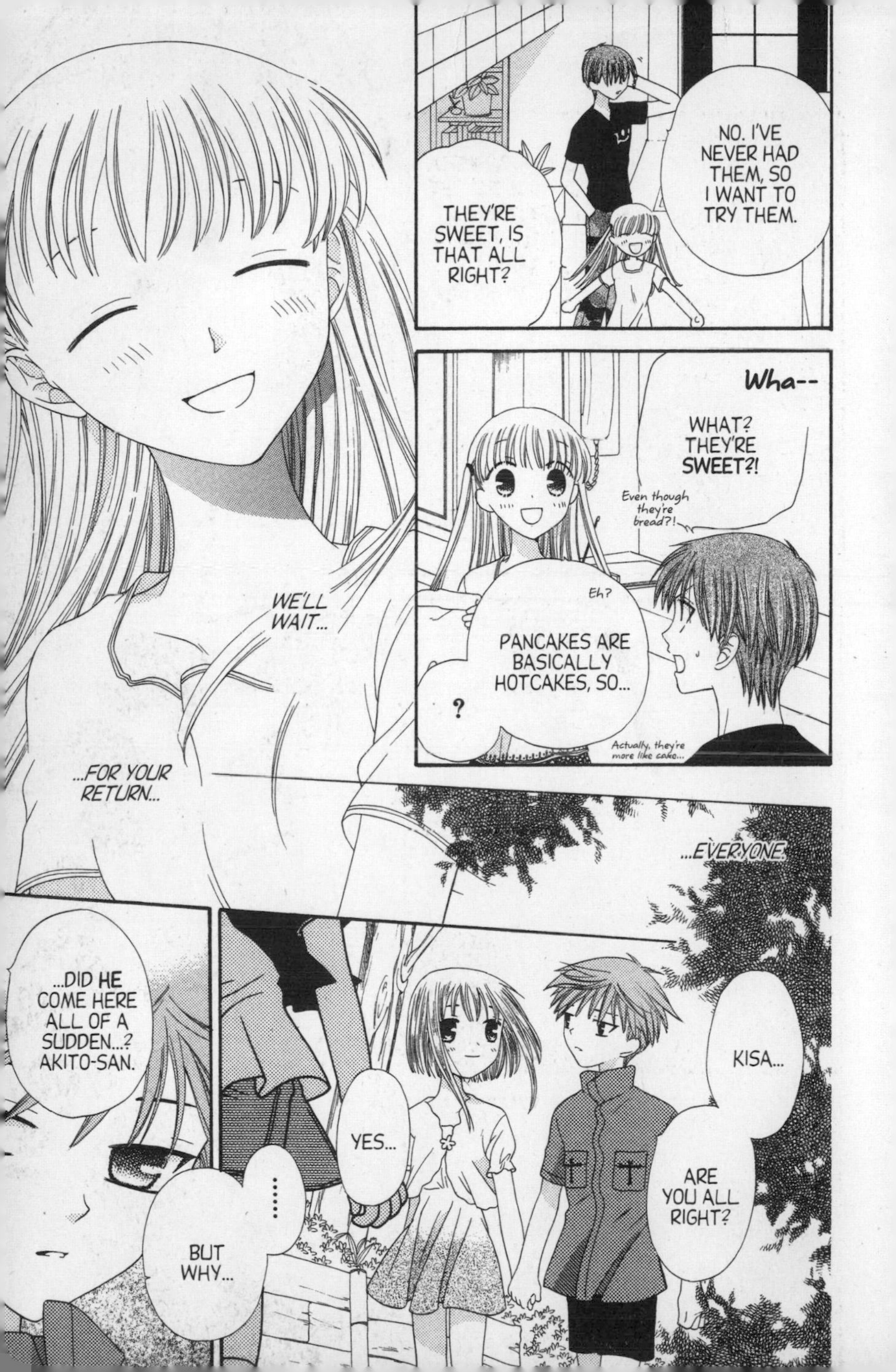
NO. I'VE NEVER HAD THEM, SO I WANT TO TRY THEM.
THEY'RE SWEET, IS THAT ALL RIGHT?
Wha--
WHAT? THEY'RE SWEET?!
Even though they're bread?!
Eh?
PANCAKES ARE BASICALLY HOTCAKES, SO...
?
Actually, they're more like cake...
WE'LL WAIT...
...FOR YOUR RETURN...
...EVERYONE.
KISA...
ARE YOU ALL RIGHT?
YES...
......
BUT WHY...
...DID HE COME HERE ALL OF A SUDDEN...? AKITO-SAN.

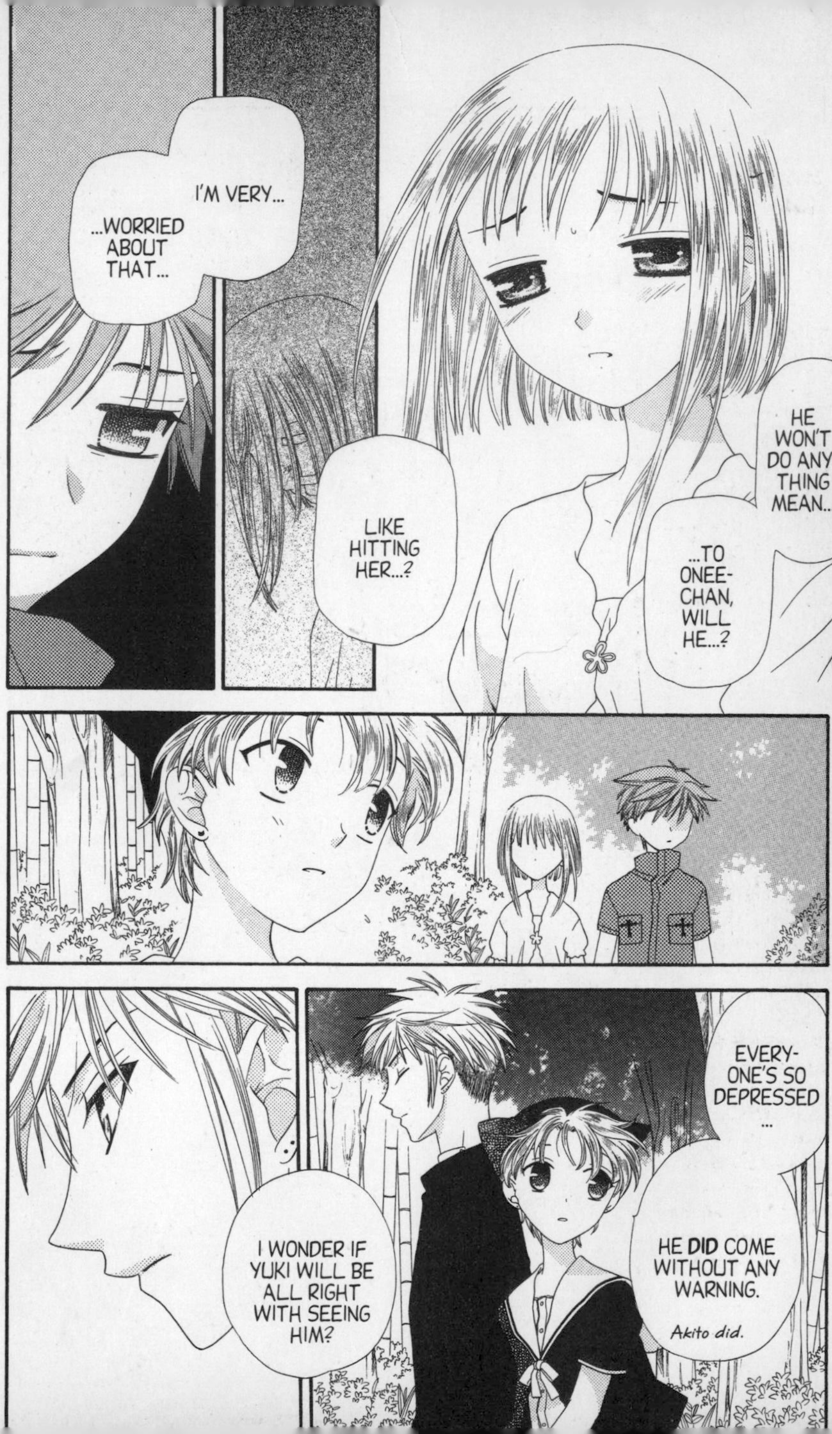
HE WON'T DO ANYTHING MEAN...
...TO ONEE-CHAN, WILL HE...?
LIKE HITTING HER...?
I'M VERY...
...WORRIED ABOUT THAT...
EVERYONE'S SO DEPRESSED ...
HE DID COME WITHOUT ANY WARNING.
Akito did.
I WONDER IF YUKI WILL BE ALL RIGHT WITH SEEING HIM?

**Makoto-kun of the Takei-san family**

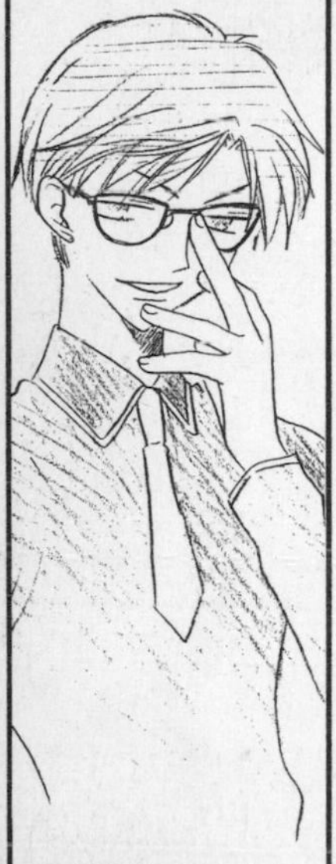

I think he's probably a capable man... (If he wasn't, how would he have become ASB president?). He's a young master from extremely good lineage. How's that for vague? He likes pretty things, so his bedroom etc. are arranged very aesthetically, but with such high tension. I wonder if he eats breakfast? Takei will soon be graduating from high school, too.

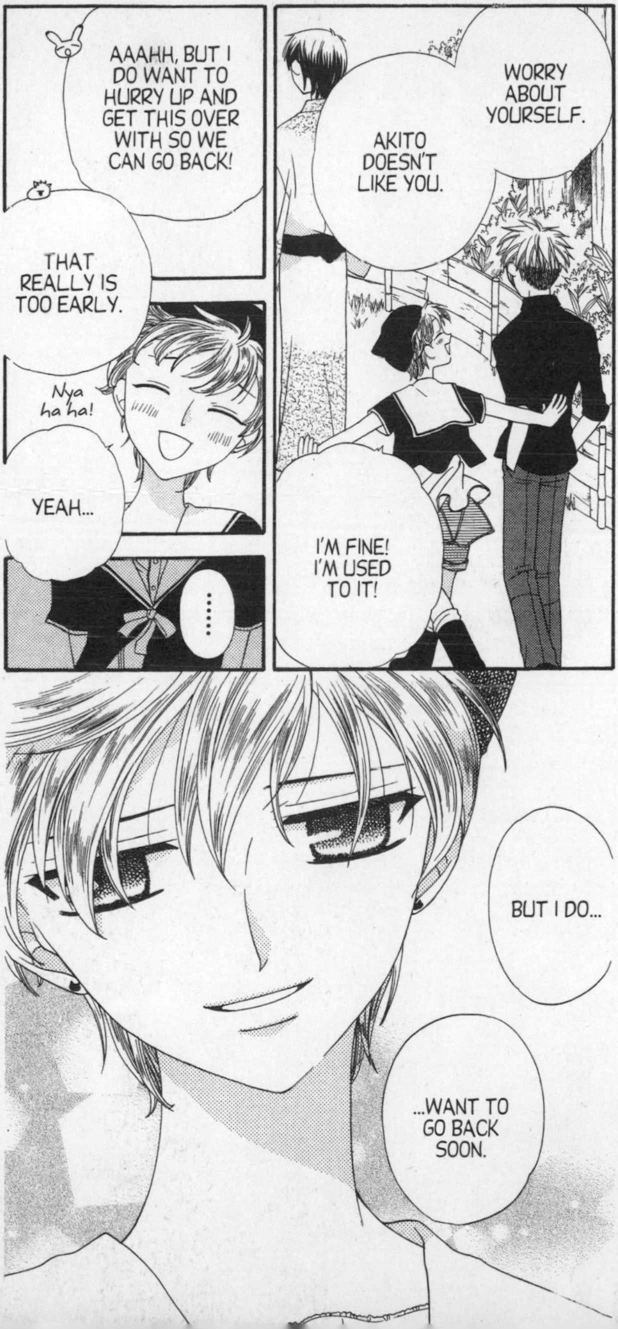
WORRY ABOUT YOURSELF.
AKITO DOESN'T LIKE YOU.
I'M FINE! I'M USED TO IT!
AAAHH, BUT I DO WANT TO HURRY UP AND GET THIS OVER WITH SO WE CAN GO BACK!
THAT REALLY IS TOO EARLY.
Nya ha ha!
YEAH...
......
BUT I DO...
...WANT TO GO BACK SOON.

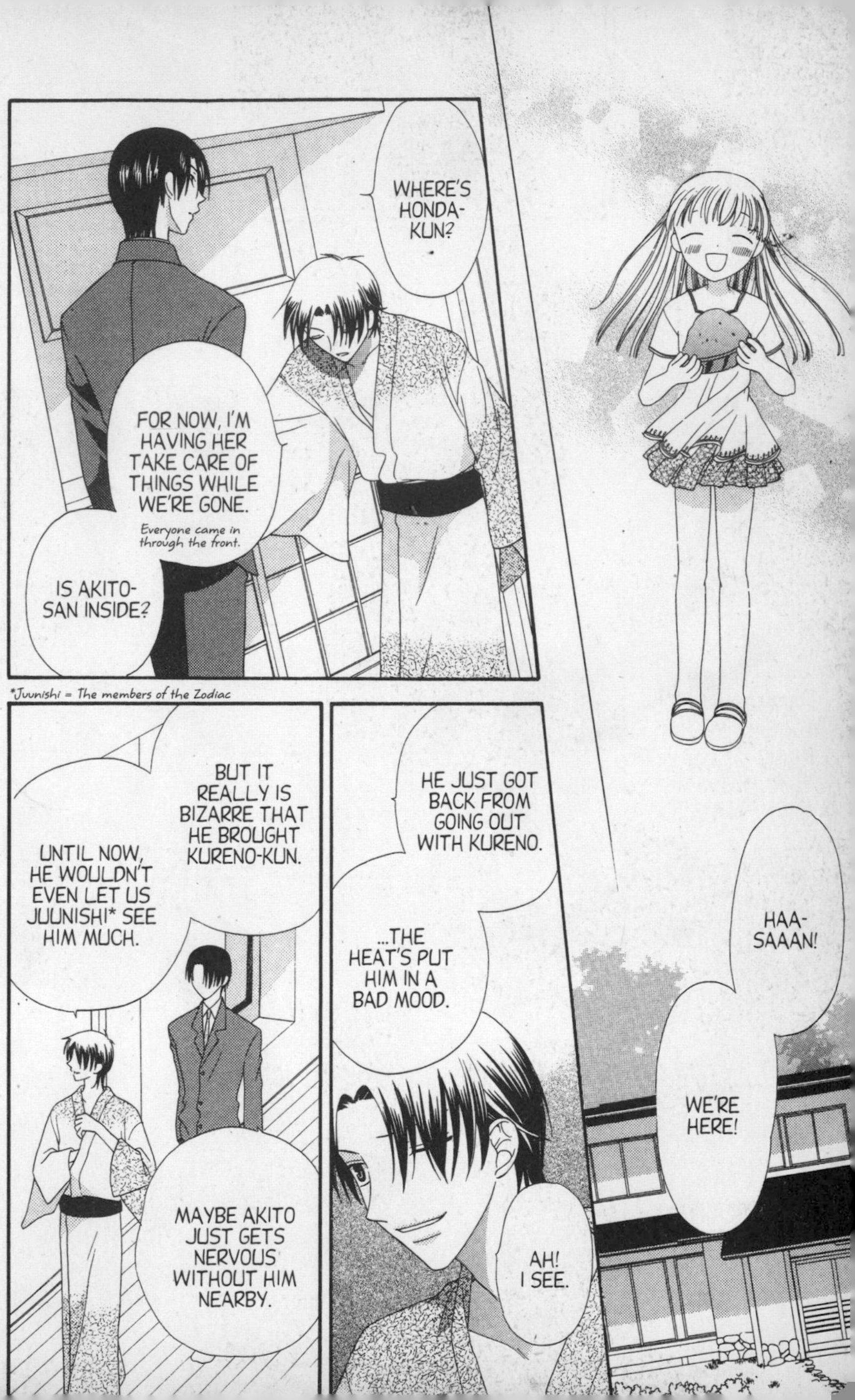
WHERE'S HONDA-KUN?
FOR NOW, I'M HAVING HER TAKE CARE OF THINGS WHILE WE'RE GONE.
Everyone came in through the front.
IS AKITO-SAN INSIDE?
HE JUST GOT BACK FROM GOING OUT WITH KURENO.
...THE HEAT'S PUT HIM IN A BAD MOOD.
AH! I SEE.
BUT IT REALLY IS BIZARRE THAT HE BROUGHT KURENO-KUN.
UNTIL NOW, HE WOULDN'T EVEN LET US JUUNISHI* SEE HIM MUCH.
MAYBE AKITO JUST GETS NERVOUS WITHOUT HIM NEARBY.
HAA-SAAAN!
WE'RE HERE!

*Juunishi = The members of the Zodiac

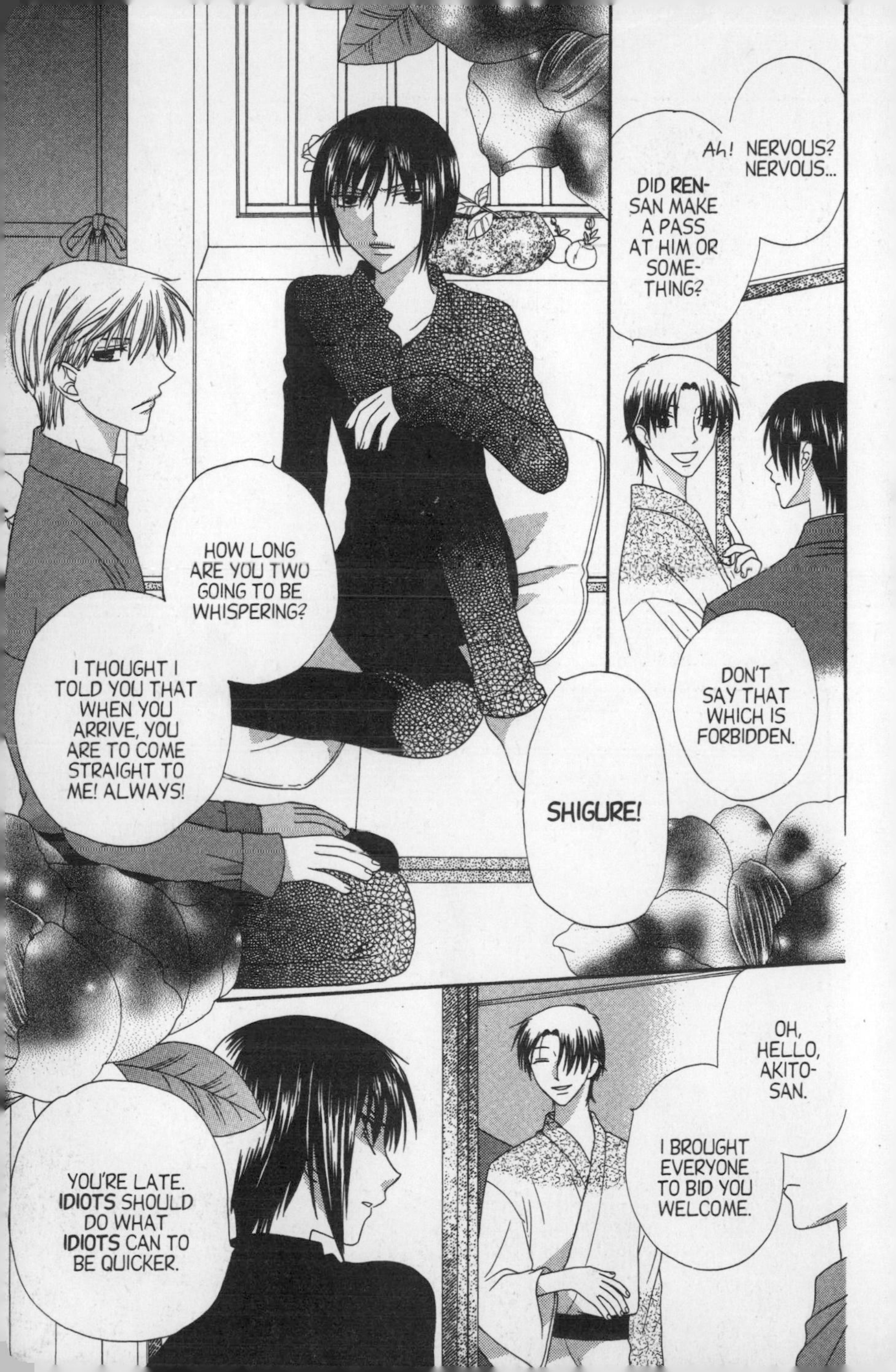

Ah! NERVOUS? NERVOUS...
DID REN-SAN MAKE A PASS AT HIM OR SOME-THING?
DON'T SAY THAT WHICH IS FORBIDDEN.
SHIGURE!
HOW LONG ARE YOU TWO GOING TO BE WHISPERING?
I THOUGHT I TOLD YOU THAT WHEN YOU ARRIVE, YOU ARE TO COME STRAIGHT TO ME! ALWAYS!
OH, HELLO, AKITO-SAN.
I BROUGHT EVERYONE TO BID YOU WELCOME.
YOU'RE LATE. IDIOTS SHOULD DO WHAT IDIOTS CAN TO BE QUICKER.

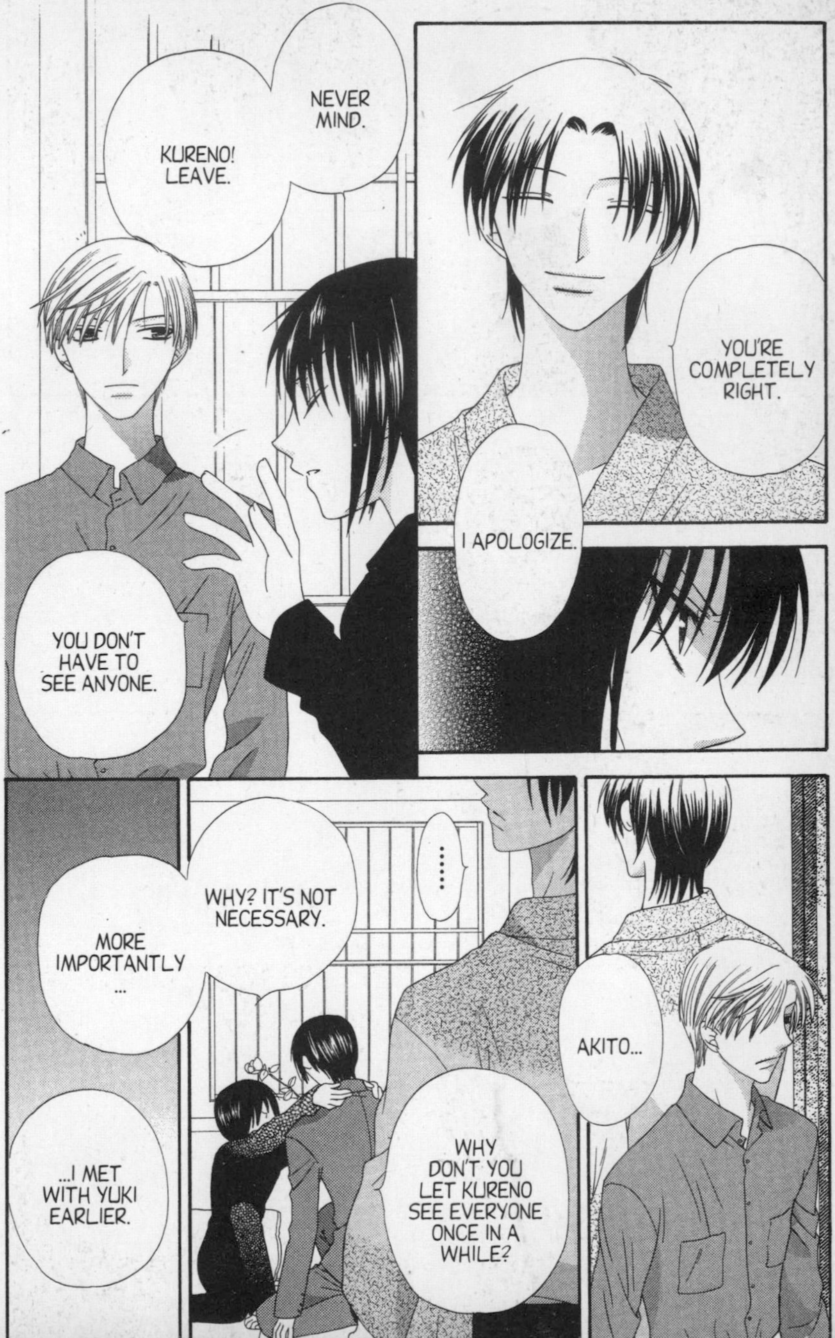
YOU'RE COMPLETELY RIGHT.
I APOLOGIZE.
NEVER MIND.
KURENO! LEAVE.
YOU DON'T HAVE TO SEE ANYONE.
AKITO...
WHY DON'T YOU LET KURENO SEE EVERYONE ONCE IN A WHILE?
......
WHY? IT'S NOT NECESSARY.
MORE IMPORTANTLY ...
...I MET WITH YUKI EARLIER.

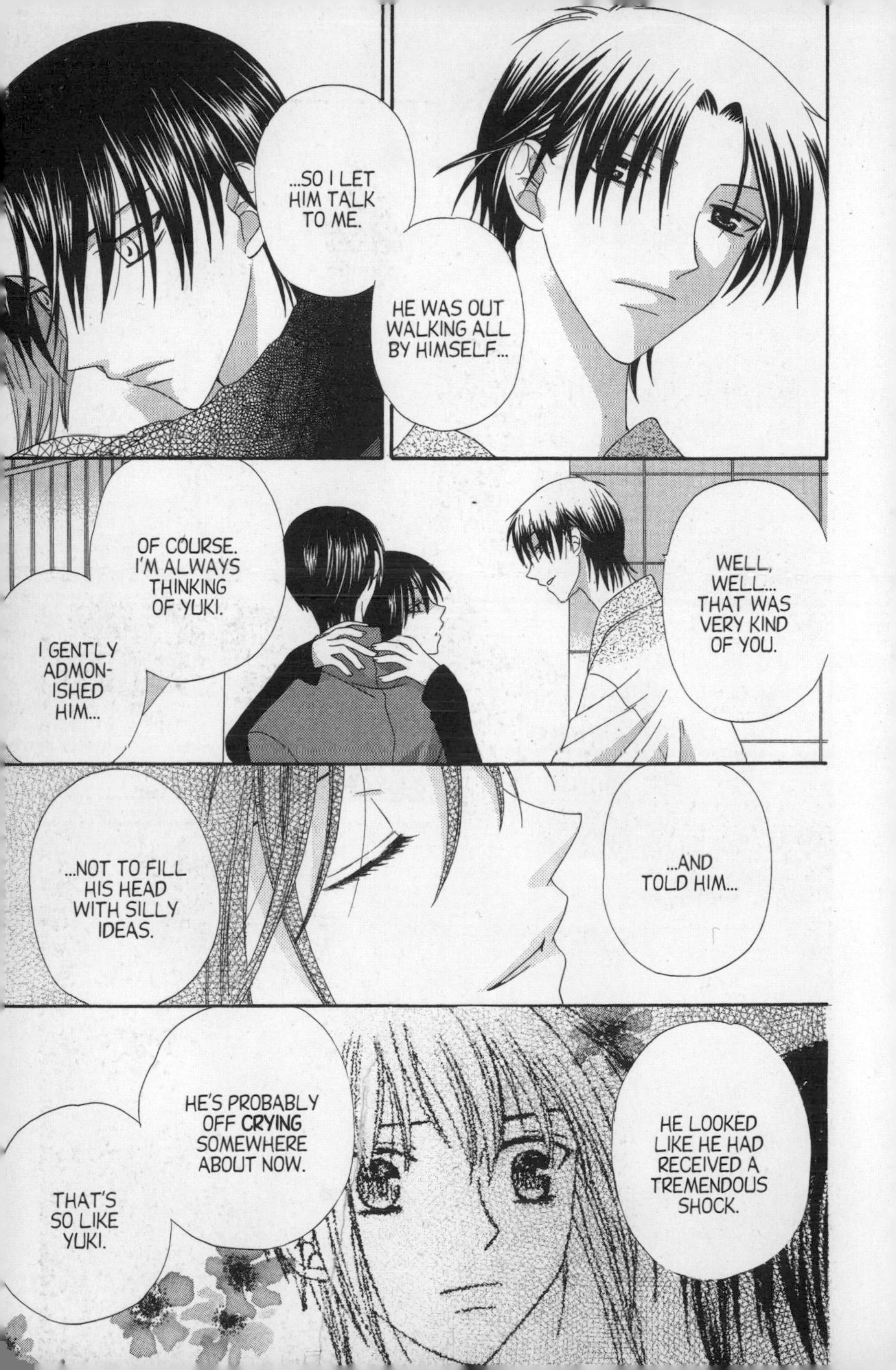
HE WAS OUT WALKING ALL BY HIMSELF...
...SO I LET HIM TALK TO ME.
WELL, WELL... THAT WAS VERY KIND OF YOU.
OF COURSE. I'M ALWAYS THINKING OF YUKI.
I GENTLY ADMONISHED HIM...
...AND TOLD HIM...
...NOT TO FILL HIS HEAD WITH SILLY IDEAS.
HE LOOKED LIKE HE HAD RECEIVED A TREMENDOUS SHOCK.
HE'S PROBABLY OFF **CRYING** SOMEWHERE ABOUT NOW.
THAT'S SO LIKE YUKI.

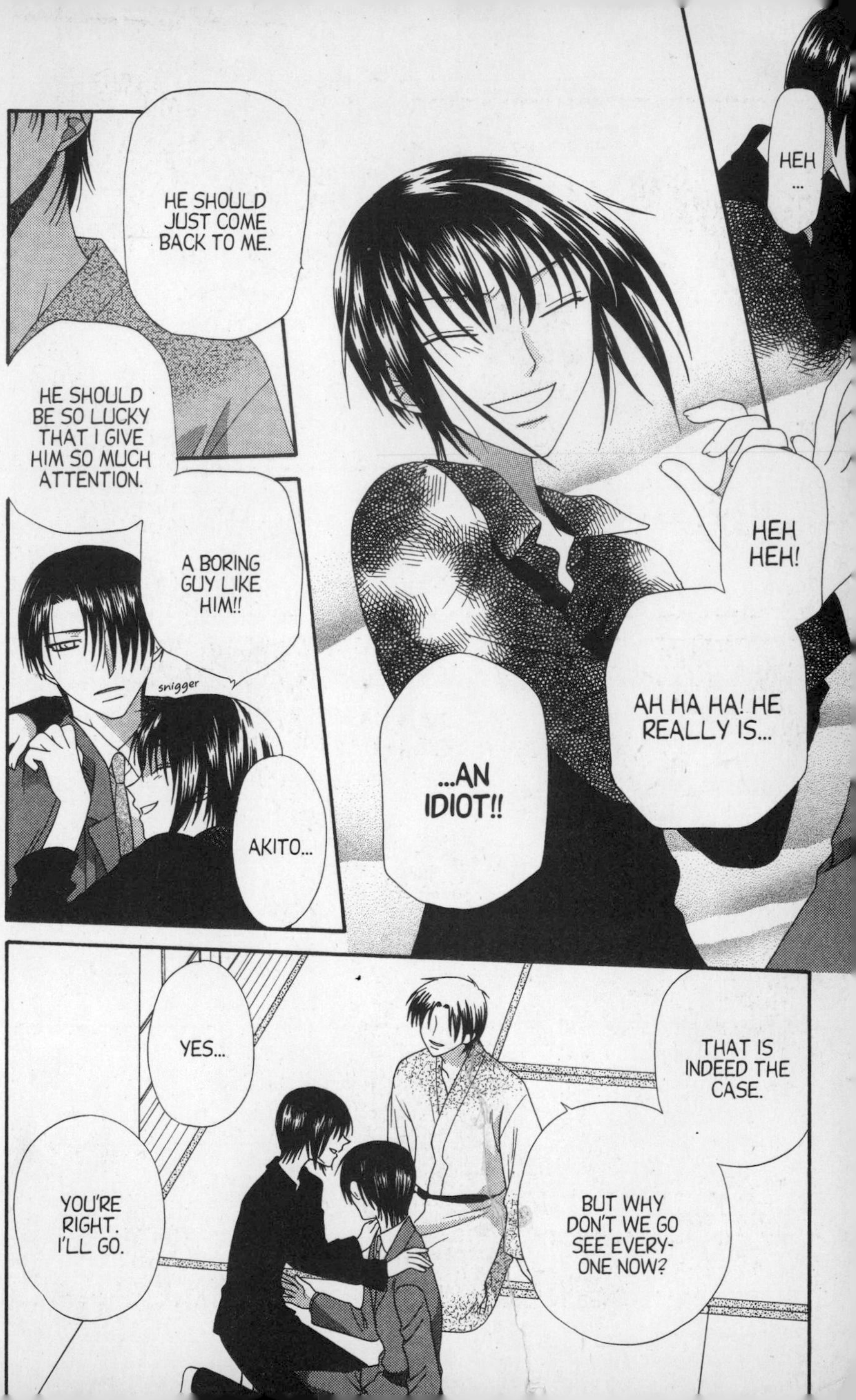
HEH ...
HEH HEH!
AH HA HA! HE REALLY IS...
...AN IDIOT!!
HE SHOULD JUST COME BACK TO ME.
HE SHOULD BE SO LUCKY THAT I GIVE HIM SO MUCH ATTENTION.
A BORING GUY LIKE HIM!!
snigger
AKITO...
THAT IS INDEED THE CASE.
BUT WHY DON'T WE GO SEE EVERY-ONE NOW?
YES...
YOU'RE RIGHT. I'LL GO.

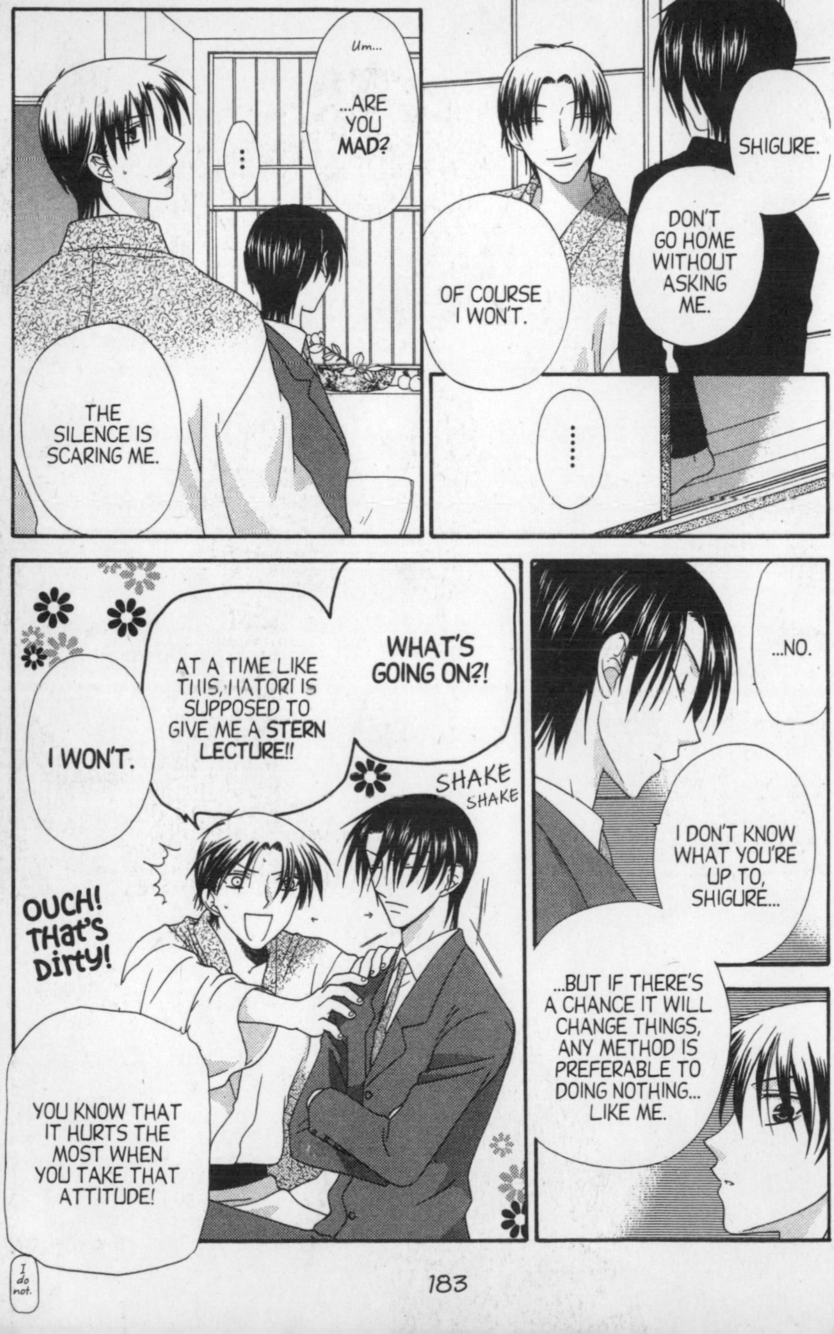
SHIGURE.
DON'T GO HOME WITHOUT ASKING ME.
OF COURSE I WON'T.
......
Um...
...ARE YOU MAD?
...
THE SILENCE IS SCARING ME.
...NO.
I DON'T KNOW WHAT YOU'RE UP TO, SHIGURE...
...BUT IF THERE'S A CHANCE IT WILL CHANGE THINGS, ANY METHOD IS PREFERABLE TO DOING NOTHING... LIKE ME.
WHAT'S GOING ON?!
AT A TIME LIKE THIS, HATORI IS SUPPOSED TO GIVE ME A STERN LECTURE!!
SHAKE
SHAKE
I WON'T.
OUCH! That's Dirty!
YOU KNOW THAT IT HURTS THE MOST WHEN YOU TAKE THAT ATTITUDE!
I do not.

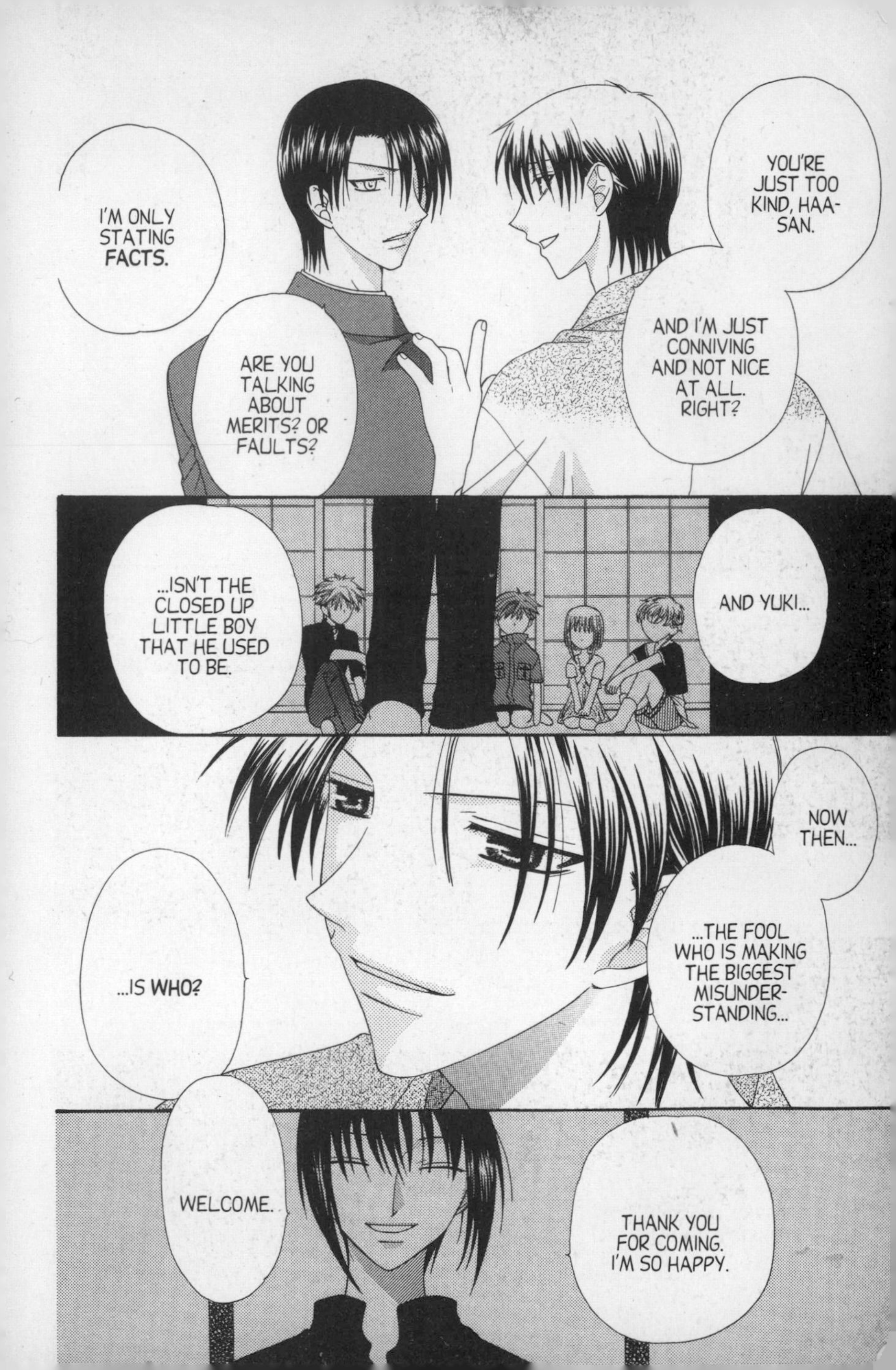
YOU'RE JUST TOO KIND, HAA-SAN.
AND I'M JUST CONNIVING AND NOT NICE AT ALL. RIGHT?
I'M ONLY STATING FACTS.
ARE YOU TALKING ABOUT MERITS? OR FAULTS?
AND YUKI...
...ISN'T THE CLOSED UP LITTLE BOY THAT HE USED TO BE.
NOW THEN...
...THE FOOL WHO IS MAKING THE BIGGEST MISUNDERSTANDING...
...IS WHO?
WELCOME.
THANK YOU FOR COMING. I'M SO HAPPY.

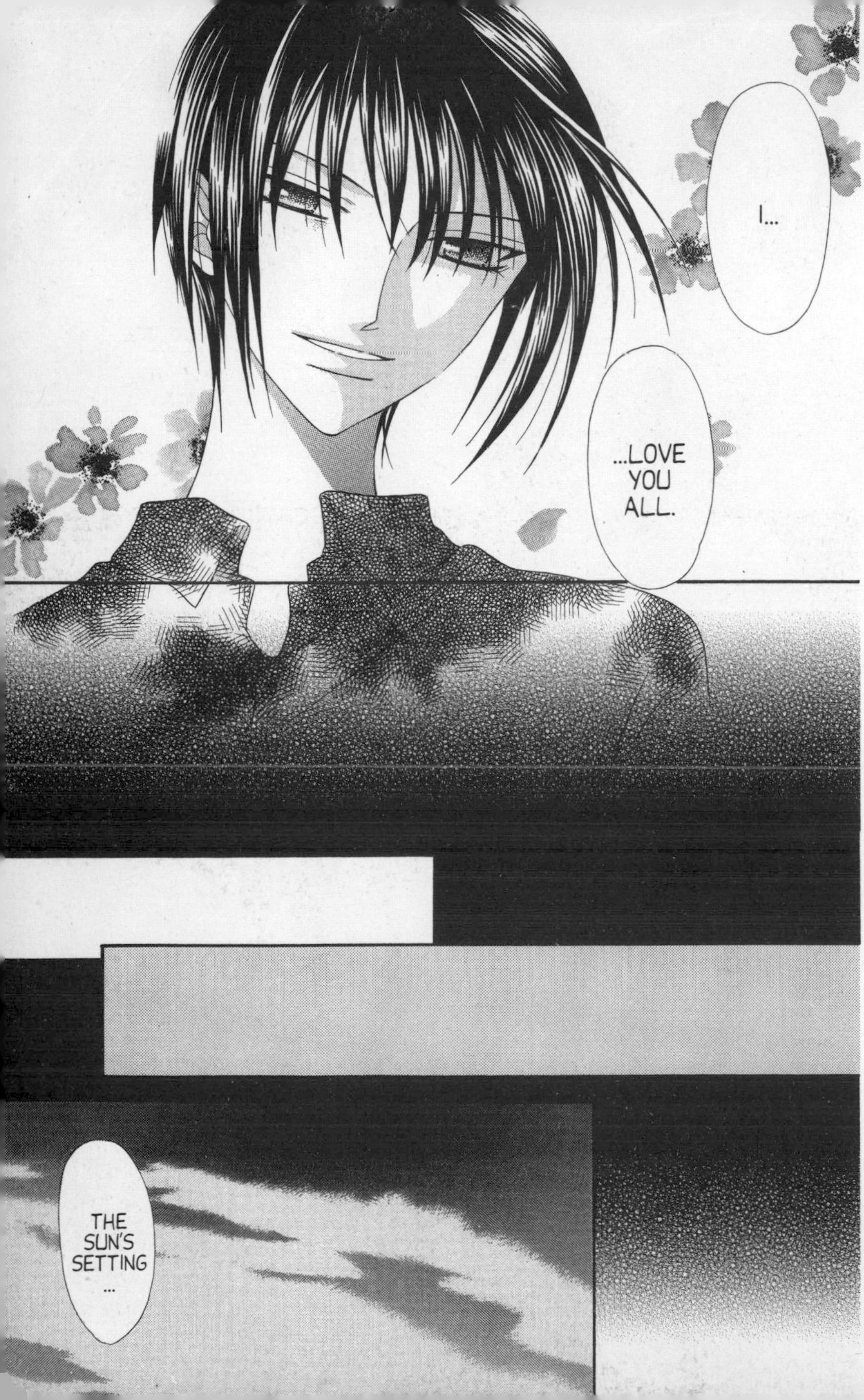
I...
...LOVE YOU ALL.
THE SUN'S SETTING ...

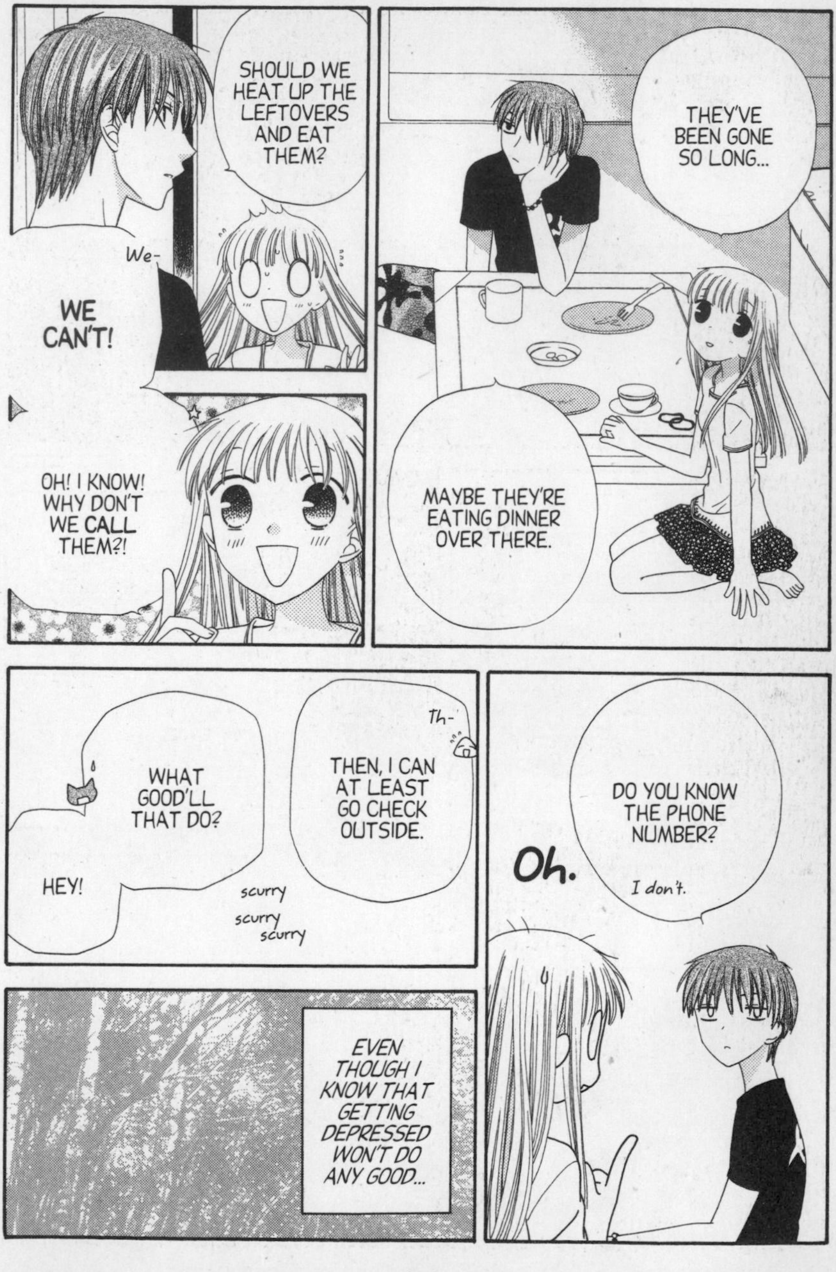
THEY'VE BEEN GONE SO LONG...
MAYBE THEY'RE EATING DINNER OVER THERE.
SHOULD WE HEAT UP THE LEFTOVERS AND EAT THEM?
We-
WE CAN'T!
OH! I KNOW! WHY DON'T WE CALL THEM?!
DO YOU KNOW THE PHONE NUMBER?
Oh.
I don't.
Th-
THEN, I CAN AT LEAST GO CHECK OUTSIDE.
scurry
scurry
scurry
WHAT GOOD'LL THAT DO?
HEY!
EVEN THOUGH I KNOW THAT GETTING DEPRESSED WON'T DO ANY GOOD...

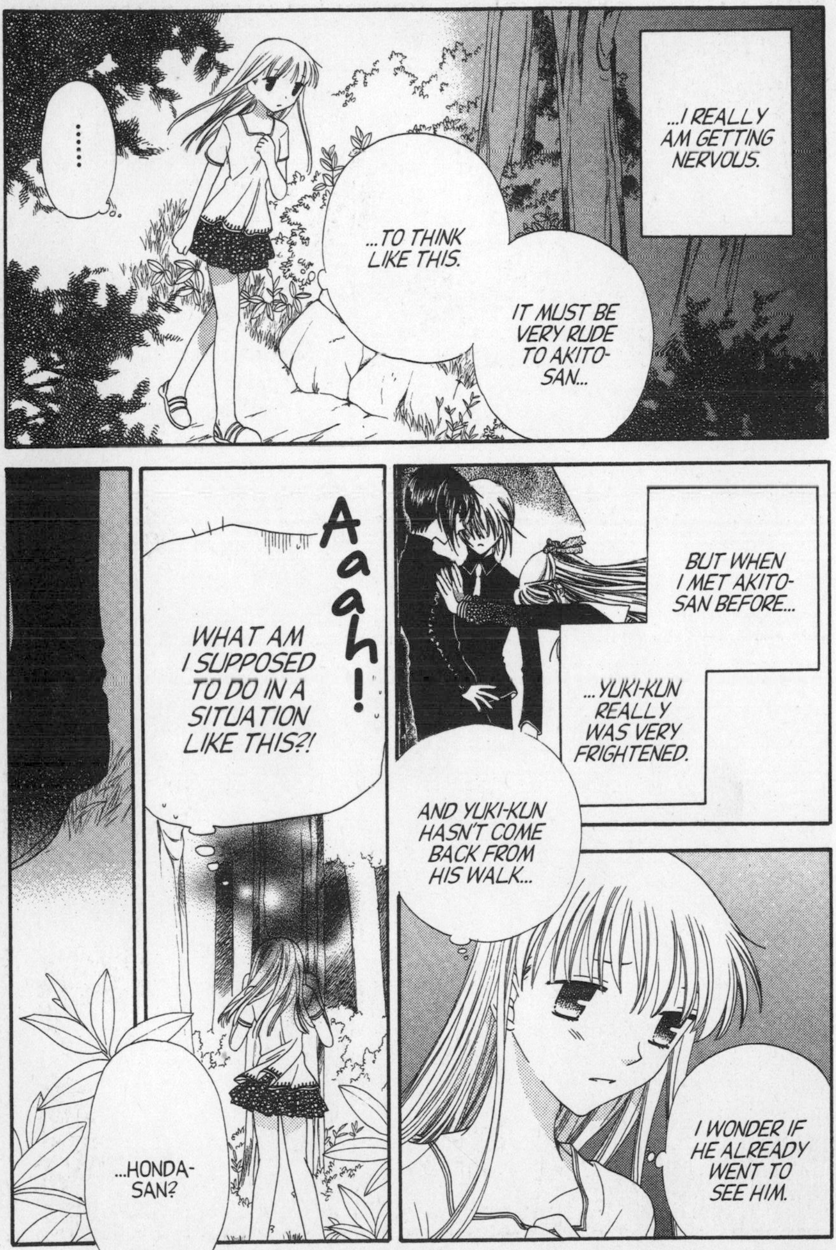

...I REALLY AM GETTING NERVOUS.
...TO THINK LIKE THIS.
IT MUST BE VERY RUDE TO AKITO-SAN...
......
BUT WHEN I MET AKITO-SAN BEFORE...
...YUKI-KUN REALLY WAS VERY FRIGHTENED.
AND YUKI-KUN HASN'T COME BACK FROM HIS WALK...
I WONDER IF HE ALREADY WENT TO SEE HIM.
Aaah!
WHAT AM I SUPPOSED TO DO IN A SITUATION LIKE THIS?!
...HONDA-SAN?

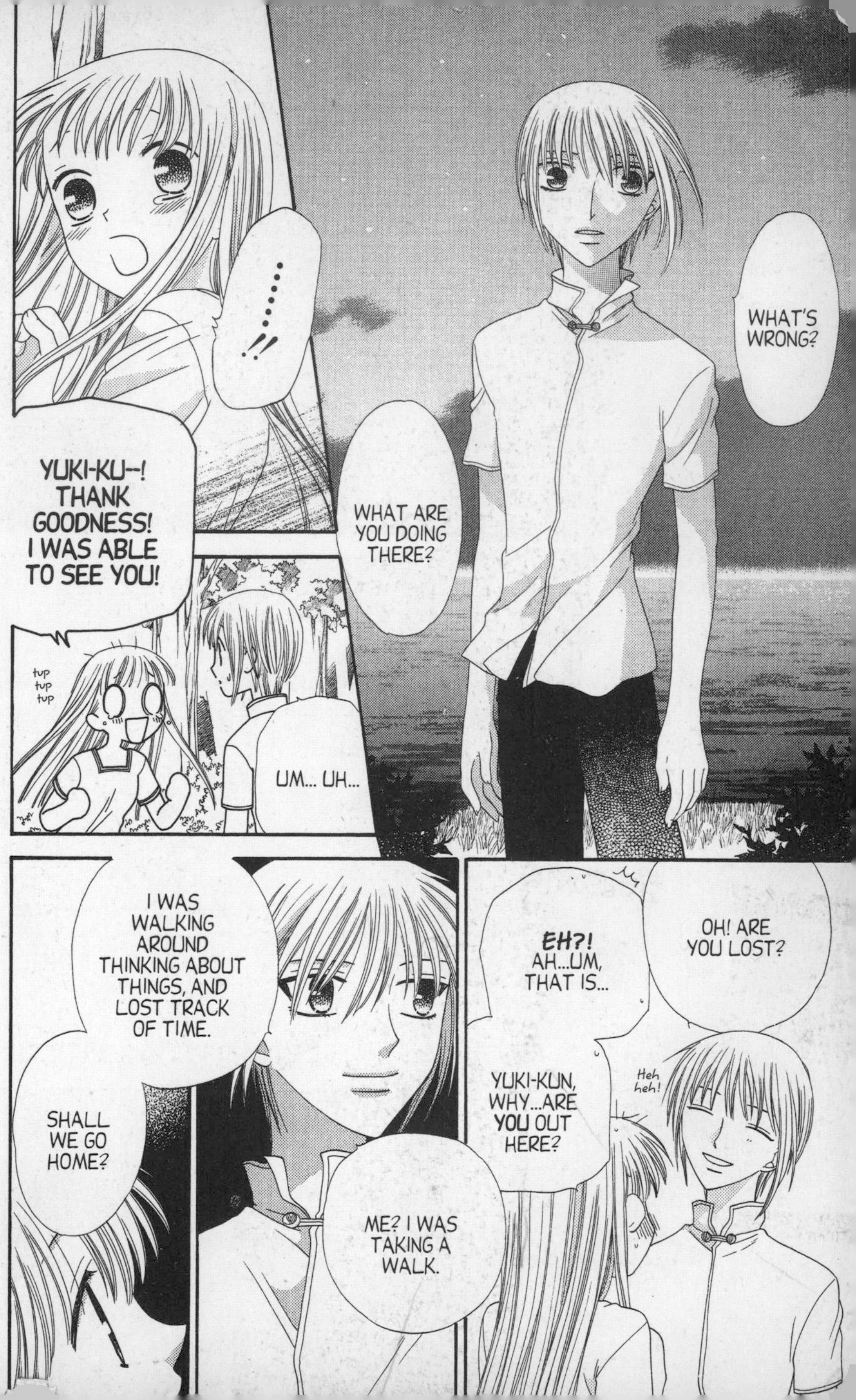
WHAT'S WRONG?
WHAT ARE YOU DOING THERE?
......!!
YUKI-KU--! THANK GOODNESS! I WAS ABLE TO SEE YOU!
tup tup tup
UM... UH...
OH! ARE YOU LOST?
EH?! AH...UM, THAT IS...
Heh heh!
YUKI-KUN, WHY...ARE YOU OUT HERE?
ME? I WAS TAKING A WALK.
I WAS WALKING AROUND THINKING ABOUT THINGS, AND LOST TRACK OF TIME.
SHALL WE GO HOME?

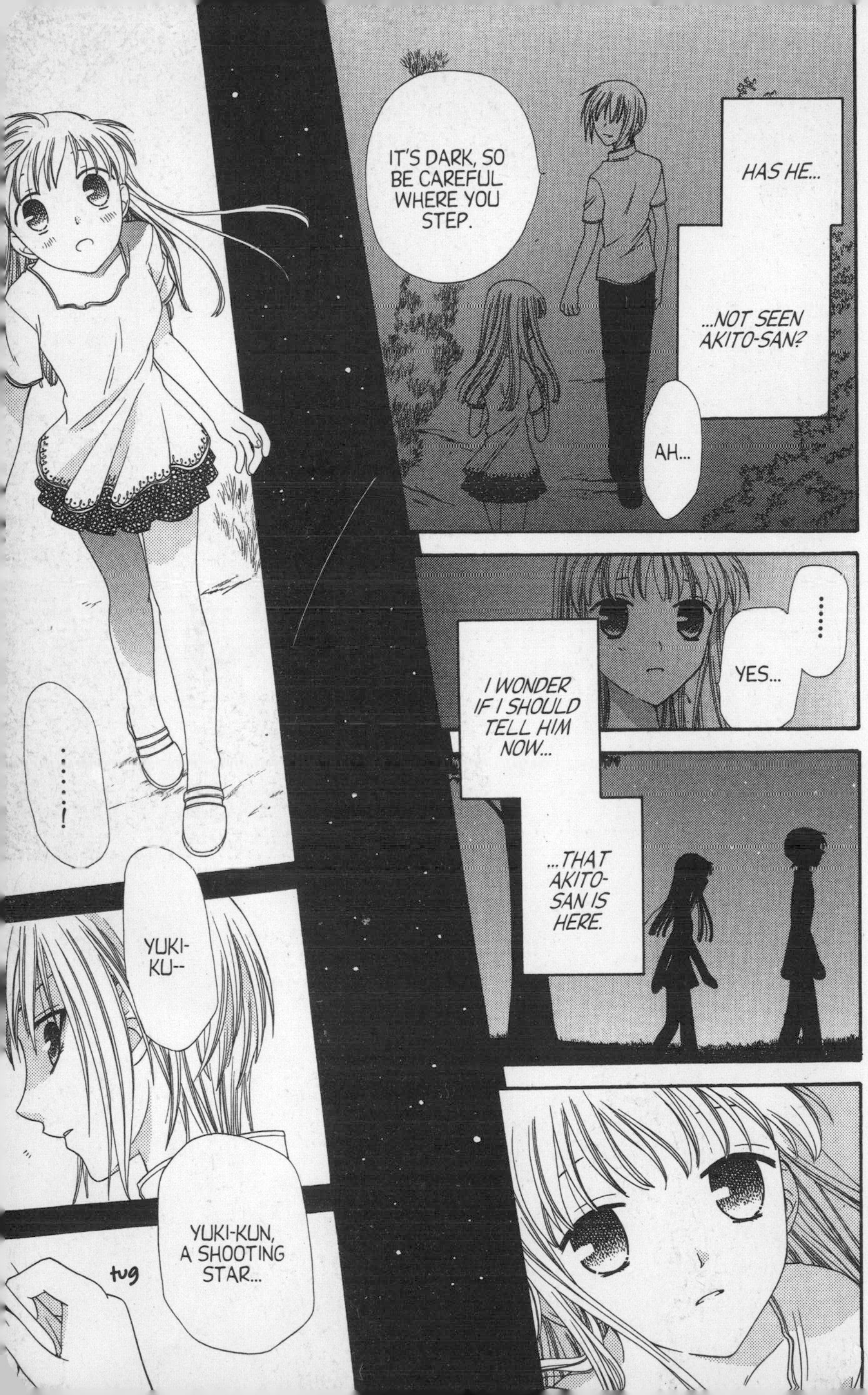
HAS HE...
...NOT SEEN AKITO-SAN?
AH...
IT'S DARK, SO BE CAREFUL WHERE YOU STEP.
......
YES...
I WONDER IF I SHOULD TELL HIM NOW...
...THAT AKITO-SAN IS HERE.
......!
YUKI-KU--
YUKI-KUN, A SHOOTING STAR...
tug

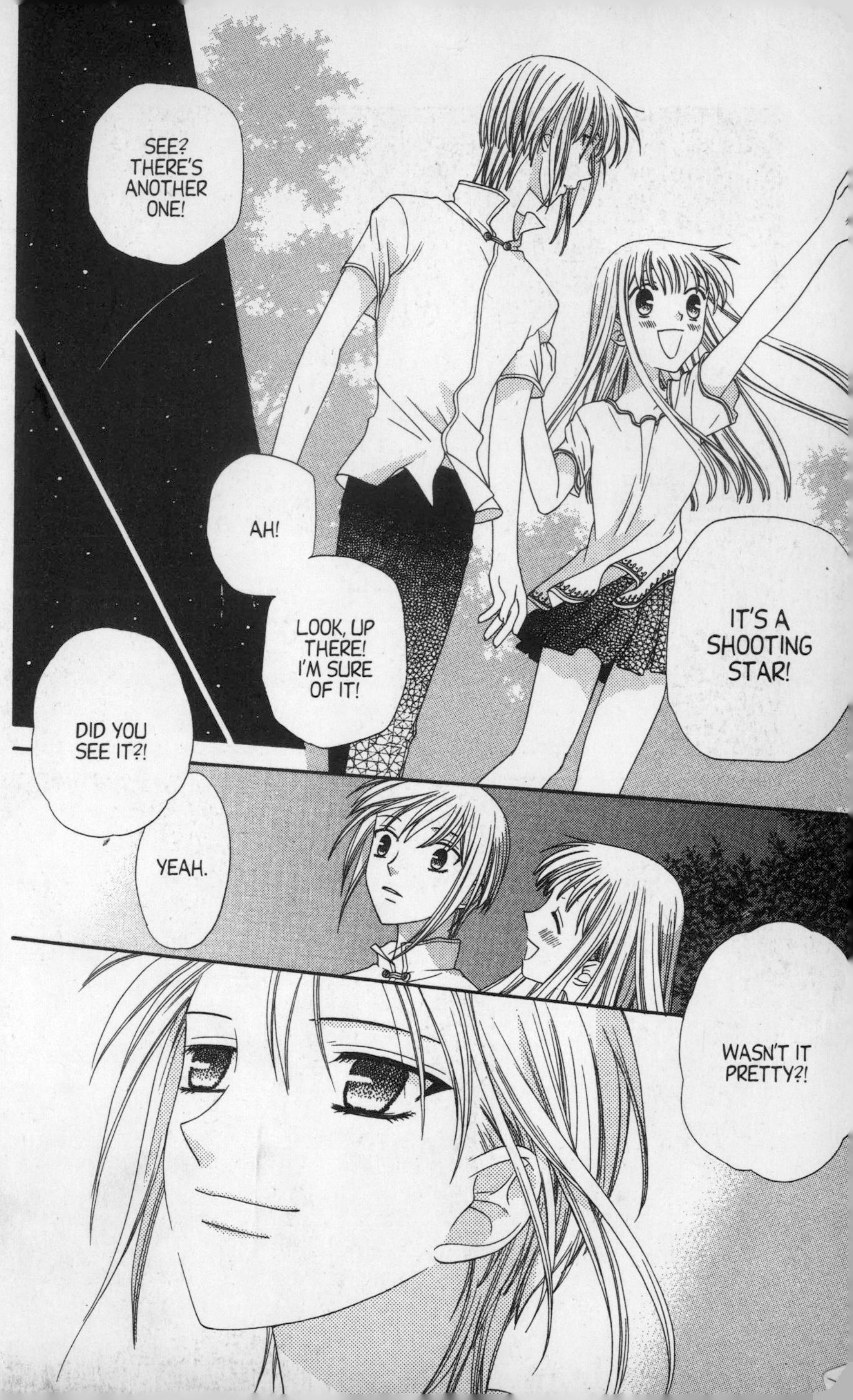
AH!
LOOK, UP THERE! I'M SURE OF IT!
IT'S A SHOOTING STAR!
SEE? THERE'S ANOTHER ONE!
DID YOU SEE IT?!
YEAH.
WASN'T IT PRETTY?!

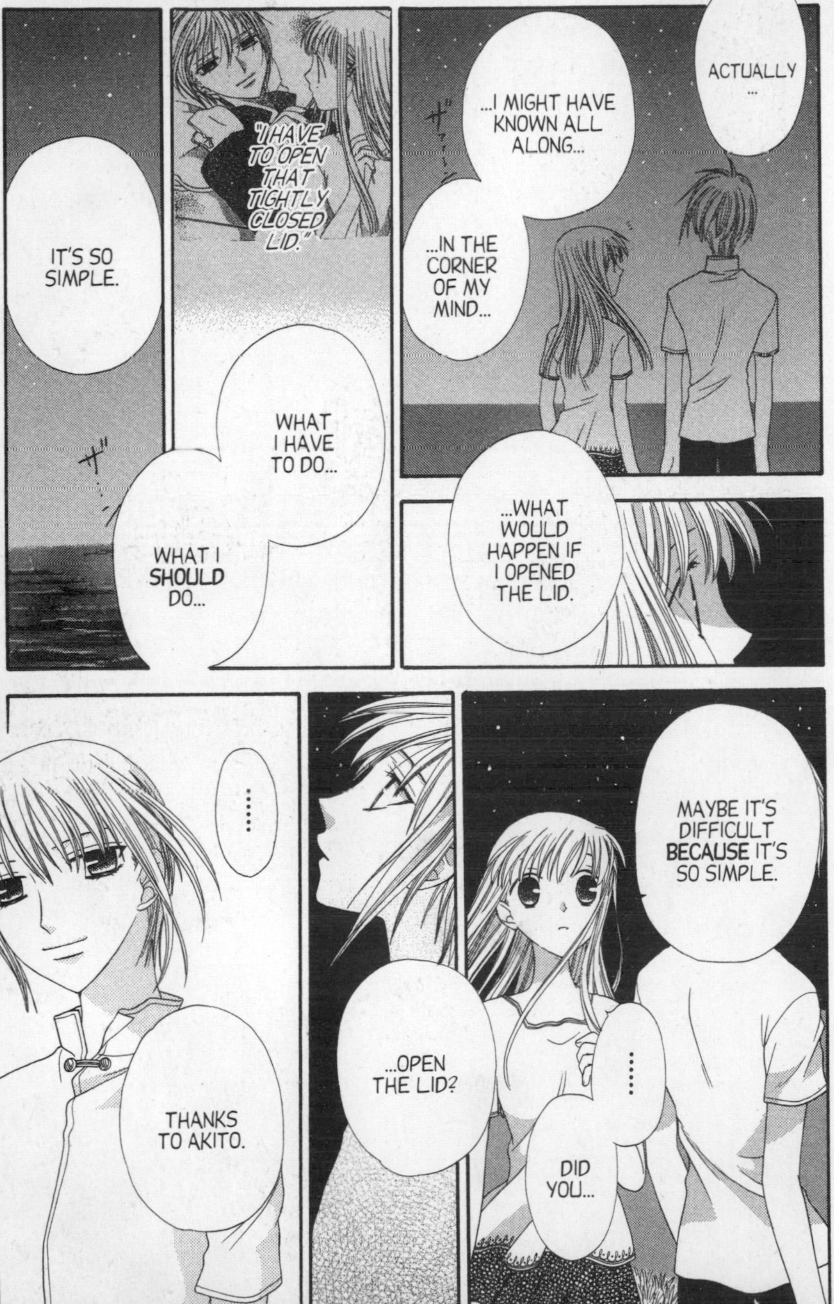
ACTUALLY ...
...I MIGHT HAVE KNOWN ALL ALONG...
...IN THE CORNER OF MY MIND...
...WHAT WOULD HAPPEN IF I OPENED THE LID.
"I HAVE TO OPEN THAT TIGHTLY CLOSED LID."
WHAT I HAVE TO DO...
WHAT I SHOULD DO...
IT'S SO SIMPLE.
MAYBE IT'S DIFFICULT BECAUSE IT'S SO SIMPLE.
......
DID YOU...
...OPEN THE LID?
......
THANKS TO AKITO.

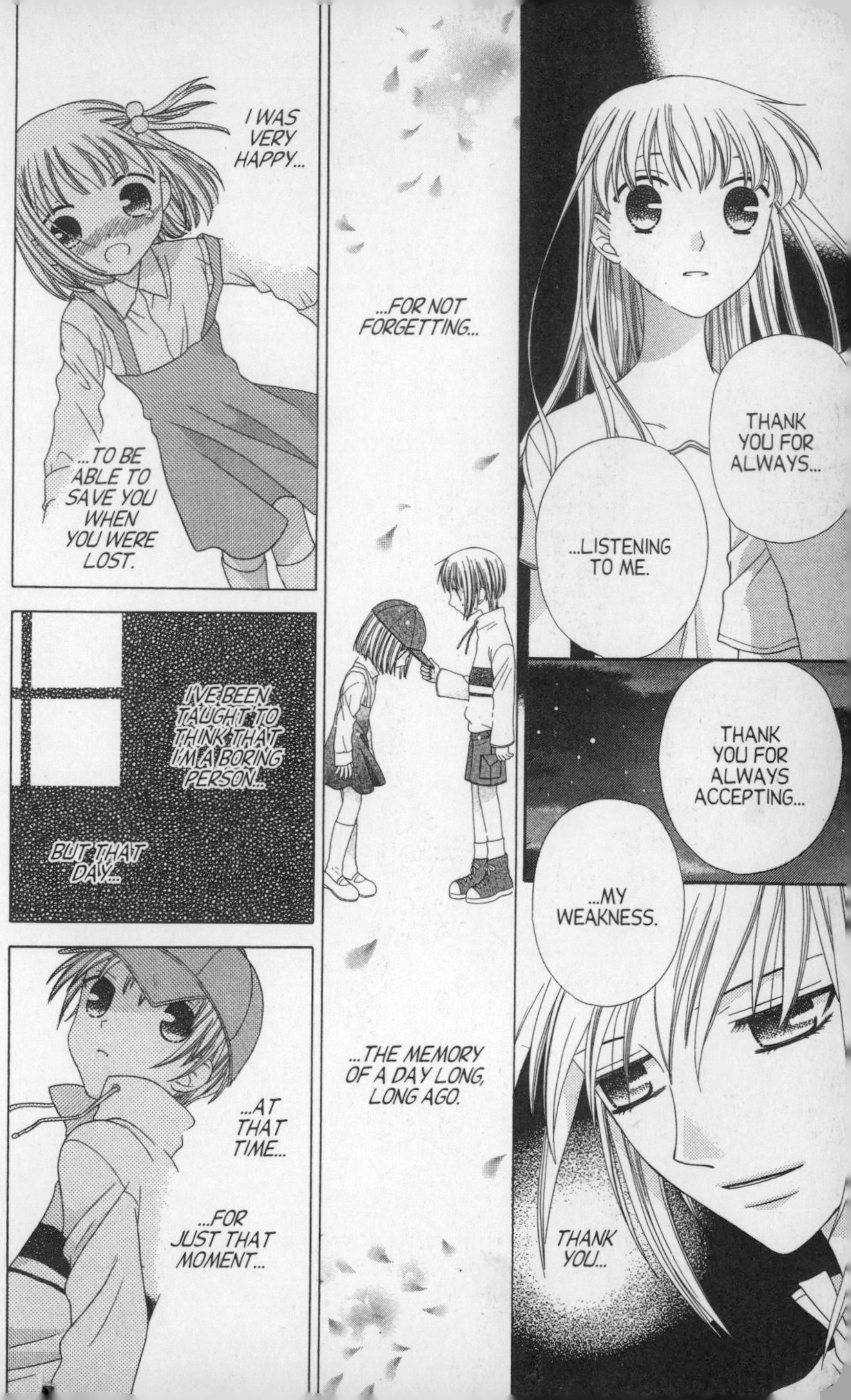
THANK YOU FOR ALWAYS...
...LISTENING TO ME.
THANK YOU FOR ALWAYS ACCEPTING...
...MY WEAKNESS.
THANK YOU...
...FOR NOT FORGETTING...
...THE MEMORY OF A DAY LONG, LONG AGO.
I WAS VERY HAPPY...
...TO BE ABLE TO SAVE YOU WHEN YOU WERE LOST.
I'VE BEEN TAUGHT TO THINK THAT I'M A BORING PERSON...
BUT THAT DAY...
...AT THAT TIME...
...FOR JUST THAT MOMENT...

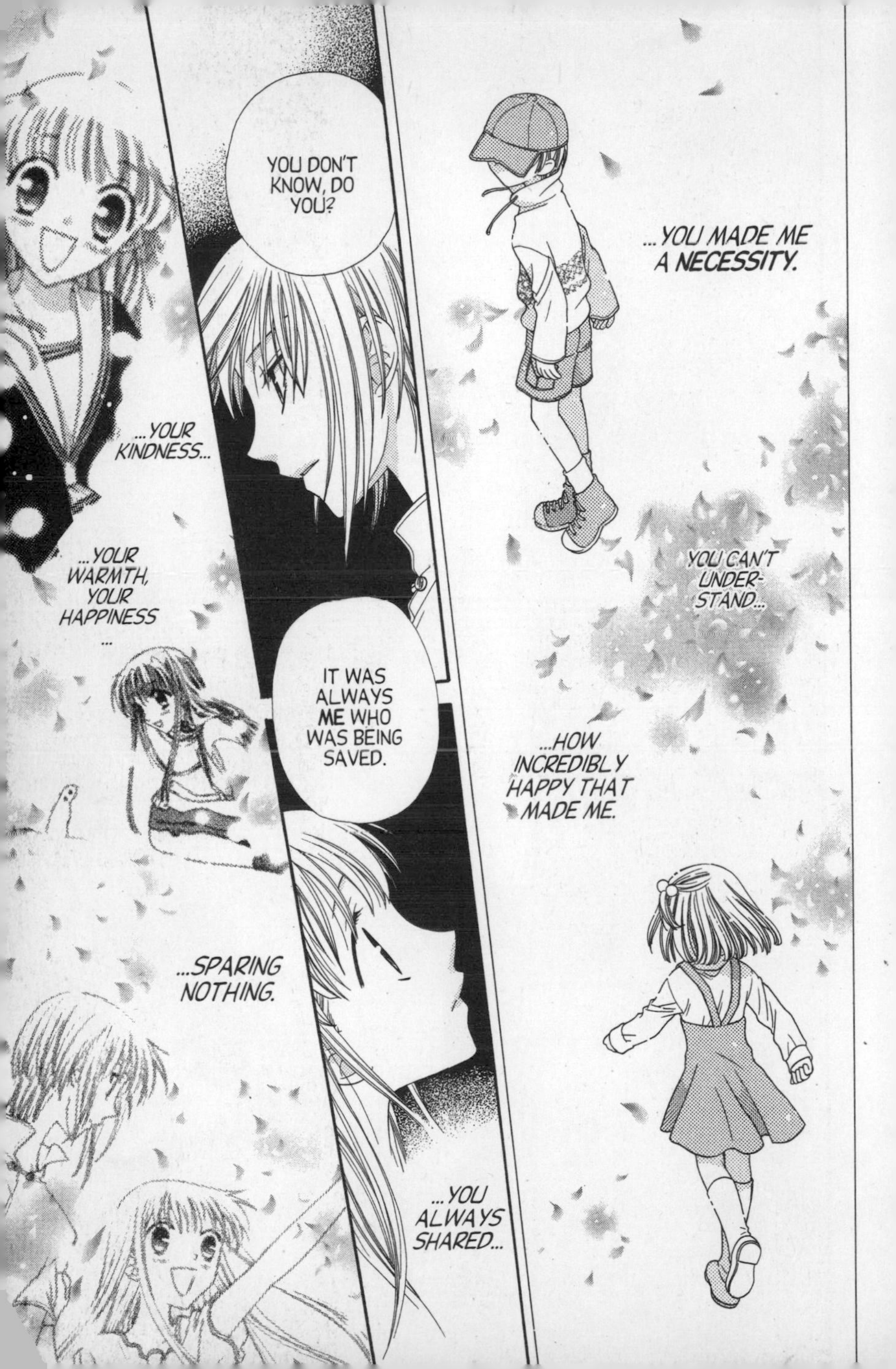
...YOU MADE ME A NECESSITY.
YOU CAN'T UNDER-STAND...
...HOW INCREDIBLY HAPPY THAT MADE ME.
YOU DON'T KNOW, DO YOU?
IT WAS ALWAYS ME WHO WAS BEING SAVED.
...YOU ALWAYS SHARED...
...YOUR KINDNESS...
...YOUR WARMTH, YOUR HAPPINESS...
...SPARING NOTHING.

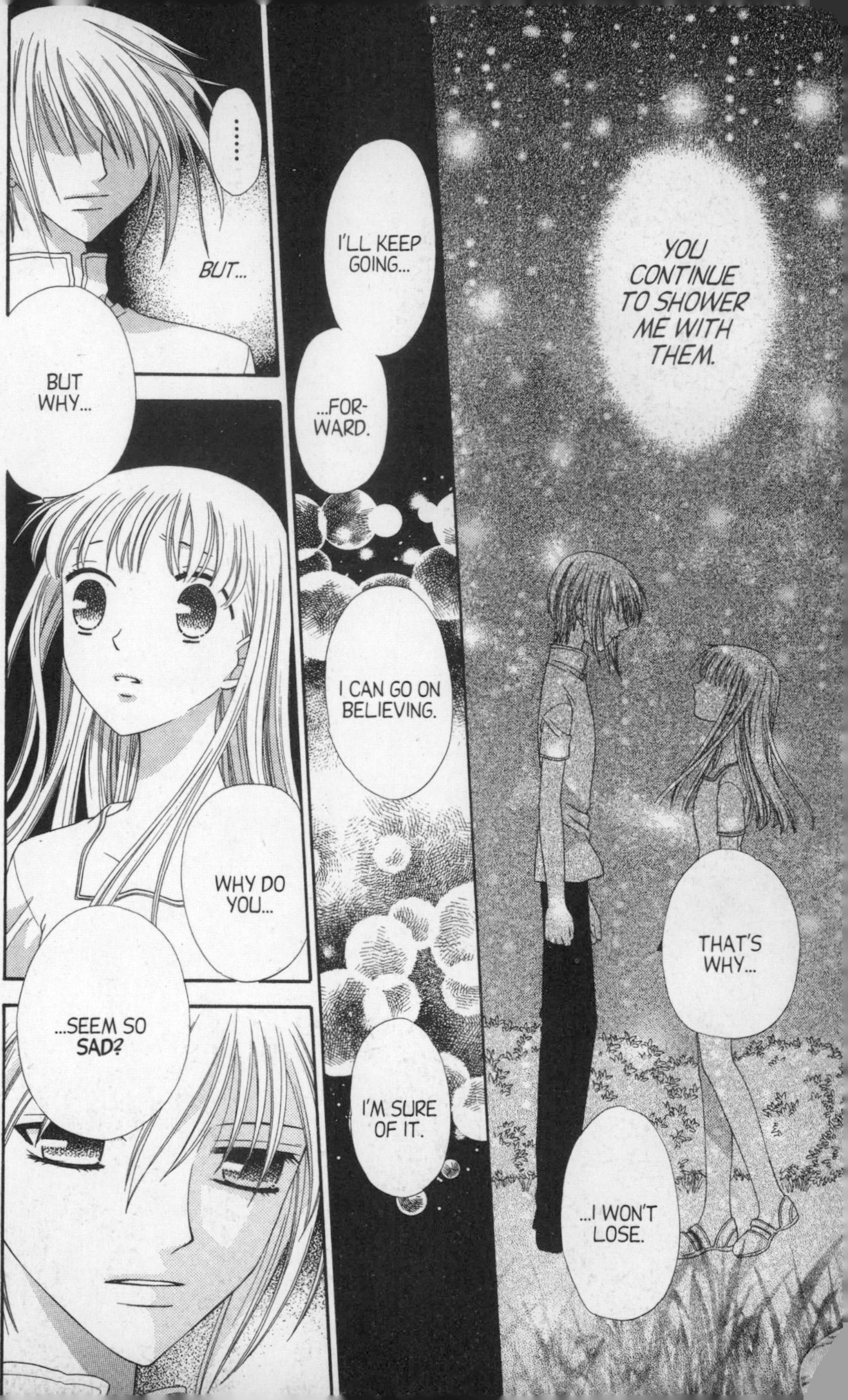
YOU CONTINUE TO SHOWER ME WITH THEM.
THAT'S WHY...
...I WON'T LOSE.
I'LL KEEP GOING...
...FOR-WARD.
I CAN GO ON BELIEVING.
I'M SURE OF IT.
......
BUT...
BUT WHY...
WHY DO YOU...
...SEEM SO SAD?

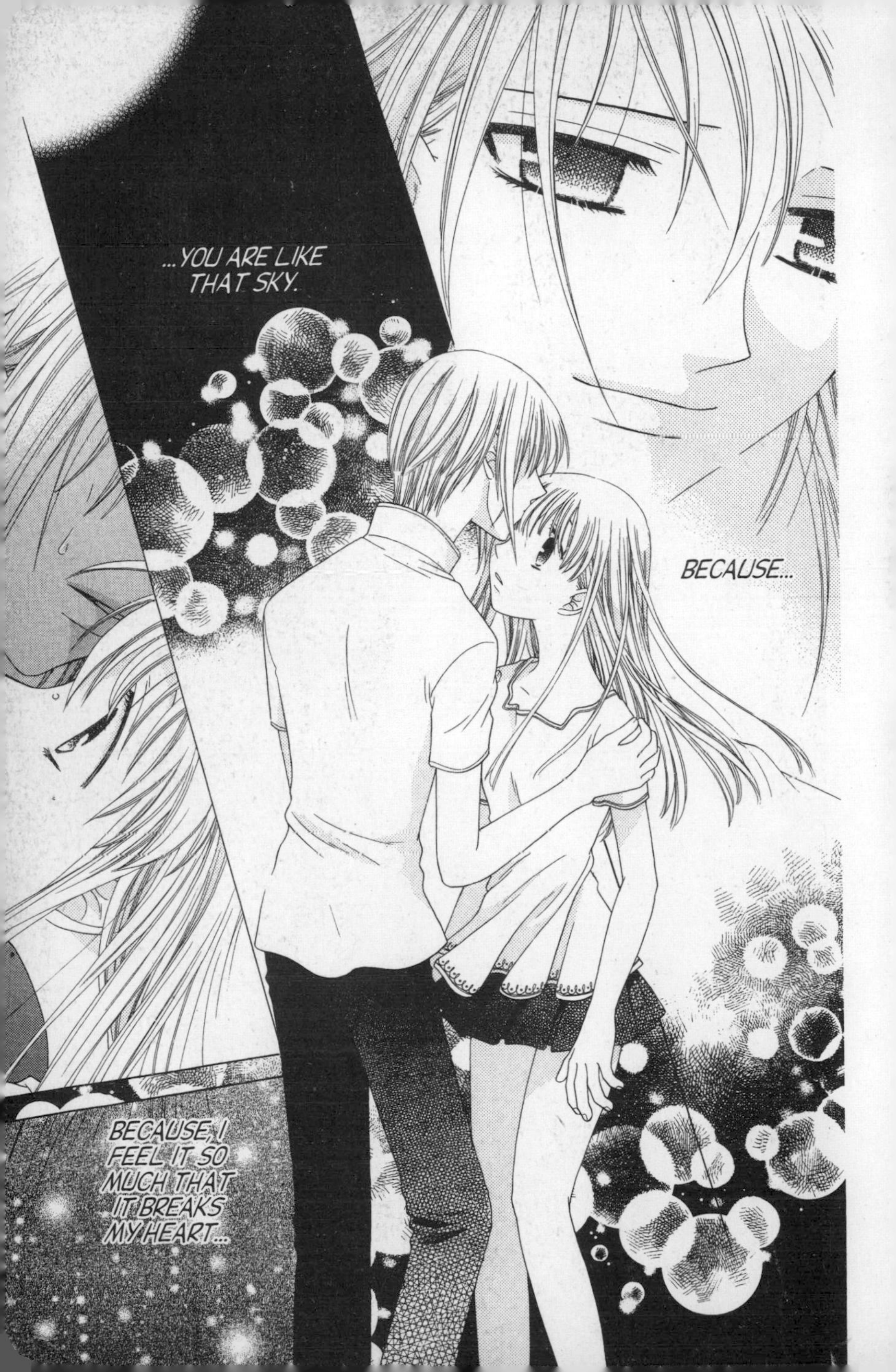

BECAUSE...
...YOU ARE LIKE THAT SKY.
BECAUSE, I FEEL IT SO MUCH THAT IT BREAKS MY HEART...

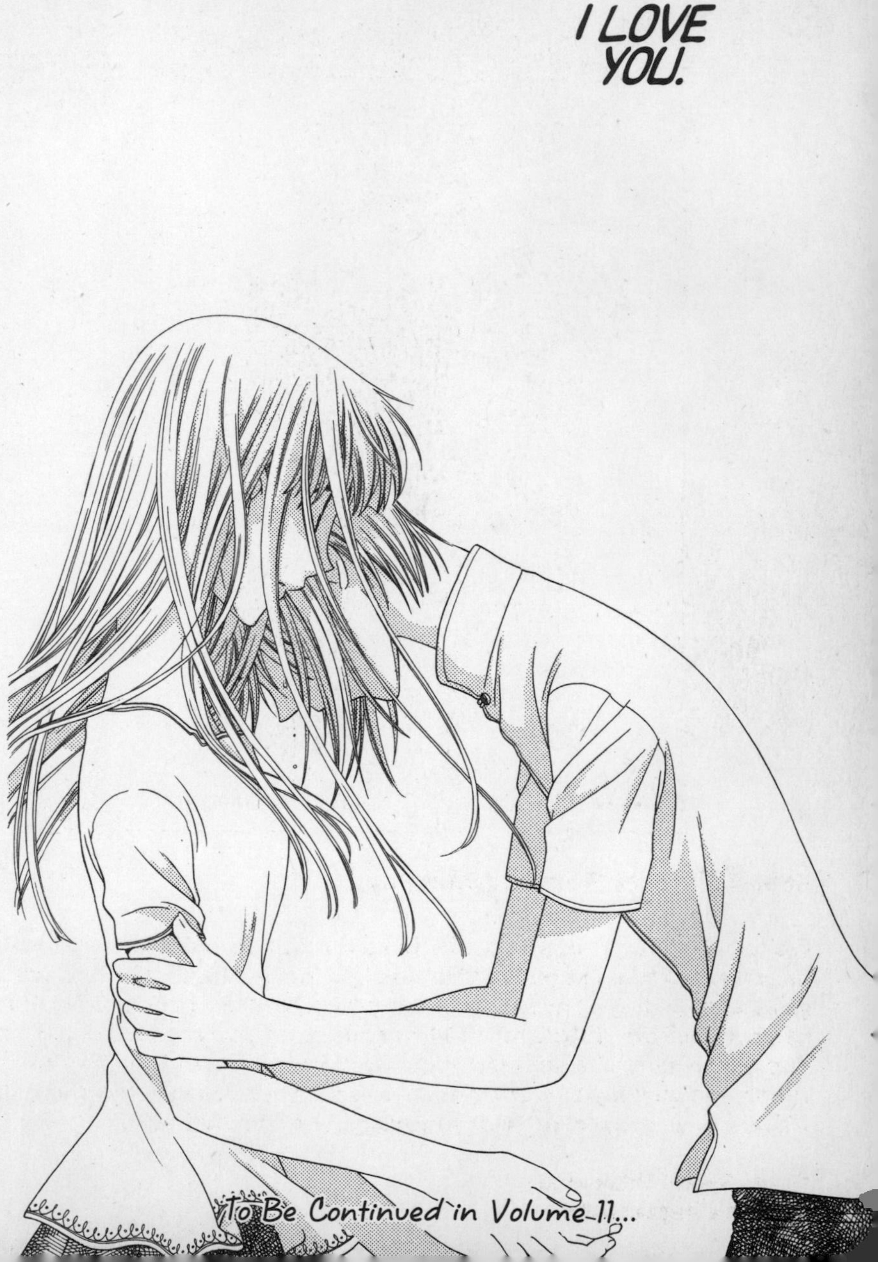
I LOVE YOU.
To Be Continued in Volume 11...

# Next time in...

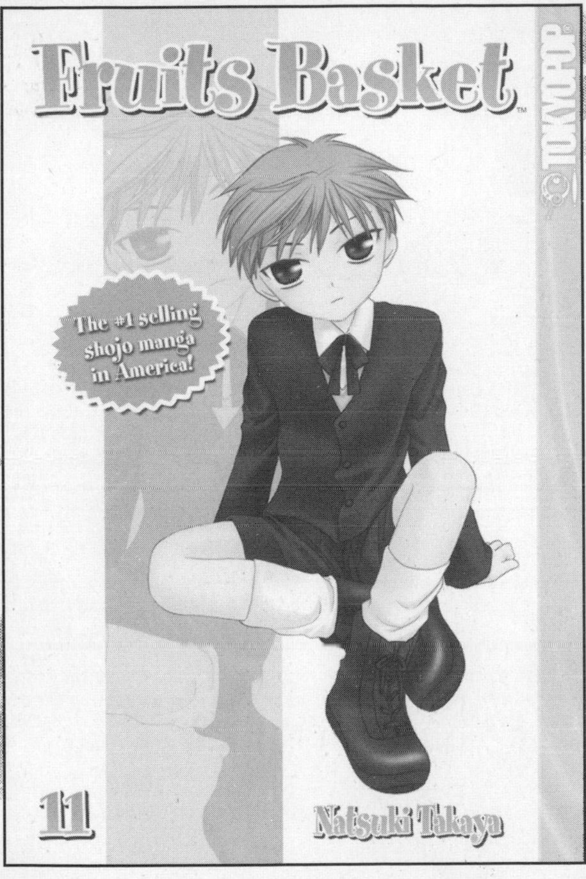
Fruits Basket
TOKYOPOP
The #1 selling shojo manga in America!
11
Natsuki Takaya

## Secrets Under Summer Skies...

While at the Sohma vacation home, Tohru is caught in a whirlwind of familial strife. Can she relax and put the "fun" in dysfunctional? None of the Sohmas are going to make it easy, including an angry horse that attacks Tohru. Could this be a new member of the Zodiac? Meanwhile, in a fierce argument with Akito, Kyo reveals his true feelings for Tohru. Will Akito tell Tohru about Kyo's secret crush? And speaking of secrets, Akito makes a major announcement--one that will reveal his true identity and change the Sohma family forever!

**Fruits Basket Volume 11**
**Available August 2005**

# Year of the Tiger: Hear Me Roar

...

## Tiger

**Years*:** 1938, 1950, 1962, 1974, 1986, 1998, 2010, 2022, 2034
**Qualities:** Courageous, Loving, Dynamic, Sincere
**Grievances:** Aggressive, Emotional, Unpredictable
**Suitable Jobs:** Manager, Explorer, Racecar Driver, Independent Film Director
**Compatible With:** Horse, Dog, Dragon
**Must Avoid:** Monkey
**Ruling Hours:** 3 AM to 5 AM
**Season:** Spring
**Ruling Month:** February
**Sign Direction:** East-Northeast
**Fixed Element:** Wood
**Corresponding Western Sign:** Aquarius

While the thought of having a Tiger chasing after them may have been encouragement enough for the Ox to come out ahead of the Tiger, a lesser-known variation of the Zodiac tales has the animals all trying to convince their peers why they deserved the coveted top spot. When asked, the Tiger proclaimed, "I am strong and powerful!"

For anyone born under the Tiger's banner, they are blessed with an aggressive nature coupled with the ability to share great love. Playful by nature, Tigers can't stand staying still for too long and are always active. Like many of the animals, Tigers are can be short-tempered and selfish, yet they are risk takers to the core. They love questioning authority, but have poor judgment.

While enthusiastic about where their lives are leading, Tigers are balls of contradictions as they are constantly struggling to ensure that they are neither rash with their decisions nor too hesitant.

A hard rope to walk, but should they manage, they will be quite successful in their lives. Through it all, though, Tigers enjoy leading carefree lives full of unexpected twists and turns that propel them further into the unknown--something they love every minute of.

A woman born in this year will be highly attractive and capable of expressing herself quite easily. She will have a lively personality and be easy going. She will spend a considerable amount of time in the mornings dressing to impress and her closet will reflect this by being packed full of the latest fashions. Tigers love being the life of a party and are great company to have. Though for them, being ignored is like a sin.

**Celebrity Dragons:**
Tom Cruise
Bridget Fonda
Jodie Foster
Alyson Hannigan
Steve Irwin
Jon Bon Jovi
Lindsay Lohan
Demi Moore
Mary-Kate and Ashley Olsen
Tigger (Winnie The Pooh)

* Note: It is important to know what day Chinese New Year's was held on as that changes what Zodiac animal you are. Example: 1989 actually began on February 6 and anyone born before that date is actually an Ox.

# Fans Basket

Hello, loyal fans! As usual, here's a beautiful batch of fan art! Your drawings always manage to cheer me up on a bad day. So, unless you want me to get really grumpy (Haru-style), keep sending them in!
- Paul Morrissey, Editor

**Vax Liu
Age 15
Lockport, NY**

Here we have some of the boys at the dojo. No doubt a fight is about to break out. Unlike Haru, I give this sketch a thumbs up!

Hiro and Kisa

**Maya Garcia
Age 14
Santa Monica, CA**

This is adorable, Maya. It's always great to get fan art of Kisa. It seems like *everyone* draws Tohru.

Furba A.k.A Fruits Basket

Tohru Honda

**Chi
Age 11
Spokane, WA**

Chi is another young reader of *Fruits Basket*. I love the use of gray "tones" in this sketch. They almost look like watercolors. And I can't believe Chi's only 11!

**Fruits Basket has fans of all ages--from 10-year-old girls to 31-year-old Brandons! I really liked your sketch, Brandon. I wish everyone else could see its original pink and purple colors, though!**

**Brandon W.**
**Age 31**
**Los Angeles, CA**

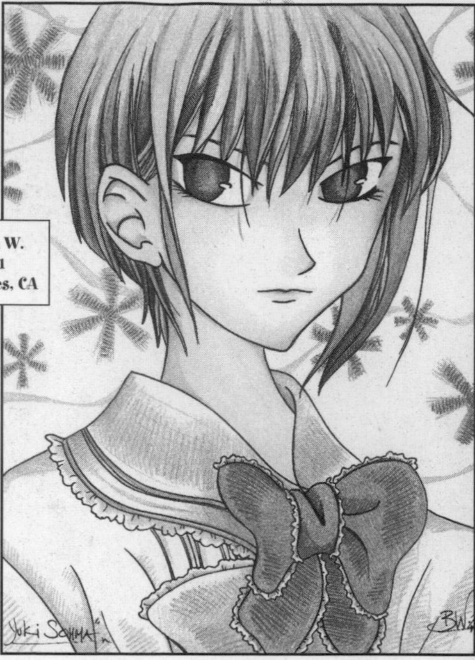
Yuki Sohma

**Good news: This sketch really catches the tone of *Fruits Basket.* Bad news: This sketch was originally done in vibrant color. It still looks great in black and white, though.**

**Abbis**
**Age 18**
**Amherst, NY**

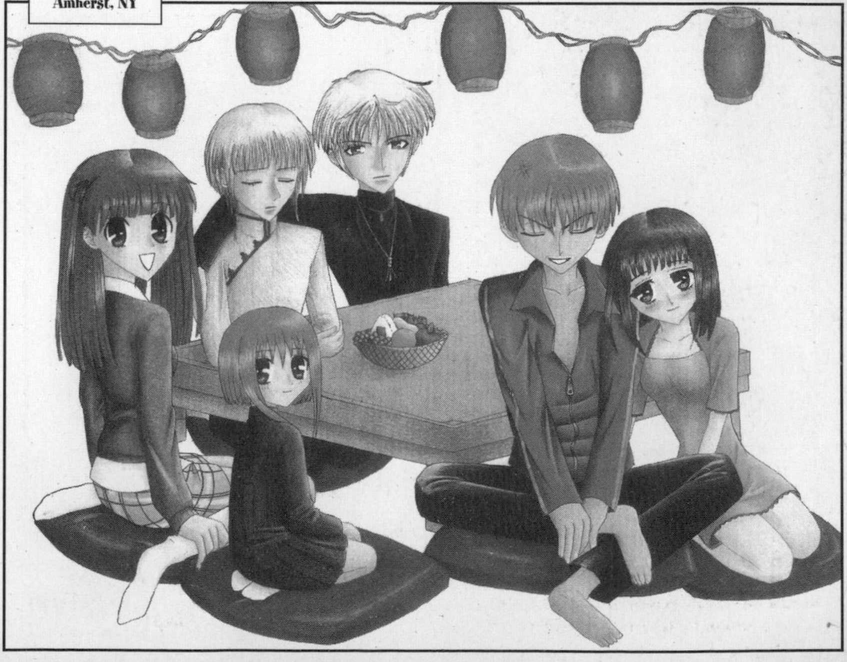

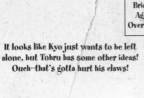

Briana Lambert
Age: Under 18
Overland Park, KS

It looks like Kyo just wants to be left alone, but Tohru has some other ideas! Ouch--that's gotta hurt his claws!

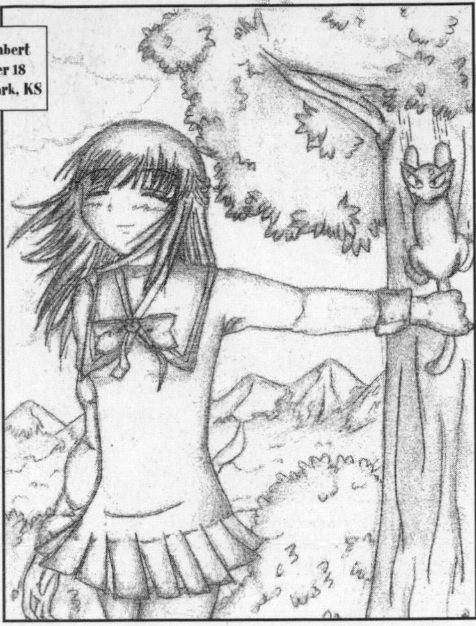

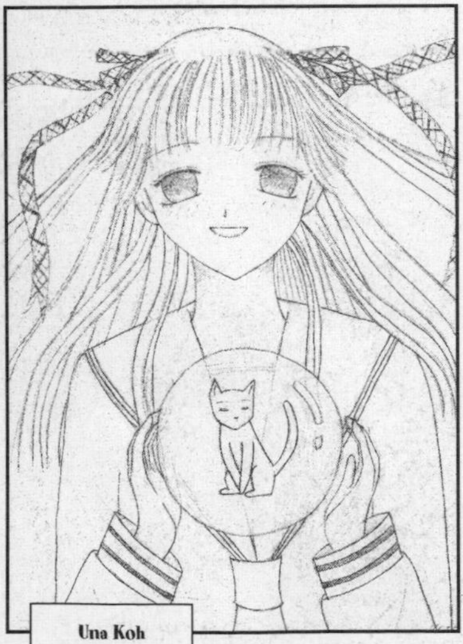

Una Koh
Age 16
Mesa, AZ

Hmmm... Here's an interesting scene. Tohru is looking into a crystal ball...and she sees Kyo! I wonder what this says about her future... Well, keep reading *Fruits Basket* to find out!

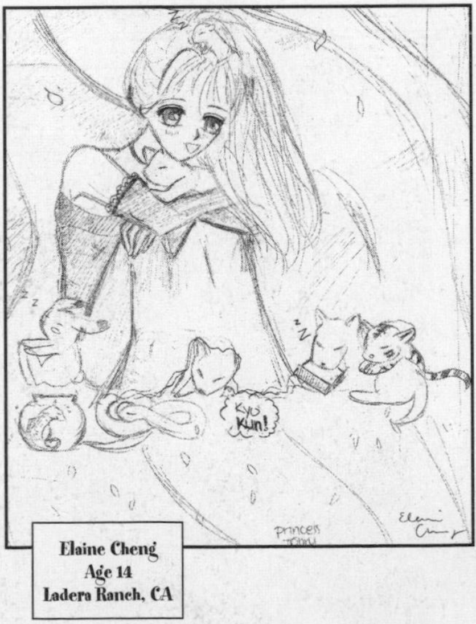
Kyo Kun!

Elaine Cheng
Age 14
Ladera Ranch, CA

Very cute, Elaine. It's naptime for everyone but Tohru. My favorite is Hatori snoozing in his fishbowl. Do sea horses sleep?

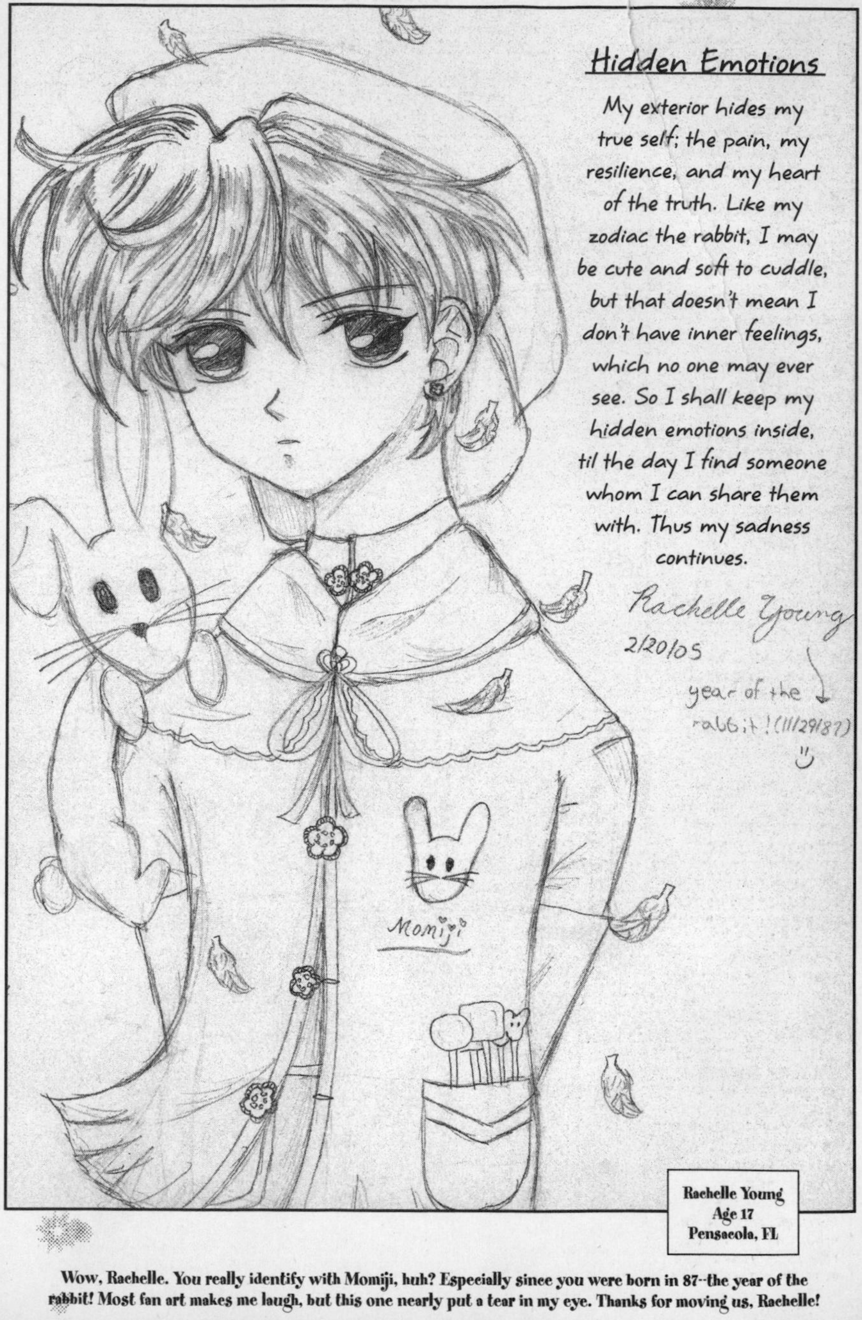
Hidden Emotions
My exterior hides my true self; the pain, my resilience, and my heart of the truth. Like my zodiac the rabbit, I may be cute and soft to cuddle, but that doesn't mean I don't have inner feelings, which no one may ever see. So I shall keep my hidden emotions inside, til the day I find someone whom I can share them with. Thus my sadness continues.
Rachelle Young
2/20/05
year of the rabbit! (11/29/87)
Momiji

**Rachelle Young**
**Age 17**
**Pensacola, FL**

**Wow, Rachelle. You really identify with Momiji, huh? Especially since you were born in 87--the year of the rabbit! Most fan art makes me laugh, but this one nearly put a tear in my eye. Thanks for moving us, Rachelle!**

Do you want to share your love for *Fruits Basket* with fans around the world? "Fans Basket" is taking submissions of fan art, poetry, cosplay photos, or any other Furuba fun you'd like to share!

How to submit:

1) Send your work via regular mail (NOT e-mail) to:

"Fans Basket"
c/o TOKYOPOP
5900 Wilshire Blvd.
Suite 2000
Los Angeles, CA 90036

2) All work should be in black-and-white and no larger than 8.5" x 11". (And try not to fold it too many times!)

3) Anything you send will not be returned. If you want to keep your original, it's fine to send us a copy.

4) Please include your full name, age, city and state for us to print with your work. If you'd rather us use a pen name, please include that, too.

5) IMPORTANT: If you're under the age of 18, you must have your parent's permission in order for us to print your work. Any submissions without a signed note of parental consent cannot be used.

6) For full details, please check out our website: http://www.tokyopop.com/aboutus/fanart.php

Disclaimer: Anything you send to us becomes the exclusive property of TOKYOPOP Inc. and, as we said before, will not be returned to you. We will have the right to print, reproduce, distribute, or modify the artwork for use in future volumes of Fruits Basket or on the web royalty-free.

Annie Rong
Age 10
Urbana, IL

**Wow, Annie! You're only 10? Lovely work--especially the clothes. You have a nice, loose style. Don't ever stop drawing!**

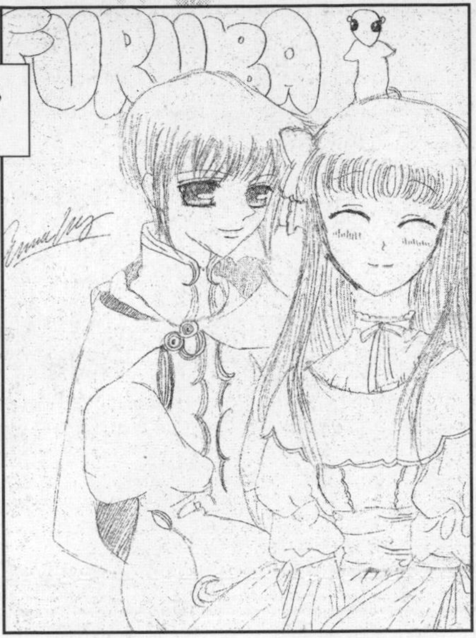

McKenna Powell
Age 15
North Ogden, UT

**I love the falling petals in your sketch, McKenna. And your pencils have a very unique feel. Thanks for sharing your talent!**

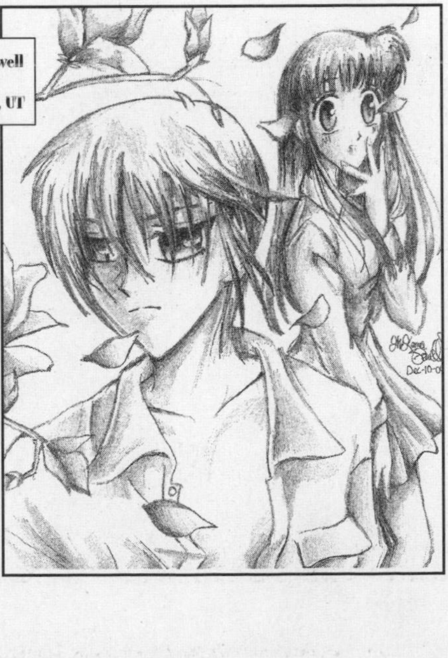

# TOKYOPOP SHOP

WWW.TOKYOPOP.COM/SHOP

## HOT NEWS!

Check out the
TOKYOPOP SHOP!
The world's best
collection of manga in
English is now available
online in one place!

## SAKURA TAISEN

## BECK: MONGOLIAN CHOP SQUAD

*Princess Ai*
and other hot
titles are
available at
the store that
never closes!

## PRINCESS AI VOL. 2: LUMINATION

- **LOOK FOR SPECIAL OFFERS**
- **PRE-ORDER UPCOMING RELEASES**
- **COMPLETE YOUR COLLECTIONS**

# SPOTLIGHT

TOKYOPOP MANGA SUPPLEMENT

## SAKURA TAISEN

BY OHJI HIROI & IKKU MASA

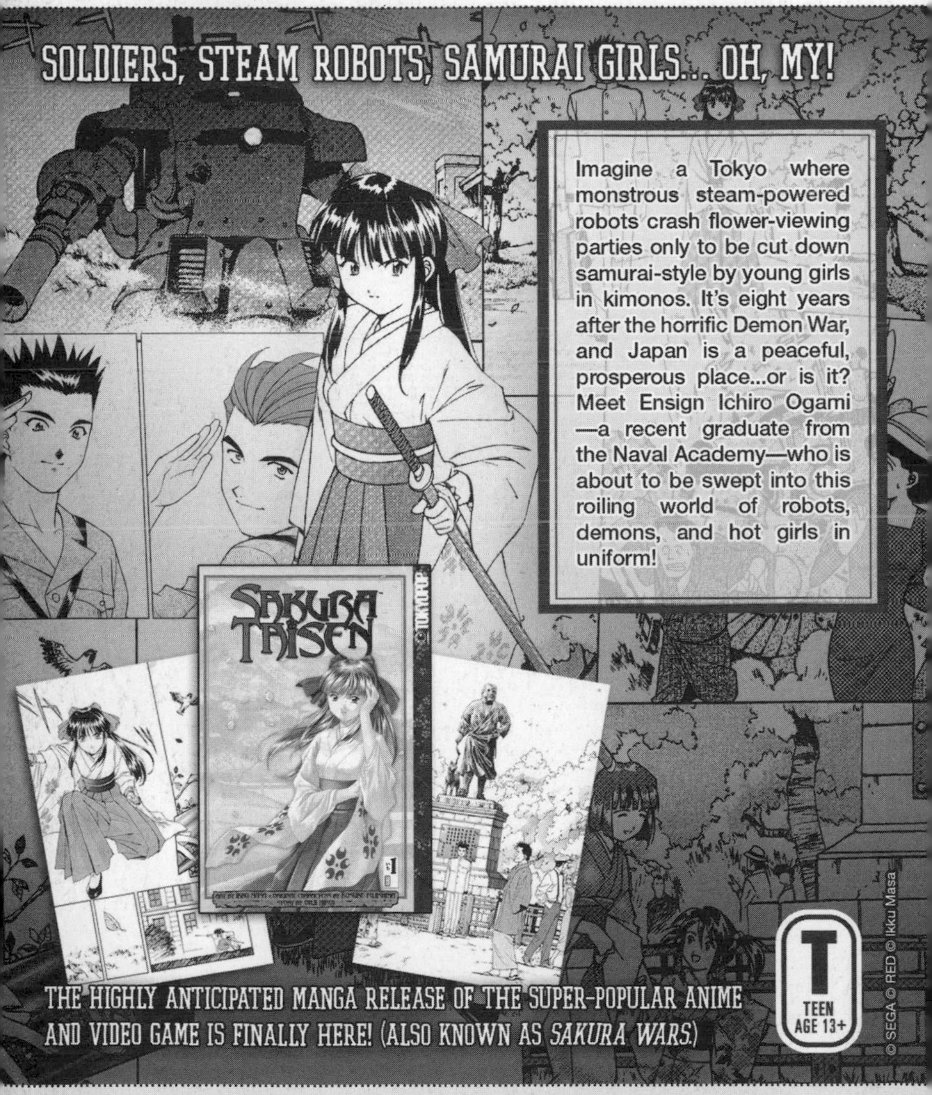

SOLDIERS, STEAM ROBOTS, SAMURAI GIRLS... OH, MY!
Imagine a Tokyo where monstrous steam-powered robots crash flower-viewing parties only to be cut down samurai-style by young girls in kimonos. It's eight years after the horrific Demon War, and Japan is a peaceful, prosperous place...or is it? Meet Ensign Ichiro Ogami—a recent graduate from the Naval Academy—who is about to be swept into this roiling world of robots, demons, and hot girls in uniform!
SAKURA TAISEN
THE HIGHLY ANTICIPATED MANGA RELEASE OF THE SUPER-POPULAR ANIME AND VIDEO GAME IS FINALLY HERE! (ALSO KNOWN AS *SAKURA WARS*.)
T
TEEN AGE 13+
© SEGA © RED © Ikku Masa


FOR MORE INFORMATION VISIT: WWW.TOKYOPOP.COM

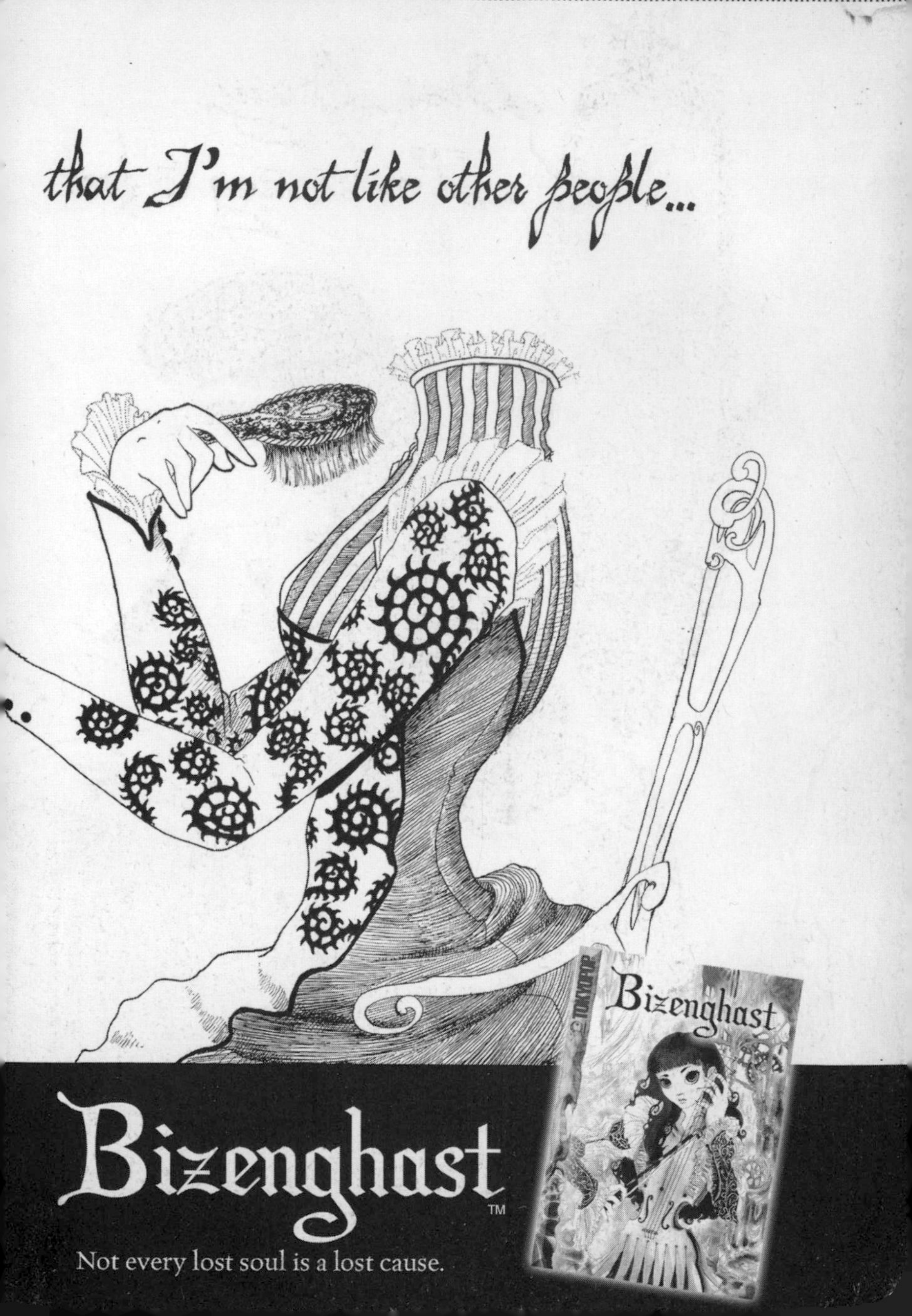
that I'm not like other people...
Bizenghast
TOKYOPOP
Bizenghast™
Not every lost soul is a lost cause.